PRENTICE HALL STUDIES
IN INTERNATIONAL RELATIONS

ENDURING QUESTIONS IN CHANGING TIMES

Charles W. Kegley, Jr., *Series Editor*

In the era of globalization in the twenty-first century, people cannot afford to ignore the impact of international relations on their future. From the value of one's investments to the quality of the air one breathes, international relations matter. The instantaneous spread of communications throughout the world is making for the internationalization of all phenomena, while the distinction between the domestic and the foreign, the public and the private, and the national and the international is vanishing. Globalization is an accelerating trend that is transforming how virtually every field of study in the social sciences is being investigated and taught.

Contemporary scholarship has made bold advances in understanding the many facets of international relations. It has also laid a firm foundation for interpreting the major forces and factors that are shaping the global future.

To introduce the latest research findings and theoretical commentary, a new publication series has been launched. *Prentice Hall Studies in International Relations: Enduring Questions in Changing Times* presents books that focus on the issues, controversies, and trends that are defining the central topics dominating discussion about international relations.

Between Two Epochs

What's Ahead for America, the World, and Global Politics in the Twenty-First Century?

J. MARTIN ROCHESTER

University of Missouri, St. Louis

Prentice
Hall

Upper Saddle River, NJ 07458

Library of Congress Cataloging-in-Publication Data

Rochester, J. Martin.
    Between two epochs ; what's ahead for America, the world, and global politics in the
  twenty-first century? / J. Martin Rochester.
        p. cm. — (Prentice Hall Studies in international relations. Enduring questions in
      changing times)
    Includes bibliographical references and index.
    ISBN 0-13-087110-9
      1. International relations.   2. World politics—21st century.   I. Title: Between 2 epochs.
  II. Title.   III. Series.
JZ1305 .R63 2002
327—dc21

                                               00-069880

VP, Editorial Director: Laura Pearson
Senior Acquisitions Editor: Heather Shelstad
Assistant Editor: Brian Prybella
Editorial/production supervision
  and interior design: Mary Araneo
Director of Marketing: Beth Gillett Mejia
Editorial Assistant: Jessica Drew
Prepress and Manufacturing Buyer: Ben Smith
Cover Art Director: Jayne Conte
Cover Designer: Bruce Kenselaar

This book was set in 10/12 New Baskerville by A & A Publishing Services, Inc.,
and was printed and bound by Courier Companies, Inc. The cover was
printed by Phoenix Color Corp.

© 2002 by Pearson Education, Inc.
Upper Saddle River, New Jersey 07458

Printed in the United States of America

10 9 8 7 6 5 4 3 2 1

ISBN   0-13-087110-9

PRENTICE-HALL INTERNATIONAL (UK) LIMITED, *London*
PRENTICE-HALL OF AUSTRALIA PTY. LIMITED, *Sydney*
PRENTICE-HALL CANADA INC., *Toronto*
PRENTICE-HALL HISPANOAMERICANA, S.A., *Mexico*
PRENTICE-HALL OF INDIA PRIVATE LIMITED, *New Delhi*
PRENTICE-HALL OF JAPAN, INC., *Tokyo*
PEARSON EDUCATION ASIA PTE. LTD., *Singapore*
EDITORA PRENTICE-HALL DO BRASIL, LTDA., *Rio de Janeiro*

To my mentor, Bill Coplin,
to my students, who have been his students,
and to Andy and Dennis,
good friends who remind me weekly that,
in trying to solve the world's problems,
humor is a valuable tool.

Contents

Preface

The philosopher Hegel once observed that the owl of Minerva only rises at night, that by the time we begin to understand fully some reality, it is already fading from view and giving way to another reality. Night has fallen on the twentieth century and given way to a new day, but it is not yet clear what this new day looks like in terms of its basic features, particularly those relating to world affairs. What has been a familiar world of nation-states whose main organizing principle has been sovereignty is being transformed before our eyes into "a new world order" whose character is less well defined. As I comment in Chapter 1, "Like the passengers on a large ship, humanity seems to be undergoing passage through unfamiliar and somewhat treacherous straits. We have left one international system [the Cold War system] behind and are seeking to establish our bearings in a new system." For sure, some recognizable elements of the recent past remain—notably, the ongoing struggle for power and wealth among countries pursuing their national interests. Yet, alongside these much-traveled currents are some uncharted waters—represented by the growth of multinational corporations, the spread of the Internet and globe-circling technologies, and other developments—which, we cannot be sure, may amount to either small eddies or a giant sea change in the way human beings relate to each other on the planet. It is the main thesis of this book that we are, in fact, *between two epochs*, one whose roots go back over 300 years ago to the birth of the nation-state and the other which seems to be, in James Rosenau's words, an emergent "post-international politics" era.

This book was inspired by the many students I have had the good fortune to teach over the years in my World Politics course. From the first time I taught this course in 1972, the lecture which always seemed to bring out the best in me and in them was the last one of the semester, when I would invite them to take out their crystal balls and speculate about what "world order" might look like in "the year 2000 and beyond." What was not only likely but desirable? Would (should) the contemporary state system persist? Would (should) we be moving in the direction of regionalism and possibly world government, or perhaps in the opposite direction, toward more localized grassroots governance? Little did I know thirty years ago that the new millennium would arrive so quickly, with so many questions unanswered and the world seemingly moving in so many different directions at once. *Between Two Epochs* is an attempt to engage students in further critical thinking about some of the most profound empirical and normative questions of our time, questions having to do with how people will be organized politically and will govern their affairs, toward what ends. It should find a broad audience not only in international relations courses but in political science courses generally and, indeed, will be of potential interest to anyone concerned about the future of humankind.

The organization of the book has the following logic. Part One tries to lay out "the puzzle," that is, the challenge of making sense today out of what seem to be not merely complex trends but contradictory, paradoxical ones. Part Two tries to "put the pieces together," offering a way out of the conundrum by suggesting how we might best conceptualize world politics in the early twenty-first century. Part Three provides some concluding futuristic reflections, mindful of Rene Dubos's caution that "trend is not destiny." Throughout the book, I have tried to apply high standards of scholarship, including endnotes containing numerous citations of various works I drew on, without burdening the reader unduly with jargon and esoterica; the notes have been placed at the rear for purposes of streamlining the body of the text. There is also an appendix that contains chapter-by-chapter "discussion questions for the twenty-first-century chat room," which the reader may wish to take a stab at beforehand or consult following each chapter. A selected bibliography accompanies each set of questions, to encourage further inquiry.

I am indebted to not only my students but also many colleagues and staff in the Political Science Department and the Center for International Studies at the University of Missouri-St.Louis, particularly Bob Baumann, for providing critical support for this project. Special thanks go to Beth Gillett, Director of Marketing, and her associate Wayne Spohr, both of whom provided the initial stimulus for this undertaking as well as constant encouragement along the way. Thanks go also to Mary Araneo for shepherding the manuscript through the production process with meticulous care. I'd like to thank the following Prentice Hall reviewers for their comments and suggestions: Neil Richardson, University of Wisconsin, Madison; Steve Chan, University of Colorado; Barry Hughes, University of Denver; and Karen Mingst, University of Kentucky. And, of course, I could not have completed this enterprise without the willingness of my family—Ruth, Stephen (Shiya), and Sean—to tolerate my lengthy absences on weekends and other occasions, what must have seemed like a millennium if not eternity to them, when I was toiling away at my office researching and writing the manuscript. I feel truly fortunate to have such a wife and children by my side as a new century dawns.

J. Martin Rochester

PART ONE
THE PUZZLE

CHAPTER 1

Introduction
A New World Order, or Disorder?

The world is leaving one epoch, the Cold War, and entering a new one.
—Mikhail Gorbachev, premier of the Soviet Union, in a
statement published in Pravda, December 5, 1989.

Don't be like the student who was asked "which is worse, ignorance or apathy?"
and who responded "I don't know and I don't care!"
—a statement I first heard uttered by Charles Yost, former
U.S. Ambassador to the United Nations, at a World Affairs
Council meeting in St. Louis in 1980, entreating citizens
to become more informed and more involved
in the discussion of international issues.

Go forth to meet the shadowy Future.
—Henry Wadsworth Longfellow, *Hyperion*, 1852

It is a special moment. We have just begun not only a new century but a new millennium. No other generation will experience such a moment for another thousand years. This moment also comes as we are all still attempting to make sense of the "new world order" or, as some would say, "disorder" in the post-Cold War era that we now live in. The Cold War, which dominated and provided a handy label for the post-World War II period, ran roughly from 1945 to 1990. It is hard to know how long the post-Cold War period will last, and by what label it will come to be known. This book is aimed at assisting lay persons, particularly undergraduate students and most especially American students, to understand the contours of the post-Cold War world, although the author must in all humility offer a twofold caveat here at the outset. First, if the truth be known, teachers no less than students are struggling to grasp fully the nature of the international system that has replaced the Cold War system; while professors clearly bring a much deeper perspective to an examination of world politics than the average college freshman or sophomore, there is considerable uncertainty even among the most veteran observers as to how this still newborn system will evolve. What British prime minister Winston Churchill once said about Russia—"it is a riddle wrapped in a mystery inside an enigma"[1]—would seem to apply doubly to the current international scene. Second, while the author is speaking mainly to an American audience, one thing we can say for certain is that, given the almost inexorable dynamics of interdependence, the lives of Americans and non-Americans are likely to be increasingly, mutually intertwined, like it or not. The purpose of this book, then, is to help students get a handle on *their* world, to engage in critical reflections on broad political trends that are likely to shape the human condition, including life in the United States, in the twenty-first century.

UNWRAPPING THE PUZZLE

As I have written elsewhere, "like the passengers on a large ship, humanity currently seems to be undergoing passage through unfamiliar and somewhat treacherous straits. We have left one international system behind and are seeking to establish our bearings in a new system."[2] One is reminded of the remarks once uttered by another former British prime minister, Harold Macmillan, near the beginning of the Cold War: "As they left the Garden of Eden, Adam turned to Eve and said, 'we live in an age of transition.'"[3] History is an unfolding process, and the world, arguably, is forever in transition. So what's new? There is a sense that this time, with the fall of the Berlin Wall in 1989 and the subsequent developments in the decade or so since, we have been witnessing not just the end of a distinctive *half-century* pattern of world politics that followed World War II, but rather a much more radical and profound turning point in human affairs, i.e., possibly the passing of a historical epoch that has extended *well over three hundred years* and has defined "modernity."

I am referring here to the unraveling of the very fabric of the nation-state system itself that, at least from a Western perspective, has been the primary framework for human political organization for the past several centuries, as far back as the Peace of Westphalia that ended the Thirty Years' War in Europe in 1648.[4] Prior to Westphalia, the main mode of political organization in Europe was feudalism, a crazy-quilt pattern of duchies, walled cities, landed manors, kingdoms, ecclesiastical territories, and assorted other entities tied together in a complex web of overlapping hierarchies of authority and multiple loyalties, with the Holy Roman Emperor on much of the continent having nominal dominion over all secular matters and the Pope over all religious matters, but in reality neither having enough power to regulate local rulers. The so-called Westphalian state system that replaced the feudal order in Europe and eventually spread out across the globe[5] was what we now take for granted as the natural order of

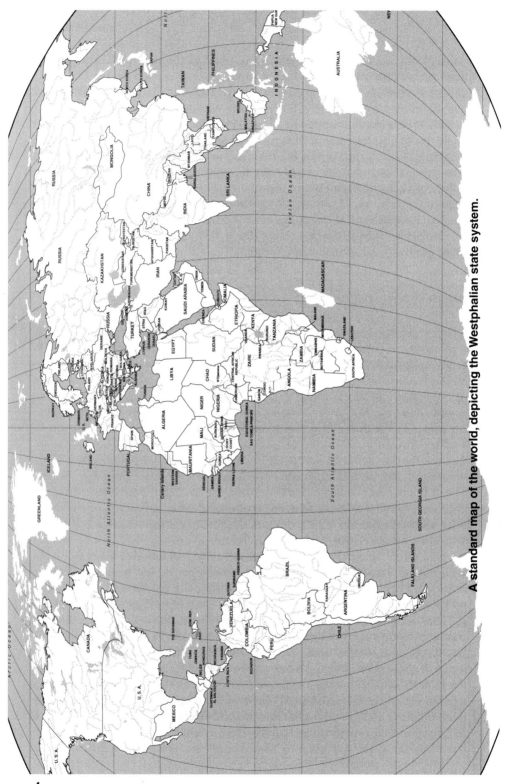

A standard map of the world, depicting the Westphalian state system.

things—a collection of clearly identifiable political units, each with a relatively well defined set of territorial boundaries and population over which a central government exercises sovereign rule through executive, legislative, and judicial institutions based in its national capital. By "sovereignty" is meant the existence of a single supreme authority that can claim the exclusive right to rule over that patch of real estate and people and that recognizes no higher authority outside those boundaries (whether it be the UN, the Pope, or any other body). In other words, these are the almost 200 entities one finds demarcated by dark, thick borders on a world map today, ranging from such large states as China and the United States to much smaller ones such as Micronesia and Palau, all of which are juridical equals in the eyes of the international community. Recognition of a new state by the international community has ordinarily meant official certification that there is a national government capable of exercising control over all activities within its borders and competent to represent its citizens in its external relations. Although the number of such states has varied during the life of the Westphalian system, the essential structural logic has remained generally intact. The academic field of international relations has reflected that logic, hinging on the critical distinction made between *domestic* and *foreign* concerns and focusing much of its attention on inter-state relations, including diplomacy, war, international organization, international law, and foreign policy-making.

There are currently more nation-states than ever, complete with their national flags, national anthems, national constitutions, and gross national products, suggesting the Westphalian state system is alive and well. However, there is a feeling that while in some respects the nation-state has never been more vibrant as a human institution, in other respects it has never been more at risk. It is just that—a "feeling in the air," more an impression than a clear-cut, empirically demonstrable fact. But one cannot help reading the daily newspaper or watching the evening news on television without noticing all kinds of happenings that simply do not square with a Westphalian view of the world. Whether it is the latest merger of two giant multinational corporations, or the latest collapse of an African country into civil war and anarchy (what is euphemistically called a "failed state"), or the latest report of an oil spill or acid rain damage that transcends country boundaries, or e-mail exchanges in cyberspace that recognize no borders whatsoever, we seem to be experiencing increasingly a set of phenomena which are far messier than the well-defined images represented on a classroom wall map or globe. Some observers have gone so far as to suggest that we are going back to the future, that we are on the brink of an emergent "new feudalism" and "new medievalism."[6]

Let us briefly glance at a few concrete examples of what the latter observers have in mind, drawn from recent news headlines:

- "The New Europe: Living Without Borders" (*New York Times*, December 24, 1998), noting the 1999 start-up date of the new Euro that was created as a common currency by eleven European countries to replace French francs, Italian lire, German marks, and other individual national currencies. The plan is expected to be fully implemented by 2002.

- "The Shadow Bankers: Currency Traders Now Control the Fate of the Dollar" (*Newsweek*, October 23, 1989), noting that "the collective might of the world's private currency traders [speculators engaging in billions of dollars of currency exchanges daily] has simply overwhelmed the power of central banks [national governmental banks, such as the U.S. Federal Reserve Bank] to control the course of the dollar."

- "DaimlerChrysler Makes Debut" (*New York Times*, November 18, 1998), noting the transatlantic merger of two corporate giants as Germany's Daimler-Benz (makers of Mercedes-Benz) bought up one of the "Big Three" American automakers, Chrysler, with the merged company to be headquartered in Stuttgart, Germany, but using English as its official language.

- "BP Agrees to Buy AMOCO in Biggest Industrial Merger" (*St. Louis Post-Dispatch*, August 10, 1998), noting that British Petroleum's purchase of the American Oil Company (a storied icon of American business much like Chrysler had been) created the third largest oil company in the world and the biggest firm in Britain.

- "Ford, By Buying Volvo Car Unit, Hopes to Sell More Luxury Autos" (*New York Times*, January 29, 1999), noting that Ford, which had already purchased British-based Jaguar and Aston Martin in recent years, acquired Swedish-based Volvo partly to keep pace with DaimlerChrysler and other competitors.

- "Ben and Jerry's Caves Into Pressure, Sells to Unilever" (*St. Louis Post-Dispatch*, April 13, 2000), noting that Unilever, the giant British-Dutch conglomerate that already owned such well-known American brand names as Good Humor and Breyers, had added the environmentally friendly Vermont company to its ice cream holdings, at the same time that, "making sure all the bases were covered," it also bought Slim-Fast Foods.

- "The Italian Who Wants to Buy Belgium" (*Newsweek*, February 1, 1988), noting that Carlos De Benedetti, a wealthy Italian financier, had made a bid for a Belgian holding company that influenced one-third of the entire Belgian economy, leading Belgians to respond "as though they had been invaded" and raising the question "can an entire country be the target of a hostile takeover?"

- "This Bud's Not For You: Tiny Brewer Thwarts Global Push by Budweiser" (*New York Times*, June 30, 1995), noting the failure of St. Louis-based Anheuser-Busch, the world's largest brewer, to acquire a small state-owned brewery in the Czech Republic, whereupon, undaunted, the maker of the signature brand it calls "The American Beer" concluded new agreements with Chinese and Japanese distributors to tap into the vast Asian market.

- "Airline Alliance: Europe's Carriers Unite to Survive" (*St. Louis Post-Dispatch*, October 7, 1993), noting that "Europe's major airlines, for decades as much symbols of national sovereignty as their countries' flags, are crossing borders and even continents in a mad scramble to prepare for the next century." Air France and most other national airlines, which have long been government-owned and operated, are increasingly not only opening up ownership to private domestic investors but are also permitting a degree of foreign ownership as well (e.g., the proposed "marriage" of Swissair, KLM Royal Dutch, SAS, and Austrian Airlines into a single carrier, and KLM's purchase of 49 percent of U.S.-based Northwest Airlines).

- "The Cries of Welfare States Under the Knife" (*New York Times*, September 19, 1997), noting the pressures many national governments feel these days to cut taxes and regulations, including gutting unemployment benefits and occupational safety, minimum wage, and other laws so as to position themselves to attract and retain private business and investment in what has become a competitive global marketplace.

- "Not Just Governments Make War or Peace" (*New York Times*, November 28, 1998), noting the role played by a transnational nongovernmental pressure group, the International Campaign to Ban Land Mines, in getting governments to agree to the 1998 Ottawa Treaty outlawing antipersonnel mines, as well as the hiring of a private foreign firm, Sandline International of Great Britain, by the government of Papua New Guinea to help defend the state against secessionist forces (much like the use of foreign mercenaries by monarchs in earlier times).

- "A New State for Inuit: Frigid But Optimistic" (*New York Times*, January 29, 1999), noting that Quebec is not the only region of Canada seeking greater autonomy from the central government. Nunavut, "770,000 square miles of snow and ice roughly the size of western Europe," where the "wind-chill sometimes sinks to minus 94 Fahrenheit" and "caribou outnumber the 25,000 residents [mostly ethnic Inuits] more than 25 to 1," did not go so far as to declare total independence from Canada, settling instead for limited self-governance in domestic affairs.

- "With Mixed Feelings, Iran Tiptoes to Internet" (*New York Times*, October 8, 1996), noting the Faustian bargain confronting the Tehran government, as "the Islamic Republic is in a quandary over just how extensive its electronic links with the outside world should be. It is eager to propagate its theocracy and become a source for questions of Islamic law. But the government fears that everyone from die-hard supporters of the deposed Shah to Western pornographers will storm in via cyberspace."

- "It's Not the Only Alien Invader" (*New York Times Sunday Magazine*, November 13, 1994), noting that "alien species" of plants and animals are being inadvertently transported globally by sea and air, arriving from faraway exotic locales in imported fruits, hand luggage, shipments of used tires, and through other ways, threatening the habitats of native species "unable to compete with zoology's cosmopolitan class."

Not everyone is in agreement about what these sorts of disparate events add up to and whether they portend a sea change in human affairs. There is a lively debate going on in the academic community. The future of the nation-state has been the focus recently of most annual conference programs of the International Studies Association, a major professional society of international relations scholars; for example, the theme of the 1998 meeting, coinciding with the 350th anniversary of the Peace of Westphalia, was "The Westphalian System in Global and Historical Perspective." The eighteenth-century French philosopher Voltaire supposedly once remarked that the Holy Roman Empire in medieval Europe was neither holy, nor Roman, nor an empire. Today the "new world order" is being questioned as to not only how worldly (non-parochial) and orderly (peaceful) it is but also how truly new it is.

Skeptics who would question whether the early twenty-first century is a "Westphalian moment" that is ushering in a whole new set of worldviews and governance arrangements would point out that the Westphalian model of a world of independent states as the dominant actors interacting on the world stage in pursuit of their individual national interests, like billiard balls on a pool table,[7] has always been an oversimplified representation of the reality of world politics, and that a lot of what we are seeing today is not wholly novel. They would note that interdependence is not a completely new phenomenon (witness the high levels of trade among European states on the eve of World War I),[8] that transnational relations (interactions between private individuals and groups across national boundaries) have existed since the very beginnings of the nation-state system (witness the early wanderings of missionaries and spice merchants as well as the organized efforts by an international network of abolitionists to curb the slave trade),[9] that sovereignty has often been merely a theoretical abstraction or formal-legal concept while in actual practice a bit of a joke (witness the subjugation of Eastern European states as satellites of the Soviet Union during the Cold War, or the long-standing economic penetration of less-developed countries by American and other foreign interests), and that there has never "been any golden age of state control"[10] (witness the spread of the Spanish flu in 1918–19, a transnational epidemic that killed some 20 million people worldwide, similar to though not nearly as deadly as the Black Plague, which killed over one-third of Europe's population in the fourteenth century and reduced average life expectancy at one point to 17 years of age). Still, notwithstanding the skeptics' arguments, one would have to say that the degree of "messiness" that is evident today is of a higher magnitude than has previously characterized the state system. If those of us living in the new millennium are not witnesses to the end of the Westphalian state system as we have known it, perhaps at the very least we may well be seeing, to use another Churchillian phrase, the beginning of the end.

It is the main thesis of this book that humanity, for better or worse, is in transition between two epochs, between the Westphalian one and the post-Westphalian one. The bedrock concepts that have guided the study and practice of international relations for centuries—sovereignty, national interests and national security, citizenship, and so forth—continue to exert a powerful hold on us, even as they often seem at odds with everyday events. One of the greatest challenges facing educators today is precisely to explain to students (and to ourselves) how, on the one hand, these traditional notions we have used to make sense of world affairs are still fundamental to understanding how the world works, yet at the same time are becoming increasingly problematical if not somewhat irrelevant in an age of economic globalization, cyberspace, and other developments that are blurring national borders and identities. The world has never been a simple place, and education has always been about learning to cope with ambiguity. It is just that now the extent of the ambiguity appears to be increasing daily. The challenge of trying to reconcile two concurrent, seemingly incompatible realities was captured beautifully by the early-twentieth-century American novelist F. Scott Fitzgerald: "The test of a first-rate intelligence is the ability to hold two opposing ideas in the mind at the same time and still be able to function." That is the task before us in the twenty-first century, and that is the rationale of this book, which hopefully will leave the reader with something more than "a feeling in the air."

CRITICAL QUESTIONS

Ultimately, this book is about the governance of human affairs. We can rightly speak today of a global economy, a global society, and a global ecosystem, yet there is no global government. There seems to be a growing incongruity between economic, social, and ecological space on the one hand, and political space on the other. While some individuals call for world government or at least improved "central guidance" mechanisms—to cope with nuclear proliferation and other planetary concerns—and although one can see possible stepping stones in that direction now being laid in the form of increased intergovernmental institution-building beyond the nation-state at both the regional and global levels, such as the European Union and the World Trade Organization, one can also find trends occurring in the opposite direction, as manifested by the breakup of Yugoslavia and the Soviet Union. Given the questionable feasibility and desirability of world government at present, there is growing interest instead in "global governance," in how national, subnational, and transnational actors relate to each other and how "some preliminary scaffolding" can be constructed to permit the nation-state to continue to function and meet the needs of people in a world where the Westphalian mode of organization seems increasingly dysfunctional.[11] By scaffolding is meant international regime-making: the development of norms, principles, rules, and organizations that can promote a degree of cooperation and stability in international life.[12] Increasingly, there is a call not only for order but for a *just* order based on an equitable distribution of resources. A new scholarly journal in the international relations field is called *Global Governance*; it seeks to examine the "contribution of international institutions and multilateral processes to economic development, the maintenance of peace and security, human rights, and the preservation of the environment."

Much of this book will focus on *empirical* questions, i.e., we will engage in an objective, descriptive analysis of current trends in world politics in order to obtain as accurate a picture of reality as possible. There is little point in reflecting on saving the planet unless one first has a fairly firm grip on what the planet looks like. But we will also engage in some *normative* analysis as well, i.e., we will contemplate not just "is" questions but also "ought" questions calling for value judgments more than factual judgments. Everywhere governments are struggling to meet the rising expectations of mass publics, with variable success. Two main questions arise. First: *what should be the proper role of government; that is, what matters should be handled by government, and what should be left to the private sector ("civil society," as the nongovernmental arena is now commonly called)?* Second: *to the extent government should concern itself with some set of issues, what level of government is best equipped to address the problem?* With regard to the first question, there has been a growing trend toward deregulation, privatization, and reliance on markets, voluntary associations, and nonstatist approaches. The stress here is on reinvigorating civil society, including what some see as an emergent "global civil society" of transnational interest groups and movements of various sorts.[13] In answer to the second question, it has been noted that "the state [the nation-state] has become too big for the small things [such as overseeing education], and too small for the big things [such as controlling global warming]. The small things call for delegation downwards to the local level. . . . The big things call for delegation upwards, for coordination between national policies, or for transnational institutions."[14] Hence, a favorite phrase today—think globally, act locally.[15]

Where does all this leave the nation-state? For the moment at least, as former United Nations Secretary-General Boutros Boutros-Ghali reminded us in a speech about the shape of the post-Cold War international order, "the foundation-stone of this work [global governance] is and must remain the State."[16] Boutros-Ghali is referring to the obvious fact that we still live in nation-states, however tenuous they may be, and this is not likely to change anytime in the immediate future, although whether change occurs, and how much and how fast, is up to us. In regard to the question posed in the subtitle of this book— what's ahead for America and the world in the twenty-first century?—nothing is foreordained. In order to think through what the future might hold, we need

"I really envy you your ability to think _globally_."

Thinking globally, acting locally.   (© The New Yorker Collection 1983 Donal Reilly from cartoonbank.com. All Rights Reserved.)

to grapple with the paradoxes we have been circling around in this chapter, particularly the existence of the forces of globalism alongside localism, and statism alongside nonstatism. We are now ready to proceed with our investigation.

THE PLAN OF THE BOOK

The organization of this book is as follows: In **Part One ("The Puzzle")**, in Chapters 2–4, the author will continue to lay out the conundrum as one would sort through the pieces in a jigsaw box, further developing many of the themes introduced in Chapter 1. Chapter 2 will provide an overview of the contemporary international system in broad outline, going beyond the preliminary sketch furnished thus far. Chapter 3 will delineate the complexity of the contemporary system in greater detail and will address some conceptual issues relating to the "paradigm debate" in the international relations field, examining the competing assumptions of the "billiard ball" (a.k.a. realist or neorealist) school, which leans toward a Westphalian worldview, and the "cobweb" (a.k.a. liberal or neoliberal) school, which leans toward a post-Westphalian worldview.

Chapter 4 will offer an alternative formulation to both the Westphalian and post-Westphalian worldviews. **Part Two ("Putting the Pieces Together")** will attempt to provide some coherence and synthesis, as we try to make sense out of what may at times appear to be chaos. We will utilize the distinction between high, middle, and low politics, with Chapter 5 focusing on the high-politics of military security issues (including a mini-case study on the negotiations surrounding the 1993 Chemical Weapons Convention), Chapter 6 focusing on the middle-politics of economic issues (including a mini-case study of the Uruguay Round negotiations leading to creation of the World Trade Organization in 1995), and Chapter 7 focusing on the low-politics of environmental issues (including a mini-case study on the negotiations surrounding the 1987 Montreal Protocol and its subsequent amendments), although we will see how such distinctions are increasingly breaking down. Finally, in **Part Three ("Solving the Puzzle")**, Chapter 8 will conclude our inquiry by engaging the reader in some crystal-ball gazing as we speculate about the long-term probability and desirability of alternative "world order models" and the near-term prospects for improved global governance, examining the implications for America and the world in the twenty-first century.

CHAPTER 2

An Overview
of the Contemporary
International System

It was the best of times, it was the worst of times.
—Charles Dickens, *A Tale of Two Cities,* 1859

A pessimist is an optimist with experience.
—Anonymous

I still can vividly recall sitting in a paneled room at the International Studies Association annual meeting in Washington, D.C., in April of 1986, attending a session featuring two American diplomats engaging two Soviet diplomats in a speculative discussion about "The Future of U.S.–Soviet Relations"—this at a time when Soviet leader Mikhail Gorbachev had just come to power in the Kremlin, when U.S. President Ronald Reagan was continuing to characterize the USSR as the "evil empire," and when his own secretary of defense was quoted as saying tensions were such that "we are no longer in the postwar era but the prewar era." One of the Russian diplomats started his comments by uttering what he took to be an old Romanian proverb, that it is always hard to predict anything, especially the future. Indeed, who in that room, or for that matter any room anywhere at that moment, can claim to have remotely predicted that within a half-decade the world would witness the end of the Cold War and the end of the Soviet Union itself, with hardly a shot being fired?[1] It is fair to say that most people—scholars, practitioners, and laymen alike—shared former Carter administration National Security Advisor Zbigniew Brzezinski's 1986 view that "the American-Soviet conflict is not some temporary aberration but a historical rivalry that will long endure."[2] Yet, by December 1989, the Berlin Wall that had symbolized the Iron Curtain separating the free and non-free worlds had collapsed, and the Soviet Red Army Chorus had taken Washington, D.C. by storm in leading President Bush and a throng of dignitaries at a Kennedy Center gala in a stirring rendition of "God Bless America"; by December 1991, the USSR had self-destructed into Kazakhstan, Uzbekistan, Kyrgystan, and assorted other independent republics.

Despite our recent failure at predicting even five-year trends, long-term forecasting is becoming a growth industry as we mark the *fin de siècle*. Observers are seeking to prophesy whether the American Century (the name given to the twentieth century by *Time* founder Henry Luce in recognition of U.S. ascendancy as a world power) will continue into the twenty-first century, whether it will give way to the Pacific Century (which looked like a reasonable bet until the recent stumbling of the Japanese and other Asian economies), or whether it will be replaced by a "post-international politics" century altogether.[3] Among prognosticators, one can find optimistic as well as pessimistic readings of the human condition generally and the American condition in particular. The optimists include the likes of Charles Maynes, who has decried "the new pessimism"[4]; Julian Simon, who posits "no limit in sight," environmental or otherwise, for America and the rest of the planet[5]; Max Singer and Aaron Wildavsky, whose *The Real World Order* envisions the current "zone of peace" inhabited by the United States and other Northern Hemisphere states (Yugoslavia aside) eventually extending into and replacing the current "zone of turmoil" inhabited by much of the South[6]; Allan Goodman, whose *A Brief History of the Future* heralds the twenty-first century as an era that "will encompass the longest period of peace, democracy, and economic development in history"[7]; John Mueller, who foresees "the obsolescence of major war,"[8] and James Lee Ray, who sees "the end of international war" altogether[9]; and Francis Fukuyama, who by 1989 had already proclaimed that "the end of history" had occurred with the final triumph of western liberal democracy and free-market capitalism over all other competitors.[10] The pessimists include John Mearsheimer, who, a year after Fukuyama's pronouncement, was already lamenting "why we will soon miss the Cold War"[11]; Samuel Huntington, who has hypothesized about the "clash of civilizations" pitting "the West vs. the rest" as the successor to the East-West ideological axis of conflict[12]; Robert Kaplan, who writes of "the coming anarchy" stemming from ecological and other catastrophes, citing contemporary Rwanda as a metaphor for how both the South and the North will evolve[13]; Paul Kennedy, who, at times writing in a doomsdayish tone reserved usually for biologists, finds us wholly unprepared for the twenty-first century[14]; and Robert Heilbroner, who finds "the human prospect" rather dim, given what he sees as a persistent "what has posterity ever done for me?" attitude held by publics everywhere[15] (in contrast to the ancient invocation supposedly offered by leaders of the Iroquois Confederacy prior to every council meeting, that "in our every deliberation we must consider the impact of our decisions on the next seven generations").[16]

Rather than engaging in such cosmic, millennial thinking exercises, the author has taken on a more modest, but amply challenging, task here. This

Two competing visions of the future. Should we be optimistic or pessimistic?
(TOP: Jeffrey Aaronson/Network Aspen; BOTTOM: Mal Hancock)

chapter will attempt to summarize the main features of the contemporary international system currently, at the turn of the century, and then analyze their near-term implications for American foreign policy, with a view particularly to examining whether the system is hospitable or inhospitable to the kind of global multilateralism the United States helped to give birth to in the twentieth century. We are interested here not so much in the future of the United Nations as in the more general subject of global governance and the potential for global institution-building of some sort.

It is worth remembering that the world does not revolve around governments making "great global choices among grand alternatives." Policymakers, John Ruggie notes, "do not get to choose on the future of the state system; they confront choices on exchange rates, . . . terrorist attacks on airport lobbies and embassy compounds, and garbage that floats down a river or is transported through the air [and, one might add, whether or not to pay one's UN dues]. If change comes it will be the product of micro practices. Hence, if we want to understand change or help to shape it, it is to these micro practices that we should look."[17] Similarly, Roger Hilsman observes: "A government does not decide to inaugurate the nuclear age, but only to try to build an atomic bomb before its enemy does. It does not make a formal decision to become a welfare state, but only to take each of a series of steps—to . . . alleviate the hardship of people who have lost their jobs in a depression with a few weeks of unemployment compensation, or to lighten the old age of industrial workers with a tentative program of social security benefits."[18] As Hilsman suggests, small decisions at times can set in motion some rather revolutionary forces. It is also important to understand that small decisions are not taken in a vacuum. Hence, we need to look at the larger environment in which decision-makers have to operate today.

SYSTEMIC CONSTRAINTS AND OPPORTUNITIES
SURROUNDING GLOBAL INSTITUTION-BUILDING

If the "New World Order" proclaimed by George Bush in 1991—centered around a universal commitment to the rule of law and the peaceful settlement of disputes in international affairs—has not yet materialized, a new world order has nonetheless begun to take shape. The exact shape of this international system remains uncertain, since it is a work in progress, subject to numerous "micro practices." But at least one thing is clear: the relatively neat, tidy *bipolar* era following World War II which featured two superpowers engaged in a great geopolitical struggle, presiding over two fairly cohesive blocs (the Western developed capitalist democracies of the First World pitted against the East-bloc developed communist states of the Second World), separated by a Third World of "nonaligned" developing countries, is gone; trends in the direction of a more complicated system which were already partially discernible toward the later stages of the Cold War are becoming more pronounced and accelerated. This complexity is marked by at least four key properties: (1) a growing diffusion and ambiguity of power, with the term "superpower" in question and the term "power" itself increasingly problematic; (2) a growing fluidity of alignments, with the old East-West (communist vs. noncommunist) and North-South (rich

President George Bush helped lead a global coalition during the Gulf War that turned back Iraq's invasion of Kuwait in 1991, ending "the first post-Cold War crisis" and proclaiming the birth of "the new world order." (The fine print on the poster contains a reference to Japan's Sony corporation having recently purchased Columbia Pictures.) (J. Vint Lawrence)

vs. poor) axes of conflicts giving way to West-West, South-South, and assorted other fault-lines; (3) an ever expanding agenda of newly salient issues facing national governments, with economic, environmental, and other concerns competing for attention with traditional military-security issues and, like the latter, enmeshing states in ever more intricate patterns of interdependence; and (4) a growing importance of multinational corporations (MNCs), international nongovernmental organizations (NGOs), intergovernmental organizations (IGOs), and other nonstate actors, which are increasingly competing with states in shaping outcomes in world politics.

Perhaps the central question of our time is whether—based on the first two trends (the breakup of the postwar power and bloc structure)—we are witnessing merely the déjà vu transformation of the international system from bipolarity back to the more normal, pre-1945 historical pattern of multipolarity, *or* whether—based on the other two trends (the new agenda of issues and the new set of actors)—we are on the brink of a much more fundamental, epic transformation, namely, as suggested in Chapter 1, a change not only *in* the Westphalian system but *of* the Westphalian system and its centuries-old underlying operating principles. Let us consider these four trends one by one.

The Growing Diffusion and Ambiguity of Power

By the 1970s, one could already see superpower slippage and the increasingly problematical nature of the exercise of power. The Vietnam War ended in 1973, marking the failure of "the greatest power on earth" to defeat "a band of night-riders in black pajamas"[19] despite utilizing 500,000 troops and the latest military technology. The Soviets suffered their own Vietnam-style debacle in Afghanistan in 1979, when seemingly backward Mujahedeen rebels repelled a Red Army invasion. Sandwiched between these two episodes, the oil crisis of 1973 saw a group of less-developed countries, some of which were tiny "statelets" and all of which were devoid of the assets traditionally associated with international influence, threatening for awhile to bring the industrialized world to a standstill over price hikes and boycotts. These were all harbingers of other setbacks and humiliations that were to follow in the next decades. While some observers refer to the United States in the post-Cold War era as the lone superpower left in a unipolar world,[20] it would seem more accurate to say we are now living in a post-hegemonic, "post-superpower age" where at times the United States has behaved more like a "subpower," due to lack of usable resources or resolve or both.[21] Although some analysts see the United States as capable of dealing with threats to international order through its own unilateral action, others argue, more cogently, that Washington cannot afford except on rare occasions to be the lone global policeman and must settle for the role of "sheriff of the posse."[22]

In the post-Cold War era, there are at least five power centers.[23] One is the United States, whose much-publicized "decline" in the 1980s (noted in such works as Paul Kennedy's *The Rise and Fall of the Great Powers*[24]) has been halted, with America now accounting for over 25 percent of world industrial output and one-third of world military spending, less than the extraordinary position it enjoyed in the immediate aftermath of World War II but impressive nonetheless; it would not be a stretch to call the United States an, if not *the*, "indispensable nation" as Secretary of State Madeleine Albright dubbed it in 1998.[25] A second is Japan, second-ranked in gross national product (GNP) despite recent economic woes. A third is the European Union, led by Germany, Britain, and France, moving toward a single market, and possibly further down the road a single European "supranational" state, larger than the United States. A fourth is China, representing one-fifth of humanity and experiencing the highest economic growth rates of any state in the past decade. A fifth is the Russian Federation—the main successor state to the Soviet Union, still the largest piece of real estate on the planet, blessed with vast natural resources, and, together with the United States, accounting for 95 percent of the global stockpile of 35,000 nuclear weapons. To this pantheon can be added the so-called middle powers, such as India, Brazil, Nigeria, Canada, Australia, and the Nordic countries.[26]

The construction of a meaningful pecking order in international relations has become a trickier exercise than in the past, however, as those states with sizable military arsenals that can be projected well beyond their borders (traditionally labeled "great powers") now find it far more awkward to employ those resources against lesser actors and almost impossible to employ them against each other. Indeed, although we are not there yet, as Libya and other relatively small or underdeveloped "rogue" states close in on acquiring ABC arsenals (particularly biological and chemical weapons, the "poor man's" weapons of mass destruction which are more readily obtainable than atomic weapons), the international system may become a "unit veto" system of the kind that was only fantasized about in the 1950s, where each state has the ultimate instrument of warfare.[27] (The American Ambassador to the United Nations reported to the U.S. Congress in 1995 that Iraq, even though it did not have substantial delivery capabilities, had produced "enough biological warfare agents to kill every man, woman, and child on Earth."[28])

One cannot discount the continuing importance of military power, as seen in the success of the U.S.-led coalition during the 1991 Gulf War against Iraq; Kenneth Waltz argues for the primacy of military power even in the post-Cold War era, noting that "no state lacking in military ability to compete with other great powers has ever been ranked among them."[29] Still, the contemporary era may mark the acceleration of a process underway for some time, namely the eclipse of military potential as the main source of control in the international system. At the same time that such resources as oil and investment capital have become part of the currency of power, traditional military resources have become somewhat devalued. Even a traditional "realist" thinker such as Henry Kissinger has commented that "the issues susceptible to solution by military action are in decline" and that military power "is less and less relevant to most foreseeable international crises."[30] The old saw attributed to Frederick the Great, that diplomacy is only as effective as the number of guns backing it up, has always been open to debate, and all the more so today. The United States, for example, is hardly going to threaten to nuke China over human rights transgressions, or Saudi Arabia over petroleum price increases, or other rival states over most matters at issue today in world politics. Resources are less fungible than previously, power more issue-specific. At times "soft power" ("the projection of a set of norms and their embrace by leaders in other nations") may trump hard power.[31] The kind of "polyarchy" that Robert Dahl years ago associated with the governance of New Haven, Connecticut, seems an apt characterization of the contemporary international system.[32]

If one must be careful not to exaggerate the power of the United States or any other single actor today, one should also not lose sight of the degree of stratification which persists in the international system. The system *is* stratified, even if stratification does not lend itself to predicting winners and losers quite so easily as in the past. Just six states (the United States, Russia, France, Germany, the UK, and China) account for 75 percent of all military spending worldwide, down somewhat from their 85 percent share in 1960, but still constituting a large concentration of firepower; if one adds Japan, which has recently joined the ranks of top spenders, seven states claim more than three-quarters of global arms expenditures. The United States, Russia, and China together account for one-third of all military manpower on the globe. Regarding economic resources, the eleven largest countries in GNP terms—the G-7 states (the Group of Seven leading industrialized democracies which convene annual economic summits as a kind of First World board of directors) plus Russia, China, India, and Brazil—account for 70 percent of the planetary product, comparing favorably with the power distribution in the immediate postwar period.[33] As for soft power, even if Asian, Islamic, and other states may be resisting Western values, an American cultural onslaught seems nonetheless to be pressing forward, with CNN in over 140 countries (being challenged by MTV), Coca-Cola in over 160 (consumed some 600 million times daily), McDonalds in over 100, the worldwide web in almost as many (and the most likely of all American innovations to become universal), and English fast expanding its reach as the dominant language of commercial and scientific communication. In short, notwithstanding the fragmentation of power, there would still appear to be, at least on paper, the makings of a "concert of power"—a small, manageable coalition of states capable of moving the international system and forging a degree of world order through a judicious blend of carrots and sticks if they were so disposed.[34]

The Growing Fluidity of Alignments

John Mearsheimer, waxing nostalgic, has said that the Cold War gave a kind of "order to the anarchy of international relations."[35] Clarity yes, order maybe. Former Israeli Foreign Minister Abba Eban seems more on the mark: "The Cold War, with all its perils, expressed a certain bleak stability: alignments, fidelities, and rivalries were sharply defined."[36] Clarity itself became more muddled as the Cold War system progressed; tight bipolarity had given way to loose bipolarity by the 1960s, and the latter had been superseded by "bimultipolarity" by the late 1970s, perhaps best exemplified by the failure of the United States to persuade many of its allies (and even Puerto Rico) to boycott the 1980 Olympic Games in Moscow in protest against the Soviet invasion of Afghanistan despite President Carter calling the Soviet action "the greatest threat to world peace since World War II."[37] Still, to the very end of the Cold War, indeed well into the 1990s, the main categories which international law texts as well as most other international relations treatises comfortably fell back on in conceptualizing world affairs were "Western," "Marxist," and "Third World" perspectives. These trichotomous, polarizing tendencies of the Cold War have now been replaced by a far more complex set of relationships, with many sources of conflict and cross-cutting cleavages to be found in the post-Cold War world. The contemporary international system is messier than its predecessor, but would seem a tad less Armageddon-prone.

It is possible that the East-West conflict could be revived in some form if communism as a belief system is resuscitated by the failure of capitalism to deliver the goods in societies undergoing capitalist transitions, but for now Marxist-Leninism has been overtaken by "Market-Leninism."[38] Any East-West axis of conflict that might reemerge is more likely to be motivated by a Russo-Sino reaction to NATO (North Atlantic Treaty Organization) expansion and other perceived U.S. ambitions than by rival ideologies. Just as the East-West conflict has disappeared as East bloc states have moved ideologically toward the West, the North-South conflict—which came to compete for attention with the East-West conflict during the Cold War era—also shows signs of possibly losing its defining character despite the persistence of the rich-poor gap. Parts of the Third World recently have been seeking to revive the NIEO ("New International Economic Order") debate of the 1970s, this time couching demands for aid and technology transfer in the language of sustainable development and environmentalism (e.g., tropical rain forest countries requesting assistance in preserving their biodiversity, particularly plant species which have valuable medical applications). However, given the growing economic diversity within the developing world, Southern solidarity likely will be increasingly difficult to maintain as some of the more industrialized members gravitate toward the North. When 108 members of the Non-Aligned Movement met in 1992 in Bandung, Indonesia, they had to search hard for a rationale for their continued existence, just as the eighth UN Conference on Trade and Development held in Cartagena, Colombia, around the same time "witnessed the end of the formal role of the alliance that created the NIEO and the Group of 77 [the name given to the coalition of less developed countries]."[39] The staying power of the Non-Aligned Movement and UNCTAD, which still exist even though they are barely functioning, is testimony to the role of inertia in human relations. As for the North, increasing economic competition between technologically advanced states threatens to make West-West conflict almost as volatile an arena as East-West conflict had been. Instead of East-West and North-South, there is the First World and the "Two-Thirds World," the latter constituting what some now call the "Global South"—the collection of former communist states and third world, fourth world (super-poor), or middle-income less developed countries (LDCs) as well as newly industrializing countries (NICs) and next NICs trying to join the global elite.

If the East-West and North-South conflicts were "the two dominant struggles of our time" in the last half of the twentieth century, what then are replacing them as the central global dramas? What new descriptive categories in the post-Cold War era might replace the vernacular of first, second, and third worlds and other such terminology that dominated discourse during the Cold War? Will the critical divisions occur in the form of competing civilizational entities built around culture (the "West vs. the rest"—Islamic fundamentalism, militant Hinduism, and other nonwestern traditions) as posited by Huntington,[40] or emergent continental blocs (the North American Free Trade Association, the European Union, and the Pacific Rim) built around economic relationships, or some other permutations? In any event, it does seem premature to declare either "the end of history" or "the end of geography."[41] Based on recent cases such as Yugoslavia and Rwanda, there is evidence that a series of relatively isolated conflicts will increasingly define world politics and that these localized and regionalized conflicts may be hard to fit into any larger global, system-wide Weltanschauung. Perhaps "unalignment" is the order of the day.[42] Yet global issues such as nuclear proliferation and the globalization of the international economy will not go away, and the very absence of polarized friction in the contemporary system can provide the grease to mobilize a coalition in support of global institution-building in a manner that was not as possible previously— again, though, only if the will to lead is present.

An Expanding Agenda of Issues

Closely related to power and alignment trends, although potentially far more revolutionary in impact, is the increased blurring of the line between "high politics" (having to do with vital, core interests) and "low politics" (having to do with not-so-vital, non-core interests). In the contemporary international system, "national security" has taken on a newer meaning, no longer equated almost exclusively with military issues. Although it may remain the overriding goal of nation-states, *security* has been broadened to include economic, ecological, and other *welfare* dimensions that have gained rising visibility on the agendas of governments.[43] This trend is rooted in long-term historical processes: mass democracy and the public appetite for improved material well-being led to the growth of the welfare state in the twentieth century, while technology over time internationalized these concerns as it became clear that they could not be fully satisfied through unilateral national action. It was already apparent by the 1970s, as Stanley Hoffmann noted, that we were witnessing "the move from a world dominated by a single chessboard—the strategic-diplomatic one (which eclipsed or controlled all others)—to a world dispersed into a variety of chessboards."[44] Such "complex interdependence"[45] was interrupted briefly during the realpolitik revival of the early 1980s—when the Cold War heated up under

"Rambo" Reagan and there was a preoccupation with military matters—only to be resumed at a more accelerated pace in the 1990s, freed from Cold War constraints.

That interdependence has become a cliché does not make it any less real a phenomenon. There is some disagreement over whether welfare issues have now achieved primacy over military issues, considering that finance ministers in recent years have been getting the kinds of front-page newspaper headlines once reserved for defense ministers and foreign ministers. Playing on the famous nineteenth century Prussian military strategist von Clausewitz, economics is being called "the continuation of war by other means,"[46] particularly among highly developed societies, which may intensify their economic competition but, presumably, are unlikely to wage shooting wars against each other given the destructiveness of armed combat in the nuclear age. That system transformation occurred in 1989 without major war as the engine of change (unlike 1815 following the Napoleonic Wars, 1919 following World War I, and 1945 following World War II) was unprecedented in the life of the Westphalian state system, defying all realist theory and raising the question of whether there had been a change of seismic proportions in the international landscape. Although there obviously was considerable conflict during the Cold War, the period since 1945 up to the present has been characterized as "the long peace," i.e., the longest continuous stretch of time since 1648 in which there has not been a single recorded instance of direct great-power exchange of actual hostilities. Indeed, during most years of the 1990s and into the 2000s, there have been very few inter-state wars occurring anywhere on the planet, great or small.[47]

Of course, civil wars have proliferated, sometimes drawing in outside actors based on "humanitarian intervention" or other motives. The Yugoslav conflict is a reminder that war in its most savage form can still occur even among people living in relatively highly developed societies, with life expectancy and literacy rates comparable to those in the United States. The Yugoslav case also shows how convulsions in international economic relations can contribute to escalation of tensions, possibly culminating in violence, since it was uneven economic development in different regions of Yugoslavia as well as disruption of traditional East bloc trade ties that was one catalyst for the country's breakup in the 1990s and the strife that followed. There is reason to believe that not only will the world continue to be faced with "teacup wars"[48] in which major actors are only peripherally involved, but one also cannot rule out larger wars between great powers themselves. The specter of Moscow dispatching a Russian warship to the Mediterranean in 1999, in order to provide a symbolic show of support for their fellow Slavs in Serbia who were being bombarded by NATO planes punishing the Milosevic regime for ethnic cleansing of its Albanian population in Kosovo, could not help but conjure up harrowing reminders of the Cuban missile crisis of 1962. Classic security problems, including territorial disputes, persist, reflected in China's pressing of claims to the Spratly Islands and Taiwan, along with the machinations between Russia, Iran, and others over control of the Caspian Sea oil routes. Although such disputes are less likely to eventuate in war today than in the past, they remain a source of concern, as do less conventional security issues, such as terrorism, drug trafficking, and the spread of epidemics.[49] If Chapters VI and VII of the UN Charter (dealing with peaceful settlement of disputes and collective security between states) are anachronisms today, it is not because war is a relic but rather that there is a need to adapt those parts of the Charter, along with other international regimes, to changed conditions.

A Growing Set of Actors

The UN Charter presumed a world of states as the basis for human organization. One of the major developments in the postwar era was, in fact, the tremendous proliferation of new states mainly precipitated by the decolonialization process whereby erstwhile colonies were granted their sovereign independence. The original UN membership had more than tripled by the time the Cold War had ended in 1989, with another two dozen states added in the 1990s. However, the founders did not envision that many of these states would be of the cookie-cutter variety—microstates smaller in size than not only a typical American state but a typical American city and, in some cases, a typical American town. What was envisioned even less was the proliferation of *nonstate* actors and their growing importance if not autonomy in world politics, including subnational actors (e.g, the overseas trade missions maintained by virtually every state in the United States)[50] as well as transnational actors (e.g., the now more than 300 IGOs, 10,000 NGOs, and 35,000 multinational corporations).[51] Relating to Hoffmann's chessboard imagery, world politics can be seen as a series of issue-areas in which outcomes are determined by a congeries of forces, including both state and nonstate actors.

For example, one cannot fully understand the dynamics of the 1992 UN Conference on Environment and Development held in Rio de Janeiro (the "Earth Summit") unless one takes into account, in addition to the interplay between Northern and Southern governments, the variety of nonstate actors involved: the secretariats of the UN, World Bank, and other IGOs, nongovernmental scientific research bodies ("epistemic communities") and global environmental advocacy groups, MNCs, and a host of other players. Although "state-centric" analysts reared in the Westphalian tradition would contend that IGOs are little more than fragile collections of states that tend to be dominated from a few national capitals, and that NGOs are no match for the power of governments, the point is not that nonstate actors played the decisive role in the conference, only that they were a not insignificant part of the equation that produced several new environmental agreements.[52] To the extent that economic issues are in ascendancy relative to military security issues, we are likely to see greater play of subnational and transnational actors which are making headlines of late—private bankers, currency traders, corporate executives, World Trade Organization bureaucrats, and the like—whose behavior is not adequately accounted for by state-centric models that are based on states as unitary, rational actors pursuing their national interests. As we will discuss in Chapters 3 and 4, "two-level games" (involving interactions between national governments trying to play to both foreign officials abroad as well as domestic constituencies at home) are being further complicated by "three-level games" (involving an additional layer of lobbying by MNCs and other transnational actors trying to influence policy).[53] There is already evidence to suggest that, with the end of the Cold War, it is harder for an American president to manipulate national security symbolism (as "the leader of the free world") and for national leaders in general to mobilize their nation in support of broad national policies, whether foreign or domestic.[54] The United States, in particular, seems to be suffering again from its "weak state" syndrome—the anti-statist (anti-government) impulse historically dominant in the American political culture, overcome usually only when there is a major external threat or national crisis of some sort requiring an energetic government response—although many polities seem to be experiencing this condition.

As discussed in the opening chapter, some have associated the nonstate actor phenomenon with what they perceive as the decline of the nation-state as an institution. There is some disagreement among those who envision the demise of the nation-state as to whether the primary threat to its viability comes from *integrative* tendencies (the transnational links, perhaps best represented by cyberspace, which are causing mounting "loss of control" and erosion of sovereignty) or *disintegrative* tendencies (the proliferation of so many small, marginally self-sustaining polities, fueled especially by the surge of ethnic conflicts and separatist movements), or *both*.[55] Depending on which analyst one believes, we are witnessing the emergence of either a global village or the exact opposite—global villages. Brussels, Belgium, would seem a perfect metaphor for our time, caught between centripetal and centrifugal forces, at once the seat of the European Union (trying to serve as the center of a supranational experiment) and also the capital of a nation-state always on the edge of dissolution (trying to mediate the differences among Belgian citizens divided between the Dutch-speaking Flemish in the North and French-speaking Walloons in the South). Everything is up for grabs in global governance, including not only what level of government (ranging from subnational to supranational) is optimal but also how much government (as opposed to civil society) is optimal. Notable here is the recent observer status granted the International Red Cross by the UN General Assembly, an unprecedented measure far more potentially revolutionary than the consultative status granted NGOs by the UN's Economic and Social Council, since only territorially defined entities—would-be states, such as the Vatican and the Palestine Liberation Organization (PLO)—have enjoyed such status previously. As Susan Strange has said, "state authority has leaked away, upwards, sideways, and downwards."[56]

However, if the nation-state is withering away, someone has forgotten to tell the leaders, and for that matter the publics, in Washington and elsewhere. Even if nuclear weapons make national boundaries as dysfunctional for defense as gunpowder did the walled cities of yore, there remains almost everywhere a generalized commitment to the national security state. Likewise, even if economic elites have outgrown the nation-state as former captains of industry and commerce outgrew feudalism, and notwithstanding pronouncements about how the "the era of big government is over" in the face of growing cynicism toward government and a growing movement toward privatization, there remains almost everywhere a continued heavy reliance on the welfare state. Judging by the non-shrinking size of most national budgets and national egos (e.g., the annual U.S. federal budget for Fiscal Year 2001 stood at approximately $2 trillion, a record high), statism and nationalism would still seem very much alive.[57] The nation-state may possibly have peaked as a political form in the twentieth century, but it is rather premature to sound its death knell.

I said at the beginning of this chapter that I would attempt to resist millennial thinking. Regarding the "central question" I raised earlier about the long-term future of the Westphalian state system, there would seem no amount of scientific analysis that could answer that question. Just as it took observers some 200 years to recognize in retrospect the significance of 1648 as ushering in a new age—the term "international relations," after all, was not invented until Jeremy Bentham was credited with it in the early nineteenth century—one must leave it to historians many decades hence to determine whether 1989 was or was not truly a Westphalian moment. The owl of Minerva always rises at night. For now, suffice it to say that we are inhabiting a schizophrenic world, or what James Rosenau has called a "bifurcated" system characterized by an uneasy coexistence of "state-centric" and "multicentric actor politics."[58] The reader was forewarned at the outset to be prepared to cope with a high degree of ambiguity. Rosenau rightly speaks of "powerful tensions, profound contradictions, and perplexing paradoxes" that mark international life.[59] We will try to resolve these as best we can in the next chapter and the remainder of this book.

Before moving on, let us consider what all this means for near-term U.S. foreign policy, and especially the prospects for a "new multilateralism" which can facilitate global problem-solving. One might recall Soviet President Mikhail Gorbachev's plea in the late 1980s, as the Cold War was winding down, for "the creation of a comprehensive system of international security," with Soviet Foreign Minister Eduard Shevardnadze commenting at the time that "the dividing lines of the bipolar world are receding. The biosphere recognizes no division into blocs, alliances, or systems."[60] The world was not ready then for such thinking. Will it ever be in the foreseeable future?

THE PROSPECTS FOR A NEW MULTILATERALISM

One can detect that there are numerous systemic constraints as well as opportunities surrounding global institution-building at present. The need for global institution-building is arguably greater today than ever before, given mankind's capacity to annihilate much of the human species in a matter of minutes through nuclear weapons or in a longer time frame through ecological disaster. This need occurs at precisely the same moment when central guidance mechanisms are less feasible in some respects than in previous eras due to the recent structural changes in the international system described above. It could be argued that, if comprehensive, global approaches to world order such as the League of Nations and United Nations have failed or worked only marginally in the past, they are *a fortiori* even less likely to succeed today, given the proliferation of states as well as nonstate actors clamoring to be at the global bargaining table, the equally unwieldy proliferation of items on the agenda (ranging from CO_2 emission reductions to intellectual property rights enforcement) that tax the financial and technical capacities of even the most well-heeled and well-intentioned states and greatly complicate reaching and implementing transparent international agreements of wide scope, the absence of any one or two powers capable themselves of moving the system, and the absence of any visible, palpable system-wide crisis equivalent to World War I or II that can serve as a catalyst for the next stage of global organization. Hence, the best we can do, some say, is subglobal multilateralism or minilateralism.

Granted the obstacles to global institution-building are enormous. However, we may be underestimating the possibilities. For example, we forget how close the world has come, with the UN Law of the Sea (LOS) Convention, to producing a single set of rules governing virtually every human activity (fishing, navigation, mining, etc.) on 70 percent of the earth's surface; the LOS treaty embodies an emerging consensus in support of each coastal state exercising sovereignty over a 12-mile "territorial sea" immediately adjacent to its shoreline, and control over all living and nonliving resources in an "exclusive economic zone" extending outward another 188 miles, although there is still some disagreement over regulation of remaining ocean space such as the deep seabed, where there is potentially enormous mineral wealth. Further progress in global institution-building would not seem out of reach. Again, by global institution-building I do not mean global government but global governance—better yet, what Barry Buzan felicitously has referred to as a more "mature anarchy."[61] Even with the rise of nonstate actors, it is still states and their national governments which will have to drive this process, since ultimately it is the latter (e.g., the United States) and not the former (e.g., General Motors) which ordinarily are parties to LOS and other international regimes. About the search for world order through the development of international regimes, specifically global bodies such as the UN, Inis Claude has written: "The international organization movement . . . can be interpreted as an attempt to perpetuate the multistate system by making its continued operation tolerable; it is not so much a scheme for creating world government as for making world government unnecessary."[62] As these efforts go, so goes the state system in which the major states continue to have the largest stake. Lynn Miller puts it most plainly when he says, after all, "it is *their* system" for the most part.[63] Even though the stakes have become diffused, along with power capabilities, there would appear enough at stake, and enough power concentration remaining in the system, for some subset of states, through an enlightened concert of great powers approach to world order, to provide the collective good represented by international institution-building. The United States, not as an all-powerful hegemon but as a "veto state"[64] capable of blocking action, is clearly critical to any significant, workable broad institutional reform inside or outside the UN.

Whether or not further global institution-building is *feasible*, we need to examine more closely why it remains *desirable* from an American perspective. The argument can be made succinctly in terms of a simple cost-benefit analysis. Let us focus on the UN. On the *cost* side of the equation, the most obvious point is that the U.S. annual assessed contribution to the United Nations regular budget is on the order of $300 million (less than one-quarter the price of a single airplane such as the B-2 bomber), hardly a budget-buster; indeed, the UN yearly regular budget is less than the budget of the New York City police department, and it totals only about .00005 percent of the U.S. GNP, amounting to $0.88 out of each American's pocket.[65] If one factors in U.S. annual peacekeeping assessments, approximately $1 billion is added, while a few million dollars more annually go to extrabudgetary payments, voluntary contributions, and support for UN specialized agencies such as the Food and Agriculture Organization. All told, the United Nations system as a whole (not including the World Bank and International Monetary Fund) spends an estimated $10 billion annually. With a bureaucracy smaller in size than the state of Wyoming and the city of Stockholm, it would seem the fears harbored by some neo-isolationists in the American political system that the UN is a sprawling world government-in-waiting which could threaten U.S. sovereignty are rather exaggerated. As for other, nonfinancial costs to the United States, it is argued by some that "small states tend to treat [international organizations] as vehicles for their self-assertion"[66] and that the UN, in particular, historically has been looked to by weak states to legitimize agendas antithetical to great-power interests, which in the absence of global sounding boards would otherwise get no hearing whatsoever.[67] There is little evidence, however, that small states have succeeded in implementing such agendas in the face of major-power opposition; one need only point to the failure of the New International Economic Order, New World Information Order, and related debates in the 1970s in the UN General Assembly, where Third World militancy fell on deaf ears and was subsequently replaced by developing countries becoming eager suitors of western foreign investment in the rush to American-led globalization and Internet use. There would seem no other potential costs worth mentioning.

Given the relatively small costs incurred by the United States in global institution-building, one does not need to demonstrate huge *benefits* to justify a policy of promoting global multilateralism. Suffice it to say, the United States has the most at stake in the creation and maintenance of a stable *world* order based on some at least semiobserved rules of the game (international treaties, norms, or general principles), being the preeminent home country and host country of multinational corporations, the state with the largest number of citizens (diplomats and nondiplomats) traveling abroad, and the state with the most far-flung global transactions and interests generally. Some universal or near-universal institutional apparatus is needed to facilitate the production and operation of broad-based international regimes, unless the United States would prefer the inefficiency of negotiating and implementing bilateral regimes piecemeal with some 200 different national authorities.[68] At a minimum, the United States seems well served by most of the UN-affiliated specialized agencies (global public unions) entrusted with relatively technical, "functional" concerns; witness, for example, the 7 billion pieces of mail that cross national boundaries each year and the 700 billion passenger-miles flown annually by scheduled airlines internationally, a set of routinized transactions of which the United States has a disproportionate share and which could not occur without the Universal Postal Union and International Civil Aviation Organization.[69]

UN achievements in the peace and security area are more debatable. Reacting to the standard criticism often leveled at the UN that it is nothing more than a talk shop, Winston Churchill once noted that "jaw-jaw is better than war-war." It is hard to measure with quantitative data how much the UN has contributed to peace. At least one study has found that the UN had a fairly successful overall record between 1945 and 1975, when the organization became involved in more than half of all international crises and was effective at crisis abatement in one-third of those cases, with effectiveness increasing as the situation became more serious and more violent[70]; citing particularly the 1973 Israeli-Arab Yom Kippur War, which at one point put both Washington and Moscow on nuclear alert, one prominent realist and UN skeptic acknowledged that the organization "proved to be . . . the most effective way by which the settlement could be achieved."[71] Although the next decade saw the UN practically moribund in the security area, the end of the Cold War resulted in more peacekeeping missions being authorized between 1989 and 1993 than in the entire previous history of the organization, with numerous additional missions added as the 1990s progressed. The recent record has been mixed, with failures probably outnumbering successes, although, lest UN critics gloat, few cases have been as disastrous as the 1983 American intervention in Lebanon, when 240 U.S. Marines were killed by a terrorist bomb while they were deployed in lieu of a UN peacekeeping force rejected by the Reagan administration (in contrast with the highly successful U.S.-led multinational force which removed Iraq from Kuwait during the 1990–91 Gulf War, aided by the political cover and coalition-building advantages provided by the UN).

On balance, then, there seem few if any reasons on the surface for the United States to oppose global institution-building as a foreign policy goal, and many reasons for Washington to be sympathetic. This conclusion seems to fly in the face of the current U.S. posture toward the UN, which ranges from hostile to indifferent, symbolized by the $1 billion in arrearages owed by the United States as the foremost dues delinquent in the world body. It is ironic that the Number 1 deadbeat in the world organization is the same state credited with launching "the move to institutions"[72] in the twentieth century, with the League of Nations being the brainchild of an American president (even though Woodrow Wilson could not persuade an isolationist Congress to accept U.S. membership after World War I) and the UN being so closely associated with the United States that its Charter resides in the National Archives in Washington, D.C. I will return to the U.S.-UN relationship in Chapter 8, suggesting some "micropractices" that might be implemented in the ongoing project of global institution-building.

Henry Kissinger has noted that the major challenge facing the United States in the post-Cold War era is to carve out a role for itself in a world which "for the first time in her history . . . she cannot dominate [in terms of being a superpower, as during the Cold War], but from which she also cannot simply withdraw [in terms of isolationism, which defined America's orientation toward the world through much of its pre-Cold War existence]."[73] That is, the United States must adapt to a new multilateralism, at a time when conditions are not wholly ripe. It is the very pacific nature of the Cold War transformation, as well as the absence of any obvious singular enemy facing the United States today, that has contributed to the current mass apathy among Americans toward world affairs; Saddam Hussein and Slobodan Milosevic do not quite measure up to Josef Stalin or Adolph Hitler as a threat to the American way of life. That has made it difficult for Washington to mobilize public interest in and support for United Nations reform or other dimensions of foreign policy, which lack saliency on the public policy agenda. Whether the New World Order trumpeted at the outset of the 1990s ever materializes will depend in no small measure on the U.S. capacity to provide leadership, now vested in the administration of George W. Bush. This in turn will depend on an American public willing to reengage itself in world affairs as a nation and not just as a set of economic, ethnic, and other enclaves. A "return to normalcy" (the slogan urging a retreat back to Fortress America after World War I) does not seem appropriate to the twenty-first century.[74]

If one might be permitted a closing millennial thought, it is worthwhile quoting Abba Eban, who, after heavily criticizing the UN through much of a recent essay, concludes that "the idea of an international organization playing an assertive role in the pacification of this turbulent world may have to bide its time, but it will never disappear from view. History and the future are on its side."[75] In the next chapter we will look more deeply into these trends.

CHAPTER 3

Billiard Balls and Cobwebs

A patriot is he whose publick conduct is regulated by one single motive, the love of his country; who, as an agent in parliament, has, for himself, neither hope nor fear, neither kindness nor resentment, but refers everything to the common interest.
—Samuel Johnson, *The Patriot*, 1772

We have been more or less brought up to believe that the bonds of community, responsibility, and obligation run only to the [national] frontiers. Should we extend our vision to include all the people of our planet?
—Barbara Ward, *The Lopsided World*, 1968

CLARIFICATION OF TERMS: STATES, NATIONS, AND NATION-STATES

We have noted that over the past several centuries the world has revolved around nation-states. The term "nation-state" can be a source of confusion, so some clarification is in order here. In everyday parlance, the average person tends not to speak of nation-states but to use a number of other terms interchangeably—"nations," "states," "countries"—to refer to those entities that are distinguished by thick boundaries on world maps. Although one might casually interchange these terms, they are not exactly synonymous. Technically speaking, "state" refers to a *legal-political* entity, "nation" refers to a *cultural* or social entity, and "country" to a *geographical* entity. In defining "state" and "nation," the distinction is not merely technical; it has real importance for international relations scholars as well as policymakers and lawyers.

When we say that "state" refers to a legal-political entity, we mean an entity that has a sovereign government exercising supreme authority over a relatively fixed population within relatively well-defined territorial boundaries and acknowledging no higher authority outside those boundaries. We have noted that there are some 200 such territorial units today considered by most observers to be states. Such entities have international legal status, which enables them to enter into treaties, join intergovernmental organizations such as the United Nations, exchange ambassadors, and engage in other "official" international activities. In short, whether one uses the term or not, states are the main reference points one sees on a world map. Some states, such as the United States and Japan, are obviously well known, but other states, such as Palau (in the South Pacific), are less so. As of this writing, the latest states admitted into the UN were a foursome of small Pacific island countries—Tonga (also called the Friendly Islands), Nauru, Tuvalu, and Kiribati, each with a total population of under 100,000 people (smaller than Akron, Ohio)—bringing the total UN membership to 189. No matter how tiny or inconspicuous a state is, its sovereignty gives it at least formal equality with all other states.

A "nation," however, is conceptually and legally different. When we say "nation" refers to a cultural or social entity, we mean a group of people having some sense of shared historical experience (generally rooted in a common language, ethnicity, or other cultural characteristics) as well as shared destiny. A nation may constitute part of a state (e.g., the Basques constituting a distinct cultural group within the state of Spain), may be coterminous with the state (e.g., the American people and the United States), or may spill over several different states (e.g., the Palestinians in Israel, Jordan, Lebanon, and several other states). As one might imagine, there are many more nations than states in the world. Indeed, ultimately a nation—which has sometimes been defined as the largest unit for which one is willing to die—is a state of mind.

These distinctions are not always clear-cut. In the case of the United States, the society is composed of many nationality groups claiming different national origins (Polish-Americans, Irish-Americans, and other "hyphenated-Americans"), but because these groups over time have for the most part become assimilated into American society and have come to identify themselves as "Americans," one can say that the state and nation are one in the United States. The oneness of the state and nation is also the case in many other established states such as Sweden. Although various groups in Sweden quarrel vociferously over the political institutions of the state, they nonetheless generally consider themselves "Swedish," and do not speak of seceding to form a new state. In contrast, the Basques in Spain do not consider themselves Spaniards; the Palestinians in Israel, Jordan, and Lebanon tend not to think of themselves as Israelis, Jordanians, or Lebanese; the Kurds in Iraq, Iran, and Turkey tend not to identify themselves as Iraqis, Iranians, or Turks. In all the latter cases, the states in question are plagued by culturally diverse populations that include separatist movements intent on establishing their own independent statehood. In the 1990s, the breakups of the Soviet Union (into the Russian Federation, Ukraine, Azerbaijan, and a dozen other successor states) and Yugoslavia (into Serbia and Montenegro, Slovenia, Croatia, Bosnia, and Macedonia) were owed to ethnic faultlines that could not be contained within existing states. Many of these successor states themselves continue to experience internal ethnopolitical conflict because they still have sizeable minority groups disaffected from the general population (perhaps the most obvious recent example being the 1999 Kosovo war fought over Serb treatment of its Albanian community).

An important aspect of world politics over the years, then, has been this search by culturally distinct nations for statehood and by polyglot states for nationhood. Hence, scholars have taken to using the term "nation-state" as essentially a synonym for "state," not to add further confusion to an already confusing terminology, but rather to acknowledge the fact that over the past several centuries there has been a persistent impulse to achieve some congruence between state and national boundaries, to make the state and nation one in the minds and hearts of its people.[1]

Nationalism has often had a negative connotation. Albert Einstein was reputed to have said "nationalism is an infantile disease. It is the measles of mankind." Yet the flip side of nationalism is patriotism, commonly thought to be a virtue to be cultivated. Generations of American schoolboys and schoolgirls, for example, have been exposed at some point in their education to such famous lines as "I only regret that I have but one life to lose for my country" (uttered by Nathan Hale in 1776, just before the British hanged him as a spy during the Revolutionary War) and "Our country! in her intercourse with foreign nations may she always be in the right; but our country, right or wrong" (uttered as a toast by naval commander Stephen Decatur in 1816). Whether good or bad, nationalism has been a powerful force in world politics. Nation-states foster flag-waving through various political socialization processes targeted at their young and old alike (through assigning civics textbooks in grade school, having the national anthem played at sporting events, commemorating national independence with special holidays, and so forth), with some societies having greater success than others in inculcating a spirit of patriotism among their people. In recent years, polls show that a remarkable 80 percent of the American public favor a constitutional amendment that would ban flag-burning or any other desecration of the Stars and Stripes.[2]

As this suggests, the United States has been among the more successful nation-states in promoting a sense of national consciousness and unity, at least since the end of the U.S. Civil War in the mid-nineteenth century. In *The Americans,* Daniel Boorstin notes how the concept of the American "nation" energized the building of the first transcontinental railroad in 1868, in pursuit of the "manifest destiny" of the United States to stretch from the Atlantic to the Pacific, while a century later it was the driving force behind Americans "meeting their destiny" in outer space as the Apollo 11 spacecraft in 1969 became the first manned vehicle to land on the moon.[3] President John F. Kennedy, who in his Inaugural Address had urged Americans to "ask not what your country can do for you but what you can do for your country," in a speech to Congress on May

25, 1961 entitled "Urgent National Needs" asserted that "this Nation should commit itself to achieving the goal, before this decade is out, of landing a man on the moon and returning him safely to earth." Discussing the need at the time to demonstrate superiority over the Soviet Union, Kennedy's Secretary of Defense Robert McNamara added: "All large-scale projects require the mobilization of resources on a national scale. . . . Dramatic achievements in space . . . symbolize the technological power and organizing capability of a nation. It is for reasons such as these that major achievements in space contribute to national prestige."[4] Kennedy and McNamara could be forgiven for thinking in such chauvinistic terms, since much of the planet has been given to national braggadocio in one way or another for much of the planet's recent history. Although astronaut Neil Armstrong's first words upon landing on the surface of the moon were "one small step for man, one giant leap for mankind," the expedition was clearly no less an American show and no less driven by dreams of national glory than the Lewis and Clark expedition 150 years earlier.

To be a human being is, generally speaking, to have some bond, legal if not emotional, with some nation-state. Although there are hundreds of thousands of "stateless" people on the globe—mostly refugees who, due to displacement by civil war or other circumstances, are literally men, women, and children without a country—most people possess "nationality" (citizenship) of some sort, whether British, Pakistani, or whatever. One might think that being stateless would confer certain advantages (e.g., less likelihood of having to serve in any country's armed forces[5]), but the disadvantages of being stateless in a state system can be far weightier than the benefits. For example, among the more important functions which national governments perform is to regulate the flow of people (their own citizens as well as foreigners) across their borders, normally through a system of passports and visas. It is this system which enables, say, New Yorkers to fly to Paris and Parisians to fly to New York, since the U.S. and French governments have worked out mutual understandings on behalf of their respective nationals. Stateless persons may not be able to navigate the globe quite so freely since, if denied entry to some port of call, they have no home government to speak for them. Hence, stateless persons have good reason to want to acquire nationality.

It should be noted that each country decides for itself on whom it will confer citizenship, with different countries using different criteria. In order to have U.S. nationality—to be able to freely enter and leave the United States and to travel around the world under protection of the U.S. government, to be able, in short, to call oneself an American—one must either have been born to American parents, born on American soil (to parents of any nationality, even to illegal aliens who entered the United States without proper documentation), or naturalized through a citizenship process administered by the U.S. Immigration and Naturalization Service. Each year almost a million immigrants who have emigrated to the United States apply for U.S. citizenship, which can be granted singly or collectively, often with much accompanying hoopla, as captured in the following scene that took place in Roanoke, Virginia in September of 1998:

> The Examinations Unit [of the INS] dispensed forms, answered inquiries, accepted applications . . . and conducted naturalization interviews. . . . The week concluded with the administration of the children's oath of allegiance to 25 children from Egypt, Guatemala, China, Russia, Korea, Vietnam, the Dominican Republic, India, and Bangladesh. . . . For many adoptive parents, it was the joyful culmination of months, and sometimes years, of completing paperwork and undergoing interviews with adoption agencies, the INS, and foreign governments and officials. . . . An area school student sang patriotic songs followed by the pledge of allegiance recited by the Daughters of the American Revolution.[6]

Along the same lines, the following scene was played out in the American heartland, in St. Louis, Missouri, on the last July 4th weekend of the twentieth century:

> One by one, they stood to tell their stories. Wearing starched suits, straw hats, miniskirts, 62 of them faced the steamy packed rotunda of the Old Courthouse Friday to announce where they were from and what they were doing here. . . . They represented 25 countries, from China and Russia to the Philippines and Vietnam. Their faces glowed with nervous hope and perspiration as they prepared to pledge allegiance to the United States and renounce formal ties to their home countries forever. . . . Maybe this naturalization ceremony was special because of its timing on a holiday weekend. Maybe it was the sense of place: An historic courthouse festooned with . . . tiny American flags tucked into the light fixtures. . . . Or maybe it was special simply because it welcomed 62 new citizens to the land of the free. . . . When that moment arrived last week . . . and dozens . . . of personalities sang a seamless Star Spangled banner, everything seemed right.[7]

Similar rituals are almost a daily occurrence in countries all over the world, reflecting the universal importance attached to one's national identity. Yet, in Chapter 1, we noted that there are other almost everyday occurrences increasingly being reported in the news which do not fully square with our image of a world of nation-states, occurrences relating to multinational corporations, cyberspace, and other contemporary phenomena that seem characterized by statelessness and a world without borders or that at the very least muddle what it means to be an American or a Brit or to belong to some other such tribal grouping. When Daimler-Benz purchased Chrysler in 1998, it was traumatic for many Americans. After all, a German conglomerate headquartered in Stuttgart was not just taking control of one of the Big Three American automakers but a storied institution that seemed "as American as apple pie," a company whose chairman, Lee Iococca, as recently as the 1980s had been making fervent patriotic sales pitches to U.S. consumers from Portland to Peoria to Poughkeepsie to "Buy American" rather than buy a Mercedes Benz or some other foreign make. American companies, of course, had been penetrating foreign economies and investing in foreign firms for years—under Iococcca, Chrysler had bought a

24 percent share of Japan's Mitsubishi Motors—but Americans were not used to being on the other end of "globalization," where foreigners were gobbling up slices of Americana. Ford and General Motors, the remaining two U.S.-based automobile giants, were being challenged on their home turf not only by Daimler-Benz but also by a number of Japanese-based companies which recently had established production plants ("transplants") in the United States, notably Honda, which by the 1990s was making more cars in the United States, at its Marysville, Ohio, plant and other locations, than it was making in Japan, contributing to the United States regaining its ranking as the world's premier auto-producing country that it had lost to the Japanese a decade earlier, and leading Robert Reich in *The Work of Nations* to ask "Who is 'US'?" Reich commented: "As almost every factor of production—money, technology, factories, and equipment—moves effortlessly across borders, the very idea of an American economy is becoming meaningless, as are the notions of an American corporation, American capital, American products, and American technology."[8]

Reich wrote these words immediately prior to becoming U.S. Secretary of Labor in the Clinton administration in 1992. He was raising very provocative questions. If, for example, your employer is a patriotic sort of American who urges you to heed Iococca's appeal and "buy American," does this mean purchasing a Honda made with American labor in Marysville, Ohio, or a Ford made with Canadian labor in Oakville, Ontario (outside Toronto), where Ford has a plant that exports cars across the border? It actually gets more complicated. If you drive a Ford Escort, chances are that your transmission was made in Japan, your wiring in Taiwan, your door lift assembly in Mexico, your shock absorber struts in Spain, your rear brake assembly in Brazil, your steering gears in Britain, and assorted other parts elsewhere. (At the time Iococca made his

Is "globalization" of the international economy leading to a new patriotism?
(BERRY © NEA Reprinted by Permission.)

famous appeal, one commentator noted that "for all of [his] red, white, and blue bunkum [which included a television commercial featuring jet planes streaking across the sky emitting red, white, and blue exhaust fumes while a voice bellowed 'Here's to you, America!'], . . . Chrysler had the lowest percentage of American-made parts in its cars of any of the Big Three."[9]) So-called "global factories"—transnationalized production networks—are becoming ever more prevalent not only in the automobile sector but in other sectors as well.[10] Take the baseballs used in the all-American game of Major League Baseball— the balls are produced by Rawlings, a St. Louis-based company, but take a circuitous route before arriving at the ballpark, with the yarn and leather supplied by plants in New York and Tennessee and the final product then assembled (sewn) in Costa Rica for export back to the United States.

One can see the conceptual problems confronting consumers in trying to ascertain the national identity of various products. Even more profound questions arise, though, for the workforce that produces these goods. In particular, as growing numbers of Americans find themselves working for foreign ownership, whether Daimler-Benz in Detroit or Honda in Marysville, Ohio, or Toyota in Georgetown, Kentucky, or the multitude of other externally headquartered multinational corporations that now dot the American landscape, to what extent might this start creating divided loyalties and affect the national pysche? Put plainly, will patriotic juices flow as freely as before? Will, for example, the "good ol boys" in Tuscaloosa, Alabama, who now find themselves working in the Mercedes-Benz plant there, drawing paychecks from Germany, be as given to American flag-waving as in the past? Even if American workers remain staunchly parochial in their worldview, what about the American managerial class, both those who work for foreign corporations and those who run American corporations, especially in New York, Los Angeles, and other "global cities" where the highest echelons of multinational business are situated? Will they not increasingly develop a more cosmopolitan frame of reference? As for the members of what sometimes is called "the political class"—those individuals whose lives and livelihoods are centered in government in the national capital—who presumably are likely to be the last to distance themselves from a national creed and national symbols, will even they experience some cross-pressures? It is too soon to say whether globalization is fundamentally altering national consciousness among elites and masses in the United States and elsewhere, but there is reason to wonder whether the kind of patriotic displays depicted in the scenes from Roanoke and St. Louis will still be part of our culture at the next *fin de siècle*. Depending on one's perspective, the passing of nation-states and nationalism, should it occur, may be something to be celebrated or to be mourned.

Chapter 2 referred to "powerful tensions, profound contradictions, and perplexing paradoxes" that mark contemporary international life. That is, we encounter two competing realities today—on the one hand a Westphalian world that lies on the surface and is the more visible and familiar to the average person, reflected in the images associated with the rituals enacted in Roanoke and

St. Louis, and on the other hand a post-Westphalian world that lies somewhat beneath the surface, a bit hazy, reflected in the images conjured up by Robert Reich. Perhaps nothing illustrates more vividly these two different realities and how they operate side by side than the following simple example. The Olympic Games are perhaps the quintessential manifestation of unabashed, unbridled nationalism, complete with anthems, flags, uniforms, and other national trappings that bombard the senses as millions of viewers watch nations (more precisely, nation-states) compete in this quadrennial spectacle. Although there is much made of how it is the individual athletes who are doing the competing, and how inside and outside the Olympic Village they are encouraged to play down their ties to their respective homelands and behave in a manner consistent with the Olympic spirit that transcends nationality, nonetheless it is understood that the games are organized along national lines, i.e., only a recognized national-level Olympic committee, normally under the auspices of the government of the nation-state it represents, is permitted to field a team—the Kurds, General Motors, and other such entities need not bother to apply for admission.[11] Maybe one day the Olympics will be a "Corporate Challenge" event, as suggested in the futuristic movie *Rollerball*, but not yet. Much of the drama of the games has revolved in the past around national rivalries, such as the upset of the Soviet ice hockey team by the American team in the 1980 Winter Olympics, which set off a huge patriotic celebration in cities around the United States. However, juxtaposed against the latter reality was *another* reality that was little noticed at the time amidst all the flag-waving, namely that by 1980 it was a foreign-based company, Toyota, which through a million-dollar donation to the U.S. Olympic Committee had become the leading corporate sponsor of the U.S. team. The only greater irony would have been if, say, Stolichnaya Vodka, had been one of the chief benefactors of the U.S. winter team. Still another jarring fact was that, when President Jimmy Carter urged all nations to boycott the summer games scheduled to be held in Moscow in July of 1980, to protest the Soviet invasion of Afghanistan earlier in the year, the U.S. Olympic Committee seriously considered ignoring the plea; as it was, Puerto Rico (whose people enjoy U.S. citizenship) sent a team as did Britain and several U.S. allies whose athletes defied their government's request. One other Olympic moment that had a post-Westphalian quality to it occurred at the 1992 summer games in Barcelona, Spain, when basketball star Michael Jordan expressed reluctance to wear the U.S. national uniform on the victory stand during the gold medal ceremony because the team was outfitted by Reebok rather than the company whose products Jordan was paid to endorse; adding to the post-Westphalian flavor of the 1992 games was the fact that the host city actually thought of itself not so much a part of Spain as the center of Catalonia, a distinct cultural region which its tourist ads trumpeted as "a modern country with centuries of tradition."

In the remainder of this chapter we will probe further into the nature of these competing realities and sets of stimuli and try to see if we can reconcile what appear to be contradictory forces at work. In order to accomplish this task, it is helpful at this point to examine what scholars call competing "paradigms," that is, alternative conceptual frameworks. We will focus on two in particular, examining the assumptions of each as well as the empirical evidence that can be marshaled to support one or the other.

THE PARADIGM DEBATE IN THE STUDY OF WORLD POLITICS

In his landmark book *The Structure of Scientific Revolutions*, Thomas Kuhn noted that in most fields of study that aspire to be scientific the scholarly community tends to share at any given moment a widely accepted theoretical orientation—a paradigm—that dominates the field in terms of determining the kinds of research questions asked and puzzles investigated; in time, when the commonly held view seems increasingly at odds with empirical evidence, a competing paradigm may emerge to challenge the established one, possibly leading to a revolution in the field.[12] An example that is commonly cited is the evolution of the discipline of astronomy. The Ptolemaic paradigm, named after the second century philosopher Ptolemy who assumed that the earth was the center of the universe, with all celestial bodies revolving about it, dominated thinking about astronomy until the sixteenth century when Copernicus posited that the sun was the center of the solar system, with all planets including the earth revolving around it. Although paradigms are of particular importance to scientists, they have relevance for policymakers and laymen as well. The Copernican system not only paved the way for the modern science of astronomy, but also fundamentally changed many people's outlook about the universe. Put simply, paradigms are "ways of seeing the world,"[13] or "comprehensive perspectives that organize our overall understanding" of some set of phenomena we are trying to fathom.[14] They give general direction to our observations, steering our attention toward some things and away from others.

As applied to the study of world politics, paradigms help us "tease meaningful patterns" out of "the welter of events, situations, trends, and circumstances that make up international affairs."[15] Admittedly, international relations does not have quite as strong a claim to being a science as does astronomy or physics or chemistry—few if any professors who study world politics walk around wearing white lab coats—but we nonetheless seek to uncover general truths about how the world works no less than an Albert Einstein or a Louis Pasteur. Can we speak of a dominant paradigm that informs this enterprise? It has been said that "international studies is a contested domain" and that "there has been a genuine debate over the . . . definition of what is *really* international relations."[16] At least three major debates have shaped the field of international relations since it emerged as a distinct academic discipline around the time of World War I: (1) the debate between idealists and realists during the interwar period between the First and Second World Wars, relating to whether world order was grounded in international law and organization as opposed to power politics, and whether peaceful change was possible; (2) the debate between traditionalists and behavioralists during the 1950s and 1960s over the appropriate methodologies for analyzing international relations and whether the field could move beyond mere *wisdom* to produce reliable *knowledge*; and (3) the debate that began in the 1970s and is still ongoing between what could be called the "Westphalian" school and the "post-Westphalian" school, which is the controversy this book centers on.[17] One can cite other debates of late, having to do with such schools of thought as Marxism, feminism, post-positivism, and constructivism,[18] but we will confine our discussion here to the third discourse.[19]

To the extent one can identify a dominant paradigm in international relations, I have indicated that for quite some time it has been the Westphalian worldview which has tended to structure our thinking about such phenomena. No matter where one stood in the first two earlier debates—whether one believed the essence of international relations to be peace or war, and the proper tools of analysis to be intuition and experience or quantitative techniques—an overarching paradigmatic given all sides tended to harbor was that nation-states were the chief actors who made the world go around. By the 1970s, enough anomalies had started cropping up—the sorts of news stories we have alluded to, which did not fully comport with the dominant, conventional paradigm—to raise questions about the latter's validity and utility and to suggest the need for some rethinking; developments in the post-Cold War era have only added to this ferment. Before reaching any conclusions about whether we are witnessing a paradigm shift, we have to elaborate what is meant by the dominant Westphalian paradigm and its post-Westphalian challenger—what exactly are the assumptions of each?—and weigh each against the existing body of evidence—is one superior over the other in yielding insights and understandings about contemporary international affairs? Let us start with the conventional Westphalian worldview, and then we will focus on the rival framework.

What paradigm makes sense in the post-Cold War era? (Copyright © 1996. Reprinted with special permission of King Features Syndicate.)

A WESTPHALIAN WORLDVIEW: WORLD POLITICS
AS A GIANT BILLIARD TABLE

In Chapter 1, I noted that a metaphor frequently used to characterize international relations is that of a set of billiard balls interacting on a pool table, set in motion not in accordance with laws of physics but rather driven by principles of sovereignty, national interest, and other such state-centric properties. The balls are the nation-states; the table is the state system. Simplistic as it may seem, many international relationists have long argued that the picture conjured up by a pool cue banging the eight‚ball into the side pocket amidst other balls reverberating across the green felt surface of a mahogany wood object is an elegant, parsimonious representation of world politics. We will consider whether this is an apt metaphor, especially whether it is suited to the twenty-first century, but first it is necessary to offer some historical perspective on how the nation-state and state system came to be in the first place.

A Historical Narrative

According to most scientific estimates, the first life on our planet (algae in the oceans) appeared over 4 billion years ago. *Homo sapiens* have been around roughly one million years, evolving from the Neanderthal man and other variations of the species. In other words, the human race has been present for only the last 0.01 percent of the planet's existence. The world's first major civilizations, and recorded history, are traced back some 5,000 years, representing 1 percent of the entirety of human existence. And what we have called the nation-state system has an even shorter lineage, dating back some 350 years to the seventeenth century. The point is that, even though the average person today probably cannot imagine life on earth without nation-states, it is sobering to remember that there is nothing God-given about the nation-state as a form of human organization and that it is a relatively new institution by historical standards.

One writer has noted that "the tapestries hung in the *Palais des Nations* in Geneva, Switzerland, [the former headquarters of the ill-fated League of Nations that preceded the United Nations] . . . picture . . . the process of humanity combining into ever larger and more stable units for the purpose of governance—first the family, then the tribe, then the city-state, and then the nation—a process which presumably would eventually culminate in the entire world being combined in one political unit."[20] However, this depiction of the human story as one involving the steady, unilinear progression from small political units to bigger ones, with the timeline ultimately projecting out toward world government, does not do justice to history. The tale is considerably more complicated. The history of humanity can more accurately be read as the search for the optimal political unit, with the pendulum swinging between two extremes: almost a single universal political order (e.g., the world empires of Alexander the Great and Rome) and a set of much smaller, highly fragmented polities (e.g., the series of walled cities and other entities that typified the Middle Ages in Europe).

Centripetal (centralizing, aggregative) forces and centrifugal (decentralizing, disaggregative) forces have alternated with each other from the beginning.[21] The earliest humans lived in what amounted to extended families or kinship groups, enduring a nomadic existence and evolving eventually into hunting and gathering bands and, still later, tribes led by chieftains. When the Agricultural Revolution began by 3000 B.C., marked by the domestication of animals, territorially based organization became possible along with civilization. The first permanent settlements—the first "states," if you will—were small localized communities such as the Sumerian civilization in Mesopotamia, some of which rapidly expanded outward, normally through the use of force, annexing neighboring lands and becoming imperial in their ambition and scale. By the fifth century B.C., a variety of political forms could be found, ranging from the self-contained city-states of Ancient Greece, such as Athens and Sparta, to a feudal order in China, to sprawling empires in Persia and elsewhere. The Ancient Greeks had given much thought to constructing the ideal polity, with Aristotle opining that the optimal size was a population of no more than 100,000 persons. One of his prize pupils, Alexander the Great, ignored his advice, creating before his death, at age 33 in 323 B.C., an empire that stretched across the known world, at least that which was known to him; Alexander supposedly "wept by the riverbank because there were no more worlds to conquer."[22] Alexander's Macedonian Empire was succeeded by the more long-lived Roman Empire, whose fall in the fifth century A.D. ushered in the Dark Ages in Europe and produced a splintered landscape of some 500 entities on the continent that included independent cities, principalities, ecclesiastical territories, and other units, feebly held together by the hegemonic pretensions of the Holy Roman Emperor and the Pope. Outside medieval Europe, expansive pan-Arab and pan-Moslem impulses, fueled by cultural and technological advances under the Islamic Caliphate, contended with local suzerainties in North Africa and the Middle East, while similar centripetal-centrifugal tensions were played out in other regions as well.

In Europe these tensions were resolved by the mid-seventeenth century with the creation of the modern nation-state—a halfway house between the centralizing aspirations of the Holy Roman Empire and Papacy on the one hand and the decentralizing tendencies of the feudal system on the other. In consolidating their power against local princes and repudiating any allegiance to higher secular or religious authorities outside their territory, national monarchs on the continent seemed bent on rejecting the forces of both fragmentation and universalism. The development of nation-states was to occur unevenly, with England and France leading the way by the time of the Peace of Westphalia in 1648, others (such as Germany and Italy) not materializing until the nineteenth century, and still others (such as many societies in Africa and Asia) appearing only in the twentieth century. Along the way, many European nation-states themselves were for awhile to create their own empires through colonial rule, although no one state was able to exercise control over the entire international system. By 1914, Europeans laid claim to 84 percent of the total real estate on the planet; as one writer put it, "by 1900, European civilization overshadowed the Earth."[23] But these centralizing trends subsequently gave way to pressures for "self-determination" and decentralization, resulting most notably in the decolonialization process after World War II that brought over 100 new nation-states and over one-quarter of the human race to independence and also recreated distinct regional subsystems (so that one could talk about the politics of South Asia that included such key actors as India and Pakistan, the politics of the Middle East that included Iraq, Syria, and Egypt, and so forth). Centrifugal and centripetal forces continue to operate today with the proliferation of "ministates" or "statelets" (such as Tonga) occurring against the backdrop of persistent efforts at planetary institution-building through multinational corporations and other international organizations with global reach. Suffice it to say, then, the *Palais des Nations* tapestries in Geneva oversimplify history.

Another way of understanding the sweep of world history is as follows. Conceptualize something called "political space," that is, any group of human beings who interact on a fairly regular basis and therefore require some set of governing arrangements. Political space hypothetically could range from including just two people (say, Adam and Eve) to including the entire world (if all corners of the world were truly connected, as now seems the case). There are three basic ways in which political space can be organized for purposes of governance. One pattern or model is a *hierarchical system*, where there is a single overarching ruling authority or sovereign over the entire political space. A second is a *feudal system*, where there is a complex set of overlapping, cross-cutting hierarchies of authority and loyalties with ill-defined territorial boundaries. A third is a *state system*, where people are organized in several relatively clearly defined territorial units, each with its own exclusive body politic and government, and no single, common sovereign authority above them. A hierarchical system would seem the simplest, neatest political order. A feudal system would seem the most complicated and unwieldy. And a state system would seem something in between, in the sense that, while it is by definition "anarchic" (lacking one ruler at the top), at least the constituent units themselves have well-defined orders, each with its own sovereign.

Relating this to our historical narrative, the empires of Alexander the Great and Rome were examples of the hierarchical model. Each in its day saw itself as ruling the known world and commanding the obedience of its subjects from one end of the empire to the other, with all roads leading to, first, Macedonia and, subsequently, after Alexander's death, Rome. That neither had any control over China or Mesoamerica (in the New World) was of no real consequence, since there was virtually no contact with those peoples, who occupied a different political space; they might just as well have lived on another planet. The following passage describes very well the centuries-long dominance of

Rome and the traumatic effects that were felt when the empire eventually went into decline:

> In the year A.D. 120, an Acquitanian grape grower may have known very little about the life of a shepherdess in the hills of Cyprus; yet both owed their allegiance to the same government, that of Rome, and, more important, each no doubt perceived herself and imagined the other as living within a single world society, the Roman one. . . . The political disintegration of Europe after the fall of Rome in A.D. 476 must rank as one of the most traumatic social upheavals of all time. The highly centralized "world state," which was the only political condition within historical memory, came crashing down at the hands of those who had been subjugated within it and who had no comparable political system of their own waiting to replace it. Successive generations of Europeans looked down upon the fallen empire as the ideal to be . . . revived, since they did not even concede that the empire itself had been ended, but merely suspended, with the abdication of the last emperor.[24]

Efforts to resurrect the empire centered on two "universalistic" institutions that sought to govern Europe during the medieval era, the Catholic Church and the Holy Roman Empire. By around 800 A.D., with the Pope's blessing, Charlemagne attempted to forge a united Christendom through establishment of the Holy Roman Empire, whereupon Pope and Emperor proceeded for the next several hundred years to debate which one exactly was supreme in religious and secular affairs. The debate was mostly academic, since the reality was that the hierarchical system had died with the fall of Rome and had been replaced by a much more decentralized, fragmented, feudal system. K. J. Holsti vividly describes this pre-Westphalian European political space:

> Nation-states did not exist, there was no concept of ethnic nationhood that had any practical significance to the form of political organization, and even though kings [and queens, as in England] reigned on thrones, few ruled directly over a specified group of people inhabiting definable territories. Instead, there were many hierarchies of authority in the known areas of Europe. Some kings, to be sure, were sovereign and commanded the obedience of nobles on some questions of policy. There also existed hundreds of semisovereign walled cities and feudal lords, some of whom determined who would sit on the king's throne. The church hierarchy was an independent power on most ecclesiastical and moral issues of the day, and wielded considerable influence in secular politics as well. Kings made treaties with their vassals, and vassals made contracts with each other—sometimes at the expense of the king; individual churches, monasteries, or convents had special privileges and immunities; peasants and independent cities formed protective leagues. . . . Europe was a patchwork of small quasi sovereignties, states within states, and overlapping.[25]

John Agnew paints a similar portrait of Europe on the eve of Westphalia:

> In medieval Europe there were few fixed boundaries between different political authorities. Regional networks of kinship and interpersonal affiliation left little

The signing of the Treaty of Westphalia in 1648. (Culver Pictures, Inc.)

scope for fixed territorial limits. Violence was widespread not because state borders were clearly established but because of frequent switches in political allegiance across fuzzy boundaries. . . . Communities were united only by . . . personal obligation rather than . . . citizenship in a geographically circumscribed territory. Space was organized concentrically around many centres . . . rather than a singular centre with established territorial boundaries.[26]

Just as the fall of the Roman Empire in 476 A.D. is often cited as the beginning of the feudal era in Europe, the gathering of several monarchs and princes at a conference in the Germanic countryside in 1648, following one of the deadliest conflicts in history, is considered a watershed date signifying the end of the feudal era on the continent.[27] The Congress of Westphalia, which ended the Thirty Years' War, gave individual rulers the right to enter into treaties (in effect, to conduct foreign policy) and to determine whether Catholicism or Protestantism would be the predominant faith practiced among their subjects within their respective realms (in effect, to conduct domestic policy). In so doing, it is credited with conceiving a new mode of political organization and bringing a degree of order, if not peace, to European affairs through the creation of a state system—a set of sovereign units sharing the same political space, each with a central government exercising authority over all interactions within its borders and enjoying a monopoly power to speak for its populace outside its borders. Nobody was yet referring to these units as billiard balls. Indeed, few if any observers at the time thought in terms of paradigms, and even those who might have sensed a "paradigm shift" could be forgiven if they did not fully understand what Westphalia had wrought, what we now call international relations.

There are those who argue that Westphalia's historical significance has been exaggerated, that, for one thing, state systems were discernible in world history prior to 1648, such as the aforementioned collection of city-states on the Greek peninsula between the eighth century and fourth century B.C., and the Chinese state system around the same time; in fact, Athens joined other neighboring states to form the Delian League, an alliance of states that was a forerunner to modern international organization. However, these states did not have quite the size and characteristics that were to distinguish the members of the European state system—the *nation-states* of England, France, and the like. It is also argued that "Westphalia was but one step in the long-term erosion of the position of the emperor [and the Pope]," that the Holy Roman Empire was already in decline well before Westphalia and that it managed to hang on even after Westphalia, being formally abolished in 1806, the result of Napoleon's conquests.[28] It is true that the Westphalian state system itself was not born overnight in 1648, but was the product of a gradual historical process that could be traced back several centuries, and that it did not bloom fully until considerably later. That said, the Peace of Westphalia nonetheless was surely a pivotal moment.

If one wishes to discover the roots of Westphalia, a number of writings offer insights into the emergence of the European state system. Charles Tilly has traced it as far back as 900 A.D., noting that the growing merchant capitalist class by this time was already finding the feudal system, with its chaotic set of juridical relationships, dysfunctional in terms of facilitating expanded commerce and was beginning to cast its lot with kings and queens against the prerogatives of the landed nobility; traders were attracted to the idea of a single ruler presiding over a specified territory in which contracts could be predictably enforced and a common set of laws would apply, including a standardized currency and standard weights and measures conducive to reducing the transaction costs of doing business.[29] Bruce Bueno de Mesquita points out that the Concordat of Worms in 1122 dealt a critical blow to the notion of papal supremacy, since the Pope agreed to surrender to princes the right to appoint bishops in their territories.[30] John Herz has noted that by 1400, the invention of gunpowder had rendered the walled cities of the past no longer viable as units of political organization capable of protecting their populations.[31] Stephen Krasner argues that one could see the outlines of modern nation-states in parts of Western Europe, particularly England, by 1300 or so: "The driving force behind the elimination of feudal institutions was . . . changes in the nature of military technology and the growth of trade, which systematically favored states that could take advantage of siege guns and elaborate defenses, and organize and protect long-distance commerce."[32] Krasner adds that "entities most clearly resembling sovereign states first appeared in northern Italy. In 1000 the Pope, the Holy Roman Emperor, and the Byzantine Emperor [who had laid claim to the eastern half of the defunct Roman Empire] claimed to rule the Italian peninsula, but in fact the more than two hundred cities on the peninsula enjoyed effective de facto control of their own affairs;"[33] however, Florence, Venice, and the other Italian city-states were to prove no match militarily and economically for the large-scale, national units which were in the process of being formed in England, Spain, and Holland.[34] Other happenings that presaged Westphalia were the Protestant Reformation, led by Martin Luther's posting of his "Ninety-Five Theses" in 1517, which further undermined the authority of a universalistic Church in favor of particularistic secular rule, and the publication of Jean Bodin's *Six Books of the Commonwealth* in 1577, which first articulated the "theory of the state" based on the concept of sovereignty.

It was around Westphalia that all these historical forces seemed to converge. As Holsti states, Westphalia "represented a new diplomatic arrangement—an order created by states, for states,"[35] whose essential features were defined at the outset of Chapter 3. In an often-cited quotation, Leo Gross remarked: "The Peace of Westphalia, for better or worse, marks the end of an epoch and the opening of another. It represents the majestic portal which leads from the old world into the new world."[36] When earlier in the book the author raised the question of whether 1989 might one day be looked back upon as a Westphalian moment leading us, in a sense, back to the future—possibly to a "new medievalism" or some other new world order—it was this sort of profound change that was contemplated. We will examine whether the end of the Cold War might rate as a "portal" between two epochs, but before we get to our discussion of the post-Westphalian paradigm we need to explore further the implications of Westphalia.

Not every polity instantly qualified to become a member of the Westphalian state system. Many areas in central Europe in what was to become Germany, for example, retained vestiges of feudalism for quite some time after the seventeenth century, while others, such as China, occupied a different political space altogether. Although Christopher Columbus' discovery of the New World in the West along with Marco Polo's earlier trips to the Orient had by the time of Westphalia begun to produce a truly planetary perspective on a scale that Alexander the Great never knew, the "closing of the world frontier"[37] would not occur until the Americas and the farthermost reaches of Africa and Asia became integrated into the interstate system. The major states (the great powers) which emerged from Westphalia and which were to dominate European politics and much of world politics into the twentieth century were England, France, Prussia, Austria, and Russia; these, along with Sweden, the Netherlands, Spain, and Turkey (the Ottoman Empire, which controlled part of the Balkans and became known as the "sick man of Europe" during its long decline), comprised the initial core of the state system. Only gradually were non-European polities "recognized" as members of the "community of states," as the Westphalian mode of political organization found its way ultimately into every corner of the earth; the United States and the Latin American states were the first to achieve independence from European colonial rule, China and Japan and a handful of other long-autonomous societies were admitted into the club as sovereign equals by the latter nineteenth century,[38] and the remaining parts of the globe by the latter twentieth century.

An immediate problem facing England, France, and other countries on the continent following Westphalia was how, in their external relationships with each other, they could maintain peace and order in the absence of any centralized authority hovering over them. One answer was provided by the Dutch jurist Hugo Grotius, who became known as the father of international law and whose path-breaking work *De Jure Belli Ac Pacis* (*On the Law of War and Peace*) actually had been written in 1625, well before Westphalia, in anticipation of what was soon to transpire. Grotius conceived of a creative system of law that could operate in a decentralized, anarchical political system such as the state system, where member states through treaties and other devices might promulgate, enforce, and adjudicate a set of rules constraining each other's behavior. Over the next 350 years, rules were developed on everything from "the law of the sea" (to which Grotius himself contributed heavily) to obligations relating to rescue of astronauts in outer space. A particularly notable event in the development of international law was the Congress of Vienna following the end of the Napoleonic Wars in 1815, since it was then that the first attempt was made to reach agreement among states on a standard set of rules regarding the appointment of ambassadors and the operation of embassies, in recognition of the importance of institutionalized diplomacy in managing relations between sovereign entities. The Congress of Vienna also created the first intergovernmental organization (IGO)—the Central Commission for the Navigation of the Rhine (to regulate navigation on the Rhine River and to assure equal access for all the riparian states that utilized the waterway)—as well as more formalized multilateral conference machinery that was to be the precursor of the League of Nations and the UN—the so-called "Concert of Europe," which was designed to facilitate regular consultations among the great powers on matters of war and peace. International law and international organization eventually became globalized, even though Western states were to continue to dominate the development of these governing arrangements ("international regimes") and even though the international community continued to place more faith in the balance of power (through formation of military alliances to deter aggression) than in law and organization as a solution to the problem of anarchy and as a basis for international order. As successive generations were to discover, neither the workings of the balance of power nor the workings of international institutions proved up to the challenge of maintaining peace.

Aside from concern over external relations and the conduct of foreign policy, Westphalian statesmen had to face even more immediately the question of governance at home and how the sovereign would relate to his own domestic populace, although external and internal concerns could never be neatly compartmentalized. In 1648, sovereignty clearly resided in the monarch rather than in the people. Thomas Hobbes' *Leviathan*, written three years after the Peace of Westphalia, provided the rationale for an all-powerful government headed by an absolute monarch, exemplified by King Louis XIV, who sat on the French throne for seventy-two years until his death in 1715, and whose famous statement "*l'état c'est moi*" ("I am the state") summarized the model of internal governance that prevailed on the continent at the time. Only later, in the eighteenth century, based on the writings of John Locke and others in the Age of Enlightenment, did the idea of representative government and the consent of the governed begin to take hold. Although the early European states were absolutist, the size of government was limited by the resources the ruler could command, which required either collecting taxes from one's subjects or acquiring gold and commodities in overseas trade and conquest or seeking loans. What resources were extracted were devoted primarily to defense of the realm and expansion of the ruler's power. That was the business of government.[39] "Big government" in the form of the "welfare state," of course, did not yet exist. Certainly poverty, pollution, and other serious societal problems cried out for attention. For example, sounding very much like a modern-day Pat Buchanan or Ross Perot, one Englishman petitioned Queen Anne in the seventeenth century to ban Indian textile imports since "English workmen could not compete with Eastern labour . . . [because] the people in India are such slaves as to work for less than a penny a day whereas ours will not work for under a shilling."[40] Similarly, in 1659, one observer wrote that London was enveloped in "such a cloud of sea-coal, as if there be a resemblance of hell on earth."[41] But the government did not see itself as having any responsibility for full employment, much less clean air, so the vast state bureaucracies which were to one day include unemployment benefits offices and environmental protection agencies were still in their infancy.

Given the overriding preoccupation of Westphalian states with military security, the state bureaucracy at first consisted mainly of an army or navy and whatever tax collectors, financial advisors, and trade officials were needed to pay for the armed forces. To the extent the state dealt with economic issues, then, it was as they related to military issues. Each country sought to increase its economic wealth, mainly as a basis to support a large military establishment and expand its power, which in turn could be expected to generate additional national wealth. According to the logic of *mercantilism*, which was the prevailing economic system in the seventeenth century, the state was driven to regulate trade through tariffs and other policies that would have the effect of limiting imports and increasing exports, hence creating trade surpluses that could provide the state with gold bullion and other revenue.[42] Only in the nineteenth century, following Adam Smith's publication of *The Wealth of Nations* in 1776, was mercantilist economic doctrine to be challenged by advocates of *free trade*—a removal of governmentally imposed restrictions on the flow of goods and services—and were economic issues to take on a life of their own apart from military issues. Absolutist rulers never seemed to have enough revenue to fund their armed forces. Louis XIV was so desperate for cash that he created superfluous judgeships, councilors, and other offices for sale, contributing to the growth of the French bureaucracy. In short, in France and elsewhere during the early state-building era that followed the Peace of Westphalia, "the state made war and war made the state,"[43] a pattern that was to continue in some respects into the twentieth century.

Several writers have noted that some countries have a history of being "strong states," while others have been "weak states."[44] They are referring not to the ability of a country to project power *externally* in the international arena but rather the extent to which the political culture of the country is such that there is general acceptance *internally*, within the political system, of a large role for government, including a willingness by the citizenry to accept a high degree of governmental taxation and government regulation of economic and other activities. Joel Migdal explains that the strong state/weak state distinction has to do with "the capabilities of states to achieve the kinds of changes in society that their leaders have sought through state planning, policies, and actions. Capabilities include the capacities to *penetrate* society, *regulate* social relationships, *extract* resources, and *appropriate* or use resources in determined ways. Strong states are those with high capabilities to complete these tasks, while weak states are on the low end of a spectrum of capabilities."[45] Some states, such as France, developed a "strong state" tradition over time. As noted in Chapter 2, the United States has often been characterized as a "weak state," in terms of having a long-standing anti-statist political culture that has resulted in a relatively low level of taxation and governmental control of the economy compared to many other polities. Where there were constant military threats surrounding a country, along with concerns about economic scarcity—as in Europe after Westphalia—there was a tendency to develop a strong state. Where these challenges were less serious—as in the case of the United States, where there were no major powers on its borders (only fish to the east and fish to the west, an impotent neighbor to the north and an impotent one to the south) and an entire continent to serve as a safety valve for the economically disadvantaged seeking land and property rights— there was a tendency to get by with a weak state.

The United States has been called the first "new nation," meaning that its founding in 1776 made it the first major entity to break away from European colonial rule.[46] Recalling our clarification of terms at the outset of this chapter, it would technically be more accurate to call the United States the first "new state," insofar as it took the collectivity of thirteen ex-colonies over 100 years to develop a true sense of nationhood, with an American national identity evolving first through the Constitution that created a federal system in place of the Articles of Confederation and then through a civil war that affirmed the primacy of the national government over the individual state governments.[47] The

American political culture initially favored a weak state not only in terms of the reach of government generally—vis-à-vis the private sector or civil society—but the reach of the central government in particular—vis-à-vis Boston, Albany, and the other state capitals. The aversion to endowing Washington with excessive power and revenue, of the kind required to field a large national military establishment, contributed to the United States adopting an isolationist posture toward world affairs through much of its early history. Although the United States was to come of age as a great power by 1898, with its victory in the Spanish-American War, and although the federal government subsequently was to expand its authority considerably in the wake of the Great Depression and other national crises, America's weak-state, isolationist roots continued to be evidenced throughout the twentieth century, most notably in the country's reluctant entrance into both world wars.

The American experience illustrates the problems nation-states have encountered in both *state-building* and *nation-building*. Louis XIV was more successful at the former than the latter. Indeed, throughout much of the seventeenth and eighteenth centuries, the average peasant in France or elsewhere on the continent did not identify wholeheartedly with the state and was not inclined to respond emotionally to flag-waving and other national symbols. It was hard for Louis XIV to wave the banner of French nationalism when his wife was Spanish, his chief advisor was from the Italian peninsula, and his army consisted largely of foreign mercenaries. It was also hard to earn the loyalty of the masses when the elites appeared blind to the plight of their subjects, as reflected in the famous response of Marie Antoinette, the wife of King Louis XVI, to the local bread famine during his regime—"Let them eat cake!" Patriotism had not yet become a major impulse in the affairs of state. This was not to occur until dynastic nationalism gave way to democratic nationalism whereby sovereignty did not reside in the ruler but rather derived from the will of the people who inhabited the state. Among the factors that contributed to the downfall of monarchy as an institution in Europe was the advance of science and the reliance upon reason as a substitute for religion, which made "divine right of kings" less and less tenable as a claim to power; the ruling houses could not stand up to Newtonian physics, Cartesian geometry, and other developments that held out hope of progress, of the capacity of human beings to understand and improve the world around them.

Although the 1789 French Revolution that overthrew the monarchy was preceded a decade earlier by the American Revolution, the "shot heard around the world" that started the thirteen colonies' revolt against the British was neither as loud as the storming of the Bastille in Paris nor as revolutionary a turning point in the development of the international system. The reason was simply that France was an integral part of the European state system that dominated world politics at the time, while the fledgling United States remained on the periphery. With the French Revolution that ultimately brought Napoleon Bonaparte to power, the age of nationalism had begun. The new nationalism was based on a firmer relationship between the central government of the state and the people over which it presided, particularly a greater emotional bond between the two created by the greater involvement of the masses in the political life of the country. It was the new nationalism that enabled Napoleon—posing as a man of the people while wearing emperor's clothing—to recruit a mass *citizen* army through nationwide conscription of young Frenchmen and to mobilize the French *nation* in support of France's military adventures abroad. France was the first nation to implement a military draft, although in his wars against Britain and other European powers, even Napoleon still relied heavily on foreign mercenaries, who comprised over half of his 700,000-man army.

French nationalism had the unintended effect of arousing nationalism in other states that felt threatened. In Great Britain and other societies, the ruling class discovered that they could extract resources (tax revenues) from their publics more readily through co-opting them into contributing to defense of the nation (the "mother country") than through brute state coercion. However, rulers also found that once they appealed to a sense of nationalism, they had opened the door to democratic pressures, with the loyalty and support of the middle class and general populace likely to be solidified the more the government was perceived as being responsive to the popular will. If the rise of mass democracy meant that leaders might have to become more sensitive to public opinion in formulating policy, it also meant that they potentially could count on the total military and economic capabilities that their societies had to offer in international politics. Although full-scale democratic institutions developed only gradually and unevenly in Europe and elsewhere during the nineteenth century, rulers could increasingly claim to be acting on behalf of a mass, nationalistic following in a way their predecessors could not.

The growth of democracy, along with industrialization and economic growth, in turn led to the welfare state, as newly empowered masses, seeking a larger percentage of the economic pie, used the electoral process to articulate demands for improved material well-being within their respective countries. By the late nineteenth century, economist Adolf Wagner was articulating what became known as "Wagner's Law," or the "law of increasing state activity": as societies develop economically, the growth of the economy inevitably is accompanied by a growth in government spending for social services such as education and public health. In the twentieth century, the national security state became fully joined at the hip by the national welfare state, as the assumption took hold, at least in the industrialized democracies, that the government had an obligation to look out for not only the citizenry's physical security but also economic security—the country's overall societal standard of living and quality of life. In the United States and other Western capitalist democracies, free traders and other *laissez-faire*, market-oriented disciples of Adam Smith were to wage an ongoing debate with the followers of another Englishman—economist John Maynard Keynes, considered the father of the modern welfare state—over exactly how intrusive a role the government should play in regulating economic activity, with a rough consensus emerging in most countries around a mixed system blending free enterprise with governmental intervention. If World War I and World War II had the effect of expanding the size of the national security state, the Great Depression between the two world wars had the effect of expanding the size of the national welfare state, as these events all provided justification for an expanded governmental role in providing both guns *and* butter. Nowhere was statism to become more pronounced than in such totalitarian societies as Nazi Germany under Adolph Hitler and Communist Russia under Josef Stalin and his successors, where few debates of any kind were permitted; the eventual defeat of fascism in World War II and Marxist-Leninism in the Cold War appeared to many observers to mark the "triumph of the West"—the "unabashed victory of economic and political liberalism"[48] over its ideological competitors—although capitalist democracies, and for that matter all states, were still left to decide on how to strike the proper balance between the size of the public sector and the private sector (state and society).

War and welfare concerns in the twentieth century also spawned the further growth of intergovernmental organizations to help states manage their security and nonsecurity relationships. Commenting on the creation of the League of Nations and United Nations, Inis Claude has written that "the organizing movement of the twentieth century can be interpreted as a reaction to the increasingly terrible consequences of armed conflict"[49] and "represents a trend toward the systematic development of an enterprising quest for political means of making the world safe for human habitation."[50] Although the latter might account for the creation of the UN, the creation of the International Civil Aviation Organization, the International Monetary Fund, and other such IGOs owed more to development of the national welfare state than the national security state. John Ruggie has argued that the growth of IGOs, especially after World War II, owed mostly to one state in particular—the United States—which after 1945 shed its isolationist past and assumed the burden of *Pax Americana* as it became the military and economic leader of "the free world"; he notes that it was not so much American *hegemony* but *American* hegemony—that is, not just the sheer influence of a dominant superpower but the peculiar American brand of moralistic-legalistic leadership—which accounted for the postwar development of international organization.[51] As suggested in Chapter 2, it is this leadership that is now in question in the post-Cold War era.

As this brief historical narrative indicates, state-building and nation-building have been complex processes. In the early life of the Westphalian nation-state system, it was the state that created the nation. That is, the states were ones in which the central political authorities gradually managed to forge a sense of national identity among a group of people who happened to find themselves living within the same set of borders but who had not previously thought of themselves as "French" or "British." In the nineteenth and early twentieth century, on the other hand, the nation often created the state. Groups sharing common linguistic and other cultural bonds eventually unified into single states, with the prime examples being the loose confederation of German-speaking territories (led by Prussia) forming Germany in 1870 and the various Italian-speaking territories (led by Sardinia) forming Italy around the same time. (Garibaldi, the founding father of the modern state of Italy, captured the challenge of nation-state building, and of forging a sense of national consciousness even among an ethnically homogeneous population, with his famous utterance that "having made Italy, we now have to make Italians.") The pattern after World War II was more like that in the seventeenth and eighteenth centuries insofar as many of the societies in Africa and Asia that achieved independence from colonial powers after 1945 became states whose borders did not correspond to any natural cultural groupings but were the artificial product of imperialistic rivalries and colonial mapmakers. Hence, in countries such as Nigeria and Indonesia, the leaders who had led the independence movement were faced with the problem of getting diverse and often historically hostile tribal units to identify with the new state in which they were situated, with some leaders being more successful than others. As evidenced by the breakup of the Soviet Union and Yugoslavia, the latest trend may be a return to nationalism energizing the creation of new states.

Whether the entity in question is Slovenia (which successfully broke away from Yugoslavia in 1991) or Kosovo (which has sought to break away from Yugoslavia, thus far unsuccessfully), or the many other "self-determination" movements one finds in the world today, the Westphalian nation-state, after 350 years, still seems to be the archetypical mode of political organization that people aspire to across the globe. In the words of Robert Jackson and Alan James, "far from withering away in the twentieth century, the independent State has everywhere become the standard form of territorial political organization and all conflicting standards have been discredited and in most cases abandoned."[52] Having gotten some historical perspective on how the Westphalian nation-state system became such an ingrained fact of life, and how it became the basis for the dominant paradigm most people internalize when thinking about world politics, we now need to examine carefully the key assumptions embedded in that paradigm and how those assumptions hold up against what some see as potential contemporary challenges to the logic of a state-centric world.

Assumptions of the Westphalian Paradigm

What I have labeled the Westphalian paradigm has also been called at various times the realist or neorealist paradigm, as well as the billiard ball paradigm. Regardless of which label one uses, it is important to understand the underlying assumptions of what has been the dominant paradigm that scholars, policymakers, and lay persons alike have relied on to make sense of the world. Although it may be true that only scholars have the inclination and time to seriously study world politics phenomena in the abstract, practitioners in the U.S. State Department and elsewhere nonetheless certainly operate with all kinds of general assumptions in their heads about how the world works, as do lay persons, including college students, whether they are aware of it or not and whether the assumptions are correct or incorrect. As John Maynard Keynes once remarked, "practical men who believe themselves to be quite exempt from any intellectual influences" frequently act on the basis of ideas that sprouted from "some academic scribbler of a few years back."[53]

Perhaps no "academic scribbler" has had more of an impact in shaping our view of world politics than Hans Morgenthau, whose *Politics Among Nations* was written in 1948, immediately following World War II (happening to coincide with the 300th anniversary of the Peace of Westphalia), and quickly became the most widely used textbook in the field.[54] It has continued to exert a powerful grip on the thinking of successive generations of students of international relations. As John Vasquez has put it, *Politics Among Nations* so dominated scholarship for decades after World War II that one could characterize the entire field as "Color It Morgenthau."[55] No matter whether the methodology utilized to investigate world politics, to produce knowledge, was traditional or behavioral-quantitative in nature, research agendas tended to focus on those questions to which Morgenthau steered observers; and, in the classroom, where knowledge was disseminated, the "stuff" of international relations that professors taught and collegians learned likewise reflected Morgenthau's view of the world. One could say that Morgenthau did for the international relations discipline what Copernicus had done for astronomy, providing an overarching, coherent conception of world politics beyond what anyone previously had offered.

Certainly many thinkers over the years had attempted to furnish insights into the fundamental nature of international relations, but few offered as parsimonious and compelling an explanation as Morgenthau. Morgenthau became identified as the father of the realist school—the realist paradigm—even though traces of realist thought could be seen in the pre-Westphalian writings of Thucydides (whose *History of the Peloponnesian War* analyzed the relationships among the Greek city-states in the fifth century B.C.) and Machiavelli (whose *The Prince* analyzed the relationships among the Italian city-states in the sixteenth century), as well as other writings in the eighteenth, nineteenth, and early twentieth centuries.[56] As suggested by the title of his book, Morgenthau—a child of Westphalia—was not interested in politics among city-states but among nation-states. Based on his reading of some 300 years of history, he concluded there were certain objective laws that characterized the workings of the Westphalian state system, realities which statesmen seeking to adopt wise policies could ignore only at their peril. What exactly was the gist of his theory?

Realism contains three basic principles. First, in any political space in which a state system (rather than hierarchical or feudal) model of governance operates, as in the case of the international system, *states* are the key actors, with nonstate actors playing only a marginal role in the functioning of the system. Second, states behave as *unitary, rational* actors, pursuing their individual *national interests*, with the highest priority given to *national security* defined mainly

The billiard ball paradigm. (Josh Korenblat)

in *military-strategic* terms. Third, given the *decentralized, anarchic* nature of the state system, where in the absence of any common authority to enforce agreements and maintain order there is inherent mutual distrust, relations between states tend to be characterized by *conflict*, often involving the *threat or use of armed force.* Hence, we get the portrait of international relations as a set of billiard balls ("the United States," "Japan," and other nation-states) interacting on a large plane (the international arena), at times barely or only gently touching but frequently crashing into one another.[57] We need to examine these three assumptions, one by one, in greater detail.

Assumption 1.   The primacy of states as the lead actors in world politics is a given to most people. This is acknowledged even by writers who might resist the realist label, such as Oran Young: "Most contemporary discussions of world politics are based on the postulate that the state, in its modern form, is the fundamental political unit in the world system and that therefore it is possible to analyze world politics largely in terms of interstate relations."[58] Similarly, Hedley Bull: "The starting point of international relations is the existence of states, of independent political communities."[59] This state-centric view, according to realists, is justified not only because states enjoy sovereignty, which gives them legal-formal control over all human beings on the planet, but, more importantly, because states exercise the most actual influence on what happens in world affairs. More precisely, it is national governments—particularly the *central decision makers* in charge of the official foreign policy establishment, acting on behalf of their nation-state—which are the preeminent players. Inter-state relations is the name of the game, although it is recognized that, unlike billiard balls, some states may be bigger than others in size and impact.

But what of international organizations and other *transnational* actors which, as noted in our brief history lesson, eventually developed alongside states? What of the 300 intergovernmental organizations (IGOs), 10,000 nongovernmental organizations (NGOs), and 35,000 multinational corporations (MNCs) alluded to in Chapter 2 in our description of the contemporary world scene? Realists assume they are no more than a supporting cast, playing bit roles in the drama of world politics. Realists treat intergovernmental organizations as mere extensions of nation-states or as peripheral to the major power struggles of world politics. IGOs are viewed as created by states (mainly through treaties) and for states, i.e., as organizations whose members are nation-states and which serve as forums for inter-state diplomacy, some of which are regional in scope (e.g., the Organization of American States or the Organization of Arab Unity) and others of which are global (e.g., the United Nations or the World Trade Organization). Moreover, realists posit that the decision-making apparatus in IGOs, particularly global IGOs, tends to reflect the power structure in the international system and ultimately serves the interests of the great powers, as suggested by the ability of the major winning states in World War II, led by the United States, to acquire special voting privileges on the UN Security

Council. Realists predict that, when major powers find an IGO no longer adequately serves their interests, they will become less involved in the organization and will reduce their commitment of resources to its operation, making it even more marginalized in world affairs.

Generally speaking, realists consider NGOs, such as Greenpeace or the International Council of Scientific Unions, even less important than IGOs in world politics, since by definition, these entities are composed of *private* individuals or groups that have organized across national boundaries, and hence are even further removed from the centers of power in the Westphalian system than are IGOs; although many NGOs recently have been granted consultative status to participate in diplomatic conferences sponsored by the UN and other bodies, it is just that—merely consultative—and their capacity to form associations and to function in the international arena remains wholly dependent upon the permission of governmental authorities which can limit citizen activity if they so choose. Multinational corporations, such as Exxon or Toyota— "companies which have their home in one country but operate and live under the laws and customs of other countries as well"[60]—can be thought of as a special subset of NGOs, subject to the same constraints as other NGOs. Indeed, MNCs have often been depicted as agents of their home country and home government, with American-based MNCs especially criticized by many less developed countries over the years as an arm of U.S. "imperialism" and "neo-colonialism," serving the interests and under the control of Washington. Others see host governments recently exercising growing control relative to home governments. In any case, realists argue MNCs are hardly autonomous actors challenging nation-state dominance. We will consider later whether this is an accurate portrait of MNCs, or whether they, as well as IGOs and NGOs, are becoming serious competitors to the nation-state in shaping events on the world stage.

Assumption 2.   A hallmark of the realist paradigm is not only that nation-states are the only actors of consequence in the international system, but also that each can be conceptualized as a homogeneous, coherent unit when it comes to the formulation and conduct of foreign policy. This realist view is one that most of us accept. Every day we hear references in conversation and news reports that "the United States" or "Washington" (or "Japan" or "Tokyo") has "decided" something or "done" something in the international arena. These are not just convenient shorthand expressions but a reflection of a natural tendency to reify the nation-state, i.e., to attribute human qualities to a collectivity. States are thought to be ego-driven rational actors concerned about maximizing their national interests in response to stimuli (hostile or friendly moves and other conditions) in their external environment outside their borders. Again, according to this conventional states-as-actors perspective, states are akin to billiard balls, although a bit more purposeful—reacting to each other's moves as billiard balls impact against each other on a pool table. To use another metaphor, states are viewed as monolithic "black boxes" cranking out foreign policy decisions and behaviors based on strategic calculations, so that in order to understand state action there is little need to look inside the black box, beneath the surface, at the internal dynamics of the policymaking process; it is the external, not internal, situation that drives foreign policy. In his well-known case study of the 1962 Cuban missile crisis, *Essence of Decision*, Graham Allison commented on this standard tendency to interpret any foreign policy decision—such as the decision of the Soviet Union to place offensive nuclear weapons in Cuba ninety miles from the U.S. homeland, or the decision of the United States to blockade Cuba to prevent Soviet ships from delivering additional missiles—in terms of the rational actor model, as the deliberate response of a unified foreign policy establishment acting on behalf of the nation:

> For example, on confronting the problem posed by the Soviet installation of strategic missiles in Cuba [in 1962] ... [the] analyst frames the puzzle: Why did the Soviet Union decide to install missiles in Cuba? He then fixes the unit of analysis: governmental choice. Next, he focuses attention on . . . goals and objectives of the nation or government [the central decision makers]. And finally, he invokes certain patterns of inference: if the nation performed an action of this sort, it must have had a goal of this type. The analyst has "explained" this event when he can show how placing missiles in Cuba was a reasonable action, given Soviet strategic objectives.[61]

A corollary of Assumption 2 is that the internal makeup of a state is not critical to how it behaves in international relations. No matter whether the state is a democracy or a dictatorship, or is led by a Saddam Hussein or a George Bush, "given the same external stimuli, all states will behave in a similar manner."[62] One could predict a hostile response by a country that had just discovered enemy troops encamped near its border regardless of whether its leaders were elected or self-appointed. Realists contend that, even with the rise of the welfare state and the growing visibility of economic and nonsecurity issues on national agendas, nation-states remain obsessed above all else with the security function, with maintaining their physical security and territorial integrity against any outside threats. There is a *hierarchy* of concerns states face, with military security at the top. In Chapter 2, we noted the distinction between high politics and low politics, with the highest politics traditionally reserved for national security issues. The high politics/low politics distinction, then, refers not to the degree of politics involved but what interests are at stake for the nation. (It is hard to imagine, for example, any more high-politics a situation than that which occurred during the 1962 Cuban missile crisis, when President Kennedy estimated "the probability of disaster [which would have resulted in the deaths of at least 100 million Americans and 100 million Russians]" as "between one out of three and even."[63]) Realist theory claims that for all states, "security is more important than economics, and economics is more important than, say, human rights. According to realist theory, then, states faced with a choice between their security interests and their human rights concerns will choose security.

Likewise, they will choose economics over human rights, but security over economic goals."[64]

As a general proposition, one would expect that the more clearly some concern impinges on core national values, such as the very existence of the state, the more applicable the rational actor model as an explanation of state behavior, since (1) the more likely the problem will engage the attention and involvement of the highest-level central decision makers (those most inclined by their institutional role to define the national interest according to realist expectations) and (2) the greater decision latitude likely to be given the latter by the public within that society to act in the name of the state (i.e., the more successfully will leaders be able to manipulate their domestic environment and mobilize broad support for their policies by invoking national interest symbolism to appeal to patriotism). As evidence of the ability of even dictatorships to cultivate mass support at times of national crisis, particularly in order to repel invasion of the motherland, one need only note the success of Stalin during World War II. (Of course, it helps to win the war rather than lose it, and it helps also if the state in question is not itself torn by serious ethnic and civil strife.) If Assumption 1 discounts the importance of transnational actors, Assumption 2 discounts the importance of *subnational* actors—interest groups, political parties, bureaucratic agencies, public opinion, the mass media, and other *domestic* political forces—which are presumed to defer for the most part to the national leadership, at least on those issues of greatest significance in international relations. This holds true for open no less than closed political systems, and weak states no less than strong states; the reader will recognize the familiar adage that in foreign policy, unlike domestic policy, politics is supposed to "stop at the water's edge" and be "bipartisan."[65]

Hence, the sharp distinction realists make between domestic policy and foreign policy, which are thought to constitute two separate domains within a country's political system, the former concerned with internal affairs and being very politicized (involving a myriad of domestic interests) and the latter concerned with external affairs and being relatively apolitical (involving a set of central decision makers as fiduciaries entrusted with serving the national interest). Just as we will consider below whether Assumption 1 is still valid in a world where nonstate actors seem to be proliferating, we will also scrutinize whether the state-as-unitary-actor assumption still holds, or needs to be relaxed somewhat in a world of growing interdependence where the boundaries between national and international life seem to be blurring and the concept of security is being broadened well beyond its military connotation.

Assumption 3.   Assumption 3 is closely related to Assumption 2. I have stated the obvious repeatedly, that there is no world government, that in contrast to national political systems, which are defined by their legislatures, executive agencies, and courts, the international political system has no such central authoritative institutions—no institutions which claim the right to determine "the authoritative allocation of values" system-wide and the right to exercise "a monopoly on the legitimate use of armed force."[66] The United Nations is at best a primitive attempt at creating a world government out of a system of formally independent states. If there is a single principle all nation-states and their governments agree on, it is that each is sovereign.

Although the decentralized, anarchical nature of the international system should be obvious, realists emphasize the profound implications that result from this fact. In particular, if "international politics, like all politics, is a struggle for power,"[67] it is a struggle whose distinguishing feature is that it is unmediated by any referee. As Thucydides said about the Greek city-state system, "the strong do what they have the power to do, the weak accept what they have to accept"; and as Machiavelli said about the Italian city-state system, "the strong do what they will, the weak suffer what they must."[68] Given the absence of any umpire to regulate the behavior of the members of the international system, even those states which are not interested in self-aggrandizement but only self-defense tend to feel a need to expand their power, if only for self-help purposes. As states sense that the best way to deter aggression and preserve peace is to arm to the teeth, they find themselves caught up in a "security dilemma" whereby the pursuit of security inevitably breeds greater insecurity. Agreements can be hard to reach since there is no central authority to ensure compliance. Hence, cooperation under anarchy is difficult. Conflict is the norm. Indeed, the constant threat of the use of organized armed force is endemic to the system.

Morgenthau and other realist writers derive this generalization about the inherently conflictual character of international relations not only from the nature of the international system but also from human nature itself, of which they take a very dim view. Remember that what distinguished Morgenthau and his generation of "realist" thinkers from an earlier generation of "idealist" thinkers who tried their hand at paradigm construction after World War I was precisely their skepticism over how much cooperation was possible in human affairs. Buoyed by the creation of the League of Nations in 1919, the so-called idealist school dominated the interwar period between the two world wars[69] but was as short-lived as the League. Idealism was not so much a paradigm—a coherent theory purporting to explain reality— as it was a hortatory plea for *changing* the existing order and reforming international relations; it was more prescriptive than descriptive, suggesting how statesmen *ought* to behave rather than how they actually *did* behave. Idealists, too, viewed international relations through Westphalian, billiard ball lenses, insofar as they saw nation-states as the chief actors and saw them as unitary, rational actors concerned most about issues of war and peace; but they were much more optimistic than realists as to where reason might lead:

> Realists share the state-centric paradigm with the idealists. . . . Idealists . . . agree with the realists about the nature of the problems posed by world politics while disagreeing with them about what should be done in response. . . . Idealists proceed to liberal doctrines; for them, power can be tamed.[70]

Where the realist tradition could be traced to such writers as Thucydides and Machiavelli, the idealist tradition was rooted in such "liberal internationalist" writers as Hugo Grotius (the aforementioned father of international law, whose *On the Law of War and Peace* suggested a body of rules that sovereign states might abide by) and Immanuel Kant (whose *Perpetual Peace*, written in 1795, envisioned the possibility of a federation of democratic, pacific states sharing a harmony of interests). Idealism and realism, then, were two different strands of thought within the Westphalian framework.

It was the very failure of the idealists to anticipate and prevent World War II that gave rise to the dominance of the realist paradigm in the postwar period after 1945. Whereas the idealists argued that their ideas about building a new world order based on the rule of law and the development of international organizations had not been fully implemented in the interwar period and hence had not been fully tested, observers such as E. H. Carr (a forerunner to Morgenthau) contended that they *had* been tested but could not stand up against armies marching across Europe and halfway around the world.[71] In the same way that the Copernican worldview displaced the Ptolemaic one in astronomy, the realist worldview replaced the idealist one, which was dismissed as utopian. An important element of realist thought, as articulated by Morgenthau, was the presumption that the normal canons of morality had little place in inter-state relations, since any statesman who based decisions on criteria other than raw calculations of national interests risked engaging in either naïve sentimentality or reckless messianic crusades. In place of international law and organization as means of conflict management, realists urged reliance instead on careful statecraft ("realpolitik") and the enlightened manipulation of power, through a *balance of power* (offsetting alliances) capable of deterring would-be aggressors or—if somehow the major actors could be persuaded to collaborate—a *concert of powers* willing to police the world.[72] The realist paradigm especially resonated in the minds of American and other policymakers during the Cold War, at a time when much of international relations seemed to be consumed by high politics revolving around the great geopolitical struggle between the superpowers and their respective blocs.[73] Although the United States and the Soviet Union initially tried to work together in a concert of great powers approach to world order in the UN Security Council, they ultimately fell back on constructing competing alliance systems (NATO and the Warsaw Pact).

Toward the end of the Cold War, an interesting revival of the idealist-realist debate occurred in the international relations field between so-called "neoliberals" and "neorealists," and has continued in the post-Cold War era. Neorealists, the successors to Morgenthau, essentially accept the tenets of realism, except they have attempted to develop a more scientific basis for the theory, focusing particularly on Assumption 3 and how the structure of the international system—the distribution of power and degree of polarization—determines state behavior.[74] Neorealists argue that, if cooperation is to occur at all, it is most likely to happen in a unipolar world, dominated by a single hegemon which has the necessary resources to coerce or induce others to follow its lead through use of sticks (punishments) or carrots (rewards). Hegemony as a source of order, however, tends to break down eventually, as the hegemonic power inevitably declines because of the draining costs of maintaining large armed forces and extensive economic commitments.[75] In the absence of a hegemon, a bipolar world (of two dominant powers) is more likely to promote international stability and order than a multipolar world (of several major powers), since it is easier for two superpowers to coordinate their moves to avoid mutual annihilation between themselves and their allies than for many powers to do so; therefore, neorealists worry about how the end of the bipolar Cold War order might hurt rather than help the prospects for world peace, and that we might even "miss the Cold War."[76]

Neorealists draw on a body of literature called game theory, arguing that many situations in international relations are analogous to games of poker or chess, in which the players (statesmen) seek to make moves based on a rational calculus of what strategies are likely to maximize their gains and minimize their losses.[77] Although some games may be "zero-sum" in nature, where what one party wins the other automatically loses (e.g., where two states claim the same parcel of land but obviously cannot both exercise sovereignty over it), many games can involve the possibility of all parties winning something, albeit not all benefiting equally (e.g., where states sign an environmental treaty that improves air quality for all the parties but requires some states to bear a greater share of the costs of pollution control). Neorealists concede that all states may find it in their mutual interests to enter into agreements and produce international regimes governing trade and other relationships, but that nonetheless

> when faced with the possibility of cooperating for mutual gain, states that feel insecure must ask how the gain will be divided. They are compelled to ask not "Will both of us gain?" but "Who will gain more?" . . . [If both states achieve absolute gains, but one gains more relative to the other,] one state may use its disproportionate gain to implement a policy intended to damage or destroy the other. Even the prospect of large absolute gains for both parties does not elicit their cooperation so long as each fears how the other will use its increased capabilities.[78]

In other words, because security remains the paramount concern of nation-states, even when all states may benefit economically from, say, a free trade agreement (i.e., even when negotiations offer a "win-win" outcome), cooperation may prove difficult if some states are perceived as winning more than others in improved capabilities that could confer military advantage. Again, military concerns are assumed to trump welfare concerns. As for the role of international organizations in facilitating cooperation, neorealists believe international institutions have little effect. John Mearsheimer states the neorealist view succinctly: "My central conclusion is that institutions have minimal influence on state behavior, and thus hold little promise for promoting stability in the post-Cold War world."[79]

Neoliberals, heirs to the idealist tradition, have countered that "institutions matter," that, regardless of the structure of the international system, institutions can help nation-states realize their self-interests in reaching agreements and can help them overcome the impediments to cooperation under anarchy.[80] Neoliberals argue that if states expect that they will continually have to interact with other states in ongoing bargaining over a variety of issues, as is the case in international organizations, then they will be more likely to honor rather than cheat on their commitments since regular noncompliance will make states untrustworthy and will undermine their diplomacy. Hence, neoliberals are cautiously optimistic about the prospects for a new multilateralism alluded to in the previous chapter.

Hedley Bull and members of the "English school," based on a Grotian conception of a "society of states," add that neorealists overlook and underestimate the substantial number of international regimes in the form of widely accepted norms and understandings that do in fact exist.[81] For example, we have noted that, if nothing else, there is a universal consensus states share regarding the principle of sovereignty. This means that, above all else, "there is the goal of the preservation of the [international] system and society of states itself,"[82] so that any attempt by nonstate actors to challenge state authority and restructure the system will be met by opposition from national governments. There are many other commonly accepted practices one can cite, some of which we have already alluded to, such as the almost universal acceptance of a system of passports and visas for regulating overseas travel, along with a system of embassies and rules governing exchange of ambassadors and treatment of diplomatic personnel (e.g., when the Iranian government in 1979 participated in the hostage-taking of fifty-two Americans from the U.S. Embassy in Tehran, in the hope of extracting concessions from Washington, that action represented such a departure from the routinely honored canons of state practice governing "diplomatic immunity" that observers at the time feverishly searched through history books to discover the last time such a violation had occurred). Bull contends that this framework of reciprocal obligations does work in a crude sort of way to create a moral-legal basis for international relations, beyond what realist or neorealist theory might predict.

Where many neoliberals part company with not only neorealists but also members of the English school and idealists of yesteryear is that they view Assumptions 1 and 2 as simplistic, leading in their judgment to equally simplistic conclusions about international governance (conflict and cooperation) under Assumption 3. They believe that, despite the strong pressures that exist to preserve the Westphalian state system, "complex interdependence" is increasingly entangling states in a web of relationships that is producing a much more complicated politics than that presumed by a billiard ball paradigm, involving a host of nonstate (subnational and transnational) actors competing with states over a host of security and nonsecurity issues competing equally for attention.[83] As suggested in Chapter 2, these trends are seen as especially on the rise in the contemporary international system in the post-Cold War era, perhaps rendering the traditional Westphalian paradigm passé and necessitating an altogether new, post-Westphalian paradigm based on a "cobweb" rather than a billiard ball metaphor.

The Relevance of the Westphalian Paradigm in the Post-Cold War Era: Assessing the Empirical Evidence

Most observers still think in Westphalian terms. The mainstream view is that the more things change, the more they stay the same. That is, all that changed in 1989, with the proclamation of a "New World Order" following the end of the Cold War, was the transformation of the international system from bipolarity back to the more normal pre-1945 pattern of multipolarity. Such an analysis focuses on the first two trends identified in Chapter 2—the growing diffusion of power and the growing fluidity of alignments among *states* in their geopolitical relations— and attaches less importance to the other two trends—the expanding agenda of issues and the growing set of actors. Even those who would argue that bipolarity has been replaced by unipolarity—with the United States as the lone superpower left in the ring—nonetheless assume that it is the distribution of power and the degree of polarization among nation-states that are the key features of world politics. Typical is the following passage from Samuel Huntington, commenting on what he sees as a "uni-multipolar world" today:

> What are the implications of a uni-multipolar world for American policy? First, it would behoove Americans to stop acting and talking as if this were a unipolar world. It is not. To deal with any major global issue, the United States needs the cooperation of at least some major [regional] powers. Unilateral sanctions and interventions are recipes for foreign policy disasters. Second, American leaders should abandon the benign-hegemon illusion that a natural congruity exists between their interests and values and those of the rest of the world. It does not. At times, American actions may promote public goods, and serve more widely accepted ends. But often they will not, . . . simply because America is the only superpower, and hence its interests necessarily differ from those of other countries. . . . Third, . . . it is in U.S. interests to take advantage of its position as the only superpower in the existing international order and to use its resources to elicit cooperation from other countries to deal with global issues in ways that satisfy American interests.[84]

So the post-Cold War era may well be more complicated than the Cold War era, where friends and enemies were clearly defined, but, according to Huntington, it all still comes down to national power and interests. The basic structure of the game has not changed.

Let us review the empirical evidence in support of the continued relevance of the Westphalian paradigm. The territorial state remains the dominant form of political organization in the minds of people everywhere; most people are quite accepting of this institution, since nation-states have been around so long that the average person cannot even imagine another way in which human beings might be governed; even in the case of disenchanted groups, their goal ordinarily is to get control of national governments or to secede and create their own. There are some 200 such units, the most there has ever been in the history of the state system, with more added each passing year; few states disappear, and—although military intervention has been a common phenomenon—none has been forcibly annexed and eliminated by another state since World War II.[85] Sovereignty is universally recognized as a core value by the national governments that preside over states; try finding a national government which is willing to concede that the UN or some other external entity has authority over it. Citizenship continues to confer standing, as few people voluntarily opt to become "stateless," while flag-waving at Olympic games and in other situations still manages to tap into nationalistic feelings, as do car and beer commercials (whether the Budvar brand in the Czech Republic or Budweiser in the United States); for example, recent polls have shown that over two-thirds of Americans consider themselves either "extremely" or "very" patriotic, and almost 80 percent have an American flag in their home.[86] Despite Robert Reich's raising questions about the national identity of multinational corporations, it is "almost impossible to find any transnational corporation which has relocated its corporate headquarters to a completely different country [except as a result of a merger, such as Daimler-Benz buying up Chrysler]"[87]; MNC ownership and management tends to "stay rooted in particular national systems," and only "18 companies in Fortune's Global 500 maintain the majority of their assets abroad, and only 19 maintain at least half of their workers abroad."[88] In strong states and weak states alike, the national security state and national welfare state are still substantial, as national governmental budgets tend to remain high even in countries where there is a movement to shrink the size of government; in the United States, for example, the federal government budget did not reach the $1 trillion level until 1987, 200 years after the founding of the republic, yet within only about a decade (by 2000) was nearing the $2 trillion mark.[89] Although the incidence of interstate war may be drastically in remission, war preparation is not; while it is true that military spending as a percentage of national budgets has been declining somewhat of late, mainly as a function of the end of the Cold War, it remains quite high in most countries; in the United States, where 75 percent of the federal budget is considered "uncontrollable" (entailing expenditures on Social Security, payment of interest on the national debt, and other items that are difficult to reduce), over half of all "discretionary" spending is devoted to the Department of Defense (as opposed to parks, education, and other domestic concerns). Most national armies are citizen armies, recruited through the draft or through volunteer enlistment, rather than relying on foreign mercenaries.[90] Intergovernmental organizations, as Inis Claude has noted, are creative adaptations of the state system, allowing countries to retain sovereignty while providing mechanisms for collaborating on problems that cannot be handled unilaterally; there are now over 300 IGOs, more than ever.[91] Only nation-states ordinarily are parties to international regimes that regulate interactions (from air travel to labeling of pharmaceuticals) across national boundaries, with more than 40,000 treaties concluded in the twentieth century, most of them since 1945.[92] National regulations themselves seem to continue to multiply despite efforts at deregulation in the U.S. and elsewhere; the need for national identification cards, much less passports for foreign travel, did not even exist prior to the twentieth century; today, regulations abound (e.g., there are 41,000 regulations alone governing ground beef in the *U.S. Code of Federal Regulations,* which now numbers well over 100,000 pages).[93] As for interdependence, notwithstanding the enormous explosion in the volume of trade, communications, and other transnational transactions—obviously helped by the spread of high-speed information retrieval and other modern technology—on many measures the world is not much more internationalized than it was at the start of the twentieth century, when, prior to the two world wars, there had been momentum building toward relaxing of trade and other barriers; in the case of the United States, for example, if one looks at trade as a percentage of GNP, at overseas capital movements as a percentage of GNP, at labor migration, at the growth of international air travel and international mail flows relative to domestic flows, only of late have these indicators of interdependence reached or exceeded the level attained in earlier eras.[94] Despite the supposed "loss of control" national governments are currently experiencing due to the penetration of their economies and societies by outside forces, at least one observer goes so far as to say: "State control has actually increased over the long term: de facto sovereignty has been strengthened rather than weakened. Contemporary developed states [more so than less developed states] exercise greater de facto sovereignty than . . . their historical European ancestors."[95] Recalling that "it was not considered odd for the [Russian] tsarist government to raise the funds for fighting the Crimean War [in 1854] by floating bonds on the London market, the same market that the British government was using to cover its own expenses in the same war," another observer agrees that "it is true in some respects we live in a more nation-bound, less internationalized world than did the Europeans of the nineteenth century."[96] The American public, in particular, historically parochial and isolationist in mentality, seems to be turning more inward in the post-Cold War era; a Council on Foreign Relations survey showed that the "percentage of respondents who perceive 'foreign policy problems' to be a high U.S. government priority has dropped from almost 26 percent in 1986 to 11.5 percent in 1994."[97] It is not only Americans but masses in other countries as well who retain inward perspectives; as Huntington has pointed out, despite the shrinking and linking and "Coca-colonization" of the planet, people in many states still cling to their traditional cultures (e.g., Islamic fundamentalism in Iran and Afghanistan) and resist pressures toward a homogeneous, world-without-borders culture.[98] Even the vaunted CNN International, with a presence in over 140 countries, "reaches only 3 percent of the world's population, four-fifths of whom do not even have [regular] access to a television set."[99]

Numerous other data can be cited in support of the Westphalian paradigm that suggest it is premature to abandon that framework. The billiard ball paradigm can still help us understand much of what goes on in world politics. As one illustration, take the matter of UN Security Council reform, which is a governance concern currently under discussion in the United Nations.

The Case of UN Security Council Reform.   One could correctly predict the politics surrounding this issue by simply looking at nation-states and their relative power and interests, without any reference to the role of subnational or transnational actors or any other variables. The UN Security Council was given responsibility under the UN Charter for whatever peace and security issues came before the world body. The Council has fifteen members, including the five major winners in World War II (the United States, Russia, the United Kingdom, France, and China)—each of which claimed a permanent seat along with special veto privileges, in keeping with the "great powers" approach to world order the UN was founded on—as well as ten other states serving two-year terms on a rotating basis. Although many objections have been raised recently about the composition of the Security Council—for example, whether countries such as Japan or Germany, both of which are major UN donors, are not at least as deserving of permanent seats as the UK and France, or whether any states should even be accorded special status as permanent members—the present arrangements are difficult to alter due to the veto power enjoyed by the Big Five, which makes it problematical to eliminate any current permanent member, and the mutual distrust UN members feel toward each other, which makes it hard to reach agreement on which if any states should be added as permanent members.

One proposal has called for the British and French to give up their seats in favor of a Japanese seat and a "European Union" seat (with the European Union representing the UK, France, Germany, and its other European members); but, predictably, the British and French have objected to losing their seats, even though the EU is a supranational project in which member states are expected to gradually cede control of foreign and defense policy to EU-wide institutions. Another proposal calls for the Security Council expanding to 24 members, with two permanent seats added from the industrialized world (probably Japan and Germany), three more permanent seats added from the developing world (one state selected from Africa, one from Asia, and one from Latin America), and four new nonpermanent seats selected from various regions, all to be voted on by the UN General Assembly, the plenary body containing all 189 member states; but there remains the challenge of reaching agreement when Mexico, Brazil, and Argentina are among those vying for the Latin American seat, while India, Pakistan, and Indonesia are the chief contenders for the Asian seat, and Egypt, Nigeria, and South Africa all want the African seat. Among those states rejecting this plan is Italy, a fellow EU member with Germany, which objects to Berlin obtaining a seat over Rome and which has complained that the proposal would create a "train with 175 nations crowded into third class."[100]

It should be added that Israel has joined in the debate, complaining that it is the only UN member not eligible for even a temporary seat, since candidate countries will be drawn from each regional grouping, and Israel has not been permitted to participate in any such grouping because Arab states have banned it from its logical geographical home in the "Asian" caucus.

It is hard to know for sure how all this will play out, but a "prominent solution" that game theorists might predict out of this UN "game" is that Germany and Japan will be added from the ranks of the developed states while the various regional caucusing groups will be left to vote on which of their developing country brethren should be accorded seats, with various states given side payments to accept such an outcome. Note that this sort of analysis is based on realist-type assumptions about interstate bargaining and does not attach much importance to nonstate actors or any other factors in the equation.

However, some might say that the UN Security Council issue is an unfair test of the relative merits of competing paradigms—since it involves the deepest core values relating to national prestige, and hence is heavily tilted toward state-centric dynamics—and that many other current issues can be examined that cannot be fully understood through a Westphalian prism. The next section examines the assumptions and supporting evidence behind a cobweb, post-Westphalian paradigm, which many neoliberals see as furnishing a radically different, but much more vivid and accurate, picture of current reality than the billiard ball, Westphalian paradigm.

A POST-WESTPHALIAN WORLDVIEW: WORLD POLITICS AS A GIANT COBWEB

Where the Westphalian paradigm focuses our attention on the first two trends articulated in the Chapter 2 description of the contemporary international system—the growing diffusion of power and the growing fluidity of alignments among states in their geopolitical relations—the post-Westphalian paradigm steers us toward examining the second set of trends in the system, that is, the expanding agenda of issues and the expanding set of actors. Post-Westphalian thinkers argue that the billiard ball portrait of international relations has always been an incomplete representation of reality and that it is especially so today. Rather than viewing international relations through realist lenses as simply a contest between national units driven by the overriding concern of national security, they argue that there is a more complex set of relationships between not only national governments (which are themselves composed of often competing bureaucracies and other players) but also nonstate actors, involved not only in war and peace issues but in economic and social welfare issues as well. For example, in the air safety issue area, one can point to the role of such entities as the International Civil Aviation Organization, the International Air Transport Association, the International Federation of Airline Pilots Associations,

The cobweb paradigm. (Josh Korenblat)

and the airline interests and transportation ministries within various countries. Whereas the world of the realist or neorealist is populated primarily by soldiers, diplomats, and foreign policy strategists, the world of the post-Westphalian analyst (sometimes labeled neoliberal, pluralist, or globalist) includes multinational corporation executives, transnational labor union leaders, intergovernmental organization officials, and skyjackers. Hence, the cobweb imagery, connoting a richer, more complicated set of linkages than the billiard ball paradigm.[101]

Another Historical Narrative

We have seen in our earlier historical discussion that the trends cited by neoliberals have deep historical roots, that well before the twentieth century one could find nonstate actors existing alongside nation-states and welfare issues being addressed alongside military security issues, with growing interdependencies across national boundaries. But it is particularly in recent years that these phenomena are thought to be escalating in their importance and in their potential to alter radically the very nature of international relations as we commonly know it. Long-term historical trends which were underway as the twentieth century began, and which were at least partially interrupted and masked by World War I, World War II, and the Cold War, may now be ready to resume their trajectory at an accelerated pace, so say neoliberals. James Rosenau, calling for a "post-international politics" (i.e., post-Westphalian) paradigm, remarks:

> The state-centric structure of world affairs, in which actions and interactions are dominated by nation-states, is now rivaled by a more complex, less symmetrical set of patterns whereby international issues arise and are managed. Many of today's crucial problems—such as currency crises, environmental pollution, and the drug trade—are transnational in scope, with the result that governments are less and less able to be effective within their own domains and must, instead, contend with a multiplicity of issues sustained in part by external dynamics.[102]

Likewise, John Lukacs, also writing at the start of the post-Cold War era, commenting on both the external and internal challenges to the integrity of nation-states presented by integrative and disintegrative forces:

> Not only the configuration of great powers and their alliances but the very structure of political history has changed . . . . The very sovereignty and cohesion of states, the authority and efficacy of the governments are not what they were. . . . Are we going to see ever larger and larger political units? . . . Or are we more likely going to see the break-up of several states into smaller ones? The very texture of history is changing before our eyes.[103]

Among the first scholars to call attention to "the decline of the territorial state" was John Herz. In his 1959 book *International Politics in the Atomic Age,*

Herz envisioned how the growing "permeability" of national boundaries—the ease with which the "hard outer shell" of the nation-state could be penetrated by modern technology, whether nuclear weaponry or financial data flows or radio and television broadcasts—might erode national sovereignty. He argued that in the nuclear age the nation-state as an institution could no more provide for the physical protection of its population than the walled cities of the feudal era could perform the defense function for its populace once gunpowder was invented, that in an age of growing economic interdependence few if any nation-states could hope to be self-sufficient, and that in an age of ever more sophisticated telecommunications national governments would find it increasingly impossible to control the flow of ideas and information and sustain a distinctive national culture.[104]

The permeability of national borders was to increase over the next few decades far beyond what even Herz had foreseen, as satellite television, fax machines, and the Internet, along with electronic commerce and other technology-driven innovations rendered the territorial state ever more susceptible to external influences, although interdependence remained an uneven phenomenon, with some societies more interconnected and impacted than others. Perhaps no single event popularized the notion that the world had become highly interdependent more than the oil crisis of the 1970s, when Arab and other oil-exporting states threatened to paralyze the United States and other petroleum-dependent industrialized economies through price hikes and embargoes, which at one point left American motorists stranded in long gasoline lines waiting for daily fill-ups. The episode not only introduced the term "interdependence" into everyday conversation but also underscored the relevance of nonstate actors, such as the Organization of Petroleum Exporting Countries (OPEC), which was the IGO that coordinated the attempted power play, and the Seven Sisters, the leading oil multinationals (Shell, Mobil, and other firms), which controlled the flow of two-thirds of Western Europe's and Japan's oil supply and were in a position to allocate oil to various countries according to their own interests rather than according to the dictates of any states. Mobil and the other American-based oil giants ultimately relieved pressure on the United States by shipping additional oil supplies from Indonesia and Venezuela, but did so more out of their worry over unstable oil markets than over any felt loyalty to Washington. Again, these actors had been around for some time (OPEC since 1960 and Standard Oil, founded by John D. Rockefeller, since the late nineteenth century), but only in the 1970s did they gain sufficient visibility as to merit scholarly books and articles on their role in world politics.[105]

The 1960s and 1970s, coinciding with a period of *détente* (relaxation of tensions between the superpowers), saw a flurry of writings commenting on the growing "sensitivity" and "vulnerability" of states to outside forces as well as the rising importance of nonstate actors which had been overlooked by the prevailing state-centric paradigm; it was only around this time that one began seeing regular references to "IGOs" and "NGOs."[106] Had these merely been the musings of the flower children of the counterculture of the time, they might have been easily dismissed, but a chorus of serious scholars and practitioners gave voice to these ideas. Charles Kindleberger, a prominent economist at MIT, opined that "the state is about through as an economic unit," referring to the burgeoning multinational corporation phenomenon.[107] Similarly, Raymond Vernon of the Harvard Business School wrote *Sovereignty At Bay*, suggesting that MNCs might be the "new sovereigns," considering the power and resources at their command.[108] George Ball, U.S. Undersecretary of State in the Johnson administration, confessed "the nation-state is a very old-fashioned idea and badly adapted to serve the needs of our present complex world," acknowledging that the nation-state seemed a dysfunctional mode of organization given the manifold problems that transcended national boundaries.[109] Even the father of the realist school, Hans Morgenthau, toward the end of his life in 1974, had second thoughts about the staying power of the nation-state, confessing that "the technological revolutions of our age have rendered the nation-state's principle of political organization as obsolete as the first modern industrial revolution of the steam engine did feudalism."[110]

During the 1980s there was some retrenchment in post-Westphalian thinking, mainly due to the heating up of the Cold War during the Reagan years. But by the 1990s, with the end of the Cold War, post-Westphalian thinking returned to fashion as a spate of articles on the subject appeared. Walter Wriston, the former head of Citicorp, the largest U.S.-based bank, wrote about "the twilight of sovereignty" just as Robert Reich was asking "Who is 'US'?"—both referring to the newly coined term called "globalization."[111] Others suggested we were witnessing "the end of geography" or at least a "power shift" from states to nonstates.[112] In our earlier discussion of the billiard ball paradigm, we noted that traditionalists question how much "loss of control" national governments are experiencing due to the penetration of their economies and societies by outside forces, and can cite data which at least partially support their position that loss of control has been exaggerated. Cobweb analysts respond by pointing to their own data—for example, the kinds of daily headlines reported in Chapter 1: "Currency Traders Now Control the Fate of the Dollar," "Airline Alliance: Europe's Carriers Unite to Survive," "Cries of the Welfare State Under the Knife," "Iran Tiptoes to the Internet." They argue that even if one dismisses the growing volume of transnational transactions and the resultant cultural diffusion that is occurring worldwide—that is, even if one considers it trivial that Coca-Cola is served 560 million times a day in 160 countries, that Philip Morris makes 640 billion cigarettes a day and markets Marlboro "in every country on earth," that MTV videos are viewed in 130 countries while the "New World Order" (NWO) has taken on new meaning as a World Championship Wrestling tag-team whose exploits are broadcast to 120 countries,[113] or that the Internet is "connecting 42,000 computer networks sprawled across 84 countries" and is currently serving some 200 million users, "with a million more people becoming 'netizens' every month"[114]—one cannot as easily dismiss the enormous impacts that individuals in one country can visit upon individuals in another country today, for better or worse, through their respective actions.

The fact is that it is harder than ever for, say, the United States or any other state to manipulate Keynesian fiscal and monetary policy levers (for example, to increase government spending and to lower interest rates in times of economic recession or depression) when globalization produces pressures for fiscal and monetary discipline and austerity. Neither the U.S. Federal Reserve nor other national central banks have as much control over exchange rates and the value of their national currencies as in the past, given the ease with which private currency speculators and other investors can move their money in or out of overseas financial markets (a phenomenon variously called "the electronic herd" and "gypsy" or "casino" capitalism).[115] The Canadian government can do very little about Canada's acid rain problem through its own unilateral policies, no matter how vigorously implemented, because many sulfur dioxide and other emissions originate in the United States. It is relatively useless for Norway or Sweden to adopt antinuclear energy policies as a safeguard against nuclear disasters when neighboring France remains dependent on nuclear energy for 65 percent of its electricity and, hence, is particularly susceptible to a catastrophic accident that would likely spill over across much of Western Europe, just as the radioactivity did from the Chernobyl reactor explosion in the Ukraine in 1986. Malaysia's Petronas Twin Tower (the tallest building in the world) was shrouded in a blanket of smog in 1997 as forest fires set by peasants in Indonesia to open up farmland moved rapidly across national boundaries throughout southeast Asia. Forty percent of the world's people depend for their drinking water on 215 river systems shared by at least two nation-states, with 12 of these shared by at least five different states, so that they are at the mercy of each other's pollution control efforts. And, perhaps the most obvious example of intertwined destinies (and also the double-edged nature of technology), the mere three-and-one-half-hour time span it now takes to travel from London to New York aboard the Concorde jetliner is exceeded in earthbound travel efficiency only by the thirty-minute ride that can be taken by a nuclear warhead aboard an intercontinental ballistic missile between Moscow and New York.

True, there has never been any age of absolute sovereignty in the sense of enjoying total immunity from outside influences, but it is hard to identify an era where states have been more immediately vulnerable to decisions taken elsewhere than the present one. Take epidemics as an example. The Spanish flu in 1918–1919 did cut a wide path across national boundaries before killing 20 million people worldwide; and long before that, the ancient Aztec civilization was practically wiped out by the spread of smallpox brought by European explorers to the New World. But today's epidemics, whether AIDS or other diseases, have the potential to spread much more rapidly than was previously possible. Only recently has mankind developed the capability to destroy the entire human species, either through thermonuclear war or, more slowly, through global warming and environmental change. Furthermore, modern society, with its dependence on giant electronic grids and other such networks, is far more vulnerable to disruption on a mass scale by terrorists or other actors than ever before. There is growing concern over another sort of "epidemic"—the transmission of computer viruses that can play havoc with everything from banking transaction records to the codes governing the launching of ICBMs. As one article reports: "In a world where computers . . . are increasingly the very engine driving modern business, [we are seeing] an ominous trend toward programs that mimic viruses and pestilence in the physical world. . . . [One expert notes] 'I believe that we are indeed living in a computational ecosystem which is more and more globally cross-linked. . . . It's an amazing system, and it's very vulnerable.'"[116] The United States leads in Internet use, with two-thirds of all Internet users worldwide residing in the United States and almost 70 percent of Internet hosts stemming from North America, although American dominance will eventually shrink as people across the globe become more wired.[117]

In his classic work *1984*, George Orwell predicted that advanced communications technology would have the effect of enabling governments to exercise greater control over their populations, through maintaining data banks and invading citizens' privacy. Yet the new technologies—the world wide web, fax machines, satellite hook-ups, and other devices—seem to be having the opposite effect, promoting greater openness and democratization, even though dictatorial governments still seek to use various means, such as jamming foreign radio signals or banning satellite dishes, to manage the flow of information. Although CNN may only reach a small fraction of the world's people, it is watched by elites in hotel lobbies and in foreign offices around the globe and is gradually spreading its reach through home satellite dishes that are surreptitiously being installed even in remote rural villages. Thomas Friedman describes one scene which vividly depicts the challenges facing Islamic fundamentalist regimes or any other governments seeking to withstand foreign "cultural imperialism" through censorship:

> In South Tehran, the poorest neighborhood of the Iranian capital, some families can afford a television and some can't. When I visited Teheran in 1997, I found that some of those in South Teheran who had televisions were setting up a few chairs and selling tickets when the most popular American television show came on each week. The most popular show was *Baywatch*, a Southern California fantasy, in which all the women wear only bikinis and are 36-24-36. The Iranian government banned satellite dishes, so my Iranian friends just hid them under the laundry lines or under their 'satellite bushes,' the plants they use to cover them up on their balconies.[118]

A more poignant example of the difficulty governments now face in keeping out unwanted information and ideas is the case of "the French journal *Actuel*, which was so upset by the crackdown in Tiananmen Square [against student militants in 1989] that, having compiled a mock edition of the *People's Daily* that contained numerous accounts that the Chinese leadership did not want their people to read, sent it to every fax machine in China. . . . Given the magnitude of these communications dynamics, it is hardly surprising that people everywhere have become . . . more ready to challenge authority and more capable of engaging in collective actions that express their demands."[119] The Internet especially has the potential to disrupt national societies not only through computer viruses but also through shaking up the political system. The pre-Internet debates which occurred in the 1970s over the so-called "New World Information Order," involving differences between developed and less developed countries over the dissemination of news by a free press, now seem quite quaint given the multiple channels of communication that currently penetrate borders.

So far we have been talking here in generalities. Just as we examined the billiard ball paradigm's assumptions and evidences in some detail, we now need to look more closely at the assumptions embedded in the cobweb paradigm and the extent to which they hold up against empirical evidence.

Assumptions of the Post-Westphalian Paradigm

The assumptions of the post-Westphalian paradigm are essentially the opposite of those associated with the Westphalian paradigm. First, international organizations and other nonstate actors are often important in their own right, pursuing their own interests apart from states and competing with the latter in shaping events on the world stage; in other words, the interactions between national governments (in particular, central decision makers presiding over foreign policy establishments based in national capitals) are just one strand in the great web of human interactions, with other lines of interaction having significance as well. Second, to the extent that nation-states remain key players, they do not always behave as unitary, rational actors fixated on military security as their all-consuming national interest goal; increasingly, there are multiple issues competing for attention, with military concerns not consistently dominating the agenda and with the foreign policy process becoming more politicized as foreign and domestic issues become more and more intertwined in the wake of growing interdependence. Third, following from the first two assumptions, the threat or use of armed force, while always present, is becoming less relevant to outcomes in a growing number of issue areas; not only is international conflict taking a less violent form than in the past, but there is the potential for greater "cooperation under anarchy," although the management of international affairs may be trickier in some respects than previously, given the sheer number and range of actors and issues.

Assumption 1.   The first assumption of the post-Westphalian paradigm calls into question the primacy of nation-states as actors on the world stage. Echoing Raymond Vernon and other pioneering neoliberal thinkers, one writer notes that "the state-centered view of world affairs, the interstate model which still enjoys so much popularity in the study of international relations, has now become too simplistic," mainly because "nation-states are not the only actors on the world scene. . . . Some NGOs [nongovernmental organizations] probably have more power and influence in their respective fields than some of the smaller nation-states. The same applies to several IGOs [intergovernmental organizations] and undoubtedly to many multinational business enterprises [MNCs] which have more employees and a larger production output than most countries."[120] This point is made in Table 3.1 (page 78), which shows that multinational corporations account for roughly half of the 100 largest economic units in the world; General Motors, for example, is "bigger" than Denmark and Norway, not to mention ministates like Palau and Vanuatu. The European Union, an IGO whose collective resources exceed even that of the United States, does not appear in the table even though it is gradually acting as a single economic unit. The United Nations, were its members more willing to support collective action, would, of course, top the chart as an "entity."

Just as the number of nation-states is proliferating, so is the number of IGOs, NGOs, and MNCs. Focusing on the IGO phenomenon, there are commonly thought to be over 300 intergovernmental organizations in the world today—that is, international organizations whose members are nation-states and which ordinarily are created through treaties signed and ratified by them— although, depending on the criteria used, the number may well exceed 1,000. One scholar, counting offshoots of existing IGOs, posits that the number of IGOs grew 5000 percent in the twentieth century, from only 37 in 1909 to 1,850 by 1997, with most of the growth occurring after 1980.[121] IGOs command attention, however, not because they are easily counted but because they appear to be part of an evolutionary process at work in world politics. Rather than being viewed as experimental, failed or at best marginal responses to war and welfare problems, as realists tend to see them, intergovernmental organizations may more cogently be seen as structures which are deeply embedded in historical forces. Inis Claude, arguably the leading student of international organization, has said:

> The expectation of international organization, the habit of organizing, the taking-for-granted of international bodies . . . are permanent results of the movement [that began almost from scratch a century or so ago]. . . . We cannot ignore the successful implantation of the idea of international organization. International organization may not have taken over the system, but it has certainly taken hold in the system. The twentieth century has seen the establishment of the prescription that multilateral agencies are essential to the conduct of international affairs.[122]

We noted earlier that broad, multipurpose organizations such as the League of Nations and the United Nations were created in the twentieth century as a direct reaction to World War I and World War II, while more functionally specific IGOs such as the International Civil Aviation Organization and

TABLE 3.1   Ranking of Countries and Corporations According to Size of Annual Product

Countries are ranked according to gross national product. Corporations (headquarters in parentheses) are ranked according to total sales. Although not exactly comparable, they are sufficiently close to illustrate size relationships. Only industrial companies are included here.

Rank	Economic Entity	U.S. Dollars (Billions)	Rank	Economic Entity	U.S. Dollars (Billions)
1	United States	6,387.69	51	Philip Morris (US)	53.78
2	Japan	3,926.67	52	Pakistan	53.25
3	Germany	1,903.01	53	Chrysler (US)	52.22
4	France	1,289.24	54	Siemens (Germany)	51.05
5	Italy	1,134.98	55	British Petroleum (UK)	50.74
6	United Kingdom	1,042.70	56	Colombia	50.12
7	China (PRC)	581.11	57	Volkswagen (Germany)	49.34
8	Canada	574.88	58	Toshiba (Japan)	48.23
9	Spain	533.99	59	Unilever (UK/Neth.)	45.45
10	Brazil	471.98	60	Ireland	44.91
11	Russian Federation	348.41	61	New Zealand	44.67
12	South Korea	338.06	62	Algeria	44.35
13	Mexico	324.96	63	Chile	42.45
14	Netherlands	316.40	64	Nestle (Switz.)	41.63
15	Australia	309.97	65	Fiat (Italy)	40.85
16	India	262.81	66	Sony (Japan)	40.10
17	Switzerland	254.01	67	Honda Motor (Japan)	39.93
18	Argentina	244.01	68	Elf Aquitaine (France)	39.46
19	Sweden	216.29	69	United Arab Emirates	38.72
20	Belgium	213.44	70	NEC (Japan)	37.95
21	Austria	183.53	71	Egypt	36.68
22	General Motors (US)	154.95	72	Daewoo (South Korea)	35.71
23	Denmark	137.61	73	Iraq	35.00
24	Indonesia	136.99	74	E.I. DuPont De Nemours (US)	34.97
25	Ford Motor (US)	128.44			
26	Turkey	126.33	75	Mitsubishi Motors (Japan)	34.37
27	Thailand	120.24	76	Hungary	34.26
28	South Africa	118.06	77	Kuwait	34.12
29	Norway	113.53	78	Peru	34.03
30	Saudi Arabia	111.10	79	Texaco (US)	33.77
31	Exxon	101.46	80	Philips Electronics (Neth.)	33.52
32	Ukraine	99.68	81	Nigeria	32.99
33	Finland	96.22	82	Fujitsu (Japan)	32.80
34	Royal Dutch/Shell (Neth/UK)	94.88	83	Mitsubishi Electric (Japan)	32.73
35	Iran	90.00	84	ENI (Italy)	32.57
36	Toyota Motor (Japan)	88.12	85	Renault (France)	32.19
37	Poland	87.32	86	Chevron (US)	31.06
38	Portugal	77.75	87	Hoechst (Germany)	30.60
39	Greece	76.70	88	Procter & Gamble (US)	30.30
40	Israel	72.66	89	Peugeot (France)	30.11
41	Matsushita Electric Industrial (Japan)	69.95	90	Belarus	29.29
			91	Nippon Steel (Japan)	29.00
42	General Electric (US)	64.69	92	Mitsubishi Heavy Industries (Japan)	28.68
43	Daimler-Benz (Germany)	64.17			
44	IBM (US)	64.05	93	Pemex (Mexico)	28.19
45	Malaysia	60.06	94	Czech Republic	28.19
46	Mobil (US)	59.62	95	Morocco	27.65
47	Venezuela	58.92	96	Amoco (US)	26.95
48	Nissan Motor (Japan)	58.73	97	BASF (Germany)	26.93
49	Singapore	55.37	98	Bayer (Germany)	26.77
50	Philippines	54.61	99	Kazakhstan	26.50
			100	BMW (Germany)	25.97

Source: GNP data are from *World Bank Atlas* (Washington, D.C.: World Bank, 1995), pp. 18–19, supplemented by *The World Factbook 1995* (Washington, D.C.: Central Intelligence Agency, 1995); sales data are from *Fortune*, 132 (August 7, 1995), pp. 123ff.

other "specialized agencies" owe their existence to the expansion of interstate commerce and the need for new structures to assist national governments in promoting orderly economic relations in an emergent world capitalist economy. Regarding the latter IGOs (sometimes called "public international unions"), their arrival on the scene in the late nineteenth century—the Universal Postal Union dates back to 1878—coincided not only with the growth of an internationalist-oriented capitalist class but also with the growth of the welfare state and modern industrial society, with nation-states experiencing mounting pressures to produce a better standard of living for their citizenry and recognizing that material well-being could only be maximized through enhanced international cooperation. Other forces also contributed to IGO growth, notably scientific and intellectual elites seeking to improve the human condition through social engineering that took advantage of new technologies spanning national boundaries.[123]

States today form intergovernmental organizations for the same practical reasons that have always provided the fundamental rationale behind IGOs, i.e., problems exist that either cannot be handled unilaterally within the capabilities of a single state or can be dealt with more efficiently through collaboration with others. When a problem arises, the first inclination on the part of the affected parties is ordinarily to try to address the concern simply through formation of an international regime (some set of written agreements or informal ad hoc arrangements) short of creating an organization, since the latter is more costly; however, if the problem is viewed as an ongoing one, more elaborate machinery may be found necessary and an IGO may be born. Some problems may involve only two states and, hence, may call for merely a two-member IGO (e.g., the St. Lawrence Seaway Authority established by the United States and Canada), whereas other problems may be defined as requiring regional approaches (e.g., the European Union) or global, universal approaches (e.g., the UN). According to one observer, "the interwar period [between WWI and WWII] was clearly the high tide of universalism," in that global IGOs as a percentage of all IGOs peaked at that time, as distinct regional subsystems in Asia, Africa, and other parts of the globe did not become fully developed and did not create their own regional institutions until the decolonialization movement after World War II.[124] While regionalism remains a powerful impulse in world affairs, economic globalization and related trends are likely to provide further impetus for global IGO growth. An interesting question the international community is attempting to address is how to reconcile the missions of such regional economic IGOs as the European Union (made up of fifteen Western European states) and NAFTA (the North American Free Trade Association, made up of the United States, Canada, and Mexico), which aim to enhance the interests of their respective *regions*, with the universal free trade rules promulgated by the World Trade Organization, an IGO which is supposed to serve *global* interests.

Although IGOs are generally conceived to be instruments of cooperation, it is important to keep in mind the realist caveat that they also inevitably involve conflict, that they can be thought of as forums for managing interstate disagreements as well as mutual problem-solving, and that member states vie for control of IGOs as they attempt to use international organizations as tools for legitimizing various national policies. We have seen that the problems that give rise to IGOs can be of the high-politics or low-politics variety, with multipurpose organizations generally dealing with the former and functionally specific organizations dealing with the latter, which by definition tend to involve relatively narrow, technical, noncontroversial matters (although even setting international mail rates or sharing weather forecasting data can become greatly politicized).

There remains the question of just how much "power and influence" IGOs have relative to states. The typical IGO has at least a plenary assembly or conference in which all member governments discuss and vote on policies, along with a secretariat or bureau that is responsible for implementing decisions and running the organization's administrative apparatus. However, IGOs differ considerably in the amount of decision-making power that states vest in the organization. A few IGOs approach a supranational decision-making model, i.e., the organization is empowered to make decisions that are binding on the entire membership, requiring all member states to abide by the collective will no matter whether they are on the winning or losing side of a roll-call vote. Far more IGOs, though, are at the opposite extreme, empowered by member states merely to offer recommendations or resolutions of an advisory nature that each individual national government is free to accept or reject as it sees fit. Other IGOs fall somewhere in-between, respecting the sovereignty of individual members in most organizational matters but evidencing a degree of supranationalism in certain areas. States have generally been more willing to cooperate robustly and entrust decision-making competence in organizations having narrow, well-defined goals (functionally specific IGOs) rather than in organizations having broader, more open-ended missions (multipurpose IGOs). A number of UN specialized agencies do approximate the supranational model in some respects. In the case of the Universal Postal Union and some other organizations, governments have even allowed officials in IGO bureaucracies ("technocrats") to exercise considerable discretion in making and implementing policies on behalf of the entire membership. These IGOs can be said to have a direct impact in several fields of international activity, including health, transportation, education, social welfare, and communications. The "higher" the politics, the less supranationalism that is likely and the more likely states will want to retain sovereignty, with the most powerful states in particular seeking to impose their will on the organization, although IGO secretaries-general and other IGO officials have been known at times to play an important independent role in situations involving war and peace and other volatile concerns.

One subset of neoliberal thinkers, the so-called functionalist school, hypothesizes that as states collaborate and surrender some measure of sovereignty to IGOs in low politics issue areas, their governments will learn *habits* of cooperation that will slowly induce further collaboration and surrender of sovereignty in high politics issue areas, all leading ultimately to a possible supra-national community (i.e., a regional or world government). In other words, willingness to entrust IGOs with power to make decisions regarding, say, locust control may be the beginning of a process that could eventually "spill over" into the realm of arms control. Some functionalists emphasize that certain sectors of intergovernmental cooperation are more likely candidates for spillover than others because they create not only a desire but a need for ever more ambitious cooperation across issue areas. (An example might be a group of countries discovering that the benefits they have derived from sharing a common fishing ground cannot be sustained without additional collaboration in environmental policymaking pertaining to ocean pollution.)[125] Where realists would counter that politics can never be completely divorced from even the most seemingly apolitical, technical set of issues and—more importantly—that there are obvious limits to the extent to which national governments can be expected to relinquish political power to a higher authority in areas that bear on their very survival, neoliberals would simply reply that whether suprana-tionalism materializes or not, international institutions *do matter*, that "to analyze world politics . . . [today] is to discuss . . . the rules that govern elements of world politics and the organizations that help implement those rules."[126]

If IGOs are a bridge between governments, NGOs are a bridge between peoples. NGOs potentially pose a greater challenge to the Westphalian state system than IGOs, since, unlike the latter, NGOs are not created by states. As suggested earlier, the IGO network can be thought of as an innovative adaptation of the state system that allows nation-states to continue to function and attempt to meet the needs of their populations through joint, collaborative machinery while at the same time permitting them to retain formal sovereignty; in other words, IGOs permit a "pooling of sovereignty." On the other hand, NGOs are created by private individuals and groups, what is often referred to as civil society, with governments exercising only indirect control over these actors. Such transnational relations have existed for centuries, represented by the early travels of European explorers, missionaries, and traders. Nevertheless, it was not until the improved communications and transportation technology that accompanied industrialization in the nineteenth century that large numbers of people were able to interact more readily across national boundaries. Industrialization also created specialized economic groups for whom national frontiers were somewhat artificial and irrelevant barriers; not only business executives but also labor union activists, scientists, artists, and others were added to the ranks of transnational actors. James Field describes the emergence of the "new tribe":

> Among the humanitarians there developed an international peace movement and international campaigns for the abolition of . . . slavery, for women's rights, and for temperance. Working class groups supported the international labor movement. . . . From the managers there came a network of . . . trusts, cartels, and the like. . . . In much of this activity, of course, private and public sectors found them-

selves intertwined; governments would intermeddle, and private groups would seek governmental aid. Among the actors, governments were . . . the most visible. But while the apparatus of the state continued to grow throughout the period, and particularly from the latter part of the nineteenth century, its role . . . was less one initiating policy than of responding to conditions produced by nongovernmental factors whose influence transcended national boundaries.[127]

As transnational interactions expanded, these ties increasingly became institutionalized in the form of nongovernmental organizations designed to provide more durable bonds between transnational actors. The number of NGOs grew from only five in 1850 to 330 by 1914 to 2,300 by 1970.[128] There are now over 10,000 international NGOs in the world; using a very broad definition, one recent work counts as many as 28,000 today.[129] Some observers speak of the explosive growth of NGOs as an "associational revolution," dominated thus far by people in developed, industrialized democracies—where both the availability of financial resources and the relative individual freedom tolerated by governments encourages participation in such networks—but increasingly extending into every corner of the globe.[130]

Admittedly, NGOs such as the World Federation of Master Tailors are not likely to alter the course of world affairs. However, certain nongovernmental organizations, ranging from the Roman Catholic Church to Islamic Jihad to Greenpeace to the International Red Cross, can have significant impacts. Some 1,500 NGOs have been formally accredited to participate in UN diplomatic proceedings, sharing information and advancing proposals as part of a web of governmental, intergovernmental, and nongovernmental efforts aimed at global problem-solving. For example, Amnesty International has been so extensively relied on for accurate monitoring of human rights violations that some view it as "almost an arm of the UN."[131] Likewise, CARE and other NGOs have become major vehicles for delivering economic development assistance to poor countries, as donor governments and UN agencies often prefer channeling aid through these bodies rather than through the host governments, which are thought to be corrupt and less likely to transfer the funds to those in need at the grassroots level. Although it is true that the consultative status of NGOs usually allows them to exercise only limited influence over the actual decisions reached by IGOs, their lobbying efforts can be extremely effective in certain cases. Most notable in this regard are the many transnational agricultural, labor, and manufacturing interests groups that have been organized to promote the concerns of their members in dealing with governmental and intergovernmental officials in the European Union. It should be added that many NGOs do not enjoy a privileged consultative status in IGOs but nonetheless are active in trying to shape outcomes in the international arena, such as numerous feminist groups that showed up at the 1995 UN World Conference on Women in Beijing as well as at the 1992 Earth Summit in Rio de Janeiro. As with IGOs, NGOs are likely to be accorded greater autonomy of action by states the more an issue is characterized by "low politics." However, some argue that NGOs "are muscling their way [even] into areas of high politics . . . that were once dominated by the state."[132] Referring to the key role played by the International Campaign to Ban Landmines in lobbying for the 1998 Ottawa Treaty that outlawed such devices, the Canadian foreign minister commented: "Clearly, one can no longer relegate NGOs to simple advisory or advocacy roles. . . . They are now part of the way decisions have to be made."[133]

Multinational corporations are a special variation of NGOs. Although the beginnings of multinational corporations can be traced far back—many of the great oil and mining companies had established their overseas extractive enterprises by the late nineteenth century, Singer Sewing Machines already had an overseas factory in Scotland in 1878, Ford Motors had an assembly plant in Europe in 1911, and Woolworth, General Electric, and Otis Elevator were among other U.S. companies establishing foreign subsidiaries before World War I— the MNC phenomenon did not really take off until after World War II, when a number of factors spurred dramatic growth in direct foreign investment. First, rather than trying to break through tariff and other trade barriers to export their goods to foreign markets, many companies found it easier to gain access simply by building separate production facilities inside those countries. Second, many countries offered cheap labor, special tax treatment, lax pollution laws, and other advantages to foreign firms willing to invest in their economies, prompting many firms to build overseas plants from which they could serve not only their foreign markets but their home markets as well. Third, the new, speedier communications and travel technology as well as containerization of cargo and computerized storage of data all greatly facilitated the physical expansion of MNC operations. The bottom-line explanation for the growth of MNCs was that foreign investment was found to be enormously profitable; by the 1980s, nearly half of the *Fortune* 500 corporations depended on their international operations for over 40 percent of their profits.[134] Of course, the MNC phenomenon could not have mushroomed as it did without general acceptance of laissez-faire, liberal internationalist principles by governments in support of the idea of an open world economy, something the United States government especially promoted after 1945.

"The number of [MNCs] in the world's fourteen richest countries has more than tripled in the past twenty-five years, from 7,000 in 1969, to 24,000."[135] Today there are over 35,000 MNCs in the world, controlling over 200,000 subsidiaries. The United States continues to be the most prominent headquarters country, being the base of operations of 151 of the 500 largest industrial and service companies in the late 1990s, trailed by Japan (149); G-7 countries as a whole were headquarters for 435 of the companies listed in the *Fortune* 500. MNCs headquartered in Western Europe and Japan have been proliferating, challenging American dominance, while MNCs based in developing countries and former communist-bloc states are also beginning to gain visibility as countries everywhere are being drawn into the network. It is estimated that just 500 corporations control 70 percent of world trade, almost half of which is intrafirm (from one subsidiary to another), and the 300 largest transnational firms account for roughly a quarter of the world's productive assets.[136]

MNCs have been the subject of much debate regarding their relationship to national governments, both the host governments of countries in which they operate subsidiaries and the home government of the country in which they are headquartered. Most of this discussion will be left to Chapter 5, where we will focus on the politics of international economic relations. Suffice it to say that MNCs pose huge challenges to the functioning of the nation-state and to concepts of nationalism and statism. Although billiard ball analysts are right that MNC ownership and management thus far has tended to "stay rooted in particular national systems"—the headquarters country—we have noted how transplants, global factories, mergers, and other aspects of economic globalization are blurring the national identity of products and companies. Alliances in international relations traditionally referred to military coalitions among states, but increasingly we hear of such partnerships among MNCs based in different countries, such as the 1999 alliance formed between Air France and U.S.-based Delta Air Lines as a response to the American Airlines-led eight-member "One World Alliance" and the United Airlines-led six-member "Star Alliance," all designed to give their participants a competitive edge by integrating flight schedules and frequent flier programs. Regarding the Star Alliance, "their ad shows an elongated airplane in which the nose section is from United, the front cabin Air Canada, the midsection SAS, Varig and Thai Airways, and the tail section Lufthansa—all next to the revealing headline 'Star Alliance: The Airline Network for Earth.'"[137] In the same vein, in 1998, the American Automobile Manufacturers Association went out of existence, replaced not at the American level but at the world level by the Alliance of Automobile Manufacturers composed of General Motors, Ford, Daimler-Chrysler, Nissan, Toyota, and other firms.[138]

It is true that national governments are in a position to block mergers, alliances, and other such moves, but there is often a reluctance to do so for fear of stifling economic growth. In the case of airlines, for example, in most countries the civil aviation sector traditionally has been either directly owned by the government or strongly regulated due to national security concerns, with foreigners prohibited from purchasing majority stock ownership in a domestic airline; however, there has been a trend lately toward not only privatizing and deregulating airlines (thereby helping consumers by encouraging price competition and helping taxpayers by eliminating the need for costly government subsidies) but also permitting greater foreign ownership. As each nation-state competes for foreign investment, trying to attract multinational corporations to its shores in the hope of generating additional jobs and other benefits, it risks exposing itself to so much foreign domination that the government's own capacity to manage its national economy may be undermined. This problem has long been experienced by less developed countries, but it is increasingly a source of concern in developed countries as well, including the United States.

As the aforementioned 1973 oil embargo episode demonstrated, neither host nor home governments may be in a position to control fully the behavior of MNCs, which are driven by their own objectives and interests. Although MNCs are technically subject to the laws of the countries in which they operate, they have often been able to use their vast resources to shape the laws to their advantage or, failing that, to evade state regulation altogether. Charles Kindleberger has gone so far as to assert that "the international corporation has no country to which it owes more loyalty than any other, nor any country where it feels completely at home."[139] MNCs now find themselves involved as at least semiautonomous actors in not only world energy politics but all kinds of regional and global politics, both the low and high variety, ranging from the politics of health (shaped by Merck and other pharmaceutical firms) to the politics of food supply and distribution (shaped by Archer Daniels Midland and other agribusiness conglomerates) to the politics of global warming and chemical weapons arms control (shaped by Dupont and the large chemical companies).

While MNCs like to pose as engines of world peace and prosperity, as reflected in IBM's ad trumpeting the company as a source of "solutions for a small planet," many questions have been raised having to do with the accountability of corporate elites toward citizens (and not just toward stockholders) as they become enmeshed in global governance. (Similar concerns have been raised about NGO elites generally, as well as IGO executive heads, who are not elected through democratic processes participated in by mass publics.) Two writers, arguably exaggerating the power of MNCs, claim they "are becoming the world empires of the twenty-first century. The architects and managers of these space-age business enterprises understand that the balance of power has shifted from territorially bound governments to companies that can roam the world. As the hopes and aspirations of government shrink almost everywhere, these imperial corporations are occupying public space and exerting a more profound influence over the lives of ever larger numbers of people. . . .The modern nation-state . . . looks more and more like an institution of a bygone age."[140] One of the strongest expressions of MNC detachment from its national roots, at least in terms of aspirations, came from the chairman of a major MNC, the Dow Chemical Company, who once remarked "I have long dreamed of buying an island owned by no nation, and of establishing the World Headquarters of the Dow company on the truly neutral ground of such an island, beholden to no nation or society."[141] The detachment of the MNC from the nation-state is still just that—a dream. Most MNCs are still anchored to the home country, and national governments would still appear to be in charge of the "global shopping mall," although their custodianship is becoming ever more complicated. As one scholar notes, "the clash between the integrating forces of the world economy and the centrifugal forces of the sovereign state has become one of the most critical issues of contemporary international relations."[142]

This theme of integration (globalism) vs. disintegration (localism) is one that I have called attention to as one of the major dramas that will be played out in the twenty-first century. The airline alliances, global factories, and the MNC culture generally represent powerful globalizing forces. But alongside these transnational Spaceship Earth images of reality—what Benjamin Barber has labeled "McWorld"—there are other countertrends and opposite images more parochial and tribalistic in nature—what he calls "Jihad"[143]—that are no less threatening to the viability of the nation-state and state system. To explore how subnationalism and subgroupism are affecting business as usual in world politics, we now examine Assumption 2 in the post-Westphalian paradigm.

Assumption 2.   The second assumption of the post-Westphalian paradigm calls into question the notion that, in order to understand a state's foreign policy behavior, one can treat the state as a unitary, rational actor intent on maximizing its national interests defined mainly in military security terms and, hence, one need not look inside the state at subnational, domestic factors. A number of scholars over the years have pointed out the importance of looking not only at the specific individuals making decisions—their personalities and their psychological dispositions—but also at the domestic political environment in which foreign policy decisions are taken.[144] In democracies especially, central decision makers are constrained to an extent by public opinion, interest groups, the mass media, legislatures, bureaucratic agencies, and other pluralistic domestic influences, granted the greater the gravity of the national security threat the more likely leaders can insulate themselves from these pressures. Certainly, in a country of any size, whether a democracy or a dictatorship, one can find bureaucratic politics at work in almost any issue area. (As a telling example of the impact of bureaucratic politics on national security decisions, one need only note that during the Cold War there was constant speculation in Washington over why each new generation of Soviet long-range missiles seemed to be produced in four different models, until it was pointed out that the organization that designed Soviet missiles had four separate bureaus and each was allowed to design its own version, i.e., Soviet arms production decisions were being driven at least as much by the need to appease competing internal constituencies as by any external strategic calculations having to do with correlation of forces![145])

Neoliberals contend that the link between the international and the domestic environment has become more complex and significant in the post-Cold War era. As welfare issues increasingly compete with traditional security issues for attention on foreign policy agendas, the number of actors claiming membership in a state's "foreign policy establishment" is expanding accordingly, as is the potential for internal cleavages to affect policy. Officials in executive branch agencies as well as on legislative committees dealing with energy, agriculture, transportation, environmental, and other concerns—bodies that previously had relatively little or no connection to the foreign policy arena—now frequently find themselves involved in the foreign policy process and are turning up at diplomatic conferences in as great numbers as foreign affairs and defense officials. These newer actors are pressured usually to promote the interest of particular domestic constituencies having the most direct stake in a given sector rather than pursuing the national interest broadly defined; for example, the U.S. State Department has no natural clientele interest group it serves, whereas the same cannot be said of the Department of Agriculture, which clearly is attuned to the interests of farmers. Given these trends, it is likely to become that much harder in the future to conceptualize states as unitary, rational actors in world politics.

It may be helpful to envision a spectrum of decisions that a government such as the United States might face. At one extreme end are "pure foreign policy" decisions (say, the decision to launch a nuclear attack). At the other extreme end are "pure domestic policy" decisions (say, the decision to add more teachers in schools to reduce class size). In the middle of the spectrum are what could be called "intermestic" decisions, i.e., decisions where it is hard to distinguish between the international and domestic dimensions (say, the decision to lower tariffs against Japanese automobiles imported into the United States).[146] More and more decisions are likely to fall in the middle, "intermestic" portion of the spectrum, given the dynamics of complex interdependence. Witness the following statement by President Clinton:

> The once bright line between domestic and foreign policy is blurring. If I could do anything to change the speech patterns of those of us in public life, I would almost like to stop hearing people talk about foreign policy and domestic policy, and instead start discussing economic policy, security policy, environmental policy . . . . When the President of Mexico comes here . . . and we talk about drug problems, are we talking about domestic problems or foreign problems? If we talk about immigration, are we discussing a domestic issue or a foreign issue? If we talk about NAFTA [the North American Free Trade Agreement] and trade, is it their foreign politics or our domestic economics? We have to understand this in a totally different way.[147]

We said earlier that billiard ball analysts often think in terms of game theory, where the players are states (or, if you will, their central decision makers) engaged in strategic moves against each other. Robert Putnam has argued that when national leaders get together, "the politics of many international negotiations can usefully be conceived as a two-level game [one pitched at an international audience and the other at a domestic audience]." He says that "each national political leader appears at both game boards. Across the international table sit his foreign counterparts, and at his elbows sit diplomats and other international advisors. Around the domestic table behind him sit party and parliamentary figures, spokespersons for domestic agencies, representatives of key interest groups, and the leader's own political advisors."[148] Putnam quotes Robert Strauss, the chief U.S. official at the Tokyo Round trade negotiations in the 1970s, as saying that "during my tenure as Special Trade Representative, I spent as much time negotiating with my domestic constituents [both industry and labor] and members of the U.S. Congress as I did negotiating with our foreign trading partners."[149] Similarly, former U.S. Secretary of Labor John Dunlop is said to have commented that "bilateral negotiations usually require three agreements—one across the table and one on each side of the table."[150]

Admittedly, these sorts of domestic political pressures in the foreign policy process have always existed and are hardly new. However, there may be a deeper reason why, today especially, the conventional states-as-unitary-actors assumption may be breaking down. Many observers have noted that in the United States and the developed industrialized democracies the absence of any immediate major external military threat in the post-Cold War era, akin to the threat posed by the USSR during the Cold War, has meant there is less "glue" holding these societies together and there is more play given to internal divisions. Nationalism and patriotism may still be alive, but they are less palpable. Recalling our discussion of MNCs, globalization at the same time is also undermining national cohesion. Some observers speak of the nation-state experiencing a "crisis of authority." There is a sense of uncertainty and disorientation among publics over the future, possibly due to the dislocations caused by globalization, including the loss of long-time national symbols (e.g., Chrysler in the United States, sold to Germany's Daimler-Benz, and Rolls Royce in the UK, sold to Germany's BMW). Demands continue to be made on the national welfare state for employment, health care, and other benefits, but states (strong and weak alike) are struggling to maintain their "capacity" to meet these needs in the wake of counter-pressures to downsize government taxes and regulations. At least one study finds growing apathy and cynicism toward politics and government in virtually all developed countries.[151] There is alienation not only from the state but also from the "McWorld" consumer culture and modernity trends which are uprooting families and traditional institutions, reflected in the search for meaning by growing numbers of evangelical Christians, orthodox Jews, and persons of other religious persuasions.

One writer comments:

> The most obvious consequence of globalization is that forces of international competition, and the mixture of opportunity and personal risk that they represent, affect a widening spectrum of the population. Not just steel and textile workers, but bank clerks, journalists, creative artists, shopkeepers . . . and doctors operate increasingly in a global as well as a local marketplace. . . . Globalization may be squeezing the wages and job prospects of the more unskilled workers in rich countries. At the same time, for the educated and moneyed section of the population, the opportunities presented by globalization . . . are great. We thus have one, potentially large, disadvantaged, alienated, and powerless segment in society and another which is flourishing but has less of a stake in the success of any particular country.[152]

Another comment: "From traffic jams to water shortages, from budget crises to racial conflicts, from flows of refugees to threats of terrorism . . . people are relentlessly confronted with social, economic, and political complexities that impel them to forego their rudimentary premises [about state and nation] and replace them with more elaborate conceptions of how to respond to the challenges of daily life."[153]

One response we have seen is to reach outward, above the level of the nation-state, to explore new expansive governing arrangements in the form of such entities as the European Union and NAFTA. But another response is to reach inward, below the level of the nation-state. One can see manifestations of this impulse in the United States in the "states' rights" movement, which seeks to return more power to the grassroots away from Washington, as well as in the fact that virtually every state now has its own overseas trade offices promoting not American national interests so much as Illinois, Missouri, and 48 other interests, with even cities increasingly creating their own more localized international contacts.[154] "The traditional division between the federal government and the states on foreign policies and trade is blurring [as] the states are moving more and more into a position of leadership, with governors rather than federal officials acting as U.S. trade ambassadors."[155] It has even been suggested that American states and cities are engaged in a "civil war" of sorts, in competing with each other, and not just other countries, to attract foreign investment. In other developed countries as well, one finds decentralizing tendencies, albeit more serious, with Northern Italy going so far as threatening to separate itself completely from Southern Italy and form the new state of Pandania, over what is perceived as excessive southern economic dependence on the north. Intrastate movements that call for either secession or at least greater autonomy and self-determination on the part of subnational groups can become especially heated when based on ethnic differences of the type discussed at the outset of this chapter (e.g., French-speaking Quebec threatening to secede from Canada, and Wales and Scotland seeking greater self-rule from Britain). Ironically, the integrative trends may be feeding the disintegrative trends, insofar as relatively small entities such as Quebec, Scotland, and Wales may now feel more emboldened to carve out their own individual destinies knowing that they can expect to be included in such larger entities as the EU and NAFTA which can provide a protective economic and security umbrella for them in the world.

Less developed countries—"weak states" to begin with, given their lack of revenue to support energetic government—are experiencing still greater turmoil, including in several cases real civil wars, mostly revolving around ethnicity. It is estimated that no more than one-third of all the nation-states on the planet have ethnically homogeneous populations (where at least 90 percent of the population is of the same ethnicity)[156] so that the potential for ethnic strife is high in the post-Cold War era. Nowhere is ethnopolitical conflict a source of greater concern than in Africa, where nation-state boundaries were the artificial creations of colonial powers rather than conforming to any historical cultural groupings; after these societies achieved independence following World War II, ethnic tensions were kept in check somewhat by Cold War politics that tended to discourage boundary changes, a condition no longer applicable. We have seen how the recent proliferation of microstates has been the result of both the winding down of the decolonialization process (e.g., Palau, Tonga) as well as the ethnically induced breakup of existing states (e.g., Yugoslavia, USSR).

Some new states are so small or so lacking in financial resources as to be at best marginally self-sustaining. A *Wall Street Journal* article reported that when the former Soviet republic of Tajikistan achieved its sovereign independence from the Soviet Union and assumed its UN seat in 1993, it could only afford a one-man diplomatic corp, with its UN delegate having even to cook his own state dinners.[157] Some states are so dysfunctional as to be called "failed states," connoting the complete collapse of all authority structures within the country, such as happened in the 1990s in Somalia, where the political system was essentially being run by rival clans or gangs.[158] Perhaps Somalia is the quintessential example of "Jihad" coexisting with "McWorld." It is also an example of how civil wars have replaced interstate wars as the predominant mode of conflict attracting attention on the planet, leading us to reexamine realist assumptions about where anarchy and violence are located in the state system.

Assumption 3.   The third assumption of the post-Westphalian paradigm calls into question the realist proposition that the most fundamental difference between international politics and domestic politics is that the former occurs in a decentralized, anarchic system which is inherently war-prone, whereas the latter occurs in a centralized, hierarchical system governed by authoritative institutions and rules which mute conflict. As we have discussed, neoliberals point out that not only is "cooperation under anarchy" possible through the creation of international regimes including international organizations, but one can cite many instances, especially in the post-Cold War era, where interstate politics is more peaceful and routine than intrastate politics.

We noted in Chapter 2 that the fall of the Berlin Wall in 1989 and the events that followed were an extraordinary moment, since system transformation, from the Cold War era to the post-Cold War era, occurred without a shot being fired—something virtually unheard of in the annals of Westphalian politics. We also alluded to what has been called "the long peace"—the period from 1945 to the present, which is the longest continuous interval since 1648 in which there has been no direct exchange of physical hostilities between any major powers. Going still further back in history, there is a long-term trend in the direction of war avoidance that is discernible. One study finds that wars among great powers in the nineteenth and twentieth centuries were underway only about one-sixth of the time, compared with an estimated 80 percent of the time in the sixteenth to eighteenth centuries.[159] Today there are few interstate wars occurring anywhere, great or small—a fact that is especially impressive given the enormous proliferation of new nation-states since 1945, which has more than tripled the number of potential candidates for interstate war participation—leading some scholars to speak of "the obsolescence of major war" and "the end of international war" altogether.[160]

Is it possible that one of the "pillars of the Westphalian temple"—war—has collapsed, or is at least "decaying"?[161] Optimism about the decline in war must be tempered. Throughout "history, war has been the norm rather than the exception in relations among nations" and "over the past two centuries the only thing more common than predictions about the end of war has been war itself."[162] After all, the other long peace of recent memory—the forty-three-year peace after the end of the Franco-Prussian War in 1871— was followed by one of history's most destructive wars in 1914, even though Norman Angell's *The Great Illusion* in 1910 had claimed war had become a relic of the past insofar as it was no longer profitable even to the victors. Indeed, while there has been a declining incidence of interstate war over time, the wars that did occur in the twentieth century produced far more carnage than previously due to the growing lethality of weaponry.

Still, there is some reason for guarded optimism that conditions are ripe for the long peace to continue in the twenty-first century and for it gradually to be extended beyond the great powers. The logic here is threefold: (1) the sheer destructiveness of nuclear weapons and other weapons of mass destruction are powerful inhibiting agents, reducing the probability of great-power war to closer to zero than at any time since the Peace of Westaphalia; (2) as the trend toward greater democratization continues worldwide, this, too, will likely have an inhibiting effect, since democracies virtually never go to war against each other;[163] and (3) as economic interdependence widens, the economies of nation-states will become so interlinked that war between them will become less attractive and less thinkable. Thomas Friedman has offered a "golden arches theory of conflict prevention," arguing that no two countries which have had a McDonalds (symbolizing societies that have become mass consumption-oriented) have ever fought a war against each other, although he acknowledges that the theory becomes problematic if one counts civil wars.[164]

Whether humanity has lost the stomach for war remains a matter of speculation. Certainly the human propensity for violence is still very much in evidence in the large volume of civil strife occurring on the planet, as demonstrated by the estimated half million to one million people killed in the Rwandan fighting between Hutus and Tutsis during the 1990s, as well as millions killed in other internal conflagrations. Despite the end of the Cold War, the level of total global military spending still exceeds $800 billion, only modestly reduced from the high-water mark of the 1980s. Moreover, various countries—whether in the name of deterrence or defense—are *preparing* for ever more sophisticated, exotic forms of warfare, including thermonuclear, chemical, and biological war. This does not even take into account other, nonstate sources of political violence in the international system, such as international terrorism. Hence, it is premature to proclaim that Kant's "perpetual peace" has arrived. The contemporary international system offers some intriguing, hopeful possibilities, as post-Westphalian theorists posit, but it also presents a number of complex challenges that go beyond the historical problem of interstate war.

In Chapter 2, we briefly discussed a larger set of possibilities and challenges confronting humanity in the twenty-first century, having to do with the prospects for a "new multilateralism" and a "more mature anarchy." We have seen how post-Westphalian thinkers are much more bullish on international institution-building than are their Westphalian counterparts. One member of the post-Westphalian school offers this analysis:

> As the global system becomes more integrated, there is a demand for international public goods that neither markets nor nation-states will provide. . . . These are roughly as follows: systematic financial stability; the rule of law and dispute settlement needed for an open system of trade and investment; common standards of weights and measures; management of global communications networks like aviation, telecommunications, and sea-lanes to prevent congestion and disasters; management of environmental concerns like Antarctica, the atmosphere, and oceans. . . . All these require some sort of institutional development, beyond the nation-state. Some of these activities are largely self-regulating, since the main commercial users have a collective interest in providing the public good, as is the case with many . . . industrial standards (the International Standards Organization). . . . In some cases, there is mixed public/private sector participation, as in the International Telecommunications Union. But, mostly, there is sovereignty pooling by governments through new institutions (the European Union, the World Meteorological Organization). . . . There is a complex but rich system of governance growing up to manage globalization. . . .[165]

At the outset of this book, the term "global governance" was used to connote the complex web of relationships that are evolving in the world, including public and private actors as well as supranational and subnational levels of political activity, with nation-states remaining at the center of this mix—pulled between the forces of McWorld and Jihad. The jury is still out on how all this will play out in the twenty-first century. The jury is also out on the twin normative questions that were raised in Chapter 1—how much government do we want, and, where governmental solutions are deemed necessary, what level of government (from local control to wider control) is optimal? Post-Westphalians stress that we should be interested not merely in the question of international *order* but also *justice*. In particular, they suggest we should go beyond a Grotian "society of states" morality, which stresses the legal and other obligations states have toward each other (e.g., the obligation not to intervene in the internal affairs of any fellow sovereign state) and consider a more "cosmopolitan" morality (e.g., the obligation of people everywhere to support humanitarian intervention in civil conflicts where a government or other group is engaged in genocide or other atrocities against its own population).[166] Some argue that "human rights" should extend not only to physical security but economic well-being, and that the international community should be concerned about reducing the rich-poor gap not only *between* countries (e.g., Switzerland's per capita income is 408 times that of Mozambique) but also *within* countries (e.g., two dozen billionaires in Mexico are wealthier than the bottom 33 million Mexicans).[167] Is it right, for example, that the three richest persons on Earth should have assets that exceed the combined gross domestic products of the 48 least developed countries, or that the 225 richest individuals have a combined wealth greater than the annual income of the poorest half of the world's population?[168] Then, too, there is ongoing concern about the implications of cobweb phenomena for democracy and how to hold IGO, NGO, and MNC elites accountable no less than national goverments.[169]

The Relevance of the Post-Westphalian Paradigm in the Post-Cold War Era: Assessing the Empirical Evidence

Normative issues aside, what does one make of the empirical argument that the post-Westphalian paradigm is a more accurate representation of current reality than the Westphalian paradigm? Should the world today more properly be thought of as a giant cobweb, rather than a giant billiard ball table? Data have been cited documenting the explosive growth of transnational actors in the form of intergovernmental organizations, nongovernmental organizations, and multinational corporations, many of which command vastly greater resources than some nation-states; while IGOs may be quite compatible with the state system, and may be simply a modern adaptation of the state system, NGOs and MNCs pose more thorny challenges to the logic of a Westphalian world. Once mainly the preserve of First World, rich, industrialized capitalist societies, this global organizational network is increasingly being participated in by former Second World (Marxist) and Third World societies in the post-Cold War era; for example, the fastest rates of growth in national participation in NGOs have been occurring lately in Africa and Asia.[170] There are numerous data available showing the shrinking and linking that is occurring in terms of transaction flows and the growing sensitivity and vulnerability of national societies to external events, granted interdependence is not new and, on some dimensions, is only now attaining or exceeding the levels witnessed in the early twentieth century. For the United States, trade as a percentage of GNP increased from 10 percent in 1952 to 22 percent by the 1990s; Canadian trade expanded from 36 percent to 51 percent in that time frame; the United Kingdom from 51 percent to 53 percent; and Germany from 29 percent to 58 percent.[171] Daily foreign exchange trading in 1900 could be measured in the millions of dollars, compared with over $1 trillion a day at present, with the international financial market now called "a global marketplace that never sleeps."[172] As evidence of the growth of communication flows, "between 1980 and 1988 the number of international calls from the United States went up from 198,880 to 685,673 million . . . and [even more impressively] for Thailand it went from 873 to

12,643 million . . . and for China from 1,075 to 45,030 million";[173] Friedman notes that a three-minute call (in current dollars) between New York and London cost $300 in 1930, where today it is almost free through the Internet.[174] Interdependence in turn is generating further need for international regimes; there are more international conferences than ever, partly a function of the growth of IGOs: "between 1838 and 1860 there were two to three a year, in the decade after 1900 there were about 100 per year, in the decade after 1910 there were about 200 per year, and [by] the 1970s there were more than 3,000.[175] By the 1970s, also, the international role of "domestic" bureaucracies (the Dept. of Agriculture and the like) that found themselves members of the U.S. "foreign policy establishment" had grown to the point where "of 19,000 Americans abroad on diplomatic missions, only 3400 were from the State Department and less than half of the governmental delegates accredited to international conferences came from the State Department."[176] Nationalism still exists, but it seems less likely to eventuate in war today, at least among great powers who have the most capacity to wreak destruction, since, as one public figure has put it, "in the event of a major war in the nuclear age, you will not be dying *for* your country but *with* your country."[177] The stability of the international system is threatened today at least as much by the internal weakness of many states as by any external belligerency, as subnational ethnic conflicts far outnumber interstate wars; William Zartman, for example, observes that half of the states in Africa are "in danger of collapse, if not already gone," while Maryann Cusimano observes that "all of the thirty-five major armed conflicts taking place on the globe today are primarily internal conflicts, showing that sovereign states . . . are feeling the effects of substate challenges."[178] Global military expenditures remain high but increasingly are having to compete with nonmilitary demands; in the United States, for example, in 1955, during the early Cold War period, defense spending accounted for 58 percent of all federal government expenditures and roughly 10 percent of the GNP, whereas it is now projected to decline to less than 15 percent of federal spending and less than 3 percent of GNP.[179] Notwithstanding internal turmoil in many states, democracy seems to be on the rise: in 1974, less than 28 percent of the countries on the planet could be called democracies, whereas by 1995 61 percent could be so labeled.[180] In its 1995 annual report "Freedom in the World," Freedom House proclaimed that "never before have so many countries been trying to follow democratic rules," although some gains have since been offset by reversals as democratic institutions remain fragile in many parts of the world[181] As societies become more democratic and open, the irony is that they risk falling victim to either growing transnational penetration from above or self-determination demands from below.

The cobweb paradigm can help us understand these McWorld vs. Jihad tensions in contemporary world politics in a way which the billiard ball paradigm fails to capture. Perhaps nowhere do cobweb phenomena seem more in evidence today than in the European Union.

The Case of the European Union.   The European Union (EU), formerly called the European Community, currently consists of fifteen member states—Germany, France, the United Kingdom, Italy, Belgium, the Netherlands, Luxembourg, Ireland, Denmark, Greece, Portugal, Spain, Sweden, Austria, and Finland—that together constitute the third largest demographic unit in the world, its population of 370 million exceeded only by China and India. The key question surrounding the EU, however, is the extent to which it can be considered a *single* unit or actor. In practice, it blends elements of *supranationalism* (the EU is an IGO that has its own flag and anthem, along with decision-making procedures which in some issue areas require its member states to surrender a measure of their sovereignty to the will of the larger majority), *nationalism* (recall our earlier discussion about the insistence by the UK and France that they each retain their United Nations Security Council seat rather than relinquish it to the EU), and *subnationalism* (a key norm in the EU is that decisions be taken as close to the local level as possible, based on the principle of "subsidiarity").

The EU owes its beginning to the Treaty of Rome in 1957, which envisioned a regionally integrated economic union, partially inspired by the model of the United States, where the absence of trade and related barriers among the constituent units made for a single, large economic market that facilitated economies of scale and promoted economic efficiency and prosperity; the hope was that goods and services, labor, and capital would flow as freely between, say, France and Italy, as they did between New Jersey and New York, although few at the time harbored serious expectations of a political union. Somewhat as functionalist theorists predicted, what started modestly as a free trade area of reduced tariffs has gradually evolved into much deeper regional integration, including joint decision making on health, education, environmental and other matters, the acceptance (by most members) of a common currency (the Euro), and—based on the 1992 Maastricht Treaty—a movement toward political unification. The Maastricht Treaty, which has not yet been fully implemented, provides for a number of far-reaching changes. EU institutions, such as the Council of Ministers, the European Commission, the European Parliament, and the European Court, are to be given enhanced authority. For example, the Council of Ministers, made up of members of the national cabinet drawn from each state, is supposed to take most EU-wide decisions based on majority rule, using a weighted voting formula that favors the most populous states, while the European Commission, composed of twenty appointed administrators—"Eurocrats"—presiding over a 18,000 member bureaucracy, is given expanded powers in identifying EU-wide problems and implementing EU-wide rules. The Treaty created a new status—that of European "citizen"—enabling community nationals to live and work anywhere in EU countries without need of passports or work permits, as well as to vote and stand for municipal elections and European Parliament elections. The Treaty also called for a "common foreign and security policy," including "the eventual framing of a common defense policy, which might in time lead to a common defense."

As important decisions are increasingly being taken in Brussels, the seat of the EU, that affect people throughout the region (e.g., in 1997, the Commission enacted a ban on cigarette advertising on television in all member states), many multinational corporations, consumer and environmental advocacy associations, and other political actors are focusing their pressure group activities there and are bypassing national capitals. One respected scholar has asserted that "economic policy is no longer made at the national level in [Western] Europe."[182] As for defense policy, one would expect that states would be most reluctant to surrender sovereignty over military security affairs, although even here national leaders at a 1999 EU summit meeting announced that in the near future "a single foreign and security policy czar would speak for Europe and carry out the military will of European leaders."[183]

It needs to be emphasized that rival nationalisms persist that could still undo this impressive experiment in regional integration. For example, despite the rules dictating an end to trade barriers among the member states, French brewers until recently were prevented from selling beer in the German market because their product did not meet "beer purity" standards specified by the Germans. French wine-growers, in turn, have conducted "wine wars" against the cheaper Italian wines that have threatened to flood the French market. The Italian government has insisted that all pasta products sold in Italy must be made (as all Italian pasta is) from durum (hard) wheat. Doctors, lawyers, and other members of the professional labor force wanting to locate across national boundaries are still prohibited by language and educational training differences (there are eleven official languages spoken in the Union) that prevent professionals from meeting licensing requirements. The British, in particular, have been reluctant to sign onto the Schengen Agreement, which relaxes border controls between member states, as well as the common currency and a "European Social Charter" that would obligate London to abide by EU-wide rules governing a minimum wage, workplace safety, and other welfare provisions. Fans of the Barcelona soccer team, which has often led the "Spanish first division," have complained that there are more Dutch players than Spaniards on the team since a 1995 EU ruling that, even though teams are limited in the number of "foreigners" they can field, players from other EU countries are not considered foreigners.[184] And so on.

The likely prospect for the foreseeable future is that the European Union will continue to muddle along in what has become a kind of halfway house between a collection of sovereign states and a supranational entity. New challenges may complicate the community-building process in the future. The applications already submitted by more than a dozen European states seeking to join the Union, including eight former East bloc states as well as the likes of Turkey, Cyprus, and Malta, raise questions about the optimal size of the enterprise; how large and diverse can it become and still remain viable in terms of the capacity to reach mutually agreeable decisions? This has become known as the "widening versus deepening" dilemma, i.e., the more states that are added, the more clout the entity will have but the harder it will be to develop a closer sense of community and build more intensely integrated, supranational institutions among the membership. Further complicating the picture are some Jihad trends, in particular the aforementioned subsidiarity principle, which encourages decisions to be taken at a lower level than the supranational level where possible, including at the subnational level. There is a trend toward greater regional autonomy *within* some EU states, notably Belgium, Spain, and Italy (e.g., the parliaments of Flanders, Wallonia, and the Brussels region were permitted to ratify the Maastricht Treaty separately from the Belgian parliament).[185] Another future concern is whether the movement toward a single internal market in Europe will add to external tensions with the United States, Japan, and other nonmember states, who through the World Trade Organization are seeking access to that market, or whether it can be achieved in a way that averts trade wars.

About all this, John Ruggie has written that one can see "a Europe of many spires. . . . For their part, Eurocrats speak of overlapping layers of European economic and political 'spaces,' tied together . . . by the community's 'spiderlike strategy to organize the architecture of a Greater Europe.'"[186] This is what is meant by "the new feudalism" that some commentators see cobweb politics leading to in Europe and elsewhere, producing a much more complex set of governing relationships than those associated with the Westphalian, territorially based state system. We have seen in this chapter that whether the start of the twenty-first century is a Westphalian moment or not is in the eyes of the beholder, that one can volley arguments and bits of data back and forth to make the case for either the continued validity of the Westphalian paradigm or for the acceptance of a post-Westphalian paradigm. In the next chapter we will try to see how we can reconcile these two seemingly incompatible perspectives.

CHAPTER 4

Living with Paradoxes
Shooting Pool
and Pooling Sovereignty

The traditional agenda of international affairs—the balance among major powers, the security of nations—no longer defines our perils or our possibilities.
—Henry Kissinger, U.S. Secretary of State, in a 1975 speech

We don't want to run off into the future all by ourselves. That means the United States will have to work responsibly through international organizations.
—Bill Clinton, U.S. President, in a 1997 speech

A recurrent theme in this book is the challenge of global governance and efforts to develop international "regimes"—norms, principles, rules, and organizations—that can promote a degree of cooperation and stability in international life. Both the billiard ball paradigm and the cobweb paradigm, each in their own way, deal with problems of governance in world politics. The billiard ball paradigm focuses our attention on the continued importance of sovereign nation-states as actors on the world stage. The cobweb paradigm focuses our attention on nonstate actors as something more than merely bit players in this drama. It is at this point that we need to try to reconcile these competing perspectives.

In this chapter, very briefly, the author will develop the argument that intergovernmental organizations (IGOs) may be thought of as the key nexus points between the state-centric Westphalian culture and the more pluralistic post-Westphalian culture. It is IGOs which are likely to provide the key vehicles in the twenty-first century whereby nation-states can essentially retain their sovereignty while managing to function in a global political space in which human transactions and concerns increasingly transcend borders. Hence, the subtitle of this chapter—shooting pool and pooling sovereignty. I wish to reiterate that I am interested here not in the emergent "architecture" of Europe or any other region but rather in the broader international institutional "scaffolding" in the world at large.

GLOBAL PUBLIC POLICY AND THE GLOBAL POLITICAL PROCESS

Conceptually, think of the contemporary international system as a global polity in which there is at work a political process consisting of a number of problems or issues on the agenda, a number of different demands made by a variety of actors (both state and nonstate) in these issue areas, and a series of outcomes or outputs (regimes) produced by the interactions of these actors in the issue areas. We need to elaborate this analytical framework further. Think of regimes as "global public policy," what one writer has defined as "joint responses to common problems that . . . national governments work out with one another [which are] products of the international community as a whole."[1] Those who study public policy in a national context, which is the usual context in which the term is used, commonly point to several sequential stages that comprise the policy process: (1) agenda-setting (identifying "problems" or "issues" and getting them at least on the radar screen of the political system, so that some collective action is possible); (2) policy formulation (consideration of a menu of various possible proposals for new rules or other responses that might address the problem or issue); (3) policy adoption (selection of a particular course of action); and (4) policy implementation (putting the chosen decision into effect).[2] In our conceptualization of a global polity and global political process, we can think, then, in terms of global public policy and the stages that occur between agenda-setting and implementation on the part of the international community.

One might argue that "global policy" is an oxymoron, that it is impossible to engage in policy-making, implementation, and other such activities in a global or any international context, because policy cannot be understood except in relation to "an identifiable actor with some capacity to produce change"[3]; put another way, policy does not exist in a political system apart from some identifiable central guidance apparatus (a government or the functional equivalent) through which the policy process can occur in its various phases. Lacking a central government, the international system has no apparent apparatus for performing the various routines associated with the formation and conduct of public policy relevant to the international community as a whole.

Granted, the author is taking some liberties here. But there is ample evidence of governance occurring in the international system in the absence of government.[4] We have seen how throughout history there have been attempts to develop not just general norms and principles but a concrete body of international law based on both customary practice and treaties. It is clear that, even in the absence of a world legislature, machinery exists to create written rules that are considered legally binding, with multilateral treaties drafted by the UN International Law Commission or entities such as the UN Law of the Sea Conference. The latter produced a 200-page document, the 1982 Law of the Sea Convention, which was negotiated by more than 150 countries (at the time constituting almost the entire state system) and which contained a set of rules governing 70 percent of the earth's surface. It incorporated some elements of the traditional law of the sea going back to Grotius' time—such as the right of "innocent passage" enjoyed by all ships in the territorial waters of coastal states, the right of "hot pursuit" by coastal state vessels against foreign ships violating the laws of the coastal state, and absolute freedom of navigation of all ships on the "high seas" outside any state's boundaries—but also modified some existing rules, such as extending the width of the "territorial sea" from three to twelve miles.[5] The vast majority of countries on the planet have signed and ratified (or indicated their intention to ratify) this treaty; one of the last remaining major holdouts—the United States—has announced its acceptance of almost every provision of the treaty with the exception of the section covering deep-seabed mining, so that there is now wide acceptance of this regime. Countless other global, if not universal, agreements can be cited which codify rules of behavior countries are expected to abide by.

Some would say that the mere existence of rules is meaningless if they are routinely ignored. Indeed, the most common indictment of international law is not the absence of rules but the lack of enforcement—the complaint that international law is broken regularly with impunity because of the lack of any central policing agent. However, what is most striking about the international legal system is not how often the law is broken but how often it is obeyed, despite the lack of "traffic cops" to provide a central coercive threat of punishment against would-be offenders. To be sure, there are frequent violations of international law, notably those serious breaches that are reported on front pages of newspapers, such as the seizure of the U.S. embassy in Iran in 1979 (the aforementioned hostage crisis), the genocidal acts committed in the Bosnian and Rwandan civil wars in the 1990s, and various acts of violent aggression at odds with the UN Charter. Although people tend to notice these conspicuous failures of international law, they neglect to notice the ordinary workings of international law in the everyday life of the international system. The fact is that, if one takes into account the myriad treaties and customary rules of international law that exist today, it can be said that most states obey most rules most of the time, a standard that approximates the effectiveness of domestic law in most countries.[6]

To understand why this is so, we need to consider the basic reasons why people obey laws in any society. The first is the threat of punishment for illegal behavior (the *coercive* motive). A second is the mutual interests that individuals have in seeing that laws are obeyed (the *utilitarian* motive). A third is the internalization of the rules by the members of the society, i.e., habits of compliance; people obey the law because that is what they have come to accept as the legitimate, right thing to do (the *identitive* motive). All of these elements can operate to produce obedience to the law. Consider for a moment why most people bother to obey a stop sign at a busy intersection. One reason is the coercive element—the possibility that a police officer might stop you if you do not stop yourself. Another is the utilitarian motive—the possibility that another car might accidentally hit your vehicle if you pass through the intersection without stopping. As powerful as these two motives are, the main driving force behind the inclination to stop at a stop sign is probably the simple habitual nature of the act, which has been inculcated as part of the "code of the road." (Even if one were driving through the middle of Death Valley in California, where no police cars or other vehicles were in evidence for several miles, there would be a tendency to stop if somehow one were to encounter a red stop sign sticking out of the desert sand!)

The point is that law and order can function to some extent even in the absence of police; indeed, any society that relies primarily on coercive threats as the basis for order is one that is terribly fragile. Although habits of compliance—the most solid basis for law—are not very well developed in the international system, the mutual interests of states in having a set of rules that prescribe as well as proscribe patterns of behavior provide a foundation for the international legal order. States are willing to tolerate certain constraints on their own behavior because it is widely recognized that international commerce, travel, and other forms of international activity would be exceedingly difficult otherwise.

Neorealists correctly point out that the more powerful states are often in a position to shape the rules and impose them on the less powerful—that the golden rule often means those who have the gold (the most resources) end up ruling—but neoliberals can correctly counter that not all international regimes reflect pure power realities and that, in any event, regimes, once instituted, can serve as a brake not only on the actions of the powerless but also on the behavior of the powerful. Put simply, international politics obviously shapes international law, but international law also in turn shapes international politics, i.e., the behavior of states. After all, it is international law, specifically treaties, that are usually the basis for creating IGOs in the first place, which themselves then facilitate the further development of international law, such as the Law of the Sea Convention. Mark Zacher and Brent Sutton, in *Governing Global Networks: International Regimes for Transportation and Communications*, have shown how all states have a special stake in developing and sustaining a set of rules and institutions governing those spaces that exist outside any state's sovereign territory (the great oceans, outer space, and other parts of the "global commons") along with those spaces not neatly confined within national borders (e.g., cyberspace) which are essential for the flow of goods, information, and other transactions related to commerce. These authors describe how various transnational and subnational actors have vested interests as well and behave as pressure groups seeking to pursue their own agendas in the international arena. In focusing on international regimes in the areas of shipping, air transport, telecommunications, and postal services, Zacher and Sutton elucidate how national governments subject themselves to regimes governing inter-state relations while seeking to preserve authority over activities occurring within their territorial borders, with the United States and other powerful states not always able to dictate the outcome of such negotiations.[7] The challenge of pooling sovereignty without sacrificing autonomy will likely grow in the twenty-first century as complex interdependence grows, and the challenge will be especially great for great powers such as the United States.

A global policy process begins when one actor or set of actors seeks to have a particular "demand" (concern) acted upon by the international system as a whole, whether it is a call for a coordinated response to the AIDS epidemic or the proliferation of landmines or nuclear weapons or some other matter. Again, some problems will be viewed as calling for more narrow, bilateral, or regional responses (regimes), but other problems will elicit multilateral, global ones. Few issues in any society, particularly one as diverse as the international society, are so noncontroversial that they can be labeled purely technical or nonpolitical, although, as we have noted, one can distinguish between low-politics and high-politics issues. All issues have to compete for attention and resources, so that there is a politics at work in any public policy endeavor. The essence of the policy process in any political system is to convince others that, first, one's demand is not so much a self-serving value to be maximized as it is a critical public policy problem to be addressed and, secondly, one's preferred policy outcome is the best solution. The latter cannot be attempted until one has succeeded at the former, getting on the agenda.

Nation-states have the primary access to the global political process, but demands for global policy can originate from a variety of sources, not only individual national governments but blocs of states, subnational and transnational interest groups, and officials of intergovernmental or nongovernmental organizations. The chief structures that receive and process global policy demands are the various United Nations organs and specialized agencies; as Marvin Soroos comments, "these international bodies are the primary arenas in which global policies are made."[8] Some observers have pointed out that the proliferation of international bodies at the global and also regional levels in recent years has added enormously to an already dense web of IGOs which may be getting out of control. With these bodies offering sundry forums in which demands can be aired by their nation-state members, NGO affiliates, and others, the result is often more heat than light generated, as there is often little follow-through in terms of policy formulation, adoption, and implementation. Harold Jacobson et al. perceptively remark: "If the U.S. finds it [difficult] . . . to formulate constructive policies for the organizations to which it belongs, . . .

what must the situation be like for countries that belong to proportionately more IGOs and have much smaller bureaucracies [and resources]?"[9]

The UN has been criticized for the litany of concerns it attempts to deal with, as the entire system is overloaded. Even where there may be widespread agreement about the existence of a problem, getting agreement on the exact nature and magnitude of the problem, much less the optimal solution, can be inordinately difficult. Some problems do manage to occupy the agenda more firmly than others and to take on sufficient visibility that major efforts at policy formulation are undertaken, frequently through "commissions" or "groups of experts" which develop proposals to be decided upon by special conferences or other adoption vehicles. The most notable examples are the series of world conferences sponsored by the UN over the past three decades on the law of the sea, the environment, population, women's rights, and other issues. Such efforts, of course, do not ensure that any action of consequence will be implemented. Where international regimes are produced that have an impact, nonstate actors are often instrumental in that success. The role of nonstate actors in the global policy process is illustrated by the case of the 1973 International Convention on Trade in Endangered Species, signed and ratified by over 100 states which have agreed to limit the export and import of threatened animal and plant species. The World Wildlife Fund and a number of scientific NGOs managed to get the issue of endangered species on the global agenda by citing evidence of extinction rates, the treaty itself was drafted by the International Union for the Conservation of Nature, the parties to the treaty have relied upon TRAFFIC (an NGO thought to be an objective, neutral, technically competent actor) to monitor treaty implementation and compliance, and the UN Environmental Program has sponsored periodic meetings for purposes of updating and modifying the regime.

Although many different actors can be involved in attempts to develop global policy, global policy adoption in a given issue-area usually ultimately requires the blessing of a combination of states that have sufficiently compatible issue positions, shared salience levels (in terms of the issue being on their radar screen), and joint power capabilities as to constitute a dominant winning coalition willing and able to move the international system to action. Throughout much of the post-World War II period, the mobilization of these factors in support of global policy was frequently achieved essentially through US-USSR condominium (as in the case of arms control regimes) or, where the Soviet Union opted out of the system, through U.S. hegemony exercised in conjunction with Western allies (as in the case of the Group of Seven's influence over Third World debt repayment regimes). As power has become increasingly diffused in the international system in the post-Cold War era—given the fragmentation of power among both state and nonstate actors—the system has become more "open," but also somewhat more difficult to move in any direction. Hegemony and bipolarity have eroded but have not been replaced with any comparable mechanisms for managing agenda-setting and other global policy processes.

The question of how humanity might devise ways for improving global policy processes in the future will be left to the end of this book. We first need to improve our understanding of how these processes now work, and for that we return to game theory.

TWO- AND THREE-LEVEL GAMES

I do not wish to delve into the intricacies of game theory here, but simply to draw on the "game" metaphor as a useful analytical tool. The reader will recall the Chapter 3 discussion of how Robert Putnam has characterized many diplomatic negotiations of the sort that are pivotal to the global policy process as usually involving a two-level game: "Across the international table sit [a national leader's] foreign counterparts, and at his elbows sit [his country's] diplomats and other international advisors. Around the domestic table behind him sit party and parliamentary figures, spokespersons for domestic agencies, representatives of key interest groups, and the leader's own political advisors." The implication here is that a country's central decision makers must try to cut a deal not only with their opposite numbers—other central decision makers representing their countries (each presumably attempting to maximize what they take to be in their individual national interests)—but also with their various constituencies back home (many of which will have conflicting interests and demands that need to be reconciled), so that national leaders must attempt to forge an outcome that will be an acceptable compromise to both the relevant domestic players as well as external players. In other words, the position a nation-state ultimately adopts in such a global policy process will often be the resultant of a mix of bargains struck within and between countries.

I alluded earlier to the phenomenon of bureaucratic politics that goes on within the government of any national political system. Graham Allison, who was among the first to question the billiard ball paradigm's assumption that states behave as unitary actors, has pointed out that where one *stands* on an issue depends on where one *sits* in the bureaucracy; a member of a defense ministry will often see a different face of an issue than a member of, say, a trade ministry.[10] Although bureaucratic politics can occur in any type of political system, it is especially true that "in a state with a well-developed bureaucracy [such as the United States], the elaboration of national positions in preparation for treaty negotiations requires extensive interagency vetting. Different officials with different responsibilities and objectives engage in what amounts to a sustained internal negotiation."[11] In the United States, many bureaucratic agencies themselves have ties to a particular clientele interest group as well as a particular congressional committee which may share mutual interests in a given issue area. Such "iron triangles" (also called "subgovernments" or "policy networks") have been identified in such diverse fields as agriculture, energy, and health care.[12]

The dynamics of two-level games can be seen in the negotiations surrounding the 1982 Law of the Sea Convention, the treaty produced by the UN Law of the Sea Conference that began in 1973 and was called "the largest single legal undertaking since the time of Grotius."[13] At one level, the global policy process here could be understood as involving a dispute between those states that wished to maintain the traditional rules governing the oceans (such as each coastal state having the right to exercise sovereignty over its territorial waters three miles out from its coastline, with the remainder of ocean space being high seas open for unrestricted navigation and exploration by any state) and those states which sought changes in the existing rules (such as extending the territorial sea to twelve miles, allowing for 200-mile exclusive economic zones in which the coastal state could regulate fishing, and creating a UN Seabed Authority to regulate mining of zinc, manganese, and other minerals on the deep seabed). Major maritime powers, including the United States, became alarmed that twelve-mile territorial seas and 200-mile economic zones, especially around such vast island archipelagos as Indonesia, would endanger the principle of the open sea that allowed maximum freedom of operation for their large, far-flung navies, scientific research expeditions, and fishing fleets. Coastal states lacking such maritime prowess felt they benefited more from an "enclosure" policy that limited other countries' access to their offshore waters than from an "open sea" policy that gave free rein to anyone who had the capability to exploit the oceans. Smaller, less developed states, then, tended to advocate increased national control over their coastal waters. The latter sought to restrict certain activities on the high seas as well, urging international regulation through the United Nations to ensure that technologically superior states did not exploit the deep seabed for their exclusive gain, particularly at the expense of established LDC mineral producers such as Zambia, Zimbabwe, and Zaire ("the three Z's"). Insofar as they were calling for regime change, it was the developing countries more so than the developed ones which pushed law of the sea issues onto the global agenda. Landlocked states, some thirty in number, were also present at the conference; they were wary of all coastal states—big and small alike—and voiced concerns about how they too could share in the riches of the sea, which some called the "common heritage of mankind."

While such ocean politics could be understood at least partially in simple billiard ball terms, with each state through its leadership advancing demands that tended to favor its own national interests, beneath the surface there was a more complex reality as the law of the sea game was played at several levels. Subnational groups, such as hard-pressed U.S. fishermen, waded into the fray and muddied the waters further, frequently disagreeing among themselves over what legal positions best served the national interest of their country. For example, American fishermen on the East Coast, generally operating with small boats in nearby waters and having to compete with mechanized Russian floating fish factories, favored a 200-mile exclusive fishing zone; in contrast, West Coast tuna fishermen, plying the distant waters off the coasts of Peru and Ecuador, supported the principle of a more limited twelve-mile zone so that they would not be excluded entirely from Latin American waters. Various governmental agencies also often took conflicting positions and engaged in domestic bureaucratic politics to have their particular views accepted as official national policy. American Defense Department officials—concerned primarily about the free passage of U.S. warships on the high seas—sought to retain the traditional narrow three-mile territorial sea, although they expressed a willingness to tolerate a twelve-mile territorial limit as long as the principle of "unimpeded transit" applied to international straits falling in the extended band. Conversely, Interior Department officials—primarily concerned about managing U.S. coastal waters, including policing would-be polluters and exploiting offshore oil and natural gas resources—were less supportive of the freedom of the sea doctrine and instead wanted to expand the national zone of jurisdiction to 200 miles for certain purposes. (About one U.S. official who at first represented the Pentagon at the Conference and subsequently was shifted to the Interior Department, it was said: "When he worked for the Pentagon, other delegates would say 'Here comes Mr. Freedom of Navigation!' Then, as soon as he moved to Interior, suddenly seabed mining became the big issue.")[14] Battles between such subnational factions, both ministries and interest groups, were fought out not only in the United States but in other countries as well, reflecting Putnam's second-level game-playing. Regarding the two types of games that occurred, a Canadian official noted: "The truth is that some of our delegation meetings [within the Canadian delegation itself] were far tougher than the negotiations with other states, because understandably a Newfoundland dory fisherman wanted assurance that his interests were not being sold out to protect British Columbia salmon."[15]

The story of how the Law of the Sea Convention came to be would be incomplete without adding yet another, third level of analysis. In addition to national and subnational elements, transnational elements were also at work shaping agenda-setting, policy formulation, adoption, and implementation. The decision that gave the initial impetus to convening the Law of the Sea Conference was a UN General Assembly resolution passed in December 1967 establishing an Ad Hoc Committee to study the peaceful uses of the seabed. The nonstate actors who played a role in the global policy process at Caracas, Venezuela and other venues where the decade-long negotiations occurred included multinational mining corporations interested in tapping the wealth of the deep seabed, scientific and environmental NGOs concerned about exploring and protecting the oceans, transgovernmental coalitions formed between ministries of different countries which at times had more in common with each other than with colleagues in their own foreign policy establishment, and IGO officials such as Shirley Amerasinghe of Sri Lanka, who served as the Conference president, and the "Eurocrats" in the European Commission, who attempted to forge a common "European Community" position. Clyde Sanger provides a glimpse into the nature of NGO input into the global policy process relating to law of the sea:

> The Final Act of the conference lists 57 varieties of NGO that in some way attached themselves to . . . the conference; they were as diverse as the World Muslim Congress and the International Hotel Association. However, it does not mention the group that did outstanding work in public education . . . for delegates whose countries lacked expertise on ocean resources, pollution problems, technology transfer, and other technical subjects. This was the *Neptune* group, a coalition of the United Methodists and the Quakers. . . . The energy of this small team of workers was phenomenal. In seven years they put out 19 issues of a lively tabloid. . . . They also sponsored press briefings and conferences . . . , luncheon seminars for delegates on subjects from dispute settlement to the economics of tuna fishing, and evening panels for other NGOs and delegates. They worked with [U.S.] Senators and Congressmen on ocean legislation, and in 1982 fed their own ideas for amendments to the Convention into the conference.[16]

Few would argue that such an NGO was a lead player. Nonetheless, in combination with dozens of other nonstate actors and state actors (obviously including the major maritime powers, which brokered a compromise with developing countries), it was part of the equation that ultimately produced a global regime in 1982 that has commanded wide acceptance of a twelve-mile territorial sea, a 200-mile economic zone, and a UN Seabed Authority, with a UN Preparatory Commission (PREPCOM) still working to iron out remaining implementation problems.

Maria Cowles has expanded Putnam's analysis and helped to call attention to the importance of what amount to *three-level* games, i.e., interactions that go on not only between states (between leaders representing different national capitals) and within states (between leaders and their own various domestic constituencies) but also between actors that bypass national capitals altogether and operate at the supranational level. She has focused particularly on the European Union, where, as suggested earlier in Chapter 3, there is "an ongoing process whereby political actors such as member states, interest groups, and sub-national governments [e.g., Wales and Scotland] bargain with [EU] institutions and with one another in a multi-level system of governance to create or shape a legal framework for their activities. . . . [This model] assumes that political action takes place on a number of levels, and by actors found both above and below the nation-state."[17] For example, the EU Economic and Social Committee is composed of representatives from various groups involving agricultural, manufacturing, transportation, and business interests, with both worker and employer groups organized transnationally to lobby in support of or in opposition to various Union proposals that affect them. On a growing number of issues, Brussels—the seat of major EU-wide institutions enjoying expanding decision-making competence—is competing with London, Paris, and other national capitals in Western Europe as the locus for political action. Such policy processes across national boundaries are not nearly as well-developed at the global level, although the Law of the Sea example and others that can be cited show at least some movement in that direction.

RECONCILING WESTPHALIAN AND POST-WESTPHALIAN PERSPECTIVES

In the study of the American political system, it has been pointed out that it is simplistic to think that there is a single process that characterizes politics and decision making across all domestic policy issue areas. Theodore Lowi, for example, has offered a typology of public policy situations that distinguishes between "distributive policy," "regulative policy," and "redistributive policy," which differ in the extent to which public opinion and mass democratic pressures, as opposed to particularistic interest group or bureaucratic influences, are likely to operate.[18] Similarly, James Q. Wilson has suggested four kinds of policy processes: "majoritarian politics," "interest group politics," "client politics," and "entrepreneurial politics."[19] As one author notes, "just which policy makers are important in shaping policies tends to depend on the type of policy being made."[20]

We can apply this logic to the international political system and the global public policy process. Rather than thinking of world politics in either-or terms, as either dominated by sovereign nation-states or dominated by a new set of actors and political arrangements, it should be evident from the preceding discussion that contemporary reality does not fall neatly into a billiard ball or cobweb pattern. There is no one pattern, but several patterns. Nation-states obviously remain very important players in producing global public policy, which often can be understood in billiard ball terms as the product of interactions among national governments, particularly the most powerful ones, seeking to maximize their respective national interests on behalf of their citizenry. But at other times, nonstate actors can play an important role as well. We need to develop a typology which distinguishes between those situations and issue areas where billiard ball politics tend to predominate, and those situations and issue areas where cobweb politics tend to predominate.

It is helpful here to fall back on the familiar "high-politics"/"low-politics" distinction. I suggest the following categorization scheme for world politics: (1) "high-politics," (2) "middle-politics," and (3) "low-politics." *High-politics* situations or issues involve extremely high stakes relating to core national interest values of national security and prestige. An example would be the game, discussed in Chapter 3, that is currently being played over the composition of the UN Security Council and the determination of which states should be allowed permanent seats and veto power; as was noted, this can be largely understood as a contest between "the United States," "Britain," "France," "Japan," "India," and other aspirant countries. Most arms control negotiations fall into this category, which is defined by the predominance of first-level, billiard ball politics, although even high-politics concerns frequently can involve second-level and third-level game-playing, with IGOs, for example, serving not only as arenas or forums for inter-state diplomacy but behaving at times as autonomous players. *Middle-politics* situations or issues involve stakes which may not be quite as high as those associated with war/peace concerns and other concerns that touch the core values of states but which nonetheless are matters of great importance to the functioning of states. Middle-politics games tend to be characterized by an almost equal mix of billiard ball and cobweb elements, with an example being the global policy processes in the area of trade and international political economy, an area that is increasingly preoccupying the international political system. *Low-politics* situations or issues involve relatively narrow or technical problems, which often are significant but tend to be not quite as politicized as the first two categories in our typology. Low-politics games tend to involve the heaviest element of second-level and third-level game-playing, and are the least driven by pure billiard ball politics. Examples would be global policy processes having to do with development of international regimes for controlling the spread of infectious diseases or harmonizing mail regulations. It must be emphasized again that few, if any, issues are ever completely devoid of politics, and that the lines between high and low politics are becoming blurred, especially in the post-Cold War era as domestic and foreign policy itself is becoming blurred. Some people will take exception to my typology as simplistic. Still, thinking of world politics as a singular phenomenon, as opposed to consisting of differentiated processes as I have suggested, would seem truly simplistic. Whatever categories one chooses to adopt, at the very least it behooves us as observers to understand the complexity of global policy and global problem-solving.

James Rosenau and Mary Durfee have noted that recent trends have added "extensive layers of complexity to the anarchical structure [of world politics]. . . . [Given the proliferation of sovereign states and 'sovereignty-free' actors], power and authority are much more dispersed . . . than is presumed by the realist and, under these turbulent conditions, achieving coordinated policies designed to address and alleviate global problems is much more difficult and time consuming."[21] Understanding and improving global governance requires a new mindset, one that permits us—scholars, students, policymakers, and citizens everywhere—to live with paradoxes. Michael Brecher, the president of the International Studies Association, upon taking office in that professional society in 1999, stated:

> On the eve of a new century, it seems to me important to reaffirm that pluralism is necessary for renewal in [the international studies discipline]. . . .We must recognize that no school has a monopoly of truth and that continuing fratricide among paradigms . . . poses a grave risk that the embryonic discipline will implode. . . . Synthesis [among competing paradigms] . . . is possible. . . . Not only would syn-

thesis represent the highest scholarly achievement; it would also enhance our contribution to society, especially to foreign policy . . . decision-makers as they confront an increasingly complex environment for coping with choice in the twenty-first century.[22]

Although Professor Brecher was targeting his comments at academics, they have no less relevance for practitioners and students of international affairs generally, all of whom have the same stake in the *world* not "imploding" in their lifetime and their children's lifetime.

Having laid out "the puzzle" in Part One, we will now turn to "putting the pieces together" in Part Two as the next section of the book aims at synthesis. Chapter 5 will focus on the high-politics of military security issues, which will be fleshed out through a mini-case study on the negotiations surrounding the 1993 Chemical Weapons Convention. Chapter 6 will focus on the middle-politics of economic issues, which will be illustrated through a mini-case study on the Uruguay Round negotiations leading to the establishment of the World Trade Organization in 1995. Chapter 7 will focus on the low-politics of environmental issues, which will be illustrated through a mini-case study on the negotiations surrounding the 1987 Montreal Protocol on Substances that Deplete the Ozone Layer. In each of these chapters I will first provide an overview of the general governance problems the contemporary international system faces in the issue area in question (security, economics, and the environment), and then present the case study that deals with a particular global policy concern within that issue area.

PART TWO
PUTTING THE PIECES TOGETHER

CHAPTER 5

Challenges to the National Security State
High Politics in the Post-Cold War Era

The protection of the nation against destruction from without and disruption from within is the overriding concern. . . . Nothing can be tolerated that might threaten the coherence of the nation.
> —Hans Morgenthau, *Politics Among Nations,* 1967

Nothing like D-Day [during World War II] will happen again not because human nature has improved, but because weaponry has. Making war on that grand scale is obsolete.
> —Herman Wouk, in a 1994 *Washington Post* column "Never Again."

In the event of a major war in the nuclear age, you will no longer be dying for your country but with your country.
> —Richard Lamm, Governor of Colorado, cited in the *Christian Science Monitor,* 1985

War is on its last legs; and a universal peace is as sure as is the prevalence of civilization over barbarism. . . . The question for us is only how soon?
> —Ralph Waldo Emerson, 1849

The first Nobel Peace Prize at the beginning of the twentieth century, in 1901, was awarded to the founder of the International Committee of the Red Cross, while the last Nobel Peace Prize at the end of the twentieth century, in 1999, was awarded to *Medecins Sans Frontiers* (Doctors Without Borders). Alfred Nobel, the Swedish inventor of dynamite, had hoped that nitroglycerin's sheer destructive power would ironically be a force for peace insofar as it would make war unfightable and unwinnable and, therefore, unthinkable. As the above quotations from Herman Wouk, Richard Lamm, and Ralph Waldo Emerson suggest, many others have harbored the dream that, where international organization and law had failed, the growing destructiveness of modern weaponry itself would so fundamentally alter warfare as to render war a relic of the past. The fact that the twentieth century witnessed the greatest carnage in human history—over 100 million war-related deaths (four-fifths of which were noncombatant civilians)—may yet provide the necessary impetus for humanity's rethinking war as a tool of policy, at the same time that it stands as testimony to the difficulty of eradicating organized violence, however irrational such violence may seem.

As realists stress, war—whether war preparation, war avoidance, war fighting, or war termination—has always constituted the "highest" form of politics among nation-states. Few "games" nation-states have played over time have involved higher potential stakes than those having to do with arms races and arms control. It is hard to dispute Hans Morgenthau's statement that concern over protecting a nation's physical security and territorial integrity has typically been at the top of every country's agenda. In the American case, for example, "national security was the realm of foreign policy that most concerned the Founding Fathers. We are and have always been a nation preoccupied with security."[1] Even as the concept of security is now being broadened and as economic and other issues compete for foreign policymakers' attention, protection from military attack is still considered the foremost responsibility of a national government toward its citizens. Although nonstate actors such as the International Red Cross or Doctors Without Borders may often get involved in war-peace matters, and at times can have significant impacts, it is generally understood that this issue area remains primarily the preserve of states and statesmen along with their diplomatic and military establishments. Indeed, the twentieth century saw the expansion of the "national security state" just as it saw the proliferation of ever more deadly conventional weapons as well as weapons of mass destruction in the form of ABC (atomic, bacteriological, and chemical) arsenals. It is little comfort that, since World War II, national armies and armaments have been housed in what are called defense departments rather than war departments.

Hence, war is obviously not a relic but remains a very real part of the fabric of world politics. One should not dismiss the admonition of realists that it is well within the realm of possibility that we could still see at some point in the future a revival of the U.S.–Russian rivalry or the emergence of a U.S.–China rivalry or some other classic great-power competition that might, as has so often happened in the past, eventuate in war. Still, the nature of warfare has been changing, and with it the nature of the threats nation-states confront. This chapter examines the changing face of global violence and the new challenges to the national security state in the twenty-first century. We will also examine the special problems the contemporary international system poses for global governance in this issue area, as humanity continues its ongoing effort to develop rules regulating the outbreak and conduct of war. The chapter concludes with

The second atomic bomb test at Bikini atoll, July 24, 1946. (Department of Defense)

a case study of the negotiations surrounding the 1993 Chemical Weapons Convention that banned the possession and use of chemical arsenals. The purpose of the case study is to illustrate the politics of global problem-solving today in an area that touches the core values of states.

THE CHANGING NATURE OF GLOBAL VIOLENCE AND NATIONAL SECURITY THREATS

Much of the history of international relations since the Peace of Westphalia has revolved around inter-state war, most notably war between great powers, especially fought over real estate. Some of these conflicts have been systemic, involving much of the international system, such as the Napoleonic Wars and World War I and World War II, and some have been more confined, such as the Franco-Prussian War of 1870–71 and the Russo-Japanese War of 1904–05. Throughout the centuries, war was understood to be a legitimate, if lamentable, vehicle for expanding national power, which tended to be equated with territorial expansion. One of the most profound changes in world politics has been the recent movement away from this historical pattern.

This thinking began to change after World War II due to a variety of factors, including the development of weapons of mass destruction that made great powers gun-shy of using armed force vis-à-vis each other and the development of democratic, anticolonial norms that made the imposition of foreign rule less acceptable and hence constrained great-power use of armed force vis-à-vis weaker states. The decolonialization process led to a tripling of the number of sovereign nation-states between 1945 and 1989, most of which were quite weak. While both the United States and the Soviet Union during the Cold War sought to recruit the new nations into their respective blocs, their efforts were only mildly successful, not only because the two giants tended to neutralize each other in many areas but also because the new Third World nationalism placed limits on what even superpowers could do to cajole or coerce even tiny states into line. In particular, because of the widespread aversion to foreign rule, along with the mutual fear of conflict escalation, the two superpowers—more than great powers in the past—were inhibited from expanding their influence in the world through direct territorial annexation or occupation. Although territorial concerns continued to play a role in world politics among lesser powers—for example, the disputes between Argentina and Chile over the Beagle Channel, between Morocco and Algeria over the Spanish Sahara, and between Israel and various Arab states over lands controlled by Israel following its achieving statehood—they were not the essence of superpower competition. Soviet territorial annexation ceased with the absorption of Estonia, Latvia, and Lithuania at the very end of World War II, while the United States had long since ended its own record of territorial aggrandizement. Instead of acquiring land, the object of superpower competition was to gain influence over the foreign policies of individual Third World states through overt or covert intervention, frequently propping up governments one side favored or destabilizing governments one side opposed. The time-honored balance of power game continued to be played but in a somewhat different manner than in the past. If the world map had previously resembled a gigantic "Monopoly" board on which the players competed for property, the map in the post-World War II era looked more like a "chessboard" in which two players attempted to manipulate a set of pawns for maximum advantage.

Although it is easy to be cynical about how the superpowers attempted to substitute subtle forms of control—manipulation of puppet, satellite regimes from the outside, neocolonialist economic penetration and domination from within—in lieu of more blatant territorial incorporation and ownership, such a view fails to recognize just how much business as usual had changed. Robert Jackson describes the fundamental change in inter-state relations that had taken place:

> Until as recently as the end of the First World War the birth and death of sovereign entities and the transfer of territorial jurisdictions from one State to another was a predictable and legitimate consequence of war and peace. Today, however, it is

increasingly unimaginable owing not least to the norm of territorial legitimacy which has spread around the world and has preserved thoroughly disintegrated states, such as Chad, Sudan, Uganda, Ethiopia, and even totally anarchic Lebanon and Somalia. . . . The existing territorial pattern of sovereign statehood in all of the major regions of the world seems to have acquired a sanctity which few if any powers are prepared to violate or even dispute, presumably because they desire to avoid not only the universal condemnation but also the threat to international order which such an action would provoke. Since 1945 there have been very few significant territorial grabs anywhere in the world. . . . The survival of even the tiniest countries is internationally guaranteed today. State survival nowadays is seen as a matter of right rather than power.[2]

One reason the United States was able to mobilize virtually the entire United Nations membership to counter Iraqi aggression against Kuwait in 1991 was because, in seeking to incorporate all of Kuwait within Iraq's boundaries, Saddam Hussein was seen as violating what had become a sacred norm of international relations, that is, since 1945 no state, big or small, had dared walk into the UN General Assembly and through armed force remove the seat of another recognized member of the international community. Perhaps Saddam might have succeeded had he opted to install a puppet government in Kuwait or had been willing to settle for a smaller sliver of real estate, but his ambition exceeded the parameters of acceptable international behavior.

The point here is that not only well before the end of the Cold War were we witnessing "the move from a world dominated by a single chessboard—the strategic-diplomatic one (which eclipsed or controlled all others)—to a world dispersed into a variety of chessboards" (see the reference to Stanley Hoffmann in note 44 of Chapter 2), but we were also witnessing a transformation of the strategic-diplomatic gameboard itself. The post-Cold War era has only accentuated these trends. The good news, as I have indicated, is that inter-state war in general and inter-state war between great powers in particular is on the decline, while respect for the territorial integrity of states is on the rise. The bad news is that the threatened and actual use of violence is still prevalent on the planet, and that it tends to take a more complex, murkier form that in some respects can be harder to get a handle on than in the past. How so? First, to the extent that violence occurs *between* states, it tends to be not so much in the form of what we commonly think of as war, i.e., large-scale, all-out, sustained armed combat between organized national armies, but rather "force without war," i.e., sporadic, intermittent, limited hostilities, with ill-defined beginnings and endings. Second, the main mode of violence today is not inter-state but rather intrastate, i.e., civil wars *within* states, several of which can become internationalized as external actors are drawn into the fray, making such conflicts hybrid mixes of internal and cross-border conflagrations. Third, there is a growing concern over nonconventional, unorthodox violence and security threats posed by *nonstate* actors, including transnational terrorist and criminal organizations, which can potentially disrupt national order and world order through skyjackings, drug trafficking, cyberspace interference, and other means. Fourth, hovering over all of the latter trends, is the growing sophistication of weaponry, with countries feeling a need—whether in the name of deterrence or defense— to be prepared for ever more lethal forms of warfare, and with the worrisome specter of nonstate states possibly gaining access to these arsenals. Force without war, civil war (purely internal or internationalized), terrorism, and arms races are hardly novel elements of world politics, but what is novel is that they have seemingly displaced old-fashioned inter-state war as the focus of high politics in the Westphalian state system. While "the most recent trends show promise that classical war between states is ceasing to dominate world affairs,"[3] there is still good reason to be concerned about the planet's proclivity toward violence. Let us examine each of these four areas of concern and the challenges they present for national and international security.

Force without War

One study reports that at the end of the twentieth century "the world had fewer active conflicts than at any time since World War II."[4] Consistent with the data reported in Chapter 3 (under the discussion of the post-Westphalian paradigm), the latter study notes that there has been a continued decline in the number of inter-state conflicts and the continued absence of great-power conflict (the so-called "long peace"), with organized violence, excepting Yugoslavia, largely confined to the developing world.

Admittedly, counting the number of wars occurring at any given moment is a trickier proposition than it used to be. Distinctions between war and other forms of international violence used to be more clear-cut, because wars in the past were definable in legal terms and had fairly clear beginnings and endings. A war usually was said to start when one state issued a formal declaration of war against another state, as in World War II; it normally ended with a formal treaty of peace between the warring parties. Since World War II, however, states have tended not to issue declarations of war prior to initiating hostilities, perhaps because armed aggression is illegal under the United Nations Charter (hence, the logic of renaming war departments defense departments). The hostilities that do occur between two or more states can be isolated one-shot affairs or can go on for days, months, and in some cases years, often interrupted by periods of peace, only rarely concluding with a formal peace treaty.[5]

Barry Blechman and Stephen Kaplan have labeled such a phenomenon "force without war." They identified more than 200 different incidents during the Cold War in which the United States used armed force in some fashion short of war, and 190 such incidents in the case of the Soviet Union.[6] It is important to reiterate that the two superpowers did not exchange fire with each other and that, even when they resorted to armed force against others, it tended to be in a somewhat restrained fashion, typified by the hour-long strafing of Muammar Qaddafi's tent headquarters by U.S. jets in 1986, to send a warning to the

Libyan leader to cease sponsoring terrorism against American targets. Even when hostilities occurred that were more extensive and had all the earmarks of war, such as the Korean War during the 1950s and the Vietnam War during the 1960s, each of which cost 50,000 American lives and thousands of Asian casualties, or the Afghan War at the end of the 1970s, which likewise resulted in enormous casualties for the Soviet Red Army and their adversaries, in the end only a small fraction of the available arsenals were utilized by the losing side in these undeclared actions. Many cases of force without war can be found in the post-Cold War era. Note, for example, the border clashes between Peru and Ecuador in 1995 (over a boundary dispute dating back more than fifty years), the periodic skirmishes between India and Pakistan along the Kashmir cease-fire lines, the sporadic sorties flown by U.S. planes over Iraq following the Gulf War, the episodic fighting between former Soviet republics such as Georgia, Armenia, and Azerbaijan, and China's 1996 conduct of missile "tests" in waters within thirty miles of Taiwan's major ports (aimed at intimidating Taiwan into refraining from declaring its independence from the mainland).

As the Chinese case especially shows, in many instances force is used today more as a political instrument than as a raw military instrument. When force is applied in a surgical fashion to inflict pain or to persuade an adversary to cease or refrain from some undesired behavior, it represents a kind of "coercive diplomacy" or "diplomacy of violence."[7] Although one can find examples of force used as a delicate rather than a blunt instrument as far back as the time of Genghis Khan, it has become particularly fashionable of late as countries, particularly the most muscle-bound, search for ways to flex their muscles without shedding excessive blood in the process. Some observers argue that acts of low-level violence, such as the American bombing of Libya in 1986, have become *surrogates for war* in the nuclear age. Strategists nowadays speak of the "controlled" use of military force in "low-intensity" conflict situations or "limited wars." (The Pentagon has even resorted to euphemisms such as "peaceful engagement," the name given the American military intervention in Panama in 1989, aimed at removing Manuel Noriega from power after the dictator was linked to drug trafficking in the United States and after economic and other pressures had failed to dislodge him; he was eventually captured and extradited to the United States to stand trial, after fleeing to the Vatican embassy in Panama City and being forced out by the blaring away of loud rock music.)

In Chapter 3, I alluded to a number of explanations which have been offered to account for the long peace and the growing reluctance on the part of highly developed societies especially to engage in major war. These explanations focus on upward trends in the destructiveness of weaponry, democratization, and economic interdependence, all of which seem to be acting as inhibitors. In response to those who argue that the sheer overkill capacity of modern weapons of mass destruction has now made war pointless, at least in the eyes of Americans and others in the North who have the most to lose in an escalating conflict, skeptics point out that humanity has shown a capacity for mindless violence on a mass scale throughout history. Rome's complete destruction of Carthage in the Third Punic War arguably was the equivalent of "nuking" that society. Twenty million Soviet citizens were killed in World War II, which at least one respected scholar has argued is not much more than the Soviet Union might have lost in a nuclear exchange with the United States during the Cold War,[8] while more lives were lost in the conventional air bombing of Hamburg, Dresden, and Tokyo than were lost through the dropping of the atomic bomb on Hiroshima and Nagasaki at the end of World War II. Evan Luard has put it in these terms: "There is little evidence in history that the existence of supremely destructive weapons alone is capable of deterring war. If the development of bacteriological weapons, poison gas, nerve gases, and other chemical armaments did not deter war before 1939, it is not easy to see why nuclear weapons should do so now."[9] Indeed, China took on the United States in Korea despite the possibility of suffering nuclear retaliation by Washington, while, more recently, India and Pakistan, two nuclear-armed countries, have risked escalation in their border skirmishes. However, James Lee Ray has posited an interesting argument that it is not merely the existence of weapons of mass destruction which account for the long peace among great powers since 1945, but the internalization of a new understanding—a new norm—that major war no longer makes sense in terms of any cost-benefit calculus.[10]

In other words, the famous dictum of the nineteenth-century Prussian military strategist Karl von Clausewitz, that war is merely "the continuation of policy by other means," may no longer apply, as leaders are hard pressed to identify a national goal so important as to risk the use of armed force which could escalate conceivably toward an Armageddon-like outcome that would eliminate the very existence of the nation. It has been said that war determines not who is right but who is left. In the event of a major war between highly developed, well-armed societies in the twenty-first century, there may be no one left; even in the case of a war between a great power and a not-so-great-power, the lesser state may be able to inflict greater damage than ever before, given what many observers fear will be the growing availability of chemical and biological weapons ("the poor man's nuclear weapons"). This recalls Albert Einstein's response, when he was asked what the weapons of World War III would be: "I don't know, but I do know what the weapons of World War IV will be—rocks!"

In addition to the increasing destructiveness of weapons, which in tandem with widening democratization and deepening economic interdependence may be creating hoped-for normative progress, there are some more subtle factors as well that may be operating here. Charles Krauthammer has written: "America cannot endure casualties. It is inconceivable that the United States, or any other western country, could ever again fight a war of attrition like Korea or Vietnam. One reason is the CNN effect. TV brings home the reality of battle with unprecedented immediacy [referring particularly to the spectacle of body bags coming home in large numbers]. The other reason . . . is demographic. Advanced industrial countries [today] have very small families, and small families are less willing than the large families of the past to risk their only children in combat."[11] The demographic factor has been cited by Edward Luttwak as the chief explanation for why the "heroic warfare" of the twentieth century, which was characterized by a willingness of states and their citizenries to fight and die for a great cause, will be replaced by "post-heroic warfare" in the twenty-first century, where wars will be supported by democratic societies only so long as fatalities are kept to a bare minimum.[12] It does seem unlikely that we will ever again hear an American president speak so boldly as John Kennedy did at his inauguration in 1961, when he proclaimed that "we shall pay any price, bear any burden, meet any hardship, support any friend, oppose any foe, in order to assure the survival and the success of liberty." The end of "heroic warfare" may have potentially huge implications for the future of the nation-state and international politics. James Rosenau has argued that it may be very difficult to keep the fires of nationalism burning if the prospect of major war over core national values becomes a fading reality.[13]

The 1999 Kosovo War has been called the prototypical war of the future. The war started when Serbia (the former Yugoslavia) stepped up its campaign of oppression against Kosovo, an enclave within Serb borders comprised predominantly of ethnic Albanians. As genocidal "ethnic cleansing" of the Kosovars mounted, the United States and its NATO allies were pressured to enter the conflict in the name of "humanitarian intervention," partly to reverse the expulsion of more than a million refugees from their homes and partly to prevent a widening of the war in the Balkans that could damage Western interests. For 78 days, American and NATO warplanes bombed Serb military and industrial targets in an effort to pressure Slobodan Milosevic, the Serb leader, to surrender to Western demands for greater autonomy for Kosovo. There was a notable reluctance on the part of NATO countries to put ground troops into the conflict, for fear of excessive casualties that might dampen support for the war at home. Instead, the war was fought totally from the air, using push-button precision munitions fired from long distances, out of range from Serb anti-aircraft batteries. In almost 10,000 bombing runs, no allied airmen were killed and only two planes were lost. In the end, in response to considerable destruction of bridges, power plants, and other infrastructure, Milosevic agreed to come to the bargaining table and allow a United Nations presence in Kosovo. (Thomas Friedman, who earlier had observed that no two countries with a McDonalds restaurant had ever fought a war against each other, acknowledged that Yugoslavia and all the NATO allies served up "Big Macs," but explained away the Kosovo War as an exception that proved the rule, insofar as the West was unwilling to shed its blood for the cause, and the Serbs themselves "wanted McDonalds re-opened [i.e., wanted to return to normalcy] much more than they wanted Kosovo re-occupied."[14])

Most observers have argued that the United States and its NATO allies were extremely fortunate to have achieved victory so cheaply in Kosovo, that ground forces may be necessary in other future conflicts, and the willingness of

Limited war. (ARIAIL © NEA Reprinted by Permission.)

the United States and Western societies to endure casualties will be more severely tested.[15] After all, it only took the death of eighteen U.S. Army Rangers in Somalia in 1993 to prompt an American withdrawal from what had also been a "humanitarian intervention" mission (to provide food and other aid to the people living in a society torn by rival clans and warlords), with the pullout traced particularly to a widely televised image of an American soldier's body being dragged through the sand. The heightened sensitivity of modern societies to war casualties could be seen as well in the American experience in Bosnia, another part of the former Yugosalvia which had been torn apart by civil war in the early 1990s; in 1996, shortly after a U.S. peacekeeping force was deployed in Bosnia to separate Bosnian Muslims from Bosnian Serbs, newspaper headlines in the United States reported in huge, boldface print—the size of which in a previous era would have been normally reserved for the onset of major hostilities— that "A Land Mine Injures GI in Bosnia."[16] The author does not mean to make light of the latter casualties, only to highlight the changing culture of war. Perhaps humanity has come full circle from the days of Napoleon, when the leadership of a country first began to count on conscripting that country's youth into its armed forces as a matter of national obligation in a way that had not existed prior to the age of nationalism. Today, the United States as well as most Western European countries have moved to replace the military draft with an all-volunteer, professional army, at least partly to defuse potential public opposition to war, even though Kosovo and other cases suggest this has not made it any easier for governments to sell national sacrifice to their mass publics.[17]

Civil Wars

Civil wars clearly are not a new phenomenon. As long as there have been nation-states, there have been conflicts within states that have led to internecine fighting between rival groups. Although civil strife is not new, it has been an especially visible feature of world politics since 1945, and it has come increasingly to preoccupy the international community in the post-Cold War period. The decolonialization process after World War II produced new states often having highly unstable political systems prone to internal unrest. Civil wars have also taken place in long established states, in Latin America and elsewhere. According to Robert Kaplan, of the 80 "wars" since 1945, only 25 have been classic inter-state conflicts.[18] Similarly, K.J. Holsti estimates that "more than two-thirds of all armed conflict in the world since 1945 has taken the form of civil wars."[19] Another study, using a relatively loose definition of war, reports that between 1989 and 1997, "the vast majority [of conflicts]—97 of the 103—took place exclusively within the boundaries of a single country. The remaining 6 involved wars between opposing states [most of which had dissipated by 1997]."[20] Still another study reports that at the end of the twentieth century, 21 civil wars were ongoing while few if any "cross-border armed conflicts" were underway.[21]

As one writer states, "today's typical war is civil, started by rebels who want to change their country's constitution, alter the balance of power between races, or secede."[22]

> Current conflicts are generally struggles for the control of a state, the secession of a region, or the autonomy of a particular identity group. Most of the victims are civilians, and most of these are women and children. The typical armed conflict does not result from a state's ambitions for regional or global dominance, but from its failure to foster or maintain a society that can provide adequately for its own citizens, either for their political and social rights or for their basic physical needs.[23]

The reader will recall the earlier discussion of the Jihad phenomenon, of how, particularly in Africa, there are not only "weak" states but wholly "failed" states where governmental institutions have collapsed completely, often as a result of ethnopolitical conflict.[24] For example, I made reference to the Rwandan civil war. Floods of Hutu refugees fled Rwanda in 1994, when Tutsi rebels succeeded in winning control from a Hutu-dominated government they blamed for the slaughter of thousands of Tutsis; the Rwanda civil war continues, with the violence thus far claiming over 500,000 lives. Whereas at the beginning of the twentieth century 90 percent of all casualties in war were soldiers, the end of the twentieth century has seen 90 percent of all casualties being civilians, in large measure due to the often indiscriminate violence that characterizes civil war.

Of special consequence for international politics has been the increasing tendency over time for civil wars to become *internationalized* (to involve foreign military forces). One study found that "the percent of civil wars internationalized" rose from 18 percent in the 1919–1939 period to 27 percent in the 1946–1965 period to 36 percent in the 1966–1977 period.[25] During the Cold War, much of the internationalization was driven by the East-West geopolitical competition, with superpower interventions seeking to bolster one side or the other in places such as Vietnam, Afghanistan, Ethiopia, and Nicaragua. The Soviet Union and proxy states often assisted in "wars of national liberation," in which revolutionary groups trying to overthrow colonial rule (for example, in Angola and Mozambique) resorted to *guerrilla warfare* tactics to overcome the stronger conventional military forces of the established authorities, which in turn were trained by the United States or its regional allies in *counterinsurgency* tactics to resist the guerrillas. As the Somalia, Bosnia, and Kosovo cases show, internationalization of civil wars has continued into the post-Cold War era. However, there is an important difference between the pattern seen during the Cold War and the pattern evidenced in the 1990s. First, civil wars in the post-Cold War era tend to be rooted far more in ethnic differences than in ideological differences. Second, interventionism in the post-Cold War era has tended to be multilateral in character, often approved by regional or global organizations seeking to play a humanitarian, peacekeeping role (the McWorld counter to Jihad). Ethnic-based conflict particularly has the potential to become internationalized as refugees flee to neighboring countries to seek sanctuary, as foreign states send arms or supplies to favored factions, and as multilateral efforts are mounted to bring an end to the fighting. Later in this chapter we will examine the problems the international community has experienced in trying to be responsive to humanitarian crises.

Terrorism and Unorthodox Security Threats

The kind of indiscriminate slaughter that often characterizes civil wars is something that is the very essence of another form that violence takes today—terrorism. Although terrorism has attracted special attention of late, the term itself can be traced back at least some 900 years to Persia, where a group arose that gave us the word for "assassin." Among scholars, lawyers, and policymakers, there is no general agreement on a clear definition of terrorism. One study notes that the term had at least 109 different definitions between 1936 and 1981, and many others have appeared since.[26] The search for an authoritative definition has been likened to "the Quest for the Holy Grail."[27] It has been said that one person's terrorist is another's freedom fighter. Yassir Arafat and his followers in the Palestinian Liberation Organization (PLO), fighting against Israeli occupation of what they consider their homeland, contend that it has been hypocritical for Israeli leaders such as Menachem Begin and Yitzhak Shamir to denounce the PLO for terrorism, when Begin and Shamir themselves had engaged in violent acts, such as blowing up the King David Hotel, as participants in the Israeli pre-independence underground movements (the Irgun and Stern Gang) that struggled against the British and Arabs in the late forties.

However, if one accepts the view that "one person's terrorist is another's national liberation hero" and that the distinction depends completely on which side of the fence one sits, then any act of violence can be excused and legitimized as long as someone invents a justification. Aside from being a recipe for anarchy, this type of logic ignores the principle that not all acts of violence are equally acceptable and condonable. At a minimum, certain acts, such as the infamous shooting and pushing of wheelchair-bound Leon Klinghoffer, a Jewish-American passenger on the *Achille Lauro* oceanliner, into the Mediterranean Sea during a 1985 Palestinian hijacking, seem so barbaric and insensitive to universal standards of civilized behavior that one can reasonably label such acts terrorist in nature.

One simple, helpful definition considers terrorism "premeditated, politically motivated violence perpetrated against noncombatant targets by subnational groups or clandestine agents, usually intended to influence an audience."[28] This definition suggests that terrorism entails a combination of at least three elements. First, terrorism ordinarily involves the threat or use of *unconventional violence*—violence that is spectacular, violates accepted social mores, and is designed to shock so as to gain publicity and instill fear in the hope of extorting concessions. Terrorists generally observe no "rules" of combat whatsoever. Their tactics can include bombings, hijackings, kidnappings, assassinations, and other acts. One immediately thinks of such incidents as the murder of Israeli athletes at the 1972 Olympic Games in Munich, the 1988 explosion of Pan Am Flight 103 over Lockerbie, Scotland, that took the lives of 270 passengers, the 1997 mid-day bombing of the busiest shopping mall in Jerusalem, and the 1998 bombing of the United States embassies in Kenya and Tanzania.

Second, terrorism is characterized by violence that is *politically* motivated. The political context of terrorism distinguishes it from mere criminal behavior such as armed robbery or gangland slayings, which may be every bit as spectacular but are driven primarily by nonpolitical motives. One would not ordinarily call the Mafia, for example, a terrorist organization, even though it is heavily involved in international drug trafficking and other criminal activities, at times in league with terrorist groups. The distinction becomes somewhat blurred, though, in the case of the assassinations of government officials, such as those carried out by Colombia's Cali cartel, because the latter has been a Mafia-like criminal conspiracy to extort money through the drug trade and paralyze law enforcement through terror, in the process threatening the viability of the entire nation-state. This type of quasi-political terrorism, which has also been seen in parts of Italy and other countries, has been labeled narco-terrorism. Incidents such as the *Achille Lauro* affair, however, are more clearly motivated by political goals, ranging from the creation of a national homeland to the elimination of foreign cultural influence in a region to the total political and economic transformation of society.

A third key distinguishing characteristic of terrorism, following from the first two, is the almost incidental nature of the *targets* against whom violence is committed. That is, the immediate targets of terrorism—whether persons or property, civilian or military—usually bear only an indirect relation to the larger aims impelling the terrorist but are exploited for their shock potential. Sometimes the targets are carefully chosen individuals—prominent business leaders or government officials—while on other occasions the targets are faceless, nondescript masses—ordinary men, women, and children randomly slaughtered in airports, department stores, and other public places. The victims are chosen for their symbolic value and are merely pawns used in violence that is staged with the intent of reaching a much wider audience.

There is a fourth ingredient of terrorism one might add, having to do with the nature of the perpetrators of such violence. It can be argued, with some qualifications, that organized terrorism tends to be the work of nonstate actors, i.e., it is mainly the tactic of "outgroups"—the politically weak and frustrated [e.g., the Hizballah Islamic faction in Lebanon, the Irish Republican Army (IRA) in Northern Ireland, Shining Path in Peru, or the Red Brigades in Italy], who see terror as the best tool for contesting the sizable armies and police forces of the governments of nation-states. Although certain excessive forms of violence used by government authorities themselves are sometimes referred to as "state terrorism"—in particular the systematic torture and repression a government inflicts on dissidents within its own society, or assassinations and "dirty tricks" committed by secret state agencies abroad—the terrorism label normally does not apply to actions taken by official government bodies. Terrorists generally do not wear uniforms, although many in the past have been at least indirectly supported and sponsored by governments.[29]

The U.S. State Department has tracked trends in international terrorism over several decades. During the 1980s, there was an average of 500 terrorist incidents reported annually, with the 856 incidents recorded in 1988 marking the peak year.[30] In the 1990s, there was a downward trend, with 273 incidents reported in 1998—"the lowest annual total since 1971."[31] This may reflect the end of the Cold War, which at times provided impetus for terrorist activity, as well as the rise to political respectability of groups such as the PLO and IRA that have renounced the use of violence. It may also be a function of the development of international regimes against skyjackings and other forms of terrorism, which will be discussed in the next section. Still, there is reason for continued concern about the possibility of expanded terrorist activity in the post-Cold war era. Although there has been much rejoicing over the end of Cold War divisions and the rise of pro-democracy movements around the globe, in the process the long-suppressed aspirations of ethnic minorities and other groups within many societies have again risen to the surface, holding out the prospect of increased communal violence and resort to terror by those seeking to advance secessionist and other causes (e.g., the bombing of Moscow apartment buildings in 1999, thought to be the work of Chechnyans seeking independence from Russia).

Indeed, modern industrial society is especially susceptible to nightmarish scenarios, given such inviting targets as not only jumbo jets but giant sky-scrapers, nuclear power stations, electronic grids, and computer networks. "Cyberterrorism" that could disrupt banking and economic systems, not to mention ICBM targeting systems, is a particularly growing concern. Among the most high-profile terrorist incidents recently were the World Trade Center bombing in New York City in 1993 (when a bomb-laden van planted by Middle Eastern Islamic extremists blew up in the parking garage beneath the world's third tallest building, miraculously killing only six people, although injuring 1,000) and the nerve gas attack in a crowded Tokyo subway in 1995 (when the Japanese Aum Shinrikyo cult succeeded in killing twelve persons and injuring 5,500 others). The existence of modern communications technology enables terrorists to receive instant publicity through the world's mass media and can contribute to an epidemic effect worldwide. This same technology enables terrorists to operate on a global scale. Today's hijackers, computer hackers, and other terrorists often have strong international ties that permit them to coordinate their efforts across various regions.

Anthony Clark Arend has commented on this phenomenon of "private violence," where nonstate actors are challenging the state's claim to "a monopoly of legitimate use of violence":

> In the wake of the violence in the Middle East and Latin America, the bombings of the American embassies in Kenya and Tanzania, terrorist groups seem active as ever. Islamic Jihad, the Abu Nidal group, and a host of other terrorist organizations have been active players in international politics. . . . Private violence has also manifested itself in the behavior of other actors. International criminal organizations have developed global networks and their own norms for using force.[32]

Arend goes on to point out that private security threats are spawning private security forces. While national governments seem to find it harder to recruit citizens into their armed forces, new jobs are opening up in the private security field. Related to our discussion of post-Westphalian trends in Chapter 3, he remarks:

> States are becoming increasingly incapable of providing for the needs of their citizens as those citizens keep asking more and more from their states. . . . As [two other authors note], 'increased demands have been placed upon states by technological changes, by the internationalization of trade and finance, and by the growth of transnational interactions among sub-state and nonstate actors.' With these rising expectations on the part of populations and the inability of states to perform, 'individuals and communities have . . . begun to look elsewhere to fill these needs.' . . . One striking example of communities looking to other entities to fulfill needs has been 'the rapid rise in private security and policing throughout the advanced industrial world.' In the United States, for example, there are numerous private police forces for certain exclusive communities, commercial security operations for corporations, community security patrols. . . .

A second—and related—indicator of the growing inability of states to meet the needs of their people is the increased use of private military forces or 'mercenaries' by states themselves. As Professor Herbert Howe contended in 1998, 'the growth of private military and police capability is staggering, especially in Eastern Europe, wealthy Middle Eastern states, and threatened African states.' Employing many former state military officers and enlisted personnel, organizations such as . . . Executive Outcomes have been playing critical roles. Executive Outcomes . . . 'fielded about 600 combat soldiers in Angola and 300 men in Sierra Leone to help defeat insurgencies.' . . . *This use of private military forces by states in international conflict has implications similar to privatization of policing within states. It reflects an inability of states to perform what had been perceived to be a core function of the state—the defense of the realm* [italics mine].[33]

Maryann Cusimano speaks of all this as posing a "new security dilemma" for nation-states beyond the traditional concerns about war and peace. The new security issues, she says, include "transsovereign crime," "nuclear smuggling," and "the global drug trade."[34] Perhaps nothing sets off more alarm bells than concern about "loose nukes" in the former Soviet Union. Cusimano quotes a former director of the U.S. Central Intelligence Agency as saying that "the breakup of the Soviet Union, the opening of Russian society, and its economic difficulties have subjected the security system to stresses and risks it was not designed to withstand."[35] She notes that "organized crime has moved in as states have retreated, creating an active, black market in nuclear materials," and that "given the strains on Russian law enforcement and intelligence institutions, 'officials readily admit' that . . . smuggling along traditional trade routes (from Russia into Iran, for example) may . . . be taking place."[36] Of course, as one nuclear strategist has put it, "the best way to keep weapons and weapons-material out of the hands of nongovernmental entities is to keep them out of the hands of national governments."[37] After all, notwithstanding the growing concern over nonstate sources of violence, nation-states still retain the largest repositories of deadly arsenals. This leads, then, to a consideration of ongoing arms races among states and the efforts of the international community to curb such competition through arms control.

Arms Proliferation

Although world spending on armaments has receded somewhat from the record trillion-dollar level reached as the Cold War was winding down in 1990,[38] arms remain plentiful and are ever more costly both in terms of their killing capacity as well as actual expenditures diverted from what could be more constructive, positive investment in education, health care, and other societal needs. Even if the huge arsenals of nation-states were never used, they arguably represent a waste in human potential; if somehow nations could achieve deterrence of aggression through development of new norms rather than depending on the threat of military retaliation, the savings achieved by reducing military expenditures could make a major dent in addressing poverty and other problems that often underlie the resort to violence.[39]

In the area of conventional weaponry, nation-states today have in their possession everything from small arms to highly sophisticated missiles. By 1990, at least 52 less developed states had acquired supersonic aircraft, 71 had tactical missiles, 107 possessed armored fighting vehicles, and 81 had modern warships.[40] In June 1998, U.S. Secretary of State Albright, "citing the increasing threat to civil aviation posed by shoulder-fired surface-to-air missiles," issued a call for "an international agreement to place tighter controls on the export of such portable, easily concealed weapons."[41] Concern about concealed weapons that gun control advocates express in the American political system pale by comparison with the concern many observers harbor over concealed weapons in the international political system, which can include not only deadly conventional arms but ABC arms as well—bags of plutonium, vials of anthrax and Ebola virus, canisters of nerve gas, and the like. The United States and Russia have the largest chemical weapons arsenals (mostly mustard and nerve gases), the former having 30,000 tonnes and the latter 40,000 tonnes, although both have committed themselves to destroying these over the next decade.[42] Other countries known or thought to possess chemical weapons include Israel, Iraq, Iran, Libya, North Korea, Britain, France, India, China, and Vietnam.[43] [The Chemical Weapons Convention (CWC), which seeks to ban such arsenals, is discussed at the end of this chapter.] The United States and Russia claim to have terminated their biological weapons programs in the 1970s, although there is still some question whether they and a few other states continue to possess some stockpiles. A 1999 *New York Times* report on a book written by a senior defector from the Soviet germ warfare program indicated that there was substantial evidence of a serious accident at a Chinese biological weapons plant in the late 1980s, and that around the same time, even as Moscow under Mikhail Gorbachev was pursuing better relations with Washington, the Kremlin "ordered the arming of giant SS-18 intercontinental ballistic missiles aimed at New York, Los Angeles, Seattle and Chicago with anthrax and other deadly germs" (possibly even the HIV virus that causes AIDS).[44]

As for nuclear arsenals, seven countries currently are official members of the "nuclear club," whose membership includes only those states which have openly detonated a nuclear explosive. In addition to the United States and Russia, these include Britain, France, China, India, and Pakistan. Three former Soviet republics—Belarus, Ukraine, and Kazakhstan—have committed to turning over leftover nuclear weapons on their soil to Moscow, although this process is incomplete. Israel is widely believed to have nuclear capabilities, while a number of other states are thought to have active programs and are feared to be close to developing at least a limited capability, including Iraq, Iran, Algeria, Libya, and North Korea. Brazil, Argentina, and South Africa had active programs in the 1980s but have since renounced any intention to build nuclear weapons, as have states such as Japan and Germany, which clearly have the technological base and resources to go nuclear if they chose to but have thus far "abstained."[45] In the 1990s, the world had "over 48,000 nuclear warheads [including both strategic weapons deliverable through intercontinental ballistic missiles (ICBMs) and other long-range systems, as well as tactical weapons of shorter-range utility] . . . with total explosive power equal to 900,000 Hiroshima bombs [the equivalent of 11,700 megatons of TNT—2.2 tons for each person on earth]. If all planned cuts in nuclear weapons are implemented, in the year 2003 the world will still have as many as 20,000 nuclear weapons containing the explosive power of more than 200,000 Hiroshima bombs."[46] The United States and Russia possess by far the bulk of nuclear weaponry, with both sides having reduced their total number of strategic warheads from the peak level of roughly 11,000 each at the end of the Cold War to roughly 7,000 each by the year 2000, but not yet achieving the still deeper cuts (down to 3,500 warheads each) called for in the Strategic Arms Reduction Talks (START) negotiations undertaken between the two sides.[47]

In engaging in arms control efforts covering everything from small arms and shoulder-fired surface-to-air missiles to nuclear-tipped ICBMs, the international community today is continuing a long tradition in the Westphalian state system, that is, pursuing humanity's ongoing quest to fulfill the biblical prophecy that nations "shall beat their swords into plowshares, and their spears into pruning hooks . . . and neither shall they learn war anymore" (Isaiah 2:4). The development of arms control regimes is part of a larger set of governance concerns facing the contemporary international system in the military security issue area. As "war and peace" has become a more complicated global policy domain, given the changing nature of security threats that has just been outlined, so, too, has the politics of problem-solving, to which we now turn.

GLOBAL GOVERNANCE: EFFORTS AT DEVELOPING INTERNATIONAL SECURITY REGIMES

Although the great body of international law consists of "the laws of peace," there also exist "the laws of war." Some of these rules pertain to the *commencement* of war, i.e., the circumstances under which it is legal for a state to resort to the use of armed force against another state. Other rules pertain to the *conduct* of war, i.e., the kinds of behavior that are permissible by governments once a war is underway, regardless of how it started. If the former rules were fully effective, there would be little need for the latter.

Efforts to Regulate the Outbreak of War

Throughout history there have been attempts to regulate the outbreak of war, going all the way back to the "just war" tradition articulated by St. Augustine in the fourth century A.D. and later by Grotius in the seventeenth century; this tradition held that the use of violence was "just" as long as the purpose was not self-aggrandizement or revenge but rather correction of some larger evil, and as long as the means used were proportionate to the provocation.[48] In the eighteenth and nineteenth centuries, legal efforts were devoted more to making war a more civilized affair than actually banishing or restricting its occurrence. Not until the twentieth century, with the League of Nations Covenant and the Kellogg-Briand Pact following the ravages of World War I, were efforts made to explicitly *outlaw* war. The latter treaty, ratified by almost every nation, provided that "the settlement of all disputes . . . shall never be sought except by pacific means."[49] World War II demonstrated the hollowness of such pious denunciations of violence.

The United Nations Charter in 1945 sought to specify more clearly and more comprehensively the proscription against the use of armed force in international relations, and to provide stronger enforcement machinery should the norm be violated. It is well to recall that the architects of the Charter were the Big Five winners of World War II and that, in calling for an end to war, they were reflecting their stake in maintaining the status quo, particularly through a "concert of great powers" approach to world order based on the special privileges and responsibilities they were to enjoy on the Security Council as the self-appointed chief guardians of peace. Under the UN Charter, all member states are obligated to "refrain . . . from the threat or use of force against the territorial integrity or political independence of any state." In other words, *any first use of armed force (armed aggression)* by one state against another state—no matter how limited—is *illegal* today.

In lieu of armed force, Chapter VI of the Charter urges states to resolve their disputes peaceably and provides for extensive "peaceful settlement" procedures (conciliation, arbitration, and adjudication). Force may be used legally only under the following conditions: (1) in self-defense by an individual state or alliance of states (e.g., NATO) against the armed attack of another state, (2) in the service of the UN as part of a "collective security" operation, or (3) in the service of a regional security organization (e.g., the Arab League or Organization of American States). The concept of "collective security," inherited from the League of Nations, represents the ultimate in pooling sovereignty: the entire international community, led by the Big Five, is obligated under Chapter VII of the UN Charter to coalesce in a grand alliance against any aggressor state; only in a handful of cases has the promise of collective security been realized, most notably in the Korean War in 1950 (when the UN responded to North Korea's aggression against South Korea) and the Gulf War in 1991 (when the UN responded to Iraq's aggression against Kuwait). Although not mentioned in the Charter, "peacekeeping" (under what is sometimes referred to as Chapter VI 1/2) has become a frequently used practice whereby blue-helmeted UN troops are deployed at the invitation of quarreling governments as a neutral buffer force, as in the case of the Suez crisis in 1956 and in subsequent conflict situations in the Middle East.

Although the resort to armed force continues to be a feature of contemporary world politics, at least one respected observer contends that "the norm against the unilateral national use of force has survived. Indeed . . . the norm has been largely observed . . . and the kinds of international wars which it sought to prevent and deter [wars between states] have been infrequent."[50] Professor Henkin acknowledges that the norm against unilateral force has been less effective in the kinds of grayish areas discussed earlier in this chapter—subversion, intervention, and "force without war." The UN Charter anticipated that the main security threat would be inter-state war, and hence "the [institutional] machinery we have to combat [security] problems are wired for the sovereign military confrontations of a bygone era."[51] Anthony Clark Arend and Robert Beck, among others, have examined "the challenges to the Charter paradigm" and have called for a "post-Charter paradigm."[52]

The rules governing the outbreak of hostilities have been especially inadequate to cope with the most common form of planetary violence today—internal wars and mixed internal/external conflicts (internal wars involving outside intervention). In the case of mixed conflicts, it is not clearly one state engaged in armed attack on another state but rather a government seeking foreign support to quell a rebellion or a rebel group seeking foreign support to overthrow a government. There is no question that a foreign army's inviting itself into a domestic conflict ordinarily would constitute aggression and would be a violation of the UN Charter; but what if it is invited in by a government on the brink of collapse? A government has a legal right to invite foreign military assistance only if it can rightly claim to exercise effective control and authority (i.e., sovereignty) over its own population, the very condition that is often in dispute during a civil war. Moreover, internal wars pose special problems today for implementation of prisoner of war (POW) conventions and other rules governing treatment of combatants. In guerrilla warfare, armies do not normally confront each other across well-defined fronts, and soldiers do not even always wear uniforms. Customary distinctions between civilians and combatants are blurred, as are distinctions between neutrals and belligerents. A national government experiencing rebellion is understandably reluctant to extend to rebels the same status normally reserved for enemy soldiers, preferring to dismiss them as "rioters" or "thugs" or "terrorists" rather than legitimizing them as "freedom fighters."

I have noted that foreign involvement in civil wars in the post-Cold War era frequently has taken the form of humanitarian intervention, that is, a multilateral response by the international community triggered by either genocide and ethnic cleansing (as in the case of NATO and UN intervention to protect Kosovars in Serbia, as well as the UN's establishment of a protective zone to shield Kurdish enclaves within Iraq from attacks out of Baghdad following the Gulf War) or the collapse of civil order and the spread of starvation and disease in failed states (as in the case of Somalia and Liberia). Respect for national sovereignty tends to suffer under such conditions, where supranationalist and subnationalist impulses are at work. If the international community waits for an invitation before acting in these situations, a humanitarian response may be impossible, because no repressive regime would welcome external oversight in the first case, and there would be no functioning regime able to issue the invitation in the second case.

Although humanitarian intervention is viewed by idealists as an important new concept in world politics, realists raise concerns that it may play havoc with Westphalian ordering arrangements insofar as it contradicts Article 2, section 7 of the UN Charter, which stipulates that "nothing contained in the Charter shall authorize the UN to intervene in matters which are essentially within the domestic jurisdiction of any state." Questions have arisen about whether the recent UN-authorized interventions in Iraq to protect the Kurds and in Serbia to protect the Kosovars set troublesome precedents for outside interference in the domestic affairs of sovereign states generally.[53] Some states, such as Russia in its brutal suppression of civil strife in Chechnya during the 1990s, may be able to resist humanitarian intervention more readily than others. (What is the likelihood, for example, that the United States would be willing to tolerate external interference within its borders should, say, some Native American tribes or other disaffected groups seek greater autonomy from Washington? The United States in the 1990s was the leading proponent of enforcing a "no-fly" zone against Iraqi aircraft intimidating Kurdish villages in Iraq, yet looked the other way when Turkey, an American ally facing calls for self-determination by its own Kurdish population, strafed Kurdish camps inside Iraq's boundaries in retaliation for those camps supporting Kurdish rebels operating within Turkey.)

How much importance should the international community attach to supporting the territorial integrity of states (such as Turkey, Iraq, and Russia) as opposed to self-determination for minority nationality groups within those states (such as Kurds and Chechnyans)? A 1999 newspaper article reported on the difficult issues raised by the evolving norm of humanitarian intervention and by the international community's increasing willingness to get involved in human rights matters generally:

> At the century's last session of the Commission on Human Rights, Secretary General Kofi Annan of the United Nations unveiled a doctrine with profound implications for international relations in the new millennium. The air strikes against Yugoslavia [in the Kosovo War] . . . showed that the world would no longer permit nations to "hide" behind the United Nations charter, which has traditionally safeguarded national sovereignty. . . . The protection of human rights, he said, must "take precedence over concerns of state sovereignty." . . . Some argue that Mr. Annan has merely blessed a "given" of the political climate today: the growing importance of human rights to the United Nations and many of its members. . . . But others argue that though well-intentioned, it is naïve, dangerous, and likely to increase tensions and paralysis within the Security Council. . . .[Mr. Annan has stated that] the principle of sovereignty cannot provide "excuses for the inex-

cusable" [and that the UN Charter] "was issued in the name of 'the peoples,' not the governments, of the United Nations."[54]

Such post-Westphalian sentiments continue to come up against Westphalian realities, however, as international regimes (e.g., the two Geneva Protocols of 1977, which sought to modernize the POW and other rules governing both inter-state and intrastate wars, and the 1998 treaty establishing a Permanent War Crimes Tribunal in The Hague in the Netherlands to try government officials and other persons accused of genocide and other atrocities) still need the imprimatur of nation-states, especially the most powerful states, if they are to prove effective.

Kofi Annan's predecessor as UN secretary-general, Boutros Boutros-Ghali, was reminded of this fact in 1992, when his *Agenda for Peace* proposal for improving UN capabilities in the peace and security area fell on the deaf ears of the United States and other Security Council members. Boutros-Ghali suggested that the UN might usefully play a number of different conflict management roles in the post-Cold War era, arranged along a continuum of situations. One would be peace maintenance; where disputes have not yet erupted in actual fighting, the UN might help by maintaining a computerized early warning system and dispatching diplomats to defuse a crisis or sending troops for purposes of "preventive deployment." A second would be peacemaking; where hostilities have already started, the UN might prevent any further escalation by mounting quick efforts at mediation. A third would be peacekeeping, which would follow once peacemaking had established a cease-fire. A fourth would be peace-building; the UN could help foster conditions for a long-term, durable peace through providing such assistance as infrastructure repair, refugee repatriation, de-mining minefields, disarming rival factions and facilitating free elections where civil wars have raged, and in general promoting postwar reconstruction. A fifth would be collective security and peace enforcement; where there has been an act of aggression in violation of the UN Charter, the UN needed to have the capability to respond with either economic or military sanctions (with, ideally, the UN having a small rapid deployment force of some 60,000 soldiers).[55] These ideas, particularly the creation of a UN standing army, aroused fears in many quarters, notably on the part of conservatives in the United States wary of world government and reluctant to put American soldiers under a foreign commander.

Efforts to Regulate the Conduct of War

Over the centuries, humanity, failing to ban war altogether, has attempted to make it at least more "humane" by regulating its conduct through agreed-upon rules of engagement. Some of the efforts to inject a dose of civility into warfare have seemed paradoxical and almost comical, such as the prohibition (embodied in the Hague Convention of 1907) against the use of "dum-dum" expanding bullets and the use of "deceit" in the form of misrepresenting a flag of truce or wearing Red Cross uniforms as a disguise—especially at a time when poisonous gas and other atrocities were legally permissible. However, absurd as they might appear and as erratic as their observance has been, the laws governing the conduct of war have often succeeded in limiting the savage nature of war to some extent.

Since World War II especially, in response to arms proliferation concerns I have alluded to, numerous international regimes have been established that impose restrictions on the testing, production, stockpiling, transfer, deployment, and use of various kinds of weapons, including both conventional weapons and weapons of mass destruction. Arms control and disarmament talks have occurred in several settings, including such multilateral forums as the Geneva-based Conference on Disarmament and special sessions of the UN General Assembly, as well as bilateral forums such as the START negotiations between the United States and the Soviet Union/Russia in the 1980s and 1990s. As with the UN Charter itself, arms control regimes are imperfect, with several states refusing to ratify treaties, compliance spotty even among the legally bound parties in some cases, and many issues not covered by any agreements.

For example, one can point to the 1980 Convention on Prohibitions or Restrictions on the Use of Certain Conventional Weapons Which May Be Deemed to Be Excessively Injurious and to Have Indiscriminate Effects, which placed limits on the use of napalm, booby traps, and other devices. Only sixty countries had ratified the treaty as of 1999. The 1998 Anti-Personnel Landmine Treaty (Ottawa Treaty) specifically sought to outlaw the use of landmines in warfare. It is estimated that in over 60 countries there are currently some 100 million landmines buried in the ground, left over from various conflicts, which tend to claim innocent civilians, often children, as their main victims as the latter accidentally trigger the devices. Landmines have been called the "Saturday night special of civil wars," and Cambodia—one of the most landmine-littered landscapes in the world—has been called a "nation of amputees" as a result of its brutal internal conflict in the past two decades.[56] Landmines are reported to "maim or kill approximately 26,000 people per year, 70 per day, or almost 3 people per hour."[57] As of 1999, 64 states had ratified the Ottawa Treaty, with the United States, Russia, and China among the more conspicuous absentees.[58] More than 90 states now participate in the UN Register of Conventional Arms, which seeks to promote "transparency" in arms at the global level by obligating states to report all exports and imports of conventional armaments, in the hope that such open monitoring will contribute to an atmosphere of trust rather than paranoia in international relations. The United States participates in both the UN Registry as well as the 33-member Wassenaar Arrangement, aimed at controlling illicit trafficking in small arms and other conventional weaponry.

What about "big" arms? Interestingly, there is no clear rule of international law banning the first use of nuclear weapons in warfare. If one country were to initiate a conventional, non-nuclear attack against another country, the right of self-defense the UN Charter permits the second country includes the right to retaliate with nuclear strikes. At least that is the position the United States took throughout the Cold War, when Washington was concerned that, without the threatened nuclear deterrent, the Soviet Union might be tempted to take advantage of its superiority in tanks and conventional forces in Eastern Europe to invade Western Europe. In 1994, the UN General Assembly voted to ask the World Court in The Hague for an advisory opinion on the question: "Is the threat or use of nuclear weapons in any circumstances permitted under international law?" The General Assembly request followed a similar request made earlier by the World Health Organization, which was concerned about the health and environmental effects of using such weapons. The World Court ended up equivocating on this issue.[59]

It is fortunate that the nuclear arms race itself has been limited to a few contestants up to now. One of the most important arms control treaties since World War II is the Nuclear Non-Proliferation Treaty (NPT) of 1970. The treaty obligates states which do not have nuclear weapons to refrain from developing them, and obligates existing nuclear weapons states to refrain from transferring such weaponry to the nuclear have-nots. Although the treaty has been ratified by almost the entire UN membership, there are a few major holdouts, notably Israel, Pakistan, and India, while some signatories have been accused of trying to develop nuclear weapons in violation of their treaty commitments, notably Iraq, Iran, and North Korea. For highly technologically developed countries like Japan and Germany, which could readily create nuclear forces were they inclined to do so, denying themselves the ultimate deterrent and badge of prestige which nuclear weapons are thought to confer represents a real act of national self-abnegation, one that they may be sorely tempted to reconsider in the twenty-first century should the strategic environment change. A remarkable accomplishment was the agreement, in 1995 (as the NPT was about to expire), to renew the NPT in perpetuity. The nuclear powers had to overcome objections by many states that contended that the United States and other members of the nuclear club had not done enough to build down their own nuclear arsenals and to adopt a comprehensive ban on any future nuclear testing.

The Partial Test Ban Treaty of 1963 prohibited atmospheric testing of nuclear weapons but permitted underground testing, and was followed up in 1996 with a Comprehensive Nuclear Test Ban Treaty that was slated to take effect upon ratification by not only the members of the nuclear club but all 44 countries possessing nuclear energy reactors; this treaty has been called "the longest-sought, hardest-fought prize in the history of arms control,"[60] since a stoppage of all nuclear testing might effectively put the nuclear genie back in the bottle. However, the United States, India and some other states have yet to sign on, with the U.S. in particular expressing concerns about adequate verification mechanisms as well as adequate alternative technologies for determining whether the existing nuclear arsenals were in working order should they be needed. Under existing UN regimes that are more widely accepted, nuclear weapons are banned from being deployed in outer space, on the deep seabed, and in Antartica. In addition to these global approaches, regional nuclear weapon-free zones have been established in Latin America and the South Pacific. The United States and Russia are still involved in the bilateral START negotiations aimed ultimately at reducing their nuclear warhead inventories to below 3,000, although concern about the relative size of Chinese, South Asian, and European nuclear armaments will undoubtedly limit how far downward Washington and Moscow are willing to go. Complete nuclear disarmament is out of the question.

While complete nuclear disarmament is a pipe dream, there have been serious efforts by the international community to eliminate all biological and chemical weapons, including not only their use but their very possession. I will save the discussion of the 1993 Chemical Weapons Convention (CWC) for the next section. The 1972 Biological Weapons Convention, ratified by over 130 states, including the United States and Russia, prohibits any development, production, and stockpiling of toxins and other bacteriological weapons for use in germ warfare. Under the treaty, all existing biological weapons stockpiles were to have been destroyed. However, a major weakness of the treaty was the failure to incorporate a meaningful verification regime, so that it is difficult to judge how much compliance has actually occurred. In contrast, the UN International Atomic Energy Agency has helped to monitor NPT compliance, while the UN Organization for the Prohibition of Chemical Weapons has been established to monitor CWC compliance, although Saddam Hussein's evasion of UN inspection teams in the 1990s hunting for proof of Iraqi ABC weapons programs shows the difficulty of verification even where institutions exist.

It is worth mentioning, also, a number of international regimes that have been produced in response to international terrorism which have had the effect of limiting the use of certain weapons by terrorists in their campaigns of violence. Three global conventions specifically address crimes relating to air travel. The Tokyo Convention of 1963 obligates signatory states to effect the safe release of skyjacked passengers and crews entering their borders. The Hague Convention of 1970 goes further in requiring states to prosecute or extradite skyjackers in their custody. The Montreal Convention of 1971 extends the Hague provisions to include not only hijackers but anyone committing any acts of sabotage against airports or aircraft. Additional multilateral agreements have outlawed the hijacking of ships at sea, the theft of nuclear material, and the illicit trafficking in narcotic drugs. Loopholes in their coverage, and the fact that many states have not yet ratified these conventions, undermine the effectiveness of international law in this area, but nonetheless the international community can point to a decline over time in the number of skyjackings and other terrorist incidents. One modest but hopeful sign of growing global recognition of the need to curb unorthodox violence appeared two months after the

Achille Lauro affair. In December 1985, the UN General Assembly for the first time, by unanimous approval, passed a resolution containing a blanket condemnation of all terrorism. The resolution even managed to contain a single if vague agreement on the definition of terrorism, as acts that "endanger or take innocent human lives, jeopardize fundamental freedoms, and seriously impair the dignity of human beings." Although General Assembly resolutions are generally not binding in any legal sense, at times such statements of principles and norms—what is called "soft law"—can make an important contribution to global governance.

If one looks at the global policy process—from agenda-setting to implementation—that has produced these international regimes in the security issue area, one sees mainly state-centric, billiard ball politics at work, with national governments taking the lead role in pursuit of national interests, although some cobweb elements can be found as well. As an example of cobweb phenomena, I alluded earlier to the role played by various nonstate actors in helping to shape the skyjacking regimes, namely the International Federation of Airline Pilots Associations (IFAPA, a transnational labor union NGO which heightened awareness of the problem and lobbied governments to take steps against terrorists), the International Air Transport Association (the IFAPA's management counterpart which also engaged in lobbying), and the International Civil Aviation Organization (the IGO which provided the forum for regime development and is responsible for implementation); at a time when many Third World governments were sympathetic to terrorists, it was the IFAPA that threatened not to fly into countries harboring skyjackers, after a particularly brutal murder of a Lufthansa Airlines pilot during a 1977 skyjacking, and successfully applied pressure on governments to pass a UN General Assembly resolution condemning aerial hijacking. As another example, the International Campaign to Ban Landmines, an NGO coalition of over 800 groups in over 50 countries, is widely credited with using the Internet and the mass media to put the landmine issue on the global agenda and, along with the Canadian Department of Foreign Affairs, persuading national governments to sign the 1998 Ottawa Treaty. One observer notes that "no other issue has mobilized such a diverse coalition of states and NGOs in such a short time-frame. Such a treaty would not have been created if it was not for the aggressive measures adopted by the NGOs."[61] As a follow-up to the treaty, the United Nations Association-USA and the UN Development Program entered into an NGO-IGO "Adopt a Minefield" agreement whereby UNDP identifies minefields to be cleared and UNA identifies sponsors (schools, businesses, and community groups) who for $25,000 each can fund the de-mining of a particular area.

Clearly, nonstate actors can be part of the solution in the search for security regimes, exemplified not only by those already mentioned but also by several NGOs active in the emergency relief field, such as CARE and *Medecins Sans Frontiers,* as well as pacifist groups such as the Quakers and the "nuclear freeze" movements that sprang up in U.S. and other cities during the Cold War and "epistemic communities" that provide scientific research support such as the Stockholm International Peace Research Institute (SIPRI). Nonstate actors can also be part of the problem, exemplified not only by terrorist and criminal organizations but also by those multinational corporations which have a heavy commercial stake in the munitions business (e.g., Boeing and Lockheed Martin in the United States) and, hence, some incentive to fuel arms races in partnership with defense bureaucracies who draw up arms shopping lists and politicians who seek military spending in their local districts. Although domestic politics may not be as animated in the national security arena as in, say, the economic and environmental arenas, we have noted that politics does not completely stop at the water's edge when it comes to security concerns.[62] Focusing on bureaucratic politics, Abram and Antonia Chayes describe the arms control process as one that involves the interaction of internal and international politics, along the lines of Putnam's two-level games:

> The [treaty-making] process goes on both within each state and at the international level. . . . [The] list of the U.S. groups normally involved in arms control negotiations includes the national security staff, the Departments of State and Defense, the Arms control and Disarmament Agency, the Joint Chiefs of Staff, the Central Intelligence Agency, and sometimes the Department of Energy. . . . These groups themselves are not unitary actors. . . . Much of the extensive literature on U.S.–Soviet arms control negotiations is devoted to analysis of the almost byzantine complexity of these internal interactions.[63]

Notwithstanding the role that subnational and transnational actors often play in security affairs, the extraordinarily high stakes found in this issue area, where the fate of the entire nation may be most directly at risk, make it the one that still comes closest to the purest form of state-centric, billiard ball politics emphasized by realists. Most analysts would argue that the dynamics of the U.S.–Soviet arms race and other behaviors exhibited by the superpowers during the Cold War were grounded mainly in an action-reaction spiral revolving around mutual suspicion and hostility on the part of the two political systems, and that security politics between the United States and Russia and other states in the post-Cold War era retains this same basic quality even if allies and enemies are not as clear-cut as previously. What follows is a short case study of the 1993 Chemical Weapons Convention, which vividly illustrates the workings of billiard ball politics, dotted with some elements of cobweb politics.

THE 1993 CHEMICAL WEAPONS CONVENTION

The 1993 Convention on the Prohibition of the Development, Production, Stockpiling, and Use of Chemical Weapons and on Their Destruction (referred to here in its abbreviated form as the Chemical Weapons Convention, or CWC) obligates all states party to the treaty "never under any circumstances to develop,

A U.S. soldier wearing gear to protect against chemical weapons. (Department of Defense)

produce, otherwise acquire, stockpile or retain chemical weapons, or transfer, directly or indirectly, chemical weapons to anyone" [or] "to use chemical weapons." In addition, any states party to the treaty that have chemical weapons are obligated to destroy those arsenals within ten years following the treaty entering into force. Unlike the Biological Weapons Convention, a verification regime has been established under UN supervision. The treaty, which had first been opened for signing in 1993, took effect on April 29, 1997, six months after the sixty-fifth state (Hungary) ratified it, as stipulated in the convention. As of 2000, over 130 countries had ratified the CWC, although many others were signatories who had indicated their intention to complete ratification procedures shortly. (A treaty ordinarily does not become binding on a state unless, in addition to signing, the state ratifies it through its constitutionally mandated procedures.) The CWC is considered a landmark agreement since it is "the first comprehensively verifiable multilateral treaty that completely bans an entire class of weapons, and firmly limits activities that may contribute to the production of those weapons."[64]

Human concerns do not automatically become identified as "problems" that dictate public policy responses by the body politic. Usually the concerns have to reach a level of seriousness, sometimes even crisis proportions, particularly as perceived by powerful actors, before they are addressed. For example, biological warfare had been around throughout history—even as far back as medieval times, an attacking army laying siege to a walled city might try to achieve victory by spreading disease through the catapulting of dead animal carcasses over the castle walls—but it was not until the 1970s, after biological weapons had become capable of mass destruction, that a Biological Weapons Convention was signed. Likewise, the first skyjacking on record occurred in 1930, but it was not until the 1960s and 1970s, after a rash of such incidents threatened aviation safety and the future of air travel, that skyjacking conventions were drafted. How did concern about chemical weapons move from being an issue that attracted relatively little attention to one that eventually made it onto the global agenda and generated demands for collective action by the international community?

Our story begins long ago. One author notes that "the Manu laws of [ancient] India forbade the use of poison weapons; so, a millennium later, did the warfare regulations which the Saracens drew from the Koran."[65] The first known international agreement to limit chemical weapons dates back to 1675, shortly after the Peace of Westphalia, when the French and Germans signed a pact in Strassbourg not to use poison bullets in warfare. In 1874, the Brussels Convention prohibited the use of poisoned weapons that caused unnecessary suffering in war. This was followed by an international peace conference in The Hague in 1899, universal in scope insofar as it included many non-European states, which issued a declaration urging a ban on the use of projectiles filled with poison gases. However, it was not until the 1920s, after chemical weapons were used to brutal effect on a wide scale during World War I, that the international community made a concerted effort to address the problem beyond the earlier half-measures. Germany introduced chlorine gas on the battlefield at Ypres (Belgium) in 1915, and both sides eventually made extensive use of various chemical agents, including mustard gas, phosgene, and hydrogen cyanide, which caused serious damage to eyes, skin, and lungs.[66] As one observer put it at the time, anticipating the even more lethal nerve agents (e.g., sarin and tabun) that were to be developed subsequently, a chemical attack could reduce a "metropolis to a necropolis."[67]

The response of the international community was the Geneva Protocol of 1925, which banned the first use of chemical weapons by any state but was interpreted to permit the production, stockpiling, and use of chemical weapons in retaliation for another state's prior use. Roughly 150 countries eventually became parties to the treaty (although the United States Senate did not formally ratify it until 1975). Although thousands of tons of chemical weapons were manufactured and stockpiled by Germany, the United States, and other countries before and during World War II, they were not used in combat.[68] While the main reason for restraint during World War II was probably mutual fear of employing such unpredictable arsenals, the norms contained in the Protocol no doubt helped to reinforce inhibitions.

There was little felt need to improve upon the Geneva Protocol until the 1960s, when a number of circumstances led to chemical weapons once again being placed on the global agenda as a "global policy" problem. The widespread use of nonlethal but nonetheless toxic chemicals (herbicides and tear gases) by the United States during the Vietnam War led Hungary in 1966 to propose a UN General Assembly resolution urging strict observance of the Geneva Protocol and attention to the treaty's loopholes. The United States and the Soviet Union at the time were already about to embark on arms control negotiations over nuclear weapons (the SALT process) and biological weapons. There were reports of poison gas use by Egypt in the Yemen civil war during the 1960s, and of ever more deadly technological "advances" in the chemical weapons field that were becoming accessible even to less developed countries. As one writer states, "In retrospect, the [CWC] treaty appears to have been shaped the most . . . by what, at root, set the process going in the first place: a widespread sense that the existing regime of international law and custom which inhibited resort to toxic warfare was coming under increasing threat, and that it might well prove to be in the best interest of all states if the regime . . . were somehow strengthened."[69]

Still, had not the two superpowers in particular shared such concerns, it is unlikely that any progress would have occurred. Superpower behavior could be explained by the classic billiard ball, state-as-rational-actor paradigm: "[The U.S. and USSR] came to the conclusion that . . . there was more which they could gain by giving the weapons up than by continuing to retain and develop them. Heavily militarized anyway, and possessing a huge range of other armaments, their need for additional weapons of terror or force multiplication was hardly overwhelming."[70] Hence, they accepted Sweden's initiative in 1968 to place the issue, along with biological weapons, on the agenda of the Geneva-based Eighteen-Nation Committee on Disarmament which they co-chaired; a subsequent British proposal led to biological weapons being negotiated separately from chemical weapons. The Committee on Disarmament had been formed under the auspices of the UN in the late 1940s to deal with disarmament issues, and had originally been composed of ten states (those judged most important militarily) and then eighteen, eventually evolving by 1978 into the 40-Nation Conference on Disarmament (CD), which by 1995 had numbered over sixty states (reflecting a tendency for UN bodies to expand as national governments distrust other governments to represent their interests); the CD was conceived as an autonomous IGO rather than as a subsidiary of the UN General Assembly, one that was expected to make decisions based on a unanimity rule. Ultimately the CWC was negotiated through consensus by thirty-nine countries, along with an additional thirty-five countries participating as observers, with the drafters then inviting the entire UN membership to sign. But that is getting ahead of the story.

In the 1970s, during the policy formulation stage, the Soviet bloc submitted various proposals for chemical weapons disarmament which were rejected by the Western bloc because of the former's refusal to allow UN on-site inspections to verify compliance. Japan, Britain, and other states offered compromise proposals. Meanwhile, the non-aligned Third World bloc submitted its own proposals, emphasizing the importance of ensuring that any ban on chemical agents would not prohibit less developed countries from gaining access to the latest non-military technology produced by industry in the North. The Conference on Disarmament negotiations did not pick up steam until the late 1980s, when a UN investigation confirmed reports that Iraq, a party to the 1925 Geneva Protocol, had violated the treaty in using poison gas against both Iranian forces and noncombatants during the 1983–1988 Iran-Iraq War and had also used such weapons against its own Kurdish population to put down a revolt in Iraqi Kurdistan in 1987–1988. Further impetus for the negotiations was provided by the additional specter of chemical warfare raised during the 1990–1991 Gulf War, as well as an improved climate of trust between Washington and Moscow following the end of the Cold War.

By 1991, as a signal to the international community that they were serious about the multilateral talks in Geneva, Presidents Bush and Gorbachev announced they had reached bilateral understandings regarding the renunciation of all use of chemical weapons, the eventual elimination of the existing American and Russian chemical weapons stockpiles, and the establishment of verification machinery to monitor compliance. The latter, however, "continued to be a perplexing aspect of the overall U.S. stance towards the convention. Hitherto an advocate of the most stringent verification regimes, the U.S. delegation entered the endgame engaged in a bizarre walk-back from its previous position on challenge inspection. With the rest of the [West and former East bloc states] . . . and at least some of the Third World . . . seemingly moving to accept its super-intrusive 1984 proposal, the United States was retreating from it, apparently seeking to protect its supersecret technology development programs in . . . [the civilian sector] from liability to international inspection under the chemical treaty."[71]

In order to understand the politics of verification, around which the policy adoption phase of the CWC game revolved, one needs to introduce some cobweb elements into the story at this point. It was commonly understood that a chemical weapons ban posed extraordinary problems of verification since there was a fine line between civilian and military applications. The same chemical agents which were precursors to weapons were also used routinely in the commercial production of insecticides, lubricants, pharmaceuticals, paints, textile dyes, and other products, and hence could be found in significant quantities at any chemical plant in the industrialized world; for example, thiodiglycol and phosphorus were "dual-use" materials that could be used to make both mustard gas as well as ball point pens and soaps and detergents. Any ban on chemical weapons potentially threatened the chemical industry worldwide in terms of limiting its production and exports. At greatest risk was the U.S. chemical industry—the largest in the world, with some 20,000 chemical manufacturing plants on American soil, representing a third of the world's total chemical production capacity, employing almost a million people with a payroll of $31 billion.[72]

Wanting to avoid domestic political and economic fallout from decisions that could adversely affect the U.S. chemical industry, the U.S. Arms Control and Disarmament Agency (the lead agency heading the U.S. delegation at the CD talks in Geneva) as early as 1978 invited the Chemical Manufacturers Association (CMA) to participate in the internal U.S. policy deliberations. The CMA was the main trade association responsible for promoting the interests of the U.S. chemical industry, representing some 180 American chemical companies (including such large ones as Dow, Dupont, and Monsanto), accounting for 90 percent of all chemical production in the United States.[73] Initially, the chemical industry was lukewarm to the negotiations, wary of costly government regulations, export controls, and intrusive on-site inspections that might encourage industrial espionage and compromising of confidential business information. However, once it became resigned to the need for a treaty, it worked to protect its interests as best it could, urging a uniform industry-wide set of rules and ultimately endorsing an even more far-reaching international inspection regime than the U.S. Defense Department was willing to permit; CMA was especially fearful that, should the United States fail to become a party to the treaty, American chemical companies could stand to lose $600 million in annual export sales under the proposed sanctions for noncompliance. Commenting on how the CMA eventually came "on board," a U.S. congressman said that "had it not been for CMA, there would not have been a Chemical Weapons Convention."[74]

Discussions occurred at several levels, among state and nonstate actors, domestically and internationally. The CMA entered into discussions with counterpart trade associations in Western Europe, Canada, Australia, and Japan to forge a common industry position, and then met with a Western intergovernmental working group to coordinate a common front which the developed industrialized capitalist states could present vis-à-vis other governments in Geneva. Along the way, the CMA established strong relationships with a number of NGOs, such as the Pugwash group (a transnational assemblage of scientists, academics, and government representatives meeting in an unofficial capacity), the Stockholm International Peace Research Institute (SIPRI), and the Quakers, who together often served as an "epistemic community" providing authoritative data on the chemical weapons problem and as "brokers" in the diplomatic process. Within the official U.S. delegation, interagency disputes had to be reconciled between the Arms Control and Disarmament Agency, Defense Department, State Department, and Commerce Department, while other country delegations experienced their own bureaucratic politics. Various private interest groups lobbied national legislators in support of and against the treaty; for example, among the groups that initially articulated concerns in Washington were the National Federation of Independent Business, a small-business association worried about the burden which inspection and other treaty provisions might impose on its members, and the Chemical Weapons Working Group, an environmentalist coalition opposed to incineration of the existing U.S. chemical weapons inventories located at eight storage depots across the country.[75] A spokesperson for the latter group stated that "our position is not NIMBY—'not in my backyard.' . . . It is NOPE—'not on Planet Earth.'"[76]

Although the Chemical Weapons Convention story would be incomplete without including the role of CMA and other nonstate actors, much of the tale nonetheless centered on billiard ball politics and core nation-state concerns relating to sovereignty, security, and access to vital technologies. Since 1984, the main diplomatic forum for CWC discussions had been a special inter-state working group of the Conference on Disarmament, with the chairmanship rotating between the Nonaligned Group of 21, the Socialist Group, and the Western Group, each bringing their particular national interests and bloc interests to the bargaining table. Within the Western Group, in addition to the United States, a number of other states played key roles in drafting treaty revisions and moving the negotiations along; as one writing notes, "the United States and the Soviet Union (succeeded by Russia) were integral to the treaty's negotiation, but their roles were at times eclipsed by the contributions and actions of states such as Australia, Germany, and France, among others."[77] India and Iran headed a group of developing countries concerned about how export controls might impact their economies, as "a critical dynamic at the CD in the conclusion of the CWC negotiations was the interplay between developed and developing states."[78] Russia was receptive to eliminating its chemical arsenal and allowing UN inspection as long as the United States did the same.[79]

By 1992, as Cold War divisions had become more muted, there was growing consensus behind a "rolling text" that called for the following provisions: (1) all parties would renounce completely the development, possession, and use of chemical weapons; (2) those states already in possession of chemical weapons would be obligated to destroy those stockpiles within a prescribed timetable; (3) an inspection regime would be administered by a new UN body headquartered in The Hague, the Organization for the Prohibition of Chemical Weapons (OPCW), which was to have an Executive Council consisting of forty-one member states drawn from all geographical regions but with the most seats going to those countries having "the most significant chemical industry" (and the U.S. paying 25 percent of the annual budget); (4) governments would be obligated to submit annual national reports to OPCW documenting the manufacture of any chemicals at civilian plants which might have dual use applications; and (5) any countries refusing to become a party to the treaty would be prohibited from importing certain classes of dual-use chemicals from participating states and, in the case of major chemical exporters, would see their exports boycotted. On the controversial matter of on-site inspection, the treaty stipulated that "challenge inspections" could be demanded by any party to the treaty against any other party thought to be violating the rules, although—instead of the original proposal that called for UN teams being allowed access to suspected sites "anytime, anywhere"—there was to be "managed access," i.e., a state would be permitted up to 120 hours until it would have to admit international inspectors within its borders, and even then it would have the right to take such measures as were deemed necessary to protect national security.

In September 1992, the Conference on Disarmament in Geneva adopted the final text and, as noted at the outset of the case study, the treaty was opened for signing in 1993, with well over 100 states having now ratified the pact. All the member states in the European Union were among the initial signatories, signing the convention together at the opening ceremony in Paris in January 1993, although each state subsequently followed its own ratification timetable. The United States and Russia were also among the original signatories, but were slower in ratifying than EU members; the U.S. formally became a party in 1997 following Senate approval, after at times acrimonious domestic political debate with partisan overtones,[80] while the Russian Federation became a party shortly thereafter following approval by the Russian Duma. Three-fourths of the two dozen states thought to have chemical weapons capabilities have joined the treaty. The major holdouts are several Middle East states, including Egypt, Iraq, Libya, and Syria, which claim they are withholding their signature until Israel becomes a party to the Nuclear Nonproliferation Treaty. Problems persist in the implementation of the regime. The United States and other signatories have dragged their feet in meeting the routine inspection and reporting requirements of the treaty, and it remains to be seen how workable challenge inspections will be, especially in light of the failure of the UN to enforce challenge inspections in the case of Iraq following the Gulf War. It is also unclear whether the threat to withhold vital chemical imports from nonsignatory countries will provide the necessary incentive for them to join the regime. Moreover, the promised dismantling of their existing chemical weapons stocks by the United States and Russia has been hampered thus far by environmental protests in the former case and financial problems in the latter case.[81]

CONCLUSION

Despite an uncertain future, the Chemical Weapons Convention represents a major achievement of the international community, one involving quintessential state-centric, billiard ball politics played for the highest stakes imaginable. But we have seen that, even in this case, subnational and transnational politics became part of the equation that produced the CWC. As the "national security" issue area continues to grow in complexity, and as security issues blend with economic and other concerns, we are likely to see an increase in cobweb politics in the shaping of international regimes. In a light-hearted commentary that has deadly serious implications, David Sanger shows how it is becoming harder to separate all these concerns:

> Bad news for Chinese generals: The United States Commerce Department has just determined that the new Sony Playstation II . . . is powered by an American-made chip so powerful that Washington would have to be notified before it could be shipped to China. If the final destination were a company . . . linked to the Chinese military, a lengthy review would be required to make sure America's most sophisticated technology does not fall into the hands of bombmakers. But any Chinese officer determined to play out his fantasies on a state-of-the-art Sony—perhaps simulating a naval attack to retake Taiwan—has other options. He could simply send his teenagers over to shop at any of the five Toys "R" Us stores in Hong Kong, which is still considered a safe place to send advanced technology even though it reverted to China two years ago. The issue of the Playstation is bandied about a lot in Washington these days as one more example of how disconnected the politics of controlling high-tech exports is from the realities of a marketplace that reinvents itself every six months.
>
> The Playstation is only the tip of the chip. Over the next 12 months American computer makers are planning to roll out a series of new products . . . that blow wildly past the limits Washington has used to define a supercomputer that needs to be guarded. By the year's end, says Andrew S. Grove, chairman of the Intel Corporation, "You'll be spending $1200 at CompUSA for a computer that, if the rules aren't changed, we may not be able to ship to China." Or to Israel, Russia, India, or 50 other nations subject to strict controls. . . . The [U.S.] computer industry's top executives were visiting Capitol Hill and the White House last week asking for a relaxation of the export rules. . . . Otherwise, they warn, Europe and Japan will eat their lunch.[82]

The apparent decline of inter-state war as a pervasive constant in international relations, noted earlier in this chapter, has opened up space for non-war-peace issues to rise on national and international agendas. As suggested in Part One, economics is now being called "the continuation of war by other means." We now turn to a discussion of challenges to the welfare state in the post-Cold War era and of attempts to promote global governance in the economic arena.

CHAPTER 6

Challenges to the National Welfare State
Middle Politics
in the Post-Cold War Era

In the Cold War, the most frequently asked question was: "How big is your missile?" In globalization, the most frequently asked question is: "How fast is your modem?"
>   —Thomas Friedman, *The Lexus and the Olive Tree,* 1999

Welfare, not warfare, will shape the rules [and] . . . dictate the agenda.
>   —Josef Joffe, a 1992 essay

Nation-states have always had to deal with not only military security issues but also economic issues, if only because one's military security depended on having enough wealth to support an army. Just as the face of global violence and the nature of the challenges to the national security state have changed over time, particularly of late, so too have the workings of the world economy and the nature of the challenges to national control over economic activity been undergoing major transformation. Even though observers have long understood the importance of the link between international politics and international economics, only recently has the term "international political economy" (IPE) become a staple of the international relations field, traceable to the Arab oil embargo and other newsworthy economic happenings in the 1970s, which drew attention to economic issues as important in their own right apart from national security concerns. One can debate whether economic issues have now overtaken traditional security issues in importance, as the above quotations from Friedman and Joffe suggest, but few would deny their growing visibility on the global agenda.

The changing face of the world economy: Who's minding the store? (© Corbis/Laffont)

We can speak today of a world economy even if there is no world government. It was noted earlier that Coca-Cola is served 560 million times a day in 160 countries and that the Marlboro Man is marketed "in every country on earth." A new McDonalds goes up in some corner of the globe every 24 hours, with Japan alone having over 5,000 franchises and with the largest McDonalds on the planet now found in Beijing, China. Globalization is not to be equated simply with Americanization. Hardees, Burger King, Dr. Pepper, and countless other brand names found in American supermarkets and shopping malls are owned by companies that have their headquarters abroad. Although the United States is still the base of operations for the largest number of MNCs in the world, with General Motors, Microsoft, and other U.S. firms continuing to expand their reach into overseas markets, its lead as a headquarters country is shrinking as American businesses themselves are increasingly falling prey to corporate buyouts by foreign interests, most recently seen in Chrysler's takeover by DaimlerBenz and AMOCO's takeover by British Petroleum.

As a quintessential example of globalization, take Unilever, the giant multinational corporation that ranks as the world's leading maker of consumer goods. Its 1600 brands include such well-known products as Good Humor ice cream, Ben and Jerry's ice cream, Ragu spaghetti, Dove soap, Imperial margarine, Lipton tea, Vaseline skin lotion, Close-Up and Pepsodent toothpaste, Q-Tips cotton swabs, and Calvin Klein fragrances. Although Unilever is unusual in that it has a dual headquarters—the company leadership is based in both the United Kingdom and the Netherlands—it otherwise resembles many contemporary MNCs. As of 2000, it had 380 different manufacturing sites throughout Europe, North America, South America, and Asia, with substantial sales in every region of the world. Due to an increasingly competitive economic environment and the felt need to downsize in order to cut costs, Unilever recently announced intentions to close 100 factories, eliminate 25,000 jobs, and trim three-fourths of its brands. As just one example of how globalization impacts local communities, a small, poor municipality named Pagedale, near St. Louis, saw its Unilever plant closed, resulting in the loss of over 200 jobs and depriving the community of much of its tax base.

Despite globalization trends, the Westphalian logic that continues to dominate our view of the world still leads us, when we think of economics, to think in terms of the economic size and health of *countries*. Hence, the importance attached to such measures as gross *national* product (GNP) or gross *domestic* product (GDP) of states. (GNP is the total value of all the goods and services produced by a state's citizens or companies in a given year, no matter where the production takes place. GDP is the total value of all the goods and services produced within a state's territory in a given year, no matter the national identity of the producers.) GNP or GDP is a measure of the size of a country's economy. Based on the understanding that it is not so much countries that are well off or poorly off, but individual human beings, analysts also look at GNP or GDP *per capita* (per person), which is a measure of a country's standard of living. Obviously, a country can have a relatively high GNP but have a relatively low GNP per capita, such as India, while the converse is true as well, such as Norway. In recent years, there has been growing attention paid not only to the per capita income of countries but also to other indicators of national well-being. The UN Development Program has created a "Human Development Index" (HDI) which it has used to rank every country in the world on an aggregate measure that includes per capita income, average life expectancy, and percentage of the adult population that is literate. Table 6.1 shows the top twenty states and bottom twenty states on the Human Development Index. Not surprisingly, the countries that rank the highest on the HDI are found in the industrialized North, while those that rank the lowest are found in the less developed South, particularly in sub-Saharan Africa.

Earlier in this book I noted that post-Westphalian thinkers have raised normative issues regarding the rich-poor gap that exists not only between countries but also within countries. In addition to publishing HDI rankings of states, UNDP has collected data on per capita income, life expectancy, and

TABLE 6.1   Human Development Index Rankings

HDI Rank	Life Expectancy at Birth (years)	Adult Literacy Rate (%)	Real GDP per Capita (dollars)
High human development			
1 Canada	79.0	99.0	22,480
2 Norway	78.1	99.0	24.450
3 United States	76.7	99.0	29,010
4 Japan	80.0	99.0	24,070
5 Belgium	77.2	99.0	22,750
6 Sweden	78.5	99.0	19,790
7 Australia	78.2	99.0	20,210
8 Netherlands	77.9	99.0	21,110
9 Iceland	79.0	99.0	22,497
10 United Kingdom	77.2	99.0	20,730
11 France	78.1	99.0	22,030
12 Switzerland	78.6	99.0	25,240
13 Finland	76.8	99.0	20,150
14 Germany	77.2	99.0	21,260
15 Denmark	75.7	99.0	23,690
16 Austria	77.0	99.0	22,070
17 Luxembourg	76.7	99.0	30,863
18 New Zealand	76.9	99.0	17.410
19 Italy	78.2	98.3	20,290
20 Ireland	76.3	99.0	20.710
Low human development			
155 Benin	53.4	33.9	1,270
156 Tanzania, Rep. of	47.9	71.6	580
157 Djibouti	50.4	48.3	1,266
158 Uganda	39.6	64.0	1,160
159 Malawi	39.3	57.7	710
160 Angola	46.5	45.0	1,430
161 Guinea	46.5	37.9	1,880
162 Chad	47.2	50.3	970
163 Gambia	47.0	33.1	1,470
164 Rwanda	40.5	63.0	660
165 Central African Republic	44.9	42.4	1,330
166 Mali	53.3	35.5	740
167 Eritrea	50.8	25.0	820
168 Guinea-Bissau	45.0	33.6	861
169 Mozambique	45.2	40.5	740
170 Burundi	42.4	44.6	630
171 Burkina Faso	44.4	20.7	1,010
172 Ethiopia	43.3	35.4	510
173 Niger	48.5	14.3	850
174 Sierra Leone	37.2	33.3	410

Source: United Nations Development Program, *Human Development Report 1999* (New York: Oxford University Press, 1999), pp. 136–137. Data are for 1997.

literacy rates for different geographical regions, ethnic groups, or other categorical subgroups within a given state. Among the states that have the worst internal disparities are several "middle HDI" states not listed in Table 6.1. For example, commenting on a recent UNDP report, the *New York Times* points out that

> on Egypt, the report notes "disturbing contrasts" between rural Upper Egypt and Cairo province. While Cairo, measured as a separate state, would rank 69th in the world for human development, or just behind Turkey, Upper Egypt would stand in 125th place, below Cameroon. Upper Egypt has less than half the literacy rate of Cairo, while the average life expectancy is six years lower and incomes are 45 percent lower. . . . [In South Africa] the white and black sections of the population are not just two different peoples but "almost two different worlds." If white South Africa were a separate country it would rank 24th in the world in terms of human development, while black South Africa would be in 123rd place, just above Congo. . . . In Brazil, the report highlights the discrepancy in living standards between the more prosperous south and the impoverished northeast, where life expectancy is 17 years shorter, adult literacy 33 percent lower, and average incomes 40 percent lower.[1]

In Brazil, the richest 20 percent of the population account for roughly 65 percent of the national income, compared to 45 percent in the United States, whose income distribution pattern tends to be more egalitarian than that found in many developing countries but somewhat less egalitarian than that of many developed states. Globalization has brought uneven benefits, as some countries and some people clearly are doing better than others. There have always been rich-poor gaps, but there is some concern that these gaps may be widening in the post-Cold War era. In the world as a whole, "the number of people living on less than $1 a day appears to be rising and will reach 1.5 billion by [the early 21st century]."[2] At the same time, the number of billionaires in the world has been multiplying rapidly (e.g., during the 1990s, the number in Mexico increased from 1 to 24, and in the United States from 13 to 170).[3]

There are complex normative and empirical questions surrounding the international economy. What obligations do governments have toward their own citizens and toward foreigners in terms of improving material well-being? What are the forces driving the production and distribution of wealth on the planet? How much coordination of the world economy through international institutions is possible and desirable? This chapter seeks to provide an overview of the politics of international economic relations and the search for global governance in this issue area, concluding with a case study of the Uruguay Round trade negotiations that culminated in the creation of the World Trade Organization in 1995.

THE CHANGING NATURE OF INTERNATIONAL POLITICAL ECONOMY

The Context for Understanding Contemporary International Political Economy: The Contest Between Economic Nationalism and Liberal Internationalism from the Peace of Westphalia to the End of the Cold War

In order to understand the recent controversies swirling around the World Trade Organization and other aspects of the contemporary global economy, it is helpful first to retrace some history. In Chapter 3, in the historical narrative associated with the billiard ball paradigm, reference was made to the "mercantilist state," a description that characterized France and most other states in the early life of the Westphalian system during the seventeenth and eighteenth centuries. As Robert Gilpin has written, *mercantilism*, or "economic nationalism," took as "its central idea . . . that economic activities are and should be subordinate to the goal of state building and the interests of the state."[4] The mercantilist state was interested in economic matters mainly as they related to using government levers, particularly tariffs and other trade policies, in support of military power and conquest. Jacob Viner, an astute student of international political economy, explained the relationship between "power" and "plenty" in the following terms: "I believe that practically all mercantilists . . . would have subscribed to all of the following propositions: (1) wealth is an absolutely essential means to power, whether for security or aggression; (2) power is essential or valuable as a means to the acquisition or retention of wealth; (3) wealth and power are each proper ultimate ends of national policy."[5] The mercantilist state was far less concerned about the general welfare of the nation and citizenry at large. To be sure, monarchs had to be at least mildly attentive to their subjects' material well-being insofar as there was always the threat of domestic unrest and revolt, but Marie Antoinette's "let them eat cake" utterance reflected the prevailing mindset. The welfare state had not yet been born, as only the privileged few were thought to be entitled to enjoy the fruits of the nation's economic growth. Louis XIV and other rulers could hardly conceive of such notions as a "human development index" for their own people, much less for people living abroad.

The mercantilist model, which stressed the role of the state as a mode of organizing economic activity within and across national boundaries, was challenged by a competing model in 1776, when Adam Smith wrote *The Wealth of Nations*, which stressed the free market—laissez-faire, private enterprise, capitalist principles—as an alternative basis for economic relations. Smith became known as the father of "free trade," and his model became known as *liberal internationalism*. The liberal internationalist school of thought held that, even though national governments could be expected to pursue economic policies designed primarily to serve their own security and other national interests, there were benefits to be derived from cooperation with other states that could promote not only security but also wider prosperity. Smith argued that, in the process of inter-state competition over the distribution of the world's wealth, states shared certain mutual interests in collaborating to open up trade and investment opportunities for each other so as to maximize the special economic advantages of each country. Some countries might have particularly low labor costs, others abundant raw materials, and so forth. Ultimately, producers as well as consumers in all nations could expect to benefit from an international economy based on the most efficient use of resources. To this end, Smith called on governments to reduce tariffs and other "artificial" barriers to international economic activity and to allow goods and services to flow as freely as possible according to "natural" laws of supply and demand, so that the boundary between, say, Britain and France, would be no more an impediment to commerce than the boundary separating Paris and Marseilles.

Smith's ideas initially met with much resistance. In the United States, Alexander Hamilton was the leading early proponent of mercantilism. In his *Report on the Subject of Manufacturers*, presented to the U.S. House of Representatives in 1791, Hamilton urged that the federal government play a lead role in promoting America's industrialization and protecting domestic "infant industries" from cheap foreign producers so as to maximize national self-sufficiency and reduce U.S. dependence on foreigners; concerned not so much about the well-being of the average citizen but rather the economic assets of the nation as a whole, Hamilton stated: "Every nation . . . ought to endeavor to possess within itself, all the essentials of national supply. These comprise the means of subsistence, habitation, clothing, and defense."[6] In Germany, Friedrich List's *National System of Political Economy*, published in 1841, echoed Hamilton's economic nationalism. At a time when Great Britain had become the champion of free trade, List argued that London's liberal internationalism masked self-serving national interests; in the words of Gilpin:

> The British, List argued, had actually used the power of the state to protect their own infant industries against foreign competition . . . , and they only became champions of free trade after having achieved technological and industrial supremacy over their rivals. . . . List believed that the British were merely seeking to advance their own national economic interests by gaining unimpeded economic access to foreign markets through free trade. He regarded British promotion of what is now called an "interdependent world economy" as another expression of Britain's selfish national interests and believed that a true cosmopolitan world economy as espoused by economic liberals would be possible only when other nations became equal to Great Britain in industrial power. List . . . advocated political unification [of Prussia and other parts of Germany], development of railroads to unify the economy physically, and erection of high tariff barriers to foster economic unification, protect the development of German industry, and thus create a powerful German state.[7]

While it may well be that British support for liberal internationalism happened to square with British national interests, it was a position arrived at in London only after much internal, domestic conflict which pitted various economic groups in Britain against each other. The free trade doctrine was particularly appealing to the emergent merchant class of capitalist entrepreneurs who saw vast opportunities for economic gain once they were freed of government-imposed restrictions. However, entrenched economic interests who had benefited from the old mercantilist policies, notably aristocratic elites whose fortunes were tied to their land holdings and agricultural production, continued to seek government protection from foreign competition. As to which side in the debate best served the interests of the masses, it was not entirely clear, especially since public opinion was not yet being consulted. With the repeal of the highly protectionist Corn Laws in 1846, the internationalists won out as Britain launched an era of free trade that was to flourish over the next several decades and result in a tremendous expansion of worldwide commercial activity. Although throughout the nineteenth century, in Britain and elsewhere, liberal internationalism continued to be contested by economic nationalism, Adam Smith's dream seemed to be moving ever closer to reality. The laying of the first trans-Atlantic telegraph cable in 1866 allowed the movement of money from London to New York and back in a matter of minutes, and presaged the $ trillion a day computerized transactions that were to fuel global financial markets much later. Between 1870 and 1910, the British invested roughly a quarter of their savings overseas, in railroads, mines, and other enterprises in their colonies and in the United States. Economic ties between the major powers of Europe had become so expansive by the early 1900s that these states on the eve of World War I recorded unprecedented high levels of exports and imports as a percentage of gross national products. Some analysts went so far as to call the late nineteenth and early twentieth centuries "the belle epoque [beautiful epoch] of interdependence,"[8] while others at the time recognized interdependence as a mixed blessing, observing that "the world is, more than ever before, one great unit in which everything interacts and affects everything else, but in which also everything collides and clashes."[9]

In the first half of the twentieth century, between 1914 and 1945, a series of major "collisions and clashes" occurred that produced a revival of economic nationalism and arrested the nascent globalization trends which had been building previously. Erstwhile trading partners were trading bullets in World War I and World War II, and were trading relatively little of anything during the Great Depression in the interwar period. The combination of World War I, the Great Depression, and World War II took the Westphalian state to a new level of development, as the two world wars resulted in ever bigger military establishments (national security states) while the worldwide depression contributed to ever bigger economic establishments (national welfare states).

The welfare state was a newer creation than the national security state. The notion that national governments were obligated to concern themselves with job creation, social security, minimum wages, and other such matters that we now take for granted as the proper preserve of public policy—that the state, in other words, should be something more than a "nightwatchman" concerned merely with enforcing laws and keeping order—was rooted in the acceleration of the Industrial Revolution, the growth of the middle class, and the advent of mass democracy in nineteenth century Europe, all of which produced growing demands on government for benefits and services. Early welfare state thinking could be found in the writings of such thinkers as Jeremy Bentham, an Englishman who envisioned government playing a role in combating poverty and other social ills and whose ideas found expression in the enactment of the British Poor Law of 1834 and other reforms. Even in the United States, where historically the idea of a "strong state" and Big Government involvement in the economy has been overshadowed by a commitment to laissez-faire market principles, as early as 1886 the American Economics Association at its founding endorsed the role of the government as a problem-solver: "We regard the State as an agency whose positive assistance is one of the indispensable conditions of human progress."[10] Still, the AEA was referring more to the Hamiltonian role of the state in protecting individual property rights and facilitating commerce through road and infrastructure construction than to the role of the state as social engineer. Only somewhat later, during the Progressive Era at the onset of the twentieth-century, did reformers step up their call for the federal, state and local governments to improve working conditions, to monitor food and other products for possible consumer health hazards, and to rectify the gross inequities in income that were being produced by a capitalist system that allowed so-called "robber barons" to accumulate vast wealth.

However, it was not until the Great Depression in the twentieth century that the concept of "the welfare state" firmly took hold, associated foremost with another Englishman, John Maynard Keynes. At one point during the Great Depression, in 1933, unemployment in the United States and other countries reached 25 percent, raising questions whether markets could right themselves and resume high job growth. Keynes argued that governments everywhere should actively intervene in their national economy and engage in "fine-tuning," i.e., manipulate monetary and fiscal policy levers in response to whatever economic problems the country was experiencing, in particular stimulating the economy at a time of recession (as in the 1930s) through heavy public spending and tax and interest rate cuts and cooling the economy off at a time of inflation through the opposite measures. Franklin Delano Roosevelt's New Deal, which featured government jobs programs and other policies that eventually led to economic recovery, became the embodiment of Keynsian welfare state thinking and government intervention in the economy, although in Western Europe, even more so, efforts were made to develop "national industrial policy" around collaborative links between management, labor, and government. The "mixed economy" became the main model for industrial democracies, which remained committed to market-oriented capitalism but permitted a growing role for the state in socioeconomic planning and problem-solving as an alternative to the more extreme ideology of state ownership that the Soviet Union and some other states had adopted based on the earlier writings of Karl Marx. Marxism itself offered a third perspective on international political economy, one that viewed the global economy as revolving not so much around states and their national interests (mercantilism) or around the invisible, neutral hand of the market (liberal internationalism) but around an inherently exploitative set of relationships between capitalist classes and working classes worldwide.[11]

There remained the question of how compatible the welfare state and national industrial policy were with free trade and a liberal international economic order of the type that Adam Smith had envisioned and that had been evolving up until it was interrupted by twentieth-century war and depression. One form that government economic intervention took during the Great Depression in the interwar period was neomercantilist trade protectionism designed to shield one's own industries from foreign competition, symbolized by the infamous Smoot-Hawley Tariff Act passed by the U.S. Congress in 1930, which imposed extremely high tariff duties on agricultural and manufactured imports to the United States. Ultimately this measure proved counterproductive insofar as it sparked retaliatory tariffs by other countries and led to a general contraction of world trade and a deepening of global recession, contributing in turn to the outbreak of World War II.

The second half of the twentieth century proved more conducive to Adam Smith's ideas than the first half. After World War II, there was a new determination to lower trade and other economic barriers so that the "beggar thy neighbor" mistakes of the interwar period would not be repeated. Just as the British as the lead economy had been the champion of free trade in the nineteenth century, the United States as the dominant economy, with an interest in maximizing global market access, became the chief supporter of open borders in the postwar period. Some observers noted that the experiences of the interwar period, when there was no clear economic hegemon, showed that hegemony was a necessary underpinning for a free trade system.[12] Whether due to U.S. hegemony or simply the power of the idea of free trade, world trade did in fact increase more than twentyfold between 1945 and 1990. By 1990, imports and exports as a percentage of GNP in many countries had been restored to, and in some cases exceeded, their high pre-World War I levels, as once again it seemed global economic interdependence was poised to take off.

It is important to note, however, that through much of the post-World War II period the world economy reflected First, Second, and Third World divisions associated with the Cold War. Military security concerns continued to compete with economic concerns on national agendas in Washington and other capitals, with the former tending to dominate, given the overriding preoccupation with the geopolitical struggle between East and West. The major traders during the Cold War were two dozen Western developed capitalist (First World) states belonging to the Organization for Economic Cooperation and Development (OECD), by 1990 accounting for roughly 70 percent of all exports worldwide, selling mostly to each other. The United States was the single most active trading nation, although by the 1980s Japan and the European Union states had become major competitors, in part because Washington permitted its allies special access to the large American market as a way of solidifying the Western military alliance against the Soviet bloc (the Second World) and promoting economic prosperity in Western societies which might otherwise risk communist regimes coming to power. There was relatively little East-West trade, as Western governments imposed embargoes on the export of high technology and other items to Eastern states that might carry national security risks, while the latter themselves attempted to pursue a policy of autarky (economic self-sufficiency) within the Council on Mutual Economic Assistance (COMECON)—their counterpart to OECD—seeking to insulate themselves from Western trade winds that could upset their planned, command economies and create unwanted dependencies; during the 1980s, for example, roughly 30 percent of Soviet trade was with the West, 10 percent with developing countries, and the largest share with fellow East bloc members.[13]

Although the Western developed capitalist states during the Cold War traded mostly with each other, they came to rely on less developed countries (the Third World) as an important source of imports as well as markets for their exports. By 1990, almost one-third of the exports of OECD states were going to less developed countries. The exports supplied by the West were mostly industrial products and technology, including refrigerators, tractors and farm equipment, computers, and other items that had to be imported by developing countries to meet their modernization needs, although food and weapons were also major exports as well. To help pay for these costly imports, Third World countries exported various goods to the developed capitalist states, mostly primary products, either agricultural commodities such as coffee, bananas, or cocoa, or raw materials such as petroleum, chromium, or copper. Over time a few newly industrializing countries (NICs), such as Singapore, South Korea, Taiwan, Brazil, and Mexico, began to take advantage of cheap labor and other assets and to shift the composition of their exports away from primary commodities to labor-intensive consumer goods (textiles, shoes, toys) and semifinished or finished manufactures. Altogether, approximately 70 percent of the exports of less developed countries went to developed countries, with the less developed countries engaging in relatively little commerce among themselves, mainly because (except for the OPEC oil-producing states and a few others) they lacked sufficient purchasing power to generate a significant trade volume.[14] The pattern of strong West-West trade, limited East-West trade, and expanding West-South trade was to persist into the post-Cold War era, although, as we will discuss, the end of the Cold War produced some shifting trade winds and shifting international economic relations generally.

Trade is only one sector of the international economy. Capital is another.

Capital flows were also heavily influenced by Cold War politics during much of the post-World War II era. Foreign aid was targeted by both the United States and the Soviet Union at those states viewed as critical allies or client states. The first large-scale foreign aid program in the postwar era was the Marshall Plan administered by the United States, aimed at rebuilding the developed states in war-ravaged Western Europe. While most American foreign aid subsequently went to less developed countries, the political aims of the donor state played at least as much a role in determining aid relationships as the economic needs of the recipients. For example, during the 1980s, two-thirds of all aid was "security assistance" rather than "development assistance." Only one-fourth of all American aid went to the poorest, low-income developing countries. Between 1946 and 1987, the United States gave the bulk of its foreign aid to pro-Western or strategically placed states, with the major recipients being Israel and Egypt (each $13.8 billion), India ($11 billion), Pakistan ($6.7 billion), South Korea ($6.1 billion), Turkey ($4.3 billion), and Indonesia ($3.5 billion).[15]

As for the flow of private investment funds, the well-heeled OECD countries during the Cold War accounted for 95 percent of all foreign *direct* investment (that is, where finance capital is used by a firm, such as Ford Motors, to create new overseas enterprises or to buy up existing overseas enterprises as subsidiaries of the parent company, which exercises control over pricing, production levels, and other economic decisions of the foreign operations). Foreign direct investment multiplied rapidly after World War II, with roughly two-thirds of the total investment by OECD states targeted at other OECD states, mostly in the manufacturing, sales, and services areas. There was modest First World investment in communist economies, for example, Pepsi in the Soviet Union and Coca-Cola in China. OECD states continued their long-standing investment in the primary sector of Third World countries (mineral mining, oil drilling, agriculture, and other extractive activities) while stepping up investment in selective labor-intensive industries in the NICs of East Asia and Latin America, but these investments were dwarfed by West-West flows of capital. Developed capitalist states obviously were viewed as offering a more favorable investment climate than economically poorer and politically unstable Third World countries, where nationalistic regimes often threatened investors with expropriation of their assets, while investment in East bloc countries was limited by the East-West ideological divide. As one writer put it, "North America, Japan, and Europe [dominated] as originators and as destinations of most international investments."[16] As with trade flows, capital flow patterns were to persist in their basic structure into the post-Cold War period but with some new developments to be noted below.[17]

Hence, the second half of the twentieth century was characterized by a growing web of economic interdependence, albeit unevenly concentrated in the First World more so than the Second and Third worlds. The United States, in particular, pushed for an open world economy, constrained only by Cold War realities and by one other reality—the need to pay homage to the Keynsian welfare state and the right of national governments to adopt policies that in some instances might restrict trade and foreign investment in the name of protecting jobs, the environment, or some other values demanded by their citizenry. In an effort to reconcile the seemingly contradictory requirements of a liberal international economic order on the one hand and what amounted to liberal welfare state nationalism on the other hand, the United States and other countries, at least those in the Western camp, entered into what John Ruggie has called the "compromise of embedded liberalism."[18] That is, states agreed that they would work together to maximize free trade and open borders as much as possible, recognizing, however, that each state retained the sovereign right to pursue protectionist policies whenever conditions warranted. Through a variety of international institutions such as the General Agreement on Tariffs and Trade (GATT), the World Bank, and the International Monetary Fund (IMF), to be discussed, the hope was that states could collaborate and peaceably adjust their differences so as to avoid the mercantilism and neomercantilism of earlier eras.

The compromise of embedded liberalism—a commitment to capitalist precepts coexisting alongside statist engineering internally (through national industrial policy) and externally (through intergovernmental institutional management of differences where national policies conflicted)—worked remarkably well in the immediate post-World War II era. Buoyed by high economic growth rates in both the developed and developing world during the 1950s and 1960s, there was so much convergence around the idea of mixed economies mediated by international institutions that some observers went so far as to speak of "the end of ideology."[19] However, the 1970s saw economic growth rates slumping in the United States and elsewhere, as a period of "stagflation" (high unemployment and high inflation) occurred that befuddled Keynsian economic planners. World trade, which had climbed to $2 trillion by 1980, leveled off and remained stagnant over the next decade. Trade wars, which had been kept in check for most of the postwar period, became a growing concern.

This economic malaise led in the 1980s to rightist leaders coming to power—most notably, Ronald Reagan in the United States and Margaret Thatcher in the United Kingdom—who argued that leftist thinking was to blame for economic problems, that the welfare state had gone too far (exemplified by Lyndon Johnson's "War on Poverty"), that people had become overtaxed and overregulated by Big Government, and that what was needed was increased privatization, deregulation, and downsizing of public sector bureaucracy; included in their prescriptions were further reductions in barriers to the free flow of goods and services across national boundaries. Bumper stickers appeared on cars in American cities with the slogan "I love my country but hate my government." In a bit of irony, flag-wavers such as Reagan and Thatcher, who urged increased defense expenditures in support of the national security state, were unintentionally laying the seeds for a growing challenge to the nation-state and to the very idea of "country" by undermining the foundations of the welfare state through promotion of a borderless economy. These leaders adopted policies which ultimately produced economic expansion within their national economies and contributed to a resurgence of world trade and commercial activity by the early 1990s. The forces of globalization seemed to be on the march once again, as the economic interdependence trends that had been evolving since World War II became even more accentuated once the Cold War ended. Indeed, the seeming end of First World, Second World, and Third World divisions promised to make Western liberal democratic capitalism a universal creed, permitting the integration of the world economy in a way that had not previously been possible. However, some critics complained that, contrary to Reaganomics theory, the "rising tide" was not "lifting all boats" and that many states and many people were being left behind. The stage had been set in the post-Cold War era for yet another debate that would pit the forces of economic nationalism against the forces of liberal internationalism.

The Contest Between Economic Nationalism and Liberal Internationalism in the Post-Cold War Era: The Welfare State Under Siege

The 1990s was marked by ongoing ideological debate over how much weight to attach to the state, as opposed to the market, as the prime basis for economic organization. In the United States and most countries, there was a general understanding that what was to be avoided were either extreme Left policies (Communism, with a capital C, that meant a state-driven totalitarian repression of economic freedom) or extreme Right policies (Capitalism, with a capital C, that meant a totally market-driven, dog-eat-dog, survival-of-the-fittest, social Darwinism). Few wanted to follow the Marxist path, just as few wanted to return to the era of the robber barons; the debate was not over whether there should be some sort of safety net for those who fell between the cracks of economic growth, but rather how deep and wide the net should be. However, with the recent electoral victories of conservative parties in the United States and Western Europe, along with the defeat of communism in the Cold War, the middle ground had shifted somewhat toward the right. In order to get elected, leaders of leftist-leaning social democratic political parties began to distance themselves from their ideological roots and to co-opt some themes that business-oriented parties had successfully articulated. A new generation of leaders—Bill Clinton in the United States (running as a Democrat), Tony Blair in Britain (head of the Labor Party), Gerhard Schroder in Germany (a Social Democrat and former member of the Green Party), and Massimo d'Alema in Italy (former editor of the Communist Party newspaper)—were able to win office by reinventing and repackaging themselves as "Third Way" politicians who claimed to be forging a new consensus around the twin propositions that "the era of Big Government is over," yet government still had a critical if more modest role to play in the economic life of a country. In the 2000 U.S. presidential election, Al

Gore and George W. Bush competed neck-and-neck in their effor to see who could capture the broad middle ground, Bush offering "compassionate conservatism" as a counter to Gore's claim as Clinton's heir apparent.

Almost everywhere it seemed "Third Way" politics was in the ascendancy during the 1990s and into the new century. As one newspaper summed it up: "Britain, like Bill Clinton's America, is a transformed society, steered to a new entrepreneurial culture first by Margaret Thatcher and now through the pro-market centrism of Tony Blair; France is loudly proclaiming its loyalty to socialism [and its strong state tradition] while quietly installing a market-oriented culture; and Germany is struggling to begin reforms that would end what Chancellor Schroder has dismissively called the 'nanny state.'"[20] Headlines announced the drift to the right: "Sweden, the World's Role Model [as a Welfare State] Now Drifting as Currents Change"[21] and "To Spur German Economy, Schroder Offers Veer to Right."[22] Third Way politics was not confined to the rich industrialized countries. Witness such headlines as "A Chilean Socialist in the Clinton-Blair Mold [Elected President of Chile]"[23] and "Iran's President Would Privatize Big Industries."[24] Russia, since the Gorbachev revolution in the late 1980s, had been undergoing *perestroika*—economic restructuring and phasing out of top-heavy, inefficient state-run industries—which was remaking the former Soviet economy, although the hoped-for *glasnost* (a more open polity based on free elections and the rule of law) was still lagging. Even in China, one of the last bastions of communism on earth, wags could be found commenting that what remained of Marxism in the wake of Beijing's increasing movement toward privatization resembled "Groucho more than Karl."[25]

The current "Third Way" discourse is the latest turn in what has been a long-term historical process involving the evolution of national and international economics, a process I attempted to sum up in the previous section. Recall that the mercantilist state came into being in the first place when emergent capitalist elites in seventeenth-century Europe, frustrated by the barriers to commerce posed by the chaotic governance arrangements of the feudal era built around walled cities and other semi-sovereign entities, threw their support behind a Westphalian order based instead on centralized nation-states whose rulers could enforce contracts and impose uniform coinage and standardization of weights and measures throughout the realm. For the next several centuries, while the "state vs. market" debate unfolded, the nation-state remained the key actor in the world economy. That is to say, economic activity traditionally revolved mainly around producers in one country making goods within its borders primarily for home market consumption or perhaps for export abroad (trade). To the extent that capitalists in one country invested abroad in other economies, it tended to be in the form of *portfolio* investment, i.e., buying foreign stocks and bonds or making overseas loans, as in the case of the aforementioned British banking investments in American railroads during the latter part of the nineteenth century. Rarely did these foreign interests engage in *foreign direct investment*, i.e., seek actual ownership and control of the enterprises in another country through operation of subsidiaries, although it was noted in Chapter 3 that so-called "multinational corporations" were beginning to appear on the scene toward the end of the nineteenth century, coinciding with the movement toward a liberal international economic order—the examples cited were extractive MNCs such as Standard Oil and British Petroleum staking out claims to Middle East oil fields, and manufacturing MNCs such as American-based General Electric and Otis Elevator establishing overseas subsidiaries in Western Europe. Indeed, as early as 1902, F.A. MacKensie's *The American Invaders* was warning Europeans about increasing U.S. penetration of European economies, much as J.J. Servan-Schreiber's *The American Challenge* was to do sixty years later.[26]

Still, the cataclysmic events of the first half of the twentieth century prevented these trends from flowering. Only after World War II did the multinational corporation phenomenon really take off, when technological and other factors (discussed in Chapter 3) contributed to their growing "global reach," and only after the Cold War did their reach extend so far as to be called by some observers "imperial corporations."[27] Recalling statistics cited earlier, there are today over 35,000 MNCs, controlling over 200,000 subsidiaries. Just 500 corporations control 70 percent of world trade, almost half of which is intrafirm (from one subsidiary to another), and the 300 largest transnational firms control roughly a quarter of the world's productive assets. Although the bulk of finance capital continues to flow from developed states to other developed states, the *UN Human Development Report* noted in the 1990s that "one of the most remarkable developments of the past decade has been the acceleration in private investment flows to developing countries."[28] Likewise the World Bank's *World Development Report* observed there was "an explosion of international flows of long-term capital to developing countries in the 1990s."[29] Private investors are increasingly being looked to by developing countries as a source of capital in lieu of foreign aid as governments have become stingier with "official developmental assistance." It is important to note, however, that thus far private foreign direct investment funds mainly have been targeted at two-dozen NICs in Asia and Latin America, such as China, Malaysia, Thailand, Argentina, and Mexico. As for former East bloc states, "Western companies have . . . begun to invest [more heavily] in the old East bloc. . . . At some point investment is likely to flow in the other direction. Perhaps early in the 21st century . . . a Czech company will make *Fortune's* top 100."[30]

What should we make of all this? Although it has long historic roots, the modern multinational corporation is a relatively young actor on the world stage, whose future implications can only be speculated about. With its tentacles now connecting national economies in every corner of the planet, in every sector (agricultural, manufacturing, services), fueled by the Internet and the latest wave of technological developments, it has become the key agent for the globalization of the international economy. (The term "globalization" itself did not enter the IPE discourse until the 1990s, to connote the seeming triumph of Western liberal-democratic and capitalist principles worldwide.) The important point to be underscored here is that some see the MNC as potentially revolutionizing not only international economic relations but international relations as a whole, insofar as it appears that, just as emergent capitalist elites by 1648 had outgrown the feudal system, their contemporary counterparts recently have outgrown the nation-state, giving rise perhaps to an altogether new set of governance arrangements. It is possible that, in the twenty-first century, we may once again see war and depression on a scale which could stop globalization trends, but, as discussed in Chapter 3, cobweb analysts argue that we are on the brink of a post-Westphalian era marked by not only a new agenda of issues but also a new set of actors which are fundamentally transforming world politics. Thomas Friedman has put it this way: "The symbol of the Cold War was a wall, which divided everyone. The symbol of the globalization system is a World Wide Web, which unites everyone. The defining document of the Cold War system was 'The Treaty.' The defining document of the globalization system is 'The Deal.'"[31]

Friedman offers an interesting contrast between the imagery of the Berlin Wall vs. that of Wall Street. Whether globalization and the demise of the territorial state is the wave of the future will be determined not only by corporate and other elites but also by mass publics, where they are permitted to have a say. Surely, one of the most important and intriguing story lines to be followed over the next several decades is the tension between welfare state nationalism, which remains a potent force, and world-without-borders capitalism, which seems to be picking up ever increasing momentum—as Robert Gilpin has put it, "the clash between the integrating forces of the world economy and the centrifugal forces of the sovereign state."[32] Meanwhile, globalization is certainly playing havoc with the "compromise of embedded liberalism" and the functioning of the welfare state. As one observer notes, it threatens to undermine "the capacity of the individual . . . state to control its own economic future. At the very least, there appears to be a diminution of state autonomy."[33] Thomas Friedman has vividly described how globalization is constraining the capacity of national governments to maintain control over their national economies:

> When your country . . . recognizes the rules of the free market in today's global economy, and decides to abide by them, it puts on what I call "the Golden Straitjacket." . . . To fit into the Golden Straitjacket a country must . . . adopt . . . the following golden rules: making the private sector the primary engine of its economic growth, . . . shrinking the size of its state bureaucracy, maintaining as close to a balanced budget as possible, . . . eliminating and lowering tariffs on imported goods, removing restrictions on foreign investment, getting rid of quotas and domestic monopolies, increasing exports, privatizing state-owned industries and utilities, . . . opening its industries, stock and bond markets to direct foreign ownership and investment. . . . The Golden Straitjacket narrows the political and economic policy choices to relatively tight parameters. . . . Governments . . . which deviate too far from the core rules will see their investors stampede away, interest rates rise and stock market valuations fall.[34]

If economics is now "a continuation of war by other means," it is both countries and companies which are savagely competing in the global marketplace and which are both feeling pressures to downsize—to be "lean and mean"—in order to survive and prosper in an open world economy. In order to attract and keep the capital of the "electronic herd" (what Friedman calls both the "short-horn cattle" engaged in portfolio foreign investment as well as the "long-horn cattle" engaged in direct foreign investment related to multinational corporations), governments often find themselves in a "race to the bottom" to cut taxes and regulations, including such things as minimum wages and workplace safety rules; in seeking to offer an attractive investment climate, governments are concerned not only about enticing foreign firms which can create new jobs, but ensuring that their own native firms do not relocate overseas. While Friedman argues that globalization on balance will produce more winners than losers, he acknowledges that some parts of society will suffer, at least in the short run, as safety nets shrink along with government entitlements long enjoyed by some groups . For example, in the United Kingdom recently, "in a nation where free education is considered as much a basic right as free health care or social security benefits, the announcement [that British college students for the first time would have to pay tuition] was taken as a sign that Prime Minister Tony Blair's government is intent on dismantling many of the most sacred vestiges of Britain's old-style welfare state."[35] The end of free tuition in the UK sparked protests, although none as violent as occurred in Mexico, where the tradition of free higher education at the 275,000-student National Autonomous University "ran headlong into a new world and a new Mexico" as shrinking public spending caused a rethinking of the government's generous tuition policy, leading to masses of students occupying and closing down the huge campus for several months in 1999.[36] Especially in highly statist political cultures, such as France, threatened governmental cuts in public sector employment and social spending have been met with widespread strikes and demonstrations.

Some analysts have argued that, ultimately, there is a point at which the downsizing of the welfare state can become counterproductive in terms of attracting and keeping business within one's borders. That is, investors are not just attracted to states where there are low wages, low taxes, and low regulations. If the latter were the key magnets for capital, then states such as Somalia and Haiti would be booming economically. Clearly, firms in many instances are also looking for states which offer good roads and other infrastructure that can facilitate commerce, an educated work force that can enhance productivity, a law enforcement system that can protect and enforce contracts and property rights, and internal political stability that reduces the risk of violent upheaval (which itself ordinarily requires that rich-poor gaps not become excessively skewed).[37] This means that, even in the age of globalization, there remains the need for well-run "welfare states" that collect enough revenue and have enough "capacity" to provide the kinds of public goods that undergird a thriving economy. In Friedman's words, business does not want a bigger state, but it does want a higher quality state, "a better state, a smarter state and a faster state, with bureaucrats that can regulate a free market, without either choking it or letting it get out of control."[38]

"Control" is the critical variable. Even if there is still a place for the welfare state in the twenty-first century, loss of control over national economic policy figures to increase rather than decrease as globalization proceeds. It stands to reason, for example, that, as governments in Western Europe and elsewhere privatize state-run airlines and permit transnational ownership, their grip on a major sector of their economy becomes looser. And, as one's society is subjected to ever greater foreign economic penetration, it becomes that much harder to tweak Keynsian fiscal and monetary policy levers unilaterally. Stephen Krasner is a leading billiard ball thinker who sees things differently, claiming that "large, highly developed states" are better able than ever to "mitigate or adjust to pressures emanating from the international environment [such as dependence on foreign capital]," while "small underdeveloped states" have always been vulnerable and "remain extremely vulnerable."[39] The suggestion here is that countries like the United States are relatively immune to such external influences as the "Asian flu," which started in 1997 with a financial panic involving the plummeting of Thailand's currency and quickly spread to Malaysia and other neighboring countries as foreign investors pulled their money out of the region, leaving national economies in shambles. But the more common view is that the economies of virtually all countries, including that of the United States, are becoming increasingly hostage to external forces. Granted there has never been any golden age of state control, the multinational corporation and unprecedented capital mobility[40] pose extraordinary contemporary challenges to the viability of nation-states, even the most powerful ones. One recent book, which examines "U.S. foreign economic policy-making in an era of global interdependence," goes so far as to bear the title of *America the Vincible*.[41]

Governments can try to reassert control, but there are potential costs entailed of the type indicated by Friedman (e.g., the Malaysian government recently tried to stem the flight of foreign capital by imposing currency controls at the border, but risked alienating and scaring off investors wanting easy convertibility of their money). Admittedly, some governments may be better positioned than others to exercise an upper hand vis-à-vis corporations, but all governments may find they have their hands tied to an extent. In order to assess whether, as Raymond Vernon opined, we are witnessing "sovereignty at bay" and the emergence of "new sovereigns" in the form of giant multinational firms, let us more closely examine two sets of relationships—MNC-*host* country (government) relations and MNC-*home* country (government) relations.

MNC-Host Country (Government) Relations.   By host government is meant the government of a country in which a foreign-based MNC operates subsidiaries. For various reasons, foreign MNCs and host governments tend to have a love-hate relationship. In less developed countries (LDCs) especially, MNCs are often credited with creating jobs, introducing modern technology, and generally helping the host country's balance of payments by bringing in fresh capital and helping to develop export industries through their subsidiaries. However, Third World critics of MNCs argue that they ultimately take more out of a country than they contribute, using a variety of devices to evade host government taxes, squeezing out smaller local firms, drawing away the most talented indigenous human resources (creating a "brain drain"), and reaping enormous profits that are repatriated to the home country rather than reinvested in the host country.

In the view of the latter critics, MNCs are not only exploitative of less developed countries but are often so enmeshed in the economy of a host country that they are able to dominate its political life as well. Much like company towns, entire countries have at times been under the sway of a single company (e.g., Liberia, until recently, under the control of Firestone Rubber). Although the "one company" country is rarely if ever found today, many foreign MNCs control huge sectors of host country economies in the developing world. For example, "foreign affiliates control 32 percent of production, 32 percent of exports, and 23 percent of the employment of Brazil's manufacturing sector. In Singapore foreign affiliates control 63 percent of production, 90 percent of exports, and 55 percent of employment in manufacturing."[42]

Given their pervasive presence in less developed economies, foreign MNCs have often been able to exert considerable influence over host government domestic and foreign policy. However, as developing countries have become increasingly sensitive about foreign penetration, in some cases they have become more assertive in their dealings with MNCs. The most obvious case of host governments exercising power against MNCs was the successful efforts of OPEC countries to gain ownership of (i.e., at least 51 percent controlling interest in) the oil production facilities operated by oil companies within their borders. Although many developing countries have tried to follow the OPEC example, few have had the degree of leverage enjoyed by the oil producers, so that get-tough policies against MNCs have frequently resulted in their closing up shop in the host country and transferring their movable assets elsewhere to a more hospitable business environment.[43] In the post-Cold War era—with Marxist rhetoric about "expropriation" being out of fashion, with developing countries looking to attract increased foreign investment, and with MNCs looking for new investment opportunities—MNC-LDC relations have been marked more by mutual accommodation than antagonism, although there remains concern about the threat to state autonomy.

Sensitivity to foreign economic penetration is not confined to less developed countries. As suggested in Servan-Schreiber's *The American Challenge*, many developed countries in Western Europe and elsewhere have expressed concern over growing foreign MNC involvement in their economies. Although the governments of these countries have usually been better positioned to exercise greater control over MNC activity than their counterparts in the Third World, they have often found MNC subsidiaries within their borders resistant to their authority (e.g., the German government has had difficulty in getting subsidiaries of U.S. firms to abide by the German national policy of facilitating worker representation on corporate boards of directors). Nonetheless, developed states increasingly seem hooked on globalization. In the new Europe under the European Union, although "age-old nationalistic sentiments" still can block cross-border mergers,[44] what were once thought to be national treasures are being sold to the highest bidder, often a foreign-based MNC, as in the case of Britain's storied Rolls Royce company purchased by BMW of Germany in 1998. Even in the defense sector, a state-owned aerospace and arms enterprise such as France's Aerospatiale is in the process of being privatized and becoming part of a large European conglomerate (tentatively called the European Aerospace and Defense Company), to compete with America's giant defense contractors, Boeing and Lockheed Martin[45]; this represents quite a departure for France, which, ever since the mercantilist era of Louis XIV, has sought as much self-sufficiency as possible in its capacity to defend itself from foreign threats.[46] In Japan, which traditionally has been relatively closed to foreign investment, a slumping economy has contributed to greater wooing of foreign capital of late (e.g., by the end of the 1990s, foreign stockholders owned 45 percent of Sony stock, while General Motors, Renault, and other companies were being welcomed as potential investors in Japanese subsidiaries).

Perhaps nowhere is there a better example of foreign penetration of a developed country economy than in Canada, where U.S. companies alone in recent years have owned or controlled over 90 percent of Canada's theaters, 55 percent of its manufacturing sector, and 70 percent of its oil and gas industry, figures that help account for the fact that Canada remains America's single biggest trade partner.[47] American dominance in the area of culture is seen in the fact that "only 3 to 5 percent of all theatrical screen time in Canada goes to Canadian films; 96 percent of profits from films shown in Canada go out of the country, 95 percent to the United States; 95 percent of English-language TV drama is non-Canadian; Canadian-owned publishers have only 20 percent of the book market; 77 percent of the magazines sold here are foreign; 85 percent of record and tape sales are non-Canadian."[48] The Canadian government has been under increasing domestic political pressure to lessen foreign control, at the same time that Washington is pressuring Ottawa to open up its economy even more in return for easier Canadian access to the U.S. market.

Even in the United States, where the domestic economy is so large that foreign economic penetration accounts for only a small fraction of total economic activity, there has been growing concern over increased direct investment by foreign interests engaged in the "buying of America"[49]—such slices of "Americana" as Beverly Hills estates and hotels (by Arab interests), Rockefeller Center in New York City (by the Japanese), Holiday Inn (by the British), and, most recently, industrial icons like Chrysler (by the Germans) and Amoco (by the

British). In fact, by the mid-1980s, the United States—long the predominant home (headquarters) country of MNCs—had become the predominant host country as well, attracting more direct investment than any other single state.[50] One author notes:

> Overseas investors can now claim ownership to over one-half of the U.S. cement, tire, and consumer-electronics industries, 40 percent of the nation's gold-mining capacity and heavy-truck production, one-third of the chemical industry, . . . and a rapidly expanding percentage of the machine-tool, book publishing, automotive parts and record companies. . . . Approximately 13 percent of the jobs in Delaware and 6 percent in South Carolina are supplied by foreign companies, and the Japanese alone provide 5 percent of all civilian employment in Alaska. Foreigners own over one half of the commercial property in downtown Los Angeles, about 40 percent in Houston, one-third in Minneapolis, and 20 percent in Denver. . . . The Japanese own 6 of the 12 largest banks in California, and account for about one-quarter of the deposits and more than 30 percent of the business loans in America's most populous state.[51]

These trends were the basis for Robert Reich raising the provocative question I alluded to in Chapter 3—"Who is 'US'?". While foreign investment in the United States generally has been perceived as economically healthy in terms of job creation and other benefits, and has been encouraged by the federal government as well as state and local governments (e.g., the numerous Japanese "transplants" dotting the American landscape), certain areas of the American economy have remained off limits. In particular, where foreign direct investment is thought to create potential risks for national security, as in the communications and air transport sectors, major restrictions apply (e.g., current American law prohibits foreigners from owning more than a 25 percent stake in U.S. radio and television stations or more than a 49 percent stake in U.S. airlines). In the agricultural sector, although foreigners own less than 1 percent of the 1 billion acres of private farmland in the United States, compared with much more sizable holdings by United Brands and other U.S.-based agribusiness MNCs in Latin America and elsewhere, many states in the American farm belt have become so alarmed at the prospect of foreign takeovers that they have passed legislation that severely restricts foreign ownership of farmland.

In the case of both less developed countries and developed countries, one can see that host governments are extremely ambivalent about foreign MNCs within their borders. There is a special concern that subsidiaries controlled from abroad will become "Trojan horses," serving the interests of the home country in which the parent firm is headquartered rather than the host country. This leads, then, to a consideration of the nature of MNC-home government relations.

MNC-Home Country (Government) Relations.   If MNCs often pose problems for host governments, what about MNC relations with their *home* government? It is curious that although MNCs are commonly portrayed by Marxist and other critics as agents of home government domination of foreign lands, the evidence is mixed as to whether MNCs fully act in the interest of and under the control of their home state. As they do with host governments, MNCs tend to have a love-hate relationship with home governments as well.

It is true that MNCs typically have special bonds with the nation-state in which they are headquartered, insofar as their ownership and top management tend to be made up predominantly if not exclusively of nationals of the home country. In a few cases such as Unilever, the giant British-Dutch consumer goods conglomerate, there is joint control by two countries. However, such internationalization of ownership and management is rare. More typical is Nestle, the Swiss-based MNC, which is required to have 51 percent of its voting stock held by Swiss citizens. In a recent study based upon *Fortune's* Global 500, of the top 30 U.S. firms listed, only five had a foreigner as a member of their executive boards.[52] Ties between Japanese MNCs and the Japanese government have been so close over the years that Japan is often referred to as "Japan, Inc."

In other ways, too, notwithstanding all the talk of globalization, MNCs appear to be rooted in their home state. Statistics were cited earlier indicating that only 18 companies in *Fortune's* Global 500 maintain the majority of their assets abroad, and only 19 maintain at least half of their workers abroad. "Even the icons . . . of corporate globalization—from Coca-Cola through Ford to McDonalds—. . . [are heavily home-state oriented]. Coca-Cola has no foreign shareholdings, more than half its assets are in America, and over 40 percent of its sales are at home. Ford, which is famous for trying to produce the 'global' car, still has 80 percent of its assets in America. As for McDonalds—the corporate embodiment of global spread—two-thirds of sales and over half its assets are still in America."[53] This has led some scholars to write about "the myth of the global corporation."[54]

It is also true that MNCs have often been used as instruments of home state foreign policy. Attempts by the U.S. government to use foreign subsidiaries of American MNCs to serve U.S. foreign policy ends are well documented. For example, the U.S. government, relying on the Trading with the Enemy Act passed by Congress, used its control over IBM to prevent IBM's French subsidiary from exporting high technology from France to the Soviet Union and other East bloc states during the Cold War. More recently, in 1997, the U.S. government ordered Wal-Mart (headquartered in Arkansas) to ban the import of Cuban pajamas by its Canadian subsidiary, as part of an anti-Castro campaign waged under the Helms-Burton Amendment passed by the U.S. Congress. Just as the U.S. government "uses" American MNCs, the latter "use" the U.S. government. As one example, Jeffrey Garten describes how, in 1994, U.S.-based Raytheon "was in heated competition with a French firm for a Brazilian contract to build an environmental-surveillance system for the Amazon. Our French foe was heavily subsidized by its government, so we swung into action. [The U.S. Secretary of Commerce] made two trips to Brazil. . . . The head of NASA called his Brazilian counterpart and said our cooperation with them in outer space would be lost if the French got the deal . . . . The Export-Import Bank extended the most far-reaching financing available, and Clinton called the president of Brazil. Raytheon won—and Massachusetts got 20,000 new jobs."[55] The sense of partnership between the U.S. government and U.S. MNCs over the years is captured in the observation that in support of American business abroad, Washington "has landed Marines in half a dozen Caribbean countries, threatened to cut off aid to several dozen others from Peru to Sri Lanka, and at some point put other forms of pressure on almost every [other government]."[56]

However, tensions can arise between MNCs and their home government, in the U.S. case as well as other cases, with MNCs at times engaging in activities that are seemingly at odds with home state interests and beyond home state control. While the Raytheon example shows how governments frequently intervene on behalf of their corporations for purposes of domestic job creation, home government problems in reducing domestic unemployment are often aggravated by "runaway shops," whereby MNCs relocate their factories from the home country to another country in which the labor force can be hired at cheaper wages (e.g., American workers fear that, as trade barriers are eliminated between the United States and Mexico, U.S. companies will be increasingly tempted to shift production to subsidiaries south of the border, or will be able to use the threat of relocation as leverage to resist worker demands, because the average hourly compensation for workers in manufacturing in the United

The impact of globalization: The Smith-Corona typewriter company moves its North American operations to Mexico. (Danziger © The Christian Science Monitor. Used by permission.)

States is $14.83, compared with $1.85 in Mexico).[57] As Republican hopeful Pat Buchanan put it during the 1996 U.S. presidential primary campaign, "What's good for General Motors is not good for America if General Motors has become a transnational corporation that sees its future in low-wage countries and in abandoning its American factories."[58]

Even in regard to foreign policy concerns, MNC and home government policies are not always in synch. One need only consider the relations between U.S. oil companies and Washington. At the beginning of World War II, the U.S. State Department had difficulty getting U.S. oil companies to terminate their close ties with German companies operating in Latin America. During the 1970s, Texaco and others among the Seven Sisters were essentially pursuing their own "foreign policy" based on their individual interests, as was described earlier. By the early 1980s, Pittsburgh-based Gulf Oil had invested over $500 million in Angolan facilities and maintained a cordial working relationship with the Marxist Angolan government, at a time when 15,000 Cuban troops were helping the government ward off a pro-Western faction seeking power with the support of the Reagan administration.[59] And when the U.S. government reached agreement in 1999 with the governments of Turkey, Georgia, Azerbaijan, and Kazakhstan to collaborate on an oil pipeline route that would carry oil from the Caspian Sea to ports in the West, bypassing Russia and Iran, it was unclear whether U.S. oil companies would support the chosen route; even though the agreement was hailed by the U.S. Secretary of Energy as "a strategic agreement that advances America's national interest," one analyst reminded that "any pipeline would have to be paid for by oil companies and their partners . . . , and they have warned that they will make their decision based on commercial rather than political considerations."[60] (The latter case is a great example of how billiard ball and cobweb phenomena can collide, as there are elements of both classic inter-state sphere-of-influence geopolitics—particularly the U.S. desire to beat the drum for an oil route that would deny Russia or Iran control over important energy resources—as well as nonstate actors marching to their own drummer.)

Acknowledging the ambivalent nature of MNC-home government relations, Raymond Vernon predicted some time ago that as these relations evolve, the identity of MNCs "is likely to become more and more ambiguous in national terms. Commingling human and material resources of many nations, formulating problems and solutions on lines uninhibited by national boundaries, multinational enterprises may not be as easy to classify in terms of national association."[61] Vernon's prescience can be seen in the growing wave of "strategic alliances" forged between MNCs based in different countries, exemplified by the "One World Alliance" and "Star Alliance" coalitions recently created among competing airline interests worldwide.[62] Another observer adds "it may be only a matter of time before the buildup of overseas assets, professional recruitment in international markets, and global networking within companies transforms the culture of companies into something that is no longer 'national.'"[63] (As one example of where trends are leading, Coca-Cola in 1999, for the first time, selected as its CEO an executive who started with its international operation—an Australian named Douglas Daft—while Nestle in the 1990s was led by a German and mostly non-Swiss general managers despite being Swiss-owned.)

Although no MNC has yet established its world headquarters on an island free of any country's sovereign control or nationalistic pressures, as the head of Dow Chemical once dreamed, some see the divorce of the MNC from the nation-state as already final. "The allegiance of the world's largest corporations is purely to their bottom lines," writes one commentator,[64] echoing the remarks of a CEO of a major American multinational firm: "The United States does not have an automatic call on our resources. . . . There is no mindset that puts this country first."[65] However, before one rushes to judgment about divorce proceedings, it is well to remember that home governments still have the authority ultimately to restore control over their MNCs, given the vast regulative role that modern societies have assigned to government. The question is whether, in an age of globalization, that role is now being given over to other governance bodies beyond the level of the nation-state—a subject to be treated in the next two sections of this chapter.

GLOBAL GOVERNANCE: EFFORTS AT DEVELOPING INTERNATIONAL ECONOMIC REGIMES

Comparing regime-building in the economic sphere with that in the peace and security area, Charles Lipson comments: "Conflict and cooperation are, of course, commingled in both [sets of] issues, but . . . economic issues are characterized far more by elaborate networks of rules, norms, and institutions."[66] In Chapters 3 and 4, it was noted that governments as well as business elites have long had a felt need for a degree of order—a relatively predictable, uniform pattern of expectations—in international economic relations so as to facilitate economic activity across national boundaries. Raymond Vernon has perhaps said it best, commenting on the need for states to pool sovereignty, especially in an age of globalization: "As governments try to apply unilateral responses to . . . [economic] problems, they stand an excellent chance of damaging both their own national interests and the interests of the multinational enterprises on which they depend. The challenge is to find the multilateral approaches that can reduce the inescapable tensions to manageable proportions."[67]

Billiard Ball Politics

As mentioned in the historical context provided earlier in this chapter, there was much attention given to international institution-building in the economics issue area after World War II, as states sought to avoid the beggar-thy-neighbor, mercantilist economic warfare that produced disastrous results during the period between the world wars. While it was not an accident that the lead state in the international system with the most to gain from a relaxation of economic barriers, the United States, became the main champion of free trade and an open world economy, other states as well recognized the folly of the interwar period and were persuaded to adopt a liberalization ethos as long as it did not undermine their sovereignty and their ability to protect their national interests. The compromise of embedded liberalism after World War II was facilitated by three UN-affiliated IGOs—The General Agreement on Tariffs and Trade (GATT), the International Bank for Reconstruction and Development (the World Bank), and the International Monetary Fund (IMF)—that together formed the underpinnings for the "Bretton Woods international economic order," named after the city in New Hampshire where forty-four nations met in 1944 to draft a plan for postwar economic reconstruction. GATT was to deal with one of the "three c's" sectors of the international economy—commerce (trade)—while the World Bank and IMF were to address the other two—capital and currency.

Initial attempts to create an International Trade Organization alongside the World Bank and IMF failed when the 1947 Havana Conference could not agree on how much power to permit the trade body to have in regulating commerce. Although leaning toward free trade, the United States Congress in particular raised concerns about sovereignty. In lieu of the ITO, GATT was created in 1948 as an "interim" institution that could provide a global forum for multilateral negotiations aimed at reducing tariff and nontariff barriers. For nearly fifty years, GATT, headquartered in Geneva, Switzerland, remained the major international trade forum, with its membership of over 100 countries (predominantly First World states but including many Third World states as well as a few Second World states) responsible for more than four-fifths of all world trade. In the words of one official, "GATT . . . provided a rule of law for world trade" and represented "an attempt to banish into history the jungle of restrictions and bilateral dealings that strangled world trade in the 1930s like jungle weed."[68] It was replaced in 1995 by the World Trade Organization (WTO), a body which has occasioned a renewed debate over sovereignty and whose story is told in the case study at the end of this chapter.

Headquartered in Washington, D.C., the World Bank consists of more than 180 member states, including former East bloc states that finally joined in the 1990s. Although most foreign aid traditionally had been given bilaterally, the World Bank was conceived as an important new multilateral aid vehicle. The Bank was to obtain its funds mainly through soliciting government subscriptions and issuing interest-bearing bonds and notes purchased by governments as well as investors in the private sector. These funds were then supposed to be loaned to needy governments on relatively generous terms, particularly by the International Development Association, the "soft loan window" of the Bank, which was authorized to offer fifty-year repayment periods at low interest rates.

Although the Bank over the years has played an indispensable role in providing capital to less developed countries, many problems have arisen, not the least of which is the servicing of the more than $1 trillion debt that borrowing countries have accumulated. As suggested in the earlier discussion, developing countries increasingly have turned to the private sector, to commercial bank lenders and other investors, to meet their capital needs, as bilateral and multilateral aid flows have not kept pace with the demand for financial resources to support economic development.

The IMF was created to address currency concerns that could inhibit international trade and destabilize the international economic order. Its purpose was, first, to provide in emergency situations a central fund of hard currency reserves that could be made available to countries experiencing balance of payments deficits (i.e., had greater outflows than inflows of money in their international economic transactions) in order to ease liquidity problems and, second, to provide a central forum for negotiating adjustments in currency values in order to prevent disruptive fluctuations in exchange rates.. Between 1945 and 1971, the system operated essentially on the basis of "fixed" foreign exchange rates, with most currencies valued in relation to the U.S. dollar as well as to gold. The value of the dollar was fixed at $35 per ounce of gold, meaning that any foreigner holding dollars could redeem them for a set guaranteed amount of gold if they wished. However, after foreign dollar holdings had reached the point where they exceeded U.S. gold reserves, the dollar-and-gold standard became less tenable since the United States could not ensure its ability to back up the claim that the dollar was "as good as gold." After 1971, the international monetary system began operating on the basis of "floating" exchange rates, with the relationships between different countries' currencies determined mostly by what values they had on the open market, although there remained some intergovernmental coordination within the IMF to try to keep currency fluctuations within reasonable limits. By the 1990s, the IMF had grown to more than 180 member states, its ranks having swelled with the addition of Russia and other former East bloc countries. Headquartered in Washington, D.C., near the World Bank, the IMF and the Bank have increasingly found themselves with overlapping and duplicating missions, as each has competed to become the major global IGO in the field of international economic development.

The UN Economic and Social Council (ECOSOC) was to have been the linchpin through which all the intergovernmental machinery devoted to global economic problem-solving was to be coordinated, much like the UN Security Council was conceived as playing a pivotal role in the military security field. However, for various reasons, ECOSOC has been largely ineffective in carrying out its mandate to integrate the efforts of GATT, the World Bank, the IMF, and other UN specialized agencies. Part of the problem is that each specialized agency has had its own distinct membership, headquarters secretariat, and budget, with little incentive to pursue a common set of policies. More problematic, the UN membership has been unwilling to entrust ECOSOC with any real decision-making power. Initially composed of 18 states, including the economically most powerful ones, ECOSOC has mushroomed to 54 members, with its decision-making competence declining as its size has increased.

A lot of the politics of global governance in the economic issue area can be understood in classic billiard ball terms, that is, as a game played between nation-states, involving power, national interests, national prestige, and other elements of the Westphalian culture. In particular, developing countries have long complained that the major global institutions responsible for coordinating the world economy have been dominated by the developed states belonging to OECD, and especially in recent years by the Group of Seven (G-7), led by the United States. For example, Third World states, viewing GATT as a "club for the rich" that limited its membership to those states meeting OECD economic criteria, for many years tried to utilize the larger UN Conference on Trade and Development (UNCTAD) as their preferred forum for global trade negotiations, but failed to persuade the OECD states to take it seriously. Decision making in the World Bank is based on weighted voting. Member governments are assigned voting power according to the size of their capital contribution to the Bank; G-7 states account for almost half of the total shares in the Bank, with the United States being the largest single contributor. Likewise, OECD states, led by the United States and Japan, have dominated decision making in the IMF, having two-thirds of the votes due to a weighted voting system based on each state's financial contributions to the central fund of currency reserves. There has been an informal understanding that an American would ordinarily head the World Bank, while a European would ordinarily head the IMF. (As a vivid example of the staying power of nationalism, there was a hotly contested debate in 2000 over who should be the executive head of the IMF. One writer noted: "France has long been an ardent advocate of the idea of Europe—a Europe led by Frenchmen. And Paris has been ruthless in its determination to put its nationals in charge of everything from the IMF to the European Central Bank. At some point, however, Europe's largest nation was going to demand its turn. Given that a Frenchman has headed the IMF for . . . 32 of the last 37 years . . . the Germans figured that it was about time they got a chance."[69] The United States also had its own candidate in mind, as did other states. Suffice it to say, nobody from the developing world need apply for such positions.)

Billiard ball politics could especially be seen in the great debate over the New International Economic Order (NIEO) during the 1970s, which was played out mainly in the UN General Assembly. It pitted rich states (the 40 or so OECD member countries of the industrialized North) vs. poor states (the over 100 countries of the less developed South, referred to as the Group of 77), with each bargaining group seeking to shape global governance over trade and other economic concerns according to its own interests.[70] The UN-commissioned Brandt Report at the time captured the nature of the battle-lines:

The North including Eastern Europe has a quarter of the world's population and four-fifths of its income; the South including China has three billion people— three quarters of the world's population but living on one fifth of the world's income. In the North, the average person can expect to live for more than seventy years; he or she will rarely be hungry, and will be educated at least up to secondary level. In the countries of the South, the great majority of people have a life expectancy of closer to fifty years; in the poorest countries, one out of every four children dies before the age of five; one-fifth or more of all the people in the South suffer from hunger and malnutrition; fifty percent have no chance to become literate.[71]

The sheer size of the South's coalition, along with different levels of development within the group (e.g., the existence of Fourth World states even worse off than Third World states) made it difficult at times to forge a single Southern negotiating position. Nonetheless, the Group of 77 displayed a high level of solidarity in pushing for a new set of international economic relationships that they argued would produce a more equitable distribution of wealth. Although many differences existed in the Northern coalition as well, these states nonetheless tended to close ranks behind the principle that LDCs should rely less on global negotiations aimed at broad changes in international economic relations and more on self-help and internal reforms aimed at promoting free enterprise.

It is worth examining briefly the exact nature of the demands made by the South in regard to the NIEO, since many of these demands are still on the table today, even though the stridency of the rhetoric has subsided and even though the Group of 77 has found it harder to sustain itself as a cohesive bargaining group given the substantial socioeconomic improvements that have occurred in some LDCs (notably the NICs) since the 1970s. In the commerce sector, the South sought better terms of trade, including reductions in Northern tariff and non-tariff barriers against cheaper Southern products, such as textiles, where the imposition of so-called "voluntary export restrictions" (VERs) amounted to quotas aimed at protecting workers in industrialized countries. In the capital sector, specifically regarding foreign aid, the South urged greater efforts by the North to meet the aid target established during the UN Development Decade of the 1970s (i.e., at least 0.7 percent of the North's combined GNPs allocated for development assistance), greater Northern willingness to cancel debts of Southern countries in serious balance of payments difficulties or to negotiate longer repayment schedules, and more loans at cheaper interest rates with fewer strings attached. As for foreign private investment, the South pushed for a code of conduct for MNCs that would limit the profits companies could repatriate to their home country, prohibit MNC interference in host country domestic politics, and strengthen host country capacity to retain control over its natural resources and to regulate foreign subsidiaries. In the currency sector, the South objected to the IMF's tendency to withhold benefits from developing countries unless their governments agreed to adopt often painful "structural adjustment" policies calling for draconian cuts in their public expenditures and services aimed at enforcing sounder fiscal management. The South above all urged a greater LDC role in the governance of the IMF and other IGOs concerned with economic matters. They went so far as to propose a World Development Authority and other new bodies in which voting would be less tied to financial contributions and economic power.

The South's NIEO demands largely went unmet as the United States and other lead states during the 1980s resisted calls for what they saw as a global welfare state. By the end of the 1990s, the rich-poor gap that the Brandt Report had called attention to had, if anything, widened. The UN Development Program in 1999 reported the following statistics:

> The income gap between the fifth of the world's people living in the richest countries and the fifth in the poorest was 74 to 1 in 1997, up from 60 to 1 in 1990 and 30 to 1 in 1960. . . . By the late 1990s the fifth of the world's people living in the highest-income countries had . . . 86% of world GDP [while the bottom fifth had just 1 %], 82% of world export markets [compared to the bottom fifth's 1%], 68% of foreign direct investment [compared to the bottom fifth's 1%], and 74% of world telephone lines [compared to the bottom fifth's 1.5%].[72]

While many of the NIEO demands remain on the global agenda, in some cases being reformulated and repackaged, LDCs remain generally powerless to get these adopted as global public policy. Meanwhile, alignments have become more complicated. What is now called the Global South is a highly diversified collection of states, including not only the aforementioned bottom fifth (the forty or so countries labeled by the UN as "least developed," typified by Bangladesh and Ethiopia), but also relatively high-income OPEC countries like Saudi Arabia and Kuwait along with NICs such as Singapore, Taiwan, and Brazil and "next NICs" such as Thailand and Malaysia, as well as Russia and other former East bloc developed countries—with some of these states becoming quite integrated into the world economy and others at risk of becoming quite marginalized. As complicated as global governance of the international economy has become in billiard ball terms, it is all the more complex when one injects cobweb elements into the analysis.

Cobweb Politics

This chapter has discussed at length how MNCs are playing havoc with the nation-state, particularly the functioning of the national welfare state. There are other nonstate actors which, along with MNCs, are having enormous impacts on the workings of the world economy and on efforts to improve global governance in this issue area. Cobweb forces compete so vigorously with billiard ball forces in the economic realm that I have suggested one might think of global policy processes in this issue area as dominated by "middle politics." We have seen how the simple state-centric paradigm can help us understand a lot of what goes on in international political economy. We need to balance this with an examination of how the cobweb paradigm offers at least equal explanatory power and, with its multilayered perspective, can arguably furnish richer insights.

In discussing global governance, we need to remember that regionalism in many parts of the world constitutes an important intermediate layer of relationships between the nation-state and global IGOs. The European Union (EU), profiled in Chapter 3, can be thought of as a regional IGO, as an experiment in regional governance, in response to globalization on a regional scale. The Chapter 3 profile pointed out that, in many respects, economic policy-making in Western Europe no longer occurs at the national level but through elaborate EU-wide institutions. With the advent of the Euro as a common currency now used by most EU members, this makes it all the harder for any one member government to utilize Keynesian fiscal and monetary policy levers in the service of one's national economy (e.g., no longer can these governments independently lower interest rates in their countries in an attempt to fight recession, and no longer can they devalue their currencies in an attempt to reduce a trade deficit). EU officials, representing the European Commission, are empowered to speak for the fifteen member states at global conferences dealing with economic issues. In short, the EU for all intents and purposes is a more important actor on the world economic scene than France, Germany, Britain, or any other individual Western European state. The North American Free Trade Agreement (NAFTA), created in 1994, is a parallel regional governance arrangement on the other side of the planet, currently consisting of the United States, Canada, and Mexico. Limited at this point to putting the finishing touches on a free trade area among the three member states, it is not nearly as far along institutionally or geographically as the EU, but some envision a regional IGO that eventually stretches from the Arctic to the Andes and presides over a single economic space throughout the Western Hemisphere. Even less developed as a regional IGO than NAFTA is the Asia-Pacific Economic Cooperation (APEC) forum, created in 1989, which involves some two dozen Pacific Rim states, including the U.S. and Canada; the long-term objective of the membership is trans-Pacific free trade by 2020. There are subregional entities as well, such as the Southern Cone Common Market (Mercosur, including Argentina, Brazil, Paraguay, and Uruguay) and the Association of Southeast Asian Nations (ASEAN, including a few states in APEC). One of the great challenges for global governance in the twenty-first century is to ensure that these regional integration projects do not simply substitute economic regionalism for economic nationalism, i.e., do not undermine efforts to promote an open world economy at the global level. Then, too, remember that alongside these McWorld forces exist Jihad forces, such as the proliferation of overseas trade offices and trade missions established by state and local gubernatorial and mayoral officials in the United States, who see themselves as economic ambassadors for their particular polity.

The executive heads of the World Bank, IMF, and other IGOs, along with their secretariat bureaucracies, can be thought of as autonomous actors helping to shape global policy. Although it is true they owe their appointment to the powerful states whose resources these IGOs depend on, they nonetheless often play important roles in their own right in agenda-setting (taking initiatives in identifying problems requiring attention), policy formulation and adoption (serving as honest brokers), and, of course, implementation (administering programs and monitoring compliance). In the case of the IMF, the organization has often been criticized by developing countries for exercising excessive power over their economies in forcing taxing, spending, and interest rate reforms as a requirement for assistance. According to one newspaper account of an international trade summit meeting in Thailand in 2000, a demonstrator threw a pie in the face of the chief of the IMF, reflecting the fact that "many people in Asia have held [him] personally responsible for the region's woes."[73] The World Bank has also become increasingly intrusive in the internal affairs of developing countries, threatening to deny loans to governments which do not clean up rampant corruption or do not utilize the funds for specified socioeconomic purposes.

Moreover, the World Bank and aid donors generally (including the United States and other governments) in recent years have often bypassed Third World governments completely and instead have channeled aid to poor countries through NGOs (feminist groups, village cooperatives, or other nongovernmental entities such as CARE), on the assumption that "NGOs can better reach the grassroots level, that NGOs . . . involve less bureaucratic red tape and overhead, and that working with NGOs helps to develop the private sector."[74] One author notes that "while foreign assistance has declined over the past decade, NGOs have received an increasing share of it. In 1975, donor governments channeled $100 million through local NGOs. . . . By 1988, this figure rose . . . to $2.1 billion. . . . Governments see themselves as the sole legitimate source of political power within a given territory. While they coexist with other organizations—families, corporations, and religious groups—they ultimately seek predominance over them. Transnational links scramble this effort. They puncture the veil of state sovereignty."[75] In what may be a glimpse of growing IGO-NGO-MNC linkages in a post-Westphalian future, the *New York Times* ran a story in 1999 on how "big companies" in the name of good corporate citizenship were becoming "unlikely allies with the United Nations," as AMOCO, Cisco Systems, and other firms were funding community projects in poor countries and relying on the UN Development Program and other IGOs to help administer the projects.[76]

Few countries can count on corporate largesse to meet their development needs. The main sources of capital remain foreign aid (official developmental assistance) of the multilateral or bilateral variety and foreign private investment of the portfolio or direct variety. As foreign private investment displaces foreign aid as the bulk of international capital flows, NGOs which rate countries as to their creditworthiness are becoming highly influential nonstate actors. Thomas Friedman describes one such actor:

> Moody's is the credit rating agency that signals the electronic herd of global investors where to plunk down their money, by telling them which countries' bonds are blue-chip and which are junk. That makes Moody's one powerful agency. In fact, you could almost say that we live again in a two-superpower world. There is the U.S. and there is Moody's. The U.S. can destroy a country by leveling it with bombs; Moody's can destroy a country by downgrading its bonds.[77]

Another NGO, the International Chamber of Commerce, has played a role in developing uniform global rules and guidelines governing transactions relating to contracts on the sale of goods and other such matters. Still other NGOs operating in the economic field include transnational business lobbies representing specific industries as well as transnational labor organizations pushing for worker rights.

As an example of the myriad transnational, national, and subnational actors which find themselves congregating in global forums and participating in global economic governance today, it is instructive to look at those in attendance at the 1995 UN World Summit for Social Development held in Copenhagen, Denmark. The gathering included government officials from 180 countries (among them 117 heads of state), 2,780 NGO representatives (many of whom convened in their own special "alternative" NGO Forum), dozens of multinational corporation executives, hundreds of IGO secretariat members (from not only the World Bank and IMF but the International Labor Organization, the World Health Organization, the Food and Agriculture Organization, and other UN specialized agencies having a stake in economic issues), and 2,800 media reporters. This meeting was the latest in what one reporter characterized as a "traveling United Nations global road show—fresh from appearances in Cairo [at the 1994 world population conference], Vienna [at the 1993 UN human rights conference], and Rio [at the 1992 Earth Summit on Environment and Development] . . . a global parliament on wheels and wings."[78] The Copenhagen meeting was intended to focus attention on what might be done to alleviate global poverty and unemployment. It was not the United States or other wealthy states that put these issues on the agenda and could claim credit for organizing the meeting; the idea was first proposed by Chile's UN ambassador years earlier and was taken up by UN Secretary-General Boutros Boutros-Ghali, who called for a "new social contract" that would recognize how economic deprivation in one part of the world affected every other part. Among the proposals floated was a tax on speculative international currency transactions that would be placed in a UN development fund, as well as a new UN Economic Security Council. What was ultimately adopted by the Summit added little to existing international regimes. The conference issued a non-binding ten-point declaration reiterating the plea for rich nations to spend 0.7 percent of their

GNP on foreign aid and to provide debt relief for poor countries, and urging donor countries to earmark 20 percent of their aid for "basic needs" human services. The NGO Forum, claiming to represent "international civil society," produced its own Alternative Declaration of Principles that was far more radical in its demands.

Not surprisingly, poverty-related issues have not made their way to the top of the global agenda and resulted in major policy adoption any more than they have been given the highest priority on national, domestic agendas. Still, even though such international conferences often produce more words than actions, they nonetheless represent an attempt to raise global consciousness. The growing inclusion of NGOs seems also to mark a democratic and participatory turn in such diplomacy. The UN is not a "global parliament," even if the dapper figures in three-piece suits engaging in voting on proposals at Copenhagen and elsewhere may give the appearance of such. Yet there are times when far-reaching decisions are taken in global settings, and new regimes created that have the force of law, with the potential to dramatically reorder international economic relations. As noted in Chapter 3, there is in fact "a complex but rich system of governance growing up to manage globalization." An especially important venue where globalization is being managed today is the World Trade Organization. That the WTO has become a lightning rod of controversy lately reflects the significant issues at stake in that body. The mini-case study that follows illustrates the mix of billiard ball and cobweb politics that gave rise to the WTO and that continues to characterize governance in this area.

THE URUGUAY ROUND TRADE NEGOTIATIONS AND THE 1994 MARRAKESH AGREEMENT CREATING THE WORLD TRADE ORGANIZATION

For some eight years, from 1986 to 1994, delegates from over 100 countries met in a series of trade talks known as the Uruguay Round, which culminated in the Marrakesh Agreement that established the World Trade Organization (WTO) as the successor to GATT as the primary global trade forum. Many observers would agree that the Uruguay Round "was without question the most complex and protracted multilateral trade negotiation in history."[79] The Marrakesh treaty itself was 22,000 pages long. It was signed in Marrakesh, Morocco by 117 states on April 15, 1994. Within six months, 81 countries accounting for more than 90 percent of world trade—all the major industrialized countries as well as most major developing countries—had ratified the treaty, permitting the WTO to be born on January 1, 1995.

The preamble to the Marrakesh Agreement embodied the liberal internationalist school's view of global commerce. WTO members agreed to enter into "reciprocal and mutually advantageous arrangements directed to the substantial reduction of tariffs and other barriers to trade and to the elimination of discriminatory treatment in international trade relations." These words rested on a fragile consensus that had been forged among developed and developing countries during the Uruguay Round. To understand how that consensus was reached, and whether it can be sustained in the future, we need to examine the regime-making process from agenda-setting to implementation.

We have already seen that the story of international trade politics is centuries old, and that the modern phase of the saga began with the creation of GATT after World War II. The main principles adopted by GATT were the following: First, where governments felt a need to protect domestic industries, protection should be accomplished primarily through tariffs rather than quotas and other nontariff barriers. Second, governments should work gradually toward reduction of the general level of tariffs through multilateral negotiations based on the most favored nation principle, i.e., when one member state lowered tariffs on certain kinds of imports from another member state, all member states were entitled to the same favorable treatment with regard to their goods. Third, any trade disputes that might arise among members should be settled through established procedures of the organization rather than states taking unilateral actions that could spark trade wars.

Hence, free trade was on the global agenda long before the Uruguay Round. A series of seven GATT negotiations were conducted over the years, including the so-called Kennedy Round (1963–1967) and Tokyo Round (1973–1979), which succeeded in substantial tariff reductions, particularly on industrial goods, where tariffs were cut by an average of 35 percent from their 1945 level. However, by the early 1980s, it was clear that if the liberal trade regime was to be strengthened further, there was a need not only to involve more states but also to address protectionist practices in areas where GATT rules were weak or nonexistent, such as agriculture, textiles, tropical products, and services, and to improve dispute settlement procedures.

It was the United States that took the initiative to call for a new GATT round in 1982. The United States was concerned about a number of issues. Its overall balance of trade was experiencing a mushrooming deficit, with imports exceeding exports by over $100 billion annually. Its share of world agricultural exports had been in decline due to foreign governments' illiberal trade policies that included both export subsidies for their farmers as well as tariffs and quotas on imported foodstuffs (e.g., Japan totally banned access to its rice market to protect its rice farmers, while the European Community, later renamed the European Union, had a long-standing "Common Agriculture Policy" designed to shield European poultry, soybean, corn, and other farmers from foreign competition). As the American economy shifted increasingly from manufacturing to services—by the 1980s, two-thirds of the labor force was employed in the service sector—the United States sought greater access to foreign markets in such fields as telecommunications, banking, insurance, and publishing, where the United States enjoyed a competitive advantage. As the technology leader in many fields, the United States was also concerned about strengthening the rules relating to infringement of trademark and patent rights and preventing pirating of CDs and other copyrighted materials, which foreign producers were clandestinely reproducing in violation of World Intellectual Property Organization (WIPO) guidelines. Since it had the most open market in the world economy (except in the area of textiles and a few other products), the United States felt it was generally in its national interest to push for a regime that would encourage wider free trade. Washington threatened to retaliate against foreign governments if they did not take steps to reduce trade-distorting tariff and nontariff barriers, export subsidies, "dumping" of foreign goods in the American economy (i.e., foreign producers flooding the U.S. market with goods sold below production costs or below home market prices, to gain market share), and pirating of intellectual property.

Within the North, there was considerable dissension, especially between the United States, which wanted agriculture on the agenda, and the European Community and Japan, which did not. At OECD ministerial meetings, at G-7 economic summits, and "more discreetly through a series of meetings among the Quad (i.e., U.S., EC, Japanese, and Canadian) trade ministers,"[80] Washington was able gradually to build support for new GATT negotiations, using the stick of threatened unilateral trade sanctions and the carrot of still greater access to the rich American market as well as protected Third World markets. Within the EC itself, many members were beginning to question the wisdom of the Common Agricultural Policy, which was consuming 60 percent of the total EC budget and was strongly supported only by France and Ireland. The South also experienced dissensus. Most developing countries were wary of accepting new intellectual property restraints and opening up their markets to developed states in the service sector in return for vague promises on the latter's part to reduce voluntary export restrictions on tropical products, textiles, and other LDC labor-intensive manufactures. However, there was a growing realization in the South that statist, protectionist policies had failed to promote economic development, that the NIC experience showed how LDCs could benefit from promoting trade and foreign direct investment, and that intellectual property safeguards were vital to attracting such investment. The LDCs were less willing to accept minimum international labor and environmental standards that the United States had proposed, viewing these as potentially undermining their competitiveness and inhibiting their exports. The Cold War at the time was still raging, so that the East-West axis of conflict prevented most of the command economies of the East bloc states from participating in the market-oriented GATT.

Ernest Preeg describes the critical bargaining that preceded the beginning of the Uruguay Round in 1986:

> An informal group of industrialized countries, the "Dirty Dozen," held a series of private meetings and produced the first comprehensive ministerial declaration. For tactical reasons, the three large members—the United States, the EC,

and Japan—temporarily withdrew from the group while the smaller industrialized countries joined with about twenty moderate developing countries to further develop and circulate the draft. Other developing countries joined, the big three rejoined, and the now forty-eight participants formally constituted themselves as the G-48 [co-chaired by a Swiss and a Colombian]. . . . The cohesion of the G-48 [which included the likes of Singapore, Malaysia, South Korea, Chile, and Mexico], cutting across North/South lines, put the hardliners [a group of ten LDCs, led by Brazil and India] on the defensive and forced them to produce their own G-10 draft. . . . A separate yet overlapping country realignment that took place during the summer of 1986 related to the agricultural sector. . . . [Six] agricultural exporters—Australia, Chile, Colombia, Thailand, New Zealand, and Uruguay—submitted a joint paper calling for substantial trade liberalization in this sector. The group expanded to fourteen, adding Argentina, Brazil, Canada, Fiji, Hungary, Malaysia, and the Philippines [the so-called Cairns Group].[81]

Partly as a bone thrown to the South, to symbolize the stake that LDCs had in the talks, it was agreed that the GATT negotiations would be launched at Punta del Este, Uruguay, in September 1986. As described by Preeg, "chilling winds greeted the two thousand delegates from seventy-two countries."[82] The G-48 vs. G-10 alignments had replaced the old OECD vs. Group of 77 alignments, and even the Soviet Union had suddenly requested observer status (which, though rejected, was a portent of the winding down of the Cold War). Negotiating groups were established in fifteen areas, focusing on such topics as tariffs, nontariff barriers, agriculture, textiles, tropical products, services, intellectual property, and dispute settlement. Over the next eight years, as the talks rotated between developed and developing country sites, "economic dichotomy between North and South would fade, between East and West disintegrate. . . . Globalization would be the catchword for a brave new world of traders and diplomats."[83] Before that outcome, however, much bargaining remained to be done, and not just between nation-states based on national interest and power relationships but among a host of actors engaged in two-level and three-level games.

For example, the U.S. delegation at Punta Del Este consisted of seventy-five members, including three Cabinet-level officials (the U.S. Trade Representative, the Secretary of Commerce, and the Secretary of Agriculture), fifty-eight others from Executive Branch agencies (including State and Treasury), nine leaders of the corporate community, two labor union representatives, two farm sector leaders, and one member of Congress. "James Robinson, chairman of the American Express Company, and Edmund Pratt, chairman of Pfizer Corporation, highlighted U.S. priority interests in trade in services and protection of intellectual property. Director Rudolph Oswald of the AFL-CIO commented that the labor representatives were there 'as the heavies to complain about the $150 billion trade deficit and the two million jobs lost'"[84] and to push for fair trade as preferable to free trade. Big Labor saw the enemy not so much as foreign countries as Big Business, epitomized by Nike, which was contracting to have its tennis shoes for the American market made in Indonesia, where the average wage for experienced workers (mostly females) was $.82 a day, compared to a minimum daily wage in the United States of $33, and was considering relocating to Vietnam to produce goods even more cheaply and profitably.[85] The farm organization representatives were complaining that "by the mid-1980s, American agriculture was squeezed by the worst collapse in farm-asset values in a half century"[86]; in 1986, the Rice Millers Association had petitioned Washington to pressure Japan to open up its rice markets, while American soybean growers and other farm belt interests were applying similar pressure for Washington to move on the European front. In the backdrop was the Multilateral Trade Negotiations Coalition, a group of 14,000 private American companies generally pushing for trade liberalization, although spokespersons for some industries, such as textiles, were worried about the U.S. Trade Representative moving not too slow on free trade but too fast. Hence, U.S. negotiators at the GATT talks were trying to empathize with foreign interests articulated by their diplomatic counterparts across the table from them, while representing "American" interests, at the same time looking over their shoulder and behind their back trying to reconcile the diverse interests of various bureaucracies and pressure groups, some of which formed natural alliances with each other (e.g., DOA with the farm lobby and Commerce with the business lobby).

As the Uruguay Round talks ensued, as numerous proposals were advanced and debated, similar internal conflicts were played out within other delegations, with the domestic politics more complex the more economically developed and the more open the national society. Recalling our earlier discussion, "at the domestic level, many diverse actors, whose alliances may shift, participate in trade policymaking. The formation of coalitions between elements of the state [bureaucracy], the legislature, and other actors are affected by the structure of domestic preferences [and the nature of domestic political institutions]."[87] The end of the Cold War by 1990 only exacerbated the role of domestic politics, and also contributed to some loosening of the glue that had bound the United States with its ideological allies. Perhaps no group was more vocal and militant than French farmers. According to one commentary, "deep connections between national identity and rural heritage existed, and even among urbanites a 'quasi-religious attitude to food' was said to prevail."[88] Even so, reactions in 1992 to the U.S.-brokered Blair House accord, a side agreement which called for the EU to reduce farm export subsidies and increase market access, were unusually hostile: "French farmers staged angry protests and rioted across the country; seventy tractors surrounded the airport at Lille; three thousand farmers demonstrated in Paris, burning the U.S. flag and using sledgehammers to demolish a Coke machine; and farmers in Bordeaux attacked a McDonalds and clashed with riot police."[89]

Interest groups operated transnationally as well. Although NGOs were not permitted nearly the direct access to participation in the trade talks as they were in other UN forums, they nonetheless were heard. Earlier, in 1990, 30,000 European farmers (not just French) had marched in protest in Brussels, which at the time was playing host to GATT meetings and where the European Commission and other EU bodies were engaged in trying to work out a common European trade policy. On the pro-free trade side, the pharmaceutical sectors in the United States, European Union, and Japan consulted and mobilized across national boundaries to persuade governments to do away with barriers in this area; similarly, on the issue of strengthening intellectual property rights, "close collaboration developed between the U.S. Intellectual Property Committee, the Union of Industrial and Employers' Confederation of Europe, and the Japanese Keidanren."[90] Among the nonstate actors which played a role in policy formulation and adoption were "epistemic communities" that provided technical data and research reports on trade issues, such as the Trade Policy Resarch Centre in the UK. The GATT secretariat itself was looked to for analytic expertise, as well as relied on to chair the various working groups. According to one account, the executive head of GATT played an indispensable role in moving the proceedings along: "Peter Sutherland and his senior deputies . . . developed a detailed negotiating strategy for the complex diplomatic endgame ahead. Sutherland himself would initially remain above the day-to-day group negotiations, engaging instead in a high-visibility public campaign to keep political leaders committed to a successful outcome. He spent most of September and October [of 1993] traveling to capitals in industrialized and developing countries, explaining that December 15 was the final deadline for the Uruguay Round and that failure to take necessary decisions would be politically damaging to everyone."[91]

Ultimately the endgame occurred successfully, as the Uruguay Round concluded on December 15, 1993, with the formal signing scheduled to follow on April 15 in Marrakesh, Morocco. Even such early holdouts as Brazil and India came on board. (The agreement was almost derailed when the United States insisted that the EU eliminate its rules permitting member governments to subsidize their film and television industries and to limit non-European TV programs to 49 percent of viewing time, a practice defended most vociferously by France, but was salvaged when Washington withdrew the issue from the table.) The new international trade regime that was adopted incorporated some of the demands made by developing countries (reduction of tariff and nontariff barriers, including VERS, against textiles, tropical products, and other goods LDCs enjoyed a comparative advantage in) and some of the demands made by the developed countries, most notably the United States (liberalization of trade in services and in agriculture and elaboration of intellectual property safeguards). Although loopholes remained (e.g., import quotas on textiles and export subsidies for certain foodstuffs would not be terminated immediately but would be phased out over several years, while certain service sectors were not covered), the consensus view, as expressed in an Indonesian newspaper, was that "the success of the final stage of GATT talks reflects the recognition by world leaders from both the industrialized and developing nations that global free trade is beneficial."[92] Understandably, there was still lingering resentment on the part of some LDCs who saw the exercise as just another power play: "The agreement . . . was in truth an accord between the United States and the European Union [and Japan]. . . . It is not the GATT of the whole world but that of the rich and powerful."[93]

One of the last issues to be resolved was perhaps the single most momentous provision of the Marrakesh Agreement—the creation of the WTO in place of GATT. Although old-fashioned nationalism and power politics could be seen at work in the haggling over the governance structure of WTO, in the end an institution was created that combined Westphalian and post-Westphalian designs. Canada's trade minister originally had proposed the WTO as a successor to GATT in 1990, following informal discussions within "the Quad." The United States was at first lukewarm to a new trade organization, worried that it would limit its freedom of maneuver, but eventually accepted the WTO as part of the overall package of compromises. Policy decisions in the WTO, headquartered in Geneva, Switzerland, were to be made by consensus as much as possible, but, to avoid paralysis, could be taken if necessary by majority rule based on a one-state-one-vote formula. That is, unlike the IMF and World Bank, decision making in the WTO would not be based on weighted voting tied to economic clout; and unlike the UN Security Council, no state, however powerful, would have a veto privilege, although certain amendments did require unanimity. Regarding the new dispute settlement procedures, any state accusing another state of being in violation of the Marrakesh rules could take the latter before an independent panel of trade experts, which would be entrusted with investigating the complaint and rendering a judgment that could then be further reviewed by a three-member appellate panel; if the defendant state were found guilty of violating free trade obligations and refused to comply with the panel's judgment, member states could then legally take trade sanctions against the state in question. U.S. concerns about being subjected to a possible "tyranny of the majority" (akin to the majority of Third World and Second World states who were able to dominate the UN General Assembly in the 1970s) were offset by the assurance that in its sovereign capacity it could always withdraw from the WTO upon giving a few months' notice and that few WTO members would want to run the risk of destroying the organization by alienating the state with the largest, richest market in the world through repeated adverse rulings; besides, Washington was confident that, having the most open economy in the world, it would win more often than lose in free trade dispute cases. The ambitious nature of the new regime was reflected in the decision to call the IGO the World Trade Organization, as opposed to the Multilateral Trade Organization, which was the name considered initially.

Following the signing ceremony on April 15, 1994, it remained for the 117 participating delegations to return home and obtain the necessary ratifications that would enable the treaty to go into effect. An interesting political drama unfolded in the American political system, where coalitions of strange bedfellows formed in support of and against the treaty. On one side, opposing the agreement, were conservatives such as Jesse Helms, Pat Buchanan, and Ross Perot along with liberals such as Ralph Nader, Richard Gephardt, and the representatives of various environmental and labor union groups (the AFL-CIO, the Sierra Club, and others). The conservatives were mainly concerned about the threat to U.S. sovereignty posed by the majority-rule voting procedures in the WTO and the binding nature of the dispute settlement procedures that, in the words of Buchanan, empowered "foreign bureaucrats who will meet in secret to demand changes in U.S. laws."[94] The specific concern was that, if an act of Congress—say, legislation banning asbestos imports—was found to be in violation of the Marrakesh free trade provisions, Washington would be expected to rescind its national law or face sanctions by the world body; there was also concern for "states' rights," if California or any other state should be forced to abrogate its own legislation in deference to the WTO . The liberals were not concerned about a nascent world government so much as the failure of the Marrakesh Agreement to include adequate international labor and environmental standards that would protect American workers from a flood of cheap imports made in some cases by child or prison labor and would protect American consumers from tainted fruits and vegetables and other products that possibly threatened environmental harm; they predicted a worsening of the aforementioned "race to the bottom" if, in order to remain competitive in an open world economy, businesses and governments had to lower wages and environmental regulations. (For example, Teamsters President James Hoffa asked how American truckers could be expected to compete when "a fifteen-year old sitting on an orange crate may be driving an eight-wheeler truck from Mexico into the U.S. now that trucking safety rules at the border were being relaxed."[95])

On the other side, endorsing the agreement, were conservatives such as Newt Gingrich, Bob Dole, George Bush (as an heir to Ronald Reagan), and the Wall Street corporate community, along with liberals such as Jimmy Carter, Al Gore, and Bill Clinton. The conservatives were driven mainly by their faith in the private sector and free-market economics and the promise of expanded investment opportunities, while the liberals were driven by a commitment to internationalism and a determination to promote multilateral cooperation that could avoid future trade wars. This coalition argued that allowing China and other protectionist states into the WTO could provide a wedge to force their closed economies to become more laissez-faire and their closed political systems to become more democratic. The pro-free trade coalition won out, as it had a year or so earlier during the domestic debate over the creation of NAFTA, allowing the United States to become a charter member of the WTO in 1995 along with 80 other countries. By 2000, the WTO membership would climb to 135, with Russia and China clamoring to join.

There is an important postscript to the story. The future of WTO remains clouded for a variety of reasons. Some of the worst fears of the Buchanan-Nader coalition have been realized. For example, a panel in Geneva recently upheld Mexico's complaint that the U.S. Marine Mammal Protection Act was a violation of free trade; the legislation had been passed by Congress to prohibit the import of tuna caught with nets that killed dolphins. A WTO panel also ruled that a section of the U.S. Clean Air Act discriminated against foreign oil refiners in Brazil and Venezuela by banning certain kinds of gasoline imports thought to increase pollution.[96] While the United States itself has initiated and won some complaint proceedings against other states, a conservative-liberal axis composed of isolationist-oriented populists and statist-oriented environmentalists and labor union activists threatens to undermine American domestic support for the WTO. Similar coalitions have been forming in other countries as well, where concerns are being raised about the growing rich-poor gap some see accompanying globalization. These forces came to a head in the so-called "Battle of Seattle" in 1999, at a WTO summit meeting attended by the 135 member governments that was marked by angry street demonstrations on the part of thousands of protesters—"environmentalists, human rights activists, the anti-sweatshop movement, and a whole grab bag of groups concerned about everything from saving the sea-turtles to saving teamster jobs."[97] The protesters were attacking what they saw as an elitist alliance between "GATTzilla" (their name for the WTO) and the multinational corporations, arguing that the meetings had been largely closed to NGOs and grassroots movements and were obsessed with free trade to the exclusion of other issues. Interestingly, even though the protesters claimed to be speaking for the world's poor, the devel-

Several thousand demonstrators protest WTO trade talks in Seattle in November 1999. (AFP Photo/John G. Mabanglo)

oping countries represented in Seattle did not see it that way. Led by Brazil, India, and Egypt, the LDC governments resisted any attempt to put global labor or environmental standards on the agenda lest they be used to ban imports from developing countries, despite efforts by the Clinton Administration, under pressure from domestic constituencies, to force the issue.[98] President Zedillo of Mexico spoke for other LDCs in his statement that "self-appointed representatives of civil society" (the street protesters) were "determined to save developing countries from development."[99] There have been many protests organized since Seattle.

One can see that the WTO lately has been at the center of debates relating to rich-poor gaps both between and within states. In Seattle, Brazil was choosing to ignore the rich-poor gap within its own country (a gap so wide and so socially explosive that the tiny elite at the top increasingly purchase armored cars, and in some cases avoid traffic altogether by relying on helicopters for transportation, to avoid "carjackings and roadside robberies [that] have become a part of the risks of daily life for anyone perceived to have money"[100]), while focusing on the rich-poor gap between states. The WTO's future is clouded not only because of the volatility of domestic politics surrounding global free trade, but also because, unless decision making in the WTO is seen in the United States and other major power centers as adequately reflecting power realities in the international system, the organization risks being ignored. As Preeg states, "the international financial institutions, the OECD, and other international bodies have their executive committees or informal select groups, and if the WTO does not do likewise, serious trade deliberation could well . . . take place elsewhere, such as through Quad, G-7, and OECD mechanisms, without participation of the WTO secretariat or the majority of its members."[101] In summary, an interesting mix of Westphalian and post-Westphalian elements figures to continue to define this issue area for the foreseeable future.

CONCLUSION

If economics is now "the continuation of war by other means," one would hope that the process of dividing up the "planetary product," which by 2000 exceeded $40 trillion, will remain peaceful however inherently conflictual the politics involved. The example of French farmers destroying a McDonalds restaurant over objections to U.S. demands for agricultural trade liberalization—just one of many such violent incidents that occurred in Europe throughout the 1990s in response to fear of not merely American competition but also U.S. exports of genetically altered corn and hormone-treated beef—admittedly does not provide ringing validation for "the golden arches theory of war." In an effort to avoid food fights over genetically modified foods, a Biosafety Protocol was negotiated in 2000. One newspaper reported that "old antagonists from St. Louis-based Monsanto Co. [a leading MNC in the biotechnology field] and

Greenpeace stood with delegates from 133 nations to applaud the UN-sponsored agreement. The pact gives people protection they are demanding from the potential risk of moving genes from one species to another and of moving new genetically modified products across borders."[102] Offering a possible model of global compromise in pursuit of global governance, the regime tried to carve out a middle ground between, on the one hand, the right of France and other welfare states to ban such imports if they are thought to pose a threat to public health and, on the other hand, the right of Monsanto and other companies not to be subjected to costly labeling and other requirements in order to sell their goods abroad.

The Biosafety Protocol was added as an addendum to the Convention on Biological Diversity negotiated at the Earth Summit in Rio de Janeiro in 1992. As much as free traders would like to keep environmental issues separate from economic ones, clearly it is not always possible. Still, environmental issues have come to occupy their own distinctive place on the global agenda and are given special treatment in the chapter that follows. One observer has gone so far as to call the environment "*the* national security issue of the early twenty-first century. The political and strategic impact of surging populations, spreading disease, deforestation and soil erosion, water depletion, air pollution, and, possibly, rising sea levels in critical, overcrowded regions like the Nile Delta and Bangladesh—developments that will prompt mass migrations and, in turn, incite group conflicts—will be the core foreign policy challenge from which most others will ultimately emanate."[103] While the latter statement may somewhat overstate the importance of environmental issues—they are not likely to assume quite the "high-politics" stature of arms control matters or perhaps even the "middle-politics" stature of economic matters—it does seem safe to predict that global ecology will become a growing topic of discussion in global governance affairs in the twenty-first century. Chapter 7, then, examines ecopolitics in the United States and worldwide.

CHAPTER 7

Challenges to the National Ecological State
Low Politics in the Post-Cold War Era

The earth is finite. Its ability to absorb wastes is finite. Its ability to provide food and energy is finite. Its ability to provide for growing numbers of people is finite. And we are fast approaching many of the earth's limits.
—The World's Scientists' Warning to Humanity,
1992, at the time of the Earth Summit

There are no . . . limits to the carrying capacity of the Earth that are likely to bind at any time in the foreseeable future.
—Lawrence Summers, U.S. Deputy
Secretary of the Treasury, 1994

Good planets are hard to find.
—Graffiti found on a bridge in Rock Creek Park
in Washington, D.C. (cited in Lester
Brown et al., *State of the World* 1989)

Environmental issues had attracted the attention of humanity long before the Earth Summit in 1992. One can read accounts of air pollution as far back as ancient times, in Seneca's references to "the heavy air of Rome." In 1659, John Evelyn wrote that London was covered in "such a cloud of sea-coal, as if there be a resemblance of hell on earth." It was an English chemist, Angus Smith, who in 1872 first coined the term "acid rain," in his book *Air and Rain*. A Swedish scientist named Svante Arrhenius in 1897 predicted potentially devastating global warming as a result of growing CO_2 concentrations in the atmosphere. In 1798, the most famous doomsdayer of all, Thomas Malthus, predicted massive world famine as population growth outstripped increases in food production.[1] The term "ecology" itself is credited to a German scientist, Ernst Haeckel, writing in 1866. Environmental consciousness had appeared in colonial America as early as 1680, when William Penn decreed that for every five acres of land cleared, one had to be preserved as virgin forest. By the late nineteenth and early twentieth centuries, the U.S. government had already set aside great national parks such as Yellowstone, while Teddy Roosevelt and Progressive Era leaders, such as those in the newly formed Sierra Club, had pushed for a variety of conservation measures. International conservation efforts were manifested in treaties such as the Convention Designed to Ensure the Conservation of Various Species of Wild Animals in Africa, Which Are Useful to Man or Inoffensive, concluded among European states in 1900, to regulate wildlife in colonial Africa. Countless other examples can be cited of historical interest in environmental concerns.

However, it was not until the 1960s and 1970s that the modern environmental movement took off in the United States and elsewhere, and what could be called the "national ecological state" was born. It was not until then that environmentalism grabbed the public's attention and came to occupy a visible place on public policy agendas. Rachel Carson's *Silent Spring*, published in 1962, as much as any other work popularized ecology as a topic worthy of expanded governmental action and of increased study by k-12 schoolchildren and Ph.D. scientists. The first U.S. Clean Air Act was passed in 1963. The U.S. Environmental Protection Agency (EPA) was created in 1970 as an independent agency, apart from the Department of the Interior, to focus solely on ecological concerns; it was among the first such agencies in the world, and by the end of the century would have counterparts in almost every country on the planet. The first Earth Day was observed in 1970 as well, the brainstorm of U.S. Senator Gaylord Nelson of Wisconsin. In 1972, a small book appeared on the scene entitled *The Limits to Growth*, authored by the Club of Rome, which painted a grim portrait of a future in which unbridled economic growth and population growth worldwide would result in overconsumption and exhaustion of petroleum and other basic raw materials, leading ultimately to collapse of human civilization sometime in the twenty-first century; the only way out of this scenario, according to the authors, was a radical change in lifestyles and an acceptance of a "steady-state," no-growth model.[2] The book provided the backdrop for the 1972 UN Conference on the Human Environment, held in Stockholm, where neither developed nor developing states were enthusiastic about adopting no-growth policies. The impact of "limits to growth" thinking could be seen in President Jimmy Carter's 1979 *Global 2000 Report*, which examined the issues raised in the Club of Rome study and supported the earlier findings, despite critics calling the conclusions "globaloney" given the lack of clear scientific evidence. The quotations cited at the beginning of this chapter (the statement by a U.S. Treasury Department official, contrasted with the warning of some 1600 scientists, including over 100 Nobel laureates) are indicative of the ongoing debate over whether humanity is pushing up against limits to the "carrying capacity" of the planet or not.

The Earth Summit, held in Rio de Janeiro in 1992, on the twentieth anniversary of the first UN conference on the environment, attempted to take an intermediate position between high growth and no growth prescriptions, based on a 1987 UN-sponsored study by the Brundtland Commission entitled *Our Common Future.*[3] The full, official name of the Rio meeting was the UN Conference on Environment and Development, reflecting the view that economic growth was compatible with ecological quality so long as it was achieved in a way that was sensitive to environmental concerns. The new concept "sustainable development" was much more acceptable to the UN membership than "limits to growth" insofar as it seemed to imply less need for retrenchment and sacrifice. Rejecting the notion held by some environmentalists that "as the Dow Jones [stock market average] goes up, the Earth's health goes down,"[4] the authors of the Brundtland Commission report argued that it was often the *lack* of economic growth that was responsible for environmental degradation—as in the Sahel region of sub-Saharan Africa where attempts by peasant farmers to eke out a living by cultivating marginal lands were only destroying the landscape—and that economic development was critical to improving human well-being, assuming it could be done in a sustainable fashion.

The Brundtland Commission report opened with the observation that "the Earth is one but the world is not,"[5] denoting the reality that the biosphere may represent a single interdependent ecosystem—Spaceship Earth, where pollution and other environmental hazards transcend territorial boundaries—but the sociosphere still consists of many separate, distinctive entities, notably some 200 sovereign states, which do not fully agree on how to share the globe. In this chapter the author examines the global politics of environmental problem-solving and the challenges faced by nation-states in this area. Although it is true that environmental concerns are rising in importance as public policy issues, they generally remain relatively low on national and international agendas when compared to military security and economic concerns. As is often said, in the typical polity, public support for clean air and other environmental benefits is a mile wide and an inch deep, i.e., virtually all people want to see an improved environmental quality of life, but environmental issues still tend to possess not as high (intense) a level of salience as leaders and publics attach to pocketbook and other issues.[6] This is not to say that ecopolitics is lacking in complexity or volatility. After providing an overview of global governance in the environmental issue-area, I will focus on the tortuous negotiations preceding and following the 1987 Montreal Protocol on protection of the ozone layer, a regime hailed as "the most significant international environmental agreement in history" and "unparalleled as a global effort."[7]

THE NATURE AND MAGNITUDE OF ENVIRONMENTAL THREATS

What is sometimes called the "global problematique"—the menu of problems facing mankind today—includes many different environmental threats. In *State of the World 2000*, Lester Brown calls attention to a number of "environmental trends shaping the new century," focusing particularly on population growth, rising temperature, falling water tables, shrinking cropland per person, collapsing fisheries, shrinking forests, and the loss of plant and animal species.[8] Other observers add to the litany of concerns. It is impossible to catalog all these threats here. Instead, I offer a brief survey, dividing the menu into atmosphere-related problems, water-related problems, land-related problems, and population, food, and resource management problems. Although these dimensions are all interrelated parts of the earth's ecosystem, we can treat them separately for purposes of discussion.

The Atmosphere

The part of the atmosphere that contains oxygen and other gases which sustain life on earth is a rather thin, fragile envelope approximately ten miles high. As just noted, air pollution is not a new problem; it can be traced to human activity as far back as ancient Babylon and Rome. The Industrial Revolution, of course, accelerated the phenomenon. Since World War II, the world has seen "killer smogs in London and Los Angeles and the widespread use of gas masks in Tokyo."[9] The chief air pollutants, released into the atmosphere through the burning of fossil fuels and other sources, are carbon monoxide, sulfur dioxide, nitrogen oxide, lead, particulate matter (soot and dust), and ozone (at lower levels of the atmosphere). Although air quality in many industrialized countries has improved somewhat in recent years because of environmental measures taken by governments (e.g., in the late 1990s, Los Angeles' skies were the clearest they had been in fifty years), pollution in the North remains a serious problem. The problem is worsening in most developing countries of the South as they add automobiles and other trappings of industrialization. In India, for example, breathing the air in Bombay is said to be equivalent to smoking 10 cigarettes a day.[10] As described by Tyler Miller, Mexico City may be worse:

> Some 4 million motor vehicles, 30,000 factories . . . and leaking . . . gas from stoves and heaters spew pollutants into the atmosphere. . . . Living in the Mexico City basin is like living in a polluted gas chamber. Since 1982 the amount of contamination in the city's smog-choked air has more than tripled; breathing the air is roughly equal to smoking two packs of cigarettes a day. According to the government, in 1993 the city's residents enjoyed only 31 days when the air was considered safe to breathe. With the number of cars growing by 7 percent a year, smog is expected to get worse.[11]

Atmospheric pollutants become an international problem when, as so often happens, they cross national borders. Recent reminders are the gray haze that caused a health alert in Dallas and other Texas cities in 1998, caused by uncontrolled fires thousands of miles away in Mexico, as well as the huge blanket of smog that covered Malaysia, Singapore, and much of southeast Asia in

The sun sets over the world's tallest building, the Petronas Twin Towers, in Kuala Lumpur, Malaysia, in June 1999. Shrouded in smog, it reminded Malaysians of the thick haze that blanketed their skies as a result of Indonesian forest fires two years earlier. (Zainal Abd Halim/Reuters)

1997, which was traced to peasant farmers burning heavily forested areas in Indonesia to clear land for crops. In the case of acid rain and greenhouse gases especially, emissions into the atmosphere know no boundaries as they circle entire geographical regions and have global implications.

Treasured cultural monuments, bridges and infrastructure, as well as natural habitats in North America and Europe have been ravaged by acid rain, caused mainly by the burning of coal that produces sulfur dioxide and nitrogen dioxide emissions, which dissolve in rain droplets and then fall to the ground far from their source. Sweden and Norway have been net importers of such emissions from the United Kingdom, Germany, and other neighboring states and have suffered severe damage to their forests and lakes. Similarly, Canada has complained for years about destruction of woodlands caused by acid rain originating in the northeastern and midwestern United States. China's heavy reliance on coal as an energy source, combined with its rapid economic growth, is provoking much concern in Japan and other nearby states.

The accumulation of carbon dioxide, methane, and other gases in the atmosphere caused by the burning of oil and other fossil fuels and by deforestation and other factors is thought to produce a greenhouse effect, trapping heat and raising the earth's temperature. There is general scientific agreement that atmospheric concentrations of CO_2, in particular, have been increasing over the past century, that these are to a large extent man-made rather than the result of natural occurrences, and that a gradual warming has been occurring. It is less clear whether this global warming trend will necessarily continue in the future and whether it will produce temperature increases of sufficient magnitude to fundamentally alter agricultural and other processes, for example curtailing the growing season in the American farmbelt and other major food-producing areas. The ten hottest years on record have been since 1983, with most of them in the 1990s, and each passing year (save for a few exceptions) setting a new record. According to some predictions, the twenty-first century may see a rise in the global average temperature of 1°–4° Celsius, in which case there could be melting of polar ice caps and massive flooding of coastal cities around the world, chaotic weather patterns including unusually severe hurricanes and droughts, and other uncertain climatic effects.[12] The buildup of greenhouse gases called chlorofluorocarbons (CFCs) has also been blamed for contributing to the depletion of the ozone layer which shields us from the sun's ultraviolet rays and helps to prevent skin cancer.

Water

Much of the earth, some 70 percent, is covered with water, yet drinkable water is in short supply. Ninety-seven percent of the world's water is salt water found in the great oceans, while another two percent is tied up in the polar ice caps, leaving only about 1 percent of total water resources—found mainly in rivers and lakes—that is freshwater readily available for human consumption. With existing water tables in many countries shrinking due to droughts and accelerated usage related to expanding agricultural and industrial activity, and with worldwide water demand expected to double over the next twenty years,[13] fresh water could become "the world's scarcest resource, more valuable than petroleum."[14] Some eighty countries, mostly in Africa, the Middle East, and Asia, are now facing water shortages, with China and India facing the largest single deficits.[15] The potential for international conflict over water is heightened by the fact that 40 percent of the world's population depends for drinking water and irrigation on 215 river systems shared by at least two states; twelve of these are shared by at least five different states.[16] For example, the Nile, the world's longest river, runs through nine countries (Ethiopia, Sudan, Tanzania, and others) before ending up in Egypt. Israel shares the Jordan River basin and other major water sources with Jordan, Syria, and an aspirant Palestinian state. Syria competes also with Iraq and Turkey over use of the Tigris-Euphrates river basin. Although disputes may arise over some countries seeking to divert water from their neighbors, such mutual dependence could also produce pressures for upstream and downstream states to cooperate in preserving a common resource.

Lakes and rivers themselves are being subjected to increased pollution and deterioration of water quality. The main pollutants have been industrial effluents (including heavy metals such as lead and mercury), agricultural runoffs (including chemical fertilizers and pesticides), toxic wastes, and raw sewage. The "Blue Danube" in Europe, for example, has been renamed by some the "Brown Danube." In much of Latin America and Africa, raw sewage is emptied directly into waterways used for drinking and other daily needs. Over 1 billion people lack access to clean water for drinking and sanitation. Although muncipal treatment plants in the United States have made great strides in removing contaminants in recent decades, the EPA estimates that 40 percent of the rivers and lakes in the United States still are unfit for fishing or swimming. Even where there has been progress, it remains an ongoing challenge to sustain water habitats. As one example, it has been noted that "by any measure, the Great Lakes were indeed saved, in one of environmentalism's most dramatic successes. Only 30 years ago Lake Erie was dead, with garbage and rotting fish regularly washing onto beaches. . . . The Cuyahoga River, which feeds Erie, was so polluted with oil . . . that it caught fire in 1969." Yet the same observers note that the Great Lakes today are being threatened again by both international sources (rising water temperatures traced to global warming and "toxic chemicals that ride in on the winds from distant countries") as well as local sources (urban sprawl).[17]

Pollutants that enter rivers and lakes ultimately are discharged into the world's oceans. The oceans were once thought to be vast sinks, impervious to overfishing, pollution, or any other damage that human exploitation could possibly inflict. T. H.Huxley in 1883 wrote that the storehouses of cod, mackerel and other fish "were inexhaustible because the multitude of those fishes are so inconceivably great that the number we catch is relatively insignificant."[18] Fish populations are threatened today with decimation not only due to giant driftnets (in some cases forty miles wide) that can sweep whole sectors of the ocean, but also due to the accumulation of land-based pollutants as well as pollution at sea that includes oilspills, discharge of plastics, and overboard dumping of garbage and toxic wastes.[19] From inland wetlands to coral reefs and the deep seabed, water habitats worldwide are at risk, endangering valuable wildlife, biodiversity, and food sources along with the sheer aesthetic beauty of the earth's waterbodies.

Land

Land degradation can take several forms, including soil erosion, desertification, deforestation, and other environmental harms. It is estimated that over one-fourth of the world's land area is arid or semi-arid desert and that the deserts in sub-Saharan Africa and elsewhere are gradually expanding at an annual rate of 81,000 square miles (an area the size of Kansas).[20] The causes of desertification, aside from drought, are overcultivation of poor soils; overgrazing and denuding of grasslands by sheep, goats, and cattle; poor irrigation techniques; and deforestation (to clear land for agriculture and for firewood). Deforestation has attracted more attention on the global environmental agenda than desertification, mainly because more valuable resources are thought to be at risk. Half the forests that once covered the earth are gone. As just one example, whereas forty years ago Ethiopia had forests covering 30 percent of its territory, it now has forests in only 1 percent. Forest cover in Europe and North America is stabilizing due to reforestation efforts—there are actually more trees in the United States today than in 1900, as 6 million seedlings are planted daily[21]—but these secondary forests cannot compensate for the loss of old-growth forests in the Pacific Northwest and other areas that house rich ecosystems.

Of greater concern to many than deforestation in temperate zones is the loss of tropical rain forests, which are home to over half of the world's 1.75 million known plant and animal species. (There may be as many as 100 million species on earth, but only 1.75 million have actually been identified and catalogued.) Between 1960 and 1990, one-fifth of the tropical rain forests on the globe disappeared.[22] Based on satellite data, estimates of how much tropical deforestation is currently occurring range from the equivalent of 14 city blocks per minute to 68 city blocks per minute.[23] Half of the tropical deforestation has been occurring in just six countries—Brazil, Indonesia, the Congo (these being the three largest rain forest countries), Mexico, Bolivia, and Venezuela.[24] The rain forests are being leveled in the Amazon basin and other parts of the developing world for a variety of reasons. They are being cut or burned by large agribusiness conglomerates which operate plantations for growing coffee and other cash crops, by poor peasants engaged in subsistence farming, by cattle ranchers seeking to expand their grazing areas, by commercial logging interests, and by mining, energy, and other interests who seek to exploit forest resources, most of whom require construction of roads to provide access into and out of the forestlands, which only adds to the further invasion of these areas—all ordinarily done with the blessing of the national government in the name of "economic development."

Aside from the substantial harmful effects tropical deforestation has on global warming through the large-scale release of CO_2, the resultant loss of biodiversity through habitat destruction is thought to be even more potentially catastrophic, since many rain forest plants and animals have been found to have important medical applications, such as the rosy periwinkle (found in Madagascar), which has been used to treat childhood leukemia, and a certain frog species (found in Ecuador) whose skin secretions have morphine-like painkilling qualities. Approximately one-quarter of all prescription drugs dispensed in the United States are derived from rain forest products. An estimated 17,000 species a year are being lost due to tropical deforestation, some of which might conceivably provide a future cure for cancer or other diseases were they to be preserved.[25]

The species extinction problem is not limited to the rain forests. Overall, in various biomes throughout the world, some 50,000 species are being eliminated annually—"the greatest mass extinction since the die-off of the dinosaurs"[26]—with many others on the brink of extinction. The African elephant, the black rhino, and the bald eagle are just a few that have been characterized in recent years as endangered, as threatened with meeting the fate of the passenger pigeon. (The last passenger pigeon was reputedly a hen named Martha who died in the Cincinnati Zoo in 1914, and whose stuffed remains are on display at the National Museum of Natural History in Washington, D.C.)[27] Edward O. Wilson has remarked: "Clearly, we are in the midst of one of the great extinction spasms of geological history. . . . As a biologist, I sometimes feel like an art curator watching the Louvre burn down."[28] Expanding human populations and human settlements, whether in the Amazon jungles or in highly urbanized settings, pose major challenges for protection of natural habitats and for land use planners seeking to reconcile environmental and other concerns.

Population, Food, and Resource Management Problems

In the debates over "limits to growth" and "sustainable development," the North and the South have each pointed fingers at each other as to who is to blame for the earth's environmental problems or who poses the greater threat. The North has tended to argue that the key problem is overpopulation in the developing world—the South contributes 90 percent of the annual growth in global population—while the South has tended to argue that the major problem is overconsumption on the part of affluent societies—the United States alone, with only about 5 percent of the world's population, consumes roughly 30 percent of all the resources and accounts for 25 percent of all carbon dioxide emissions. It is estimated, for example, that the average American consumes as much energy as 20 Costa Ricans, 50 persons in Madagascar, and 70 Bangladeshi.[29] Of course, there is truth to both criticisms. If every country had a fertility rate of over 6 births per woman, as in Kenya, clearly this would put tremendous pressure on the earth's carrying capacity. At the same time, if every country attempted to emulate the United States, where one-third of all households have at least two cars, one has to wonder where the energy would come from to support such a lifestyle on a global scale and what the implications for global warming and other environmental phenomena would be.

At least since the time of Malthus, the eighteenth-century English clergyman and economist who became famous for his prediction that the world's population would inevitably outstrip its food supply and cause massive famine, the problems of population and food have been seen as inextricably linked. Although there have been pockets of famine in recent years, with an estimated 5 million children dying from starvation in Africa annually during the 1980s, and almost 1 billion people on the planet suffering from chronic malnutrition,[30] this has had less to do with inadequate food supplies than with the lack of purchasing power in poor countries and the inadequacy of food aid distribution networks. World food production since World War II has kept pace with population growth, increasing by over 2.5 percent annually between 1950 and 1990, due to advances in genetic engineering and other technological innovations, although there are some signs of late that we may be pushing up against limits in terms of available cropland and the ability of ecosystems to absorb chemical fertilizers, pesticides, and other inputs designed to enhance agricultural productivity.[31] Scientists have tried to assess the maximum number of people the earth conceivably could feed. The answer, according to one study, is in the range of 10 to 11 billion—roughly double the current world population—although this "would require some changes in food habits, as well as greatly improving the efficiency of traditional agriculture."[32] Others are less optimistic, such as David Pimentel, a biologist who has argued that we must somehow slash the world's population to 2 billion or fewer by 2100.[33] The concern of Pimentel and others is that one does not live by bread alone and that, even if hypothetically we could feed several times the current world population, unbridled population growth causes problems that go well beyond food demands.

Global population trends are a source of considerable alarm to many observers. It took several millennia for the human race to reach 1 billion in number, around 1830. Just one century later, by 1930, global population had doubled to 2 billion. And by 1999, the total had reached 6 billion. At the current annual growth rate of 1.5 percent, the earth's population could be expected to double in 40 years. By 2150, it would reach 694 billion![34] The good news is that the annual population growth rate has been declining, so there is hope that world population will eventually stabilize around 10–15 billion sometime in the twenty-first century. The bad news is that, meanwhile, we are adding some 90 million people to the planet each year, which translates into adding a city the size of Dayton, Ohio to the world's breakfast table every morning and a New York City every month, necessitating having to accommodate many more mouths to feed and people to find shelter and employment for in a world which already seems unable to provide decent living conditions for many of its already existing inhabitants.[35]

Population growth has been most dramatic in the South, where the introduction of advanced medical care since World War II has lowered death rates while birth rates have remained relatively high. Life expectancy has increased almost everywhere (although the AIDS epidemic threatens to reverse this trend in parts of Africa). Whereas most developed states of the North have become virtually ZPG (zero population growth) countries, many less developed states are experiencing population growth of more than 2 to 3 percent annually. The hope is that, as happened in the European experience, population growth rates will eventually decline as people improve their income. Large families are no longer necessary when parents have sufficient income, because fewer children are needed to work and to provide old-age security. With economic progress also comes higher literacy rates and access to education about family planning and contraceptives, along with improved conditions for women, who are no longer viewed as mere childbearers, all of which tend to lower birth rates. The problem is that of the chicken and the egg—how to produce improved economic conditions when such progress is hampered by the very population growth it could curb. Still, the case of poverty-stricken Bangladesh, where the fertility rate recently declined from an average of 7 children per family to 4.5 within just a decade due to an activist government birth control program, suggests that a country can get a handle on its population problem even without necessarily having the benefit of significant per capita income growth. Indeed, the falling annual rate of world population growth is attributable not only to a declining birthrate in the North from 2.8 children per woman in the 1950s to 1.6 today but also to a declining birthrate in the South from 6.2 children per woman to slightly less than 3 within the same time frame.

What is aggravating the population picture in the South is the fact that the age distribution in LDCs is heavily weighted toward the young, with 35 percent or more of the citizenry typically under the age of fifteen, so that there is a built-in population momentum due to the existence of so many future childbearers in the pipeline who have not yet reached childbearing age. Moreover, increasingly masses of people are moving from the countryside to the city in search of a better life. By 2005, for the first time in history, a majority of the world's people are expected to live in urban areas. By 2025, it is projected that there will be some fifty cities in the developing world having populations of over 5 million, including twenty "megacities," each exceeding 10 million, far larger than half the countries on earth (with Lagos, Nigeria and Bombay, India possibly exceeding 30 million). It remains to be seen whether governments in the South will be able to cope with overcrowding and other strains such changes figure to place on an already stretched social fabric in these societies. Urbanization poses challenges for developed and developing societies alike, relating to mass transit and other issues, but the challenges are especially acute in those societies undergoing rapid modernization. Bangkok, Thailand, one of the megacities of 10 million inhabitants, just built a sixteen-mile elevated rail system to relieve traffic jams so horrendous that motorists routinely carry portable potties in their cars. As described in a recent news article:

> Traffic jams have become one of the most debilitating and intractable side effects of urbanization and economic growth. "Most of the mega-cities in Asia are approaching gridlock for increasing portions of the day" [according to an Amer-

The skytrain running through Bangkok, Thailand seeks to alleviate some of the world's worst traffic jams. (Photo by John McDermott)

ican traffic consultant]. . . . As in many other countries, a personal car is seen by a newly emerging middle class as something of a human right. . . . In Bangkok, urban planners estimate that the average resident spends 44 days a year in traffic jams [and] that 20 percent of fuel is consumed by vehicles that are standing still. . . . Residents of Bangkok have the region's longest average round trip to work . . . at 82 minutes. To deal with emergencies, hospitals have prepared motorcycle ambulances to weave through traffic [and] police officers have been given courses in midwifery.[36]

One can debate whether or not this represents progress, but it reflects consumer sovereignty as human beings everywhere seem to want to partake of the fruits of the mass consumption culture without much regard for the ecological implications of their behavior either locally or globally. How the world can find the energy and other resources to sustain modern lifestyles on a planetary scale and can cope with the environmental fallout from such lifestyles is a major challenge for nation-states and for global governance. An interesting question is how much regulation of behavior, whether it be procreation or recreation, are human beings willing to tolerate, and at what level of governance. For example, is the world ready for a global carbon tax to dampen oil consumption and global warming and encourage use of mass transit? Should policies that prohibit the sale of nonreturnable soda bottles be left up to individual localities (as in the United States, where Michigan and some other states have adopted such conservation measures), or should they be mandated nationwide (as in Denmark) or even supranationally (as has been considered in the European Union)? And should there be any restrictions at all imposed by governments anywhere on the number of children a couple can have? This is what global governance is all about.

GLOBAL GOVERNANCE: EFFORTS AT DEVELOPING INTERNATIONAL ENVIRONMENTAL REGIMES

In *State of the World 2000*, Hilary French sums up where global governance stands in the environmental issue area compared with other issue areas:

> Ecological globalization . . . poses enormous challenges to traditional governance structures. National governments are ill suited for managing national environmental problems that transcend borders, whether via air and water currents or through global commerce. Yet international environmental governance is still in its infancy, with the treaties and institutions that governments turn to for global management mostly too weak to put a meaningful dent in the problems. . . . Although nation-states are losing ground in the face of globalization, other actors are moving to the fore, particularly international corporations and non-governmental organizations (NGOs). New information and communications technologies are facilitating international networking, and innovative partnerships are being forged between NGOs, the business community, and international institutions.[37]

As always, one must be careful not to exaggerate the importance of nonstate actors, but they do seem to be playing an especially rich role in managing global ecological concerns. A complex system is emerging in the governance of environmental affairs, with environmental problem-solving occurring at several levels—local, national, and international—and with state and nonstate actors interacting in interesting ways somewhat differently than we saw in the security and economic fields. Before analyzing this brew of state and nonstate actor politics, I will briefly describe a few of the major environmental regimes that have been produced to address problems relating to the atmosphere, water, and land.

Negotiating the World's Troubled Waters, Air, and Land: Key Regimes

Nation-states continue to play a pivotal role, if only because their governments remain the exclusive agents empowered to enter into official treaties and international legal instruments. Much of the discourse that occurs in the global ecology field revolves around the question of what obligations sovereign states have vis-à-vis each other to ensure clean air and other collective goods. In 1941, in the famous Trail Smelter case, an international tribunal was asked by the United States to consider whether Canada should be held liable for damages caused by a British Columbia smelter spewing sulfur dioxide across the border into the State of Washington; in what was perhaps the first statement of its kind on transboundary air pollution, the panel of judges found in favor of the United States, arguing that "no state has the right to use its territory in such a manner as to cause injury . . . to the territory of another."[38] This principle was reaffirmed in Article 21 of the Stockholm Declaration, one of the key outputs of the first UN global environmental conference held in 1972; Article 21 acknowledged "the sovereign right of states to exploit their resources in accordance with their environmental policies" but urged states to "insure that activities within their own jurisdiction do not cause damage to the environment of other states or areas beyond the limits of national jurisdiction [i.e., the global commons, including the high seas, the air space above the high seas, outer space, and Antarctica]." The Stockholm Declaration was an example of soft law, a normative statement hortatory in nature rather than a statement of explicit legal obligations as would be contained in a treaty. Other outputs of the Stockholm meeting included an Action Plan containing over 100 recommendations to be taken by governments to deal with environmental problems, as well as the creation of the UN Environmental Program (UNEP), the first global IGO focused on the environment.

The Stockholm conference provided tremendous impetus for the development of international environmental regimes. Although, as French notes, regimes are often weak in this area, nonetheless hundreds of international environmental agreements currently exist, the great majority of which were initiated after 1972.[39] The 1992 Earth Summit in Rio de Janeiro added further impetus to the growth of environmental regimes. The conference itself produced the Rio Declaration and the Agenda 21 Action Plan (two soft law outputs that refined and expanded upon the earlier versions produced in Stockholm twenty years earlier) as well as two treaties, a Framework Convention on Climate Change and a Convention on Biological Diversity (to be discussed).[40]

There are a number of specific international regimes that deal with atmospheric problems. UNEP and the World Health Organization (WHO) administer a Global Environmental Monitoring System (GEMS) that collects data on urban air quality from some eighty cities in over fifty countries in order to determine to what extent concentrations of particulate matter and other pollutants are increasing or not.[41] Individual countries draft their own individual national clean air plans (e.g., the U.S. Clean Air Act of 1990), only rarely consulting with neighboring states, although the acid rain issue has been an exception. Since acid rain tends to be a transborder problem confined to a particular geographic locale rather than global in its reach, international regimes in this area have been bilateral or regional in scope. For example, the United States and Canada have attempted to forge agreements, even though Canada continues to find American responses inadequate. The most ambitious efforts to combat acid rain have been undertaken in Europe. In 1979, thirty-three European countries including the Soviet Union (as well as the United States and Canada) signed the Framework Convention on Long-Range Transboundary Air Pollution, which committed the parties to study and assess acid rain damage and to explore what steps could be taken to reduce sulfur dioxide emissions. This was followed by the 1985 Helsinki Protocol, which required the same European parties to go beyond the framework convention and actually commit to reducing their SO_2 emissions by at least 30 percent from the 1980 level. More than twenty of the parties, notably Germany, agreed to join the "30% club," and have since made considerable progress in cutting sulfur emissions, although the regime's effectiveness has been hampered somewhat by the fact that the United Kingdom and some other major polluters have refused to sign the protocol and by the complication that sulfur reductions have been offset by growing emissions of nitrogen oxides and other harmful pollutants not covered by the treaty.[42]

European acid rain diplomacy illustrates what has become a common pattern in environmental regime-making, namely, starting modestly with a rather nebulous "framework convention" as a way to hook states into participating initially in the process, and then following up with a "protocol" which contains specific targets and timetables and entails real costs. It is easy to dismiss framework conventions, declarations, and other soft law kinds of outputs as little more than platitudinous preachings, but they have been shown to play a strategic role in greasing the regime process in many instances. This pattern can be seen at work not not only in regard to acid rain but also global warming and ozone layer deterioration. The ozone case, which will be examined in some detail, will be saved for last.

As contentious as acid rain politics can be, the debate over developing a single global regime on global warming has been particularly heated. The Framework Convention on Climate Change that came out of the 1992 Earth Summit, which was signed and quickly ratified by almost the entire UN membership present at the conference, contained a nonbinding set of principles that acknowledged global warming was a serious problem requiring continued monitoring, that called upon countries to try to reduce their greenhouse gas emissions to 1990 levels by 2000, and that urged industrialized countries in particular to take immediate steps to curb their emissions and to help developing countries do likewise. The Kyoto Conference in 1997 produced a follow-up Kyoto Protocol that obligated industrialized countries to meet specific targets (averaging approximately 5 percent below 1990 levels from 2008 to 2012) while LDCs for the most part were exempted from any obligations. The Protocol has yet to be ratified by many states, with the United States in particular refusing to commit until there is more definitive scientific evidence confirming the greenhouse threat and unless demands are made on China and developing countries.[43] At the most recent UN-sponsored global warming conference held in The Hague in 2000, the United States unsuccessfully proposed to meet half its emission target by counting its existing forests as "carbon sinks" offsetting its CO_2 production. Meanwhile, in the United States and elsewhere, as greenhouse emissions continue to rise well above the 1990 levels—as countries ignore the nonbinding mandate contained in the 1992 framework convention—it is becoming all the more difficult to meet the pledges made at Rio.

The main global regime covering water space, the 1982 UN Convention on the Law of the Sea (the Montego Bay Convention), was discussed in Chapter 4. To repeat, it was an amazing accomplishment of the international community to produce a single comprehensive regime covering fishing and almost all other human activities on 70 percent of the earth's surface, one that has largely been wholly accepted as customary or treaty law (except for the deep seabed mining provisions) by virtually all states, including the major maritime powers. Unfortunately, fishing disputes still arise, especially over migratory species such as tuna, while overfishing remains a problem along with destruction of dolphins and other species due to the use of driftnet devices, but at least there is a legal framework in place to resolve these disputes. Other global regimes that specifically deal with ocean pollution are the 1972 London Dumping Convention that prohibits the dumping of high-level radioactive and toxic wastes overboard and regulates other waste disposal through a permit system, and the 1973 Marpol Convention that limits oil, plastic, and other discharges from ships at sea, with "flag states" in each case supposed to report accidents or violations to the International Maritime Organization (IMO), a UN specialized agency. Although there has been progress in reducing oilspills and other oceanic hazards, these regimes suffer from the fact that many states either have not ratified the agreements or do not fully comply with the reporting and other requirements, especially "flag of convenience" states, such as Panama and Liberia, which are home to some of the largest merchant fleets in the world, since these governments allow foreign shipowners to register their vessels with them without demanding they meet costly IMO safety regulations.[44]

Ocean governance also suffers from the fact that two-thirds of all ocean pollution is land-based. Precisely for that reason, UNEP during the 1970s established several Regional Seas Programs in the Mediterranean, the Caribbean, and other areas where neighboring states shared a common resource and had a mutual interest in reducing pollution not only at sea but also originating from on-shore industrial and other activities. The Mediterranean Action Plan is the most well known of these. It involves eighteen countries that border the Mediterranean, including such traditional, bitter rivals as Israel, Syria, and Libya, as well as Greece and Turkey, in cooperation on research, monitoring, and pollution control. Member countries have established a Regional Oilspill Combatting Center and a Land-Based Sources Protocol that bans ("blacklists") or regulates ("greylists") various categories of effluents into the Mediterranean, largely funded by the north-shore developed countries. Although many pollution problems persist along with disputes over who is to blame, considerable cooperation has occurred.[45] The action plan is a good test of functionalist theory and whether engaging states in collaboration on relatively low-politics, technical matters can lead to deeper cooperation. So, too, are various river use regimes, such as the UNEP-sponsored Zambezi River action plan that has attempted to sort out riparian rights and obligations among eight different countries, including several traditional adversaries, who depend on the waterway for drinking water for 20 million people in southern Africa.

In regard to land-related concerns, desertification has not engendered much regime-making. The only global regime on the subject is the 1994 Convention on Desertification, resulting from a promise that developed countries had made at the 1992 Earth Summit to assist African countries experiencing arid conditions in return for their support on other issues; the treaty, which has been ratified by over 160 states (excluding the United States among others), has thus far failed to generate the necessary financial resources to support scientific research and technical assistance (for irrigation and land rehabilitation projects) to slow the advance of drylands. The Earth Summit gave far more attention to deforestation. Building upon a previous Tropical Forest Action Plan that the UN Food and Agriculture Organization had initiated in the 1980s, the Rio conference succeeded in issuing a Statement of Forest Principles and a Convention on Biological Diversity that affirmed the sovereign right of states to exploit their forest resources with the understanding that they were also obligated to do so in a sustainable fashion in order to protect these ecosystems and the biodiversity housed in them. The biodiversity treaty, now ratified by over 160 countries (again, not including the United States), requires less developed states to formulate plans for preserving rain forests and other biologically important areas, while obligating developed states to provide financial assistance and to ensure "fair and equitable sharing of the benefits" (e.g., profits from pharmaceutical sales) with species-rich but cash-poor countries.[46] As suggested in the survey of environmental problems, this regime does not seem to be working very well in stemming the loss of biodiversity, although Costa Rica and some other countries have set aside biospheres that they hope will be supported by ecotourism and other sustainable economic uses.

Somewhat more effective has been the U.S.-inspired 1973 Convention on International Trade in Endangered Species (CITES), which bans or restricts trade in hundreds of animal and plant species thought to be endangered. In the 1980s, poachers were killing hundreds of African elephants daily, seeking to sell the ivory to Japanese and other consumers, until ivory was added to the list of prohibited exports in 1989. In Zambia, Zimbabwe, and some other African countries, local villagers were given an incentive to help the central government catch poachers and manage game parks through programs that returned some of the proceeds from ecotourism to the grassroots level rather than all the monies flowing to the national capital. The revival of the elephant population in Zimbabwe was so successful that, by the late 1990s, the government was complaining about excessively large herds, urging a restoration of the ivory trade and permitting safari hunters to reduce herds by inviting them to shoot elephants for $10,000 per animal. In addition to international regimes, there are, of course, unilateral national conservation efforts, such as the Endangered Species Act passed by the U.S. Congress in the same year CITES took effect. (One news article reported recently that the U.S. legislation is stronger than its Canadian counterpart, but this does not help grizzly bears in the western United States who wander unknowingly across the border into British Columbia.)[47]

As mentioned at the end of Chapter 6, a Biosafety Protocol was added to the Convention on Biological Diversity in 2000 for the purpose of regulating trade in genetically modified foods. This is just one of several global regimes dealing with food and the problem of world hunger. In addition to the UN Food and Agriculture Organization (FAO), there is an International Fund for Agricultural Development, a World Food Council to coordinate global food policy, a plan to maintain a global grain reserve to be made available to food-deficit countries, and assorted other institutions aimed at promoting agricultural development and food assistance programs. Despite this infrastructure and the convening of two world food conferences, one in Rome in 1974 and one in Lucerne in 1995, the pledge made by U.S. Secretary of State Kissinger in 1974 that by the end of the decade "no child will go to bed hungry at night" remains unfulfilled.

Food, as seen in the French case, is a subject that can deeply touch national sensibilities. So, too, can population as a global issue, insofar as countries differ over whether they have too many people or too few, and, if too many, how to curb population growth. For example, the Chinese government has succeeded in dramatically lowering China's birth rate by enforcing a draconian "one child" policy in urban areas that penalizes couples who violate the law and rewards those who comply and that authorizes aborting "defective" fetuses. Japan, on the other hand, sees itself as having an alarmingly low birth rate that is expected to cause its population to decline over the next several decades, and hence has adopted policies that encourage couples to have childen. At the three UN world population conferences (Bucharest in 1974, Mexico City in 1984, and Cairo in 1994), the only regimes that emerged were a series of declarations and action plans that ultimately affirmed the sovereign right of each state to devise its own population policies, with due regard to be given to universal access to family planning and reproductive health services supported by the UN Fund for Population Activities and other agencies.[48] The UN Center for Human Settlements (Habitat) exists to provide governments with technical assistance on overcrowding and other urbanization problems. It has sponsored the UN International Year of Shelter for the homeless and a variety of other projects, including a "City Summit" in Istanbul in 1996 that attracted mayors from throughout the world and addressed everything from coping with graffiti to coping with sewage.

Numerous other international institutions and agreements can be identified in the environmental field—the 1989 Basel Convention that bans the export of hazardous wastes, the 1991 Wellington Convention that imposes a fifty-year moratorium on mining and oil-drilling in Antarctica, and so forth. Having briefly identified some of these regimes, I will now delve into the politics that define this arena.

Ecopolitics

At times it is possible to make sense out of global environmental politics by relying simply on billiard ball lenses.[49] Certainly the billiard ball paradigm provides at least a partial explanation of what transpired at the UN conferences held in Stockholm and Rio in 1972 and 1992. Delegations from 114 states attended the 1972 Stockholm conference, representing governments drawn from both North and South. The Soviet Union and most states in Eastern Europe boycotted the meeting in protest over the nonrecognition of East Germany, their Warsaw Pact ally. The United States and other developed states to varying degrees were advancing an environmental agenda calling upon less developed countries to control their population growth and to take other measures to address ecological concerns. The LDCs in turn criticized the rich industrialized states for failing to take responsibility for causing the bulk of the planet's environmental problems and for failing to provide adequate technical and financial aid transfers that might enable Third World governments to respond properly to their own national needs. Partly as a symbolic gesture to coopt the South into buying into the North's agenda, the major UN donors agreed to put the headquarters of UNEP in a Third World capital, in Nairobi, Kenya.

Although the 1992 Rio conference was considerably larger—178 states attended, more than 110 of which were represented by their head of state—and although it was much more receptive than the Stockholm conference to the coequal priorities of the environment and economic development, in many respects it was a replay of 1972. Less developed states in a self-serving way reiterated their NIEO demands for more "green" in the form of money, while developed states in an equally self-serving way reiterated their call for "green" policies in Brazil, China, and other parts of the South to curb the latter's growing contribution to deforestation, global warming, and other such trends. To be sure, there were splits within the North and within the South that made for shifting coalitions across different sets of issues. For example, the United States joined with Saudi Arabia, Kuwait, and other OPEC states to block any provisions in the Climate Change Convention that would adversely affect major oil-producing or oil-consuming economies, while Germany, Japan, Sweden and some other industrialized states joined with the thirty-two nation Alliance of Small Island States (the Maldives and others which are especially vulnerable to the sea-level rise effects of global warming) to press for tougher measures. Each country sought to have others make the greater sacrifice. In the end, some delicate compromises were reached, including pledges by LDCs to pursue sustainable development and pledges by DCs to help bring that about through the infusion of additional funds channeled through the Global Environmental Facility that had just been created by UNEP, UNDP, and the World Bank, although differences persisted between DCs and LDCs over voting power in the Facility.

Within the G-7, there remains a split between the EU and Japan on the one hand and the U.S. and Canada on the other over whether to support the Kyoto Protocol along with a global carbon tax on fossil fuel use. This is based largely on national interest considerations. Germany has been a lead state in support of sizeable CO_2 reductions, since it can easily meet its Kyoto obligations by simply closing down heavily polluting factories in the former East Germany which it would be inclined to do anyway. France relies on nuclear energy for 65 percent of its electricity while Japan also heavily utilizes nuclear energy; hence, they are more supportive of carbon taxes and other anti-fossil fuel measures than the United States, which not only has a more fossil fuel-driven economy but also is more automobile-dependent and less able to shift to mass transit given its vast continentwide highway system. Not surprisingly, China, which depends on coal for three-quarters of its total energy use as the basis for fueling its high-octane economic growth, was opposed to developing countries being saddled with obligations under the Kyoto Protocol and continues to resist any such demands. It is also not surprising, in regard to the European acid rain problem, that it was Sweden, a net importer of SO_2 emissions, and not the United Kingdom, a net exporter, which put the issue on the agenda and pressed for solutions that resulted in the Helsinki Protocol.

Describing ecopolitics in traditional billiard ball, state-centric terms, Lawrence Susskind comments that "a few powerful nations play [a] . . . dominant role in most treaty negotiations, forcing other countries and nongovernmental interests to accept secondary roles or to sit on the sidelines.[50] Just as Germany has been a lead state on the global warming issue, the United States and China have been referred to as veto states whose cooperation is crucial to the success of any global warming regime since they are the two leading emitters of greenhouse gases. Susskind adds that, for powerful and nonpowerful states alike, there is "the stubborn persistence of national sovereignty as an important goal unto itself."[51] The UN membership was unresponsive when, in 1989, twenty-four states, led by the Netherlands, France, and Norway, proposed a new supra-national UN body in the environmental field that would be empowered to make "nonunanimous" binding decisions "for the good of the world community" and proposed that the International Court of Justice in the Hague would be given jurisdiction over rule compliance.[52]

Realists and idealists alike point out that regime compliance is especially weak in the environmental area.[53] However, this may have less to do with flagrant violations or indifference to treaty obligations than to the nature of environmental treaties, which tend to involve complex national monitoring and reporting requirements entailing highly technical, costly data collection and analysis on CO_2 and SO_2 emissions, waste disposal, species extinction, and other ecological variables which many governments even with the best of intentions are ill-equipped to do.[54] I referred earlier to the existence of many small, "weak" states in the international system, whose governments lack the financial and other resources that support "state capacity" for action. The reader will recall the example of Tajikistan, whose UN ambassador was its one-man diplomatic corp, responsible for answering the office phone and cooking state dinners. One can imagine the difficulty such a government would have in meaningfully participating in environmental conferences and carrying out legal obligations in this area. Virtually all states, including the least developed ones, have some version of an EPA, but in many cases these are minimally staffed and minimally functioning bureaucracies.

It is precisely the highly technical character of much environmental problem-solving, along with its *relatively* low salience on national agendas, that sets it somewhat apart from other issue areas and, arguably, gives rise to a somewhat different, "lower" brand of politics than one finds in the military and economic spheres. Having just noted how Westphalian, billiard ball dynamics are clearly evident in ecopolitics, we now need to examine, as Hilary French suggests, cobweb dynamics and the growing role played by nonstate actors in agenda setting, policy formulation, adoption, and implementation in the environmental arena.[55] Should environmental issues in the twenty-first century attract greater attention and involve greater stakes, as many believe will happen, it is possible that ecopolitics will acquire the flavor of high politics, but it is premature to reach such a conclusion just yet.

As an example of how nonstate actors have increased their involvement in global environmental governance, one can compare their role at the 1972 UN Stockholm Conference on the Human Environment with their role twenty years later at the 1992 Rio UN Conference on Environment and Development (UNCED). In 1972, there were some 500 representatives from 250 NGOs. In 1992, there were over 25,000 representatives from 1,400 NGOs. The proliferation of NGOs between 1972 and 1992 partly reflected the growing visibility of environmentalism on the global agenda—after all, there were only 1,500 journalists at Stockholm, compared to 9,000 at Rio—but it also reflected their enhanced presence and activism at international conferences. Many of the delegates at Rio were representing NGOs that had been officially invited to participate directly in the proceedings (e.g., Greenpeace and the International

Union for the Conservation of Nature), while others participated in an informal, parallel nongovernmental Global Forum (e.g., one of my students who was part of a small Hare Krishna group).[56] Although 70 percent of the accredited NGOs were based in industrialized countries, some developing countries, such as India, the Philippines, and Kenya, also were heavily represented.[57] Not all NGOs at Rio were environmental groups. Some were business and other groups lobbying against excessive new governmental and intergovernmental regulations, although at least one corporate NGO—the Business Council for Sustainable Development, an alliance of Volkswagen, Dow Chemical, Nippon Steel, and a few other MNCs—took a pro-environmental stance.[58] James Speth describes this "global civil society" phenomenon as follows:

> Rio signaled the rise of an increasingly powerful group in international diplomacy: nongovernmental organizations (NGOs). The Earth Summit brought together an international community of scientists, policy experts, business groups, and activists representing a wide array of interests. Although far from cohesive themselves, NGOs worked together surprisingly well throughout the summit process, lobbying and educating delegates, helping draft agreements, and communicating with the 9,000 journalists who covered Rio.[59]

Echoing Speth, other observers note that efforts were made by the conference organizers to give NGOs "unprecedented" access both to the preparatory (PREPCOM) meetings as well as to the Rio sessions themselves,[60] and that Rio "represented a new level of NGO participation in global environmental politics."[61] In addition, there were numerous IGO representatives, drawn not only from UNEP, which helped to sponsor the conference, but also from UNCED's own secretariat, which was responsible for running the conference, as well as from FAO, WHO, and other UN specialized agencies involved in environmental regimes.[62] Then, too, below this transnational layer, there were quite complicated domestic politics at work within national delegations (e.g., in the U.S. delegation, there were conflicting positions to be reconciled among the Environmental Protection Agency, the Commerce Department, and other government agencies, as well as among environmentalists, oil companies, utilities, and other interest groups). Rio, in short, saw a rich set of two- and three-level games being played by a variety of state and nonstate actors.

Susskind is more cautious than Speth in evaluating the importance of nonstate actors. He argues that, while there is general agreement that in the environmental area as a whole "NGOs have been given substantial roles . . . up to and including shared responsibility for managing working sessions, and speaking (although not voting) at formal plenary meetings at which final decisions are made," "the rights accorded to NGOs, however, are unpredictable."[63] Obviously, not all nonstate actors have had equal impacts on global environmental governance at Rio or in other forums. The Hare Krishna have not been influential. However, other actors have had input at various points in the global policy process. At the front end, "most multilateral environmental treaty negotiations have been initiated by international organizations,"[64] with UNEP in particular serving as a catalyst for convening dozens of conferences since 1972. Activist NGOs have frequently succeeded in attracting world attention to certain environmental causes, notably Greenpeace, with its over 3 million members in twenty countries; Greenpeace members dramatized their "save the whales" campaign in the 1970s by sending ships to pursue a Russian whaling fleet and positioning their vessels between the harpoonists and pods of whales, while in the 1990s they helped to publicize environmental devastation caused by Shell Oil in its Nigerian drilling operations by organizing a consumer boycott of Shell gas stations in Europe.[65] Scientific NGOs ("epistemic communities") have also played a special role in the agenda-setting stage, as we will see in the role played by atmospheric research teams in alerting the world to the ozone layer problem.

Epistemic communities generally have been given a far greater consultative role in the policy process at Rio and other such environmental conclaves than they have enjoyed in such venues as the Uruguay Round trade talks or global arms control talks, where nation-state officials have been less likely to defer to "technical experts." Such actors affect global environmental governance not only in contributing to agenda setting but also in subsequent phases of the policy process, at times helping to craft regimes, to mobilize mass publics to support governmental action, and—especially in the case of LDCs—to supplement national capacity to carry out regime obligations and perform policy evaluation.[66] For example, an NGO named FIELD provided critical expertise to the member governments in the Alliance of Small Island States that enabled the latter to participate more fully in the Rio climate negotiations.[67] In the words of one commentator, "NGOs [at Rio] set the original goal of negotiating an agreement to control greenhouse gases long before governments were ready to do so, proposed most of its structure and content, and lobbied public pressure to force through a pact [the Framework Convention on Climate Change] that virtually no one else thought possible when the talks began."[68] Similarly, as noted earlier, the World Wildlife Fund has been instrumental in compiling statistics on endangered species and putting pressure on governments to add various animals and plants to the protected list of the CITES treaty, while the International Union for the Conservation of Nature was called upon to draft the treaty itself, and TRAFFIC and other NGOs have been relied upon by governments to monitor treaty implementation and compliance. It should be added that the more neutral and professional scientific NGOs are perceived to be by national governments, the greater access they are likely to be accorded to the regime process; such perceptions are enhanced when the epistemic community is composed of participants from many diverse countries.

Of course, as the global warming issue demonstrates, experts may be able to put certain issues on the global agenda and may help to propose solutions, but meaningful policy adoption and implementation may lag if the scientific community itself appears to lack consensus and if there are no politically palatable, "cheap fixes" to the problem. As Susskind reminds, "independent scientific investigations may play a role in environmental treaty making, but they are intertwined with, not separate from, political considerations."[69] Still, one cannot understand the politics of global warming without taking into account the Intergovernmental Panel on Climate Change (IPCC), an epistemic community of the world's leading climatologists that was charged by the UN General Assembly in 1988 with providing expert monitoring of climate change, and has kept the greenhouse effect on the agenda from Rio to Kyoto to the present with its alarming reports, publicized by the mass media, of rising temperatures and volatile atmospheric conditions. In support of IPCC, one finds the Climate Action Network, a global coalition of more than 250 national and local environmental groups, as well as some odd bedfellows that include MNCs in the insurance industry concerned about the potential costs associated with floods and other disasters attributable to global warming, along with firms in the nuclear and renewable energy industries hoping to benefit from curbs on fossil fuel use, such as those which belong to the World Fuel Cell Council. Pitted against these forces are the Global Climate Coalition in the United States and counterpart organizations in other countries, made up of labor union leaders and executives from the oil, coal, automobile, and other industries concerned about lost jobs and lost profits, such as members of the World Coal Institute, although some companies are breaking ranks, such as British Petroleum (the new owner of AMOCO), which recently has committed itself to exploring new energy alternatives. Clearly, while some firms chafe at environmental regulation, others accept it, either because they believe "doing good" is good business or because they envision becoming enriched if sustainable development becomes more fashionable and if they can invent and market cutting-edge "green" technologies; several of the biggest MNCs have gone so far as to urge the adoption of global uniform environmental standards, as in the packaging and labeling of various products.[70]

One writer asks: "What does it mean that top European insurance executives have begun consulting with Greenpeace about global warming?"[71] It may produce little regime change in the foreseeable future, but it may nonetheless signal the beginning of a new kind of post-Westphalian politics which features a web of NGO-MNC-IGO interactions that often bypass nation-state capitals.[72] Jennifer Clapp, in a study of the politics surrounding amendments to the 1989 UNEP-sponsored Basel Convention that restricted the export of hazardous wastes, comments that "the attempt by business leaders to influence global environmental matters has traditionally been via lobbying the state at the domestic level. . . . While this is an important aspect of industry's efforts to insure that treaties which states enter into are in accordance with industry's desires, business actors are increasingly focusing their lobby efforts at the global level as well."[73] She analyzes the two- and three-level games played over the issue of whether scrap metal and other recyclables should be included in the waste ban—a highly technical, yet multimillion dollar controversy involving not only developed and developing states but also the Bureau International de la Recuperation (composed of some 600 firms and national recycling federations in over fifty countries), the International Chamber of Commerce, and other industry groups, pitted against Greenpeace and environmental NGOs.

Just as one cannot fully understand the politics of global warming or recycling without taking into account two- and three-level games played among subnational, national, and transnational actors caught in a complex web of interrelationships, so also must one go well beyond the simple billiard ball paradigm to develop a rounder picture of the politics of acid rain, population, and other environmental concerns. U.S.-Canadian acid rain diplomacy has been shaped at least as much by subnational conflicts between midwestern and northeastern states in the United States (over which region is to blame for Atlantic seaboard air pollution) as it is by national interest calculations out of Washington and Ottawa; New York and other northeastern American states have found themselves allying with the Canadian government in calling for Ohio and other midwestern states to take action against their coal-burning utilities whose SO_2 emissions drift hundreds of miles. The multidimensional politics of ocean governance was discussed in Chapter 4; Peter Haas has authored a well-known study on the important role played by epistemic communities in the creation and execution of the Mediterranean Sea Action Plan.[74] I alluded earlier in this chapter to the welter of timber, cattle, agricultural, mining, and other interests whose activities have been contributing to tropical deforestation in Brazil and elsewhere. The cast of characters involved in this story include many different kinds of nonstate actors who have been a part of either the problem or the solution—not only MNCs such as McDonalds and Burger King which have promoted cattle ranching but also Merck and other pharmaceutical companies which have been cutting their own deals with host governments to engage in rain forest "bioprospecting" in return for royalty payment and profit-sharing, NGOs such as the World Wildlife Fund which pioneered debt-for-nature-swaps whereby conservation organizations would agree to take over payment of a country's debt if the latter would pledge to preserve certain species-rich biomes, IGOs such as the World Bank which have funded ecologically damaging road and dam construction projects in developing countries but of late have become more environmentally sensitive, and indigenous peoples whose plight has attracted media attention worldwide.[75] As discussed by Dan Morgan in *Merchants of Grain*, one cannot begin to fathom the politics of food unless one includes Cargill, Andre, and a handful of agribusiness MNCs that dominate world grain production and distribution.[76] Likewise, an analysis of population politics would be incomplete without a consideration of an assortment of nonstate actors which increasingly have become involved in the deliberations at global population conferences, ranging from women's rights, reproductive rights, and family planning organizations on the "anti-natal" side to the Catholic Church, Islamic groups, and other organizations on the "pro-natal" side, and various "lifestyle" advocacy groups (homosexual and heterosexual) in between.

Although many nonstate actors admittedly have at best a marginal impact on global governance and the kinds of regimes that emerge in the environmental field—certainly, few observers would credit gay and lesbian groups, for example, with significant impacts on global population policy—the previous discussion has suggested that some of these actors can be an important part of the political equation and that it would be equally erroneous to discount their importance as it would be to exaggerate it. For a more detailed, textured look at cobweb dynamics in the environmental issue area, let us now examine the 1987 Montreal Protocol and its subsequent amendments which have sought to protect the ozone layer.

THE 1987 MONTREAL PROTOCOL ON SUBSTANCES THAT DEPLETE THE OZONE LAYER

Richard Benedick has written: "On September 16, 1987, representatives of countries from every region of the world reached an agreement unique in the annals of international diplomacy. In the Montreal Protocol on Substances That Deplete the Ozone Layer, nations agreed to significantly reduce production of chemicals that can destroy the stratospheric ozone layer (which protects life on earth from harmful and ultraviolet radiation) and can also change global climate."[77]

Benedick should know. He was there in Montreal as the head of the U.S. delegation. He noted that the protocol was "only possible through an intimate collaboration between scientists and policymakers."[78] One can question whether it was "unique" or not—we have seen other examples of such collaboration—but this case does offer an especially vivid glimpse into the nature of contemporary ecopolitics. Benedick himself might well question whether this was a case of "low politics," since he considered it a great triumph of global cooperation against great odds, given the disagreements that existed at the start of the negotiations. Still, the very "intimate collaboration between scientists and policymakers" he refers to is a feature of regime-making that one associates much more with ecopolitics than with the politics of defense or trade and investment.

The tale begins in 1839, when the existence of ozone was first discovered.[79] However, it was not until the 1930s that a problem began to emerge, when Dupont, General Motors, and a few other companies started making new chemical compounds called chlorofluorocarbons (CFCs) as substitutes for ammonia in refrigeration, by the 1950s producing these in large quantities not only as coolants but as propellants in aerosol spray cans, as the stuff of styrofoam packaging in fast food restaurants, and for other purposes. However, only in the 1970s, after the "national ecological state" was born and global environmental consciousness had spread, did the ozone problem manage to find its way onto the global agenda, sparked by scientific studies postulating a link between CFCs and ozone layer deterioration.

A 1974 study published in *Nature*, written by Mario Molina and Sherwood Rowland (both of whom were later to win the Nobel Prize for chemistry), is widely credited with establishing the linkage. At the time, the United States was the world leader in CFC production. Dupont, which accounted for half of all CFC production in the United States, at first discounted the scientific theory and evidence. However, there was sufficient concern that Washington in 1977 unilaterally banned CFCs in most aerosol products, followed by Sweden, Norway, and other Nordic countries along with Canada adopting similar measures. CFC production worldwide dropped, but CFCs continued to be manufactured as the chemical industry in the United States and other countries mounted resistance against government regulations, exemplified by the formation of an industry lobby called the Alliance for Responsible CFC Policy. Although there was growing recognition by scientists and environmentalists that half-hearted, unilateral national policies were inadequate and had to be broadened to include a more far-ranging, multilateral regime, it was a tough sell: "The links between causes and effects were not obvious: a perfume spray in Paris helps to destroy an invisible gas 6 to 30 miles above the earth, and thereby contributes to deaths from skin cancer and extinction of species half a world and several generations away."[80]

Aside from an epistemic community of atmospheric scientists, IGOs played a key role throughout the regime process: "UNEP coordinated research, informed governments and world public opinion, and played an indispensable catalytic and mediating role during the negotiation and implementation [of the ozone regime]. . . . Other intergovernmental organizations, including WMO [the World Meteorological Organization], the World Bank, UNDP . . . and the World Health Organization, were also drawn into varied aspects of the ozone protection process."[81] UNEP was an especially critical actor, especially at the outset in putting the ozone issue on the agenda; according to one observer, "it is no exaggeration to state that it was UNEP that kept the ozone issue alive at this stage [in the late 1970s and early 1980s]."[82] UNEP sponsored a meeting in 1977 in Washington, D.C. that was attended by thirty-three nations and the European Community (EC) Commission, that produced a World Plan of Action on the Ozone Layer (a nonbinding call for monitoring and research), and that led to the creation of a Coordinating Committee on the Ozone Layer (a transnational network of scientists similar to the IPCC in the area of climate change, charged with reporting on the latest research). In early 1983, Norway, Sweden, Finland, Canada, and Switzerland formed the "Toronto Group," with the United States joining later that year; the Toronto Group's call for not merely studying the problem but taking action to eliminate CFC use was opposed by the EC (led by France and Britain), Russia, Japan, and other CFC producing and consuming countries.

In March 1985, around the same time that British scientists reported finding a "hole" (a depression) in the ozone layer over Antartica that was roughly the size of the continental United States, forty-three nations, including all the major CFC producers as well as sixteen LDCs, convened in Vienna. Three transnational industry bodies—the International Chamber of Commerce and two European federations—were present as observers, although environmental NGOs were curiously absent, not yet fully mobilized on the ozone issue. The Vienna conference produced the Vienna Convention for the Protection of the Ozone Layer. Signed and eventually ratified by virtually all the major industrial states, it was a modest framework convention which, though it simply obligated the parties to take "appropriate measures" to protect the ozone layer and to continue to monitor the problem and exchange data, paved the way for the subsequent protocol produced at Montreal two years later that would set explicit, mandatory phaseout targets and timetables.

The Reagan administration itself was ambivalent toward imposing greater restrictions on CFC use. Although the United States had joined the Toronto Group, some in the administration, wedded to laissez-faire, antiregulatory ideological principles, aired "the argument that skin cancer was a 'self-inflicted' disease attributable to personal life-style preferences, and therefore protection against excessive radiation was the responsibility of the individual, not the government." A spokesman for Secretary of the Interior Hodel urged a "personal protection" program of broad-brimmed hats and sunglasses.[83] Benedick describes the bureaucratic politics that went on within the executive branch as some two dozen government agencies "worked together in developing and promoting a U.S. position" in preparation for the Montreal Protocol talks. This "interagency minuet" revolved around the State Department chairing interagency meetings attended by EPA staff, NASA scientists, Office of U.S. Trade Representative staff, and representatives from Commerce, Energy, Interior, and other departments, each with its own agenda and set of concerns that had to be resolved in internal negotiations.[84] Summaries of policy debates had to be reported to the White House Domestic Policy Council.

In short, the ozone case showed how on certain issues the line between foreign and domestic policy had become completely blurred, and the "foreign policy establishment" had expanded to include virtually the entire federal government. Various domestic interest groups from both the industrial and environmental sectors, often with close ties to specific government agencies, sent observers to participate in a number of international meetings leading up to Montreal. "With these observer representatives, the U.S. contingent at the international meetings was by far the largest, numbering over 30"; the multi-level game-playing was such that U.S. officials "could not indicate in advance to domestic observers what they might be prepared to compromise, lest they undermine their position vis-à-vis their foreign adversaries."[85] Similar dynamics were at work within other national delegations.

Meanwhile, independent of any national delegations, various epistemic communities, NGOs, and IGOs were making their own way to Montreal. In 1986, an international research team of 150 scientists from the United States, Brazil, Canada, Australia, Japan, and several other countries, under the leadership of NASA and auspices of UNEP and WMO, finalized their data collection and published their findings showing that the accumulation of CFCs in the atmosphere had doubled between 1975 and 1985 and was steadily eroding the ozone layer. It was in a 1986 technical workshop co-sponsored by UNEP and EPA that "environmental NGOs . . . participated in the international negotiating process [over ozone] for the first time."[86] In April 1987, a well publicized meeting of scientists was held in Wurzburg, West Germany, that reinforced earlier warnings about the ozone layer problem. Also in April 1987, a preparatory meeting for Montreal was held in Geneva, where UNEP Executive Director Mostafa Tolba told the diplomatic gathering that the latest research made it "no longer possible to oppose action to regulate CFC release on the grounds of scientific dissent."[87] Pressure for action was mounting. On the eve of the Montreal meeting, in late summer of 1987, there were further media reports of an accelerated thinning of the ozone layer.

Still, forces of opposition had to be overcome within and between nation-states before scientific consensus could be converted into a political consensus supporting a strong global policy response. Sixty governmental delegations, including all the major actors from the developed and developing worlds, converged on Montreal in September 1987, along with numerous IGO and NGO representatives, including members of Greenpeace, the Natural Resources Defense Council, the International Chemical Manufacturers Association, and Friends of the Earth. The European Community Commission's bargaining position upon its arrival was to push for at most a freeze on CFC production rather than any reductions, but EC unity was shattered when West Germany, influenced by its strong domestic "green" movement, began to shift toward the Toronto Group position, which called for major reductions. (One factor that complicated negotiations was uncertainty over whether the EC Commission was or was not authorized by EC member states to speak for them; ultimately each of the 12 EC members voted individually on the Protocol.) By this time, the U.S. position, hammered out only after a "bitterly contested process [among subnational players],"[88] had changed from ambivalence to active support for an ambitious phaseout program, partly because U.S.-based Dupont was close to developing a substitute product for CFCs (hydrochlorofluorocarbons, or HCFCs) that would be less ozone-depleting and would advantage the American company vis-à-vis its European competitors in the world marketplace were an agreement to be reached. As for the Soviet position, Benedick notes that the cordial relationships that had developed between the two superpowers over arms control issues in the late 1980s carried over to environmental diplomacy, as Moscow accepted Washington's position of phasing out CFCs in the spirit of "ozone glasnost."[89] Among the developing countries, Mexico, Venezuela, Egypt, and Indonesia led the way in supporting the call for CFC elimination; Malaysia led the opposition while China and India dragged their feet, arguing that the South should not be asked to endorse a potentially costly switch away from CFCs when the problem had been caused largely by the North. (One Indian delegate labeled the ozone issue a "rich man's problem–rich man's solution."[90])

In the end, the compromise that was reached heavily tilted toward the Toronto Group position. CFC production and consumption was to be cut substantially, by 50 percent from 1986 levels by 1998, with further cuts to be made thereafter depending on scientific analyses and recommendations. Trade in products with CFC content was to be restricted with any states that refused to sign the agreement. Less developed countries were given a longer grace period of an additional ten years to phase out their CFCs and were to be given financial and technological assistance in weaning themselves off of CFCs. Each party was obligated to issue an annual report on total CFC production as well as imports and exports. In addition, the agreement contained an unusual provision for periodic review whereby further fast-track revisions of the protocol could occur without lengthy negotiations if the scientific evidence revealed the necessity for amendments. The Montreal Protocol was signed initially by twenty-four states and the EC Commission. By January 1, 1989, it had received the necessary ratifications to come into force, having been endorsed by twenty-nine states, representing over 75 percent of all CFC consumption worldwide. Mexico was the first country to ratify, and the United States was second, with the EC members, Japan, and the Soviet Union acceding shortly afterwards. China was to ratify the Montreal Protocol in 1991 and India in 1992. By 2000, both the Vienna Convention and the Montreal Protocol had attained "nearly universal" adherence as had the London and Copenhagen amendments that followed.[91]

A combination of factors produced successful policy adoption of a global regime on ozone. Although some might offer a realist, billiard ball explanation that "the rapid adoption of the Montreal Protocol was the consequence of extensive pressure applied by the USA at international negotiations," there were more complex variables at work than U.S. hegemony.[92] Benedick argues that it was a combination of not only U.S. leadership (along with the leadership of other Toronto Group states) but also the key role played by UNEP and its executive head, the force of domestic public opinion, the mobilization of environmental NGOs along with industry acquiescence, the availability of a quick, relatively cheap fix in the form of HCFCs, and the constant pressure applied by transnational espistemic communities concerned about the ozone threat. Benedick goes so far as to say that "science became the driving force behind the formation of public policy on the ozone issue,"[93] and was especially instrumental in sparking rapid ratification of the protocol and the amendments that were subsequently added.

Certainly, alarm bells set off by media reports of new scientific findings following the Montreal conference kept the world focused on the ozone issue and prompted calls for not only speedy ratification but for amendments accelerating the timetable for phaseout of CFCs. Just two weeks after the Montreal meeting, a transnational research team of sixty scientists issued a widely publicized report noting a worsening of the ozone problem, while six months later another team of over 100 scientists from ten countries reinforced the message that the ozone layer was severely deteriorating and that this was clearly tied to CFCs. When a team of British scientists confirmed these same findings, even Britain—one of the early holdouts—decided to support ratification of the Montreal Protocol, with Prince Charles providing a symbolic gesture in announcing that the British royal family would no longer use aerosol sprays propelled by CFCs.[94] The British government was also pressured by a consumer boycott of CFC-laden aerosol sprays that was organized by Friends of the Earth (FOE). FOE also helped to launch a worldwide "stratospheric defense initiative" (dubbed "styro-wars" after the "star wars" nickname used by critics of Ronald Reagan's antiballistic missile SDI, "strategic defense initiative"), getting city councils in Berkeley, California, and elsewhere to create "styrofoam-free zones" which in turn put pressure on McDonalds and other fast-food restaurants to seek alternatives to styrofoam packaging. It would be wrong to suggest that such local actions dictated global policy on CFC production, any more than "nuclear freeze" resolutions passed by municipalities in the 1970s precipitated stronger international arms control regimes, but they did provide yet another example of the growing linkages between local and global levels. The actions of FOE (as well as Greenpeace, which in 1989 "staged an 8-hour blockade holding up rail cars carrying 44,000 gallons of CFCs" destined for export from a Dupont manufacturing plant in New Jersey[95]) illustrated the growing activism of environmental NGOs well before Rio.

As the Montreal Protocol took effect in 1989, even more alarming scientific reports surfaced indicating that, even if production of *all* ozone-depleting substances (not only CFCs but also methyl bromide and halons) *totally ceased immediately*, it would still take as much as eighty years for the ozone layer to recover, given the long life of these chemicals in the upper atmosphere. In June 1990, ninety-five governments met in London to discuss moving up the target date for CFC reductions, making it a 100 percent ban, and adding methyl bromide and halons to the regime. The countries closest to the polar regions, where the ozone hole was most in evidence and hence most threatening—Australia, New Zealand, and the Nordic states—were the most outspoken about the need for more stringent measures, but few states needed swaying in the face of mounting scientific evidence. Even the representatives from private industry, which predominated among the forty NGOs in London and represented not only the chemical sector but also the automotive, electronics, refrigeration, solvent, and appliance industries, had resigned themselves to harsher measures.[96] The Montreal Protocol was formally amended to mandate a total ban on all CFCs by 2000, and a secretariat was established in Montreal to implement the regime.

No sooner did the amendment take effect than the scientific community issued yet another warning, this one especially ominous in its global reach; the report was released under the joint sponsorship of UNEP and WMO:

> For the first time, "serious levels" of ground-level ultraviolet radiation had been observed in Europe and Australia. Ozone layer values . . . registered new lows everywhere except the tropics. . . . Antarctica ozone depletion in 1991 was the most serious ever recorded. . . . Perhaps most significantly, for the first time diminished stratospheric ozone levels were recorded in the spring and summer in both Northern and Southern Hemisphere mid-latitudes, covering North America, Australia, New Zealand, and South Pacific Islands, nearly all of Europe, and large parts of Asia and South America.[97]

In the wake of this latest news, the parties to the Protocol met again in Copenhagen in 1992, and agreed to accelerate the CFC phaseout timetable to 1996 and to include halons in the ban as well. Meanwhile, LDCs complained that the promised assistance to them had not been forthcoming from Northern governments and multilateral aid channels despite the creation of a special fund administered by the World Bank and UNDP. It was left to multinational corporations to try to serve as "catalysts for change in the developing countries, both via their local affiliates and through requiring their suppliers or contractors to abstain from use of [ozone-depleting substances] . . . and often aiding them . . . by furnishing the needed technologies. Two industry associations, the Industry Cooperative for Ozone Layer Protection and the Japan Industrial Conference for Ozone Layer Protection, played prominent roles in introducing new technologies to many developing countries. Nortel assisted Mexico to an early conversion of its electronics industry; Motorola played a similar role in Malaysia. Numerous foreign firms linked up with Chinese manufacturers to produce ozone-friendly refrigerators, including Germany's Bayer AG, Sweden's Electrolux, and America's Raytheon. . . . More than forty multinational companies from eight countries . . . joined to help Vietnam's phaseout. In 1993, Germany's Hoechst opened the first substitutes factory in a developing nation, an HFC-134a plant in Brazil."[98] The world was readying for a post-CFC economy in the twenty-first century through a political process that was almost as complex as the underlying science.

There is a postscript to the ozone story that illustrates how policy implementation in the case of global regimes can often be problematical. Although in many respects the Montreal Protocol can be considered a success story, there are concerns of late that the global regime may prove to be too little, too late. In April, 2000, the European Union-sponsored European Stratospheric Experiment on Ozone and the NASA-sponsored Ozone Loss and Validation Experiment reported data revealing ozone levels over the Arctic had fallen "dramatically" during the previous winter.[99] Other worrisome findings have been reported since. Part of the problem is the aforementioned staying power of already existing CFC chemicals in the atmosphere, which could be eating away at the ozone layer for at least another fifty years. But there are other problems as well. First, compliance with the Montreal Protocol has been spotty, both in terms of the annual reporting requirements and the meeting of scheduled phaseout targets. While the United States and most major CFC producers in the developed world have generally made good on their commitments to eliminate their CFCs, a few industrialized countries, particularly Russia and the other members of the CEIT group (Countries with Economies in Transition), have claimed they lack adequate state capacity to meet their obligations; for example, Poland has had only one person specifically charged with handling Montreal Protocol implementation, compared to thirty in the Netherlands.[100] Second, the developed countries continue to lag in fulfilling their financial pledges to help developing countries shift away from CFCs. Third, related to state capacity problems, Russia, China, and India have become the largest CFC producers and the source of many "black market" exports to the West, where there is still consumer demand for cheaper CFCs in older-model car air conditioners and other products. Fourth, the HCFCs and other CFC substitutes that were developed, while more short-lived in the atmosphere than CFCs, nonetheless have some corrosive effects. Fifth, methyl bromide continues to be relatively unregulated, partly because the pesticide and other industries that utilize the chemical have been successful thus far in blocking action.[101] Hence, the effectiveness of the ozone regime, for all of its forward-looking features, remains in doubt.

CONCLUSION

Richard Benedick has suggested that the governance structure of the Montreal Protocol might serve as a "model" for future environmental regimes and perhaps global regimes generally:

> At the top of the structure is the Meeting of the Parties to the Montreal Protocol, which combines executive, legislative, and judicial functions in a single supreme decision-making body. The parties, which had numbered only 35 states at the First Meeting of parties in Helsinki in 1989, grew to 157 by the eighth assembly in San Jose, Costa Rica, in 1996. (Meetings of parties were also open to nonparty states, UN agencies, and other intergovernmental institutions and nongovernmental organizations, which could all participate in discussions but did not have decision-making privileges.) . . .The main job of the assembly is to debate and decide on adjustments or amendments to the protocol. . . . Decisions [are to be] adopted by a two-thirds majority of parties present, representing at least separate simple majorities of both industrialized and developing-country parties. . . . An Open-Ended Working Group . . . is a less formal negotiating body . . . that prepares detailed options for decisions by the Meeting of Parties [based on review of scientific, financial, and other data]. . . . The Ozone Secretariat, located at UNEP headquarters in Nairobi, . . . is responsible for convening meetings, assembling reports, [and carrying out other administrative tasks]. . . . Assessment Pan-

els . . . [comprised of] hundreds of experts from around the world, coming from universities, governments, industry, and research institutes but serving in their personal capacities [perform policy evaluation in assessing regime effects]. . . . The Implementation Committee, comprising 10 members from the state parties, has assumed a central role in a unique process of monitoring compliance.[102]

Elegant as this governance model appears, questions abound. Despite the reference to "supreme" authority, is it not the case that ultimately each state retains its sovereign right to join or not join and to remain in or leave the regime? As the number of state parties belonging to the regime approaches 200, how easy or hard will it be to forge a global consensus and reach meaningful global agreements with so many actors crowding around the global bargaining table, including many that barely have enough state capacity to pay the airfare of their delegation? Does the participation of a myriad of IGO officials and NGO representatives, some representing private industry and some representing competing interests—all claiming to speak for "global civil society"—further complicate regime-making, and how exactly will they be accommodated? On ozone and other issues, to the extent that the locus of decision making shifts to international institutions—where MNCs and other transnational actors are peculiarly well organized for lobbying and where unelected bureaucrats ("Eurocrats" and the like) can often wield considerable influence in the political process—how does one avoid a "democratic deficit"? Will major state players, such as the United States, tolerate enhanced participation of these nonstate actors, and will they accept a decision-making formula where they are not assured of veto power? If compliance is found lacking, what means exist for regime enforcement? Is the ozone case "unusual" in the stress placed on scientific data, or can we expect global problem-solving in all fields to rely increasingly on technical expertise?[103] Will high, middle, and low politics imperceptibly blend into one another as the concepts of "security" and "welfare" broaden to include environmental threats? And will people in the United States and elsewhere be willing to accept global regulation of their behavior, when even now they often complain that their national capital is too far away and unresponsive to their concerns?

All of these questions bring us back to square one, to the matter of global governance and the search for, at the very least, a "more mature anarchy." The future of global governance will be examined in Part Three, in the next, concluding chapter, when the author returns to the "critical questions" raised in Chapter 1 having to do with the possibility and desirability of improved global institution-building, or scaffolding, in the twenty-first century. In thinking through the architecture for a new world order, it is worth quoting Benedick once more:

> The ozone treaty reflects a realization that nations must work together in the face of global threats and that if some major actors do not participate, the efforts of others will be vitiated. . . . The Montreal Protocol can be a hopeful paradigm of an

evolving global diplomacy, one wherein sovereign nations find ways to accept common responsibility for stewardship of the planet and for the security of generations to come.[104]

Even if there is a compelling logic dictating a reformation in international governance arrangements, "will the need forge a way?"[105] Whether individuals and societies in the contemporary international system are prepared to find their way toward a new world order, and how distant they are willing to go, is uncertain. It was thought in 1948 that "once a photograph of the Earth, taken from the outside is available . . . a new idea as powerful as any other in history will be let loose."[106] Yet neither Sputnick's orbiting of the planet in 1957, nor the Apollo moon landing in 1969, nor thousands of satellite photos taken since have fundamentally altered our image of the human species as organized around a state system, no matter how many exhortations about Spaceship Earth have been uttered. Typical of this mindset is the recent billing of Brazil as "a developing nation on the frontiers of space" whose "equatorial location gives it a competitive edge in launching rockets [that are] faster and carry heavier payloads" than "temperate zone competitors." Brazil is building its own Cape Canaveral, at Alcantara on the eastern edge of the Amazon basin, in a tropical rain forest region some claim to be the common heritage of mankind. Brazil is also "the only developing country to be invited to join the 15-nation group building the international space station."[107] The international space station itself is a striking symbol of the continued commingling of cooperation and conflict in a world of states.

The author has noted throughout this book how, if anything, the forces of Jihad are at least as powerful as the forces of McWorld. Tip O'Neill, the late speaker of the U.S. House of Representatives, once said that all politics is local. That was an exaggeration, but one that probably resonated with the representatives of 579 cities from 171 nations at the 1996 UN-sponsored City Summit in Istanbul, many of whom signed onto Local Agenda 21 action plans to make "human settlements safer, healthier and more livable, equitable, sustainable and productive."[108] As with the example of Friends of the Earth stimulating city councils to pass "styrofoam-free zone" measures, UN Habitat's sponsorship of the City Summit reflected the growing interpenetration of global and local phenomena, going both over and under heads of state. The jumbled images of Jihad and McWorld can be seen in the following account of NGO networks connecting cities:

> In 1990, the Toronto-based International Council on Local Environmental Initiatives (ICLEI) was formed to serve as the environmental arm of the world's oldest association of municipalities, the International Union of Local Authorities. As a clearinghouse, ICLEI disseminates information about the 2,000 plus cities in 64 countries that are now working on Local Agenda 21 initiatives. . . . The New York-based Mega-Cities Project . . . was founded in 1987 to promote exchange between officials from the world's largest cities. . . . More than 100 European city

leaders convened in Aalborg, Denmark in 1994 to inaugurate the European Sustainable Cities and Towns Campaign, which is supported by several municipal associations in Europe, as well as ICLEI and the World Health Organization.[109]

The odd juxtaposition of Jihad and McWorld images can be seen as well in the current environmental battle cries "NIMBY (Not in My Backyard)!" and "NOPE (Not on Planet Earth)!"

As usual, however, the nation-state lurks in the background of all this, as "cities with Local Agenda 21s are generally those that have strong support from the national level. A 1997 survey showed that 82 percent of known Local Agenda 21 initiatives were concentrated in 11 countries with national campaigns sponsored by government or country-wide municipal associations."[110] When subnational jurisdictions have attempted to take action on the international plane independent of their national capital, the central government has ordinarily been quick to remind them that it alone is empowered to conduct foreign policy, such as Washington's recent admonition to the Maryland and Massachusetts legislatures which tried to pass sanctions bills prohibiting their state-level governments from engaging in commercial transactions with the Nigerian and Burmese governments accused of environmental irresponsibility and human rights atrocities.[111]

In Part Two, by examining various issue areas and case studies, I have tried to show how billiard ball and cobweb phenomena can be pieced together into a mosaic of contemporary world politics, and how one can reconcile what seem to be two competing, contradictory realities today—on the one hand a persistent Westphalian order and on the other hand an emergent post-Westphalian order. As we have seen, Westphalian and post-Westphalian forces contend with each other in different ways across different sets of issues. We are now ready to put the finishing touches on the puzzle we started with.

PART THREE
SOLVING THE PUZZLE

CHAPTER 8

Summing Up and Moving On
World Politics and Global Governance in the New Millennium

Time has no divisions to mark its passage. There is never a thunderstorm or blare of trumpets to announce the beginning of a new month or year. Even when a new century begins, it is only we mortals who ring bells and fire off pistols.
—Thomas Mann, *The Magic Mountain*, 1924

The age of nations is past; the task before us, if we would survive, is to build the earth.
—Pierre Teilhard de Chardin

On the eve of most revolutions, they are thought to have been impossible, whereas the morning after they are thought to have been inevitable.
—Remarks by Richard Benedick, the chief U.S. negotiator at the 1987 Montreal Protocol ozone talks, at a meeting of the International Studies Association

I made reference earlier to IBM, the computer giant, advertising itself as offering "solutions for a small planet." A modest estimate is that at the outset of the twenty-first century, there were well over 200 million people in 56 countries using the Internet, over half of whom were Americans, with the number of Net users expected to double by 2002 and with the Worldwide Web eventually becoming less an American phenomenon than a truly universal one.[1] Computers symbolize the kinds of paradoxes which mark our age. They at once hold out the promise of unparalleled social connectiveness on a planetary scale, permitting instantaneous communication with anyone anywhere anytime, at the same time that they may have the effect of producing greater personal isolation, alienation, and atomistic behavior, if one no longer needs to work in a common workplace or shop in a mall or otherwise interact face-to-face with other human beings when one has his or her own private space to operate out of at home. Robert Putnam, in his book *Bowling Alone*, has called attention to the fact that more individuals in America may be bowling than ever before, but membership in bowling leagues has been on the decline, as is the tendency to join the Elks or the Rotary Club or other such voluntary associations that represent "social capital," i.e., underlying structures that help to knit a society together and provide a sense of community.[2] Likewise, computers have the potential to maximize individual freedom and democracy, in terms of prying open closed political systems and providing global access to new information and ideas long denied to millions of the world's people, yet the same technology may be used to control or disrupt lives on a mass scale through manipulation of data banks or sabotage of banking, air traffic, and other systems by governmental or nongovernmental actors.[3]

In his book *The Lexus and the Olive Tree*, Thomas Friedman explores at length the collision of traditional culture, based upon atavistic impulses rooted in the "nation" or other mental constructs, and modern (more properly, postmodern) culture, driven by technological forces that are threatening to obliterate established ways of thinking. He has only one illustration in the entire book, but it is a striking one—a photo that depicts an Orthodox Jew, clinging to 5,000 years of history, standing by the Western Wall in Jerusalem and holding a celluar phone up to the wall so that his relative in France can say a prayer at the holy site.[4] Similar, if not so poignant, images have been presented in the preceding pages, such as photos of the world's tallest building in Malaysia and of a high-tech skytrain in Thailand towering over "Third World" huts and shanties—for better or worse, symbols of modernity in developing countries that might have been thought unimaginable a generation or so ago, yet now coexist not far from ancient Islamic mosques and Buddhist temples. There is a double-edged quality to many contemporary phenomena that makes it difficult to get a handle on the world. It is not easy to assess where humanity is headed as we begin a new century and a new millennium, to offer "solutions" to problems, and to decide whether we should be happy or sad at our prospects.

In this book, I have focused on one glaring ambiguity, a puzzle that lies at the very core of our existence today and has engendered both optimism and pessimism about the future. To recapitulate: In Chapter 1, I noted how the nation-state and state system has remained the one constant over the past several centuries as an organizing principle for comprehending how the world works (although it took awhile after their origin around 1648 and the Peace of Westphalia for "Westphalian" ideas to be internalized by elites and masses). I noted further that this is now in question, as we seem to be *between two epochs*—a Westphalian world struggling to survive and a post-Westphalian world struggling to be born. Such traditional concepts as sovereignty, national interests and national security, citizenship, and the like remain fundamental to understanding world politics, yet in some respects are becoming increasingly problematical if not

Getting wired: The clash of tradition and modernity in the post-Cold War world.
(Stock Market/Sally Wiener Grotta)

anachronistic in an age of economic globalization, cyberspace, and other developments that are playing havoc with state-centered institutions. The nation-
state has never appeared to be more robust than at present—there are more
nation-states than ever, and the range of concerns their governments are
expected to deal with continue to be on the rise—yet the nation-state has never
seemed more vulnerable as a political form. It is being buffeted not only from
above by MNCs and other transnational forces, but also from below by ethnic
and other subnational forces, these winds of change feeding on each other.
Centralizing and decentralizing, centripetal and centrifugal, tendencies have
long vied with each other in world affairs, but there is an especially schizophrenic quality to the present situation. Some see the nation-state as dysfunctional, too small to handle the big problems in life and too big to handle the

small ones. Some argue that governments at every level should be more willing to step aside and allow civil society to work its will, whether in the form of the unregulated market or nongovernmental organizations or other private agents. Among the major dramas that will be acted out in the twenty-first century are the tensions between globalism and localism and between statism and nonstatism. This has led observers to invent a new term recently—"global governance," defined by the UN Commission on Global Governance in its 1995 report *Our Global Neighborhood* as "the sum of the many ways individuals and institutions, public and private, manage their common affairs. It is a continuing process through which conflicting or diverse interests may be accommodated and co-operative action may be taken [at several levels]. It includes formal institutions . . . as well as informal arrangements that people . . . either have agreed to or perceive to be in their interest."[5] The aim of *Between Two Epochs*, as stated in Chapter 1, was to grapple with the paradoxes surrounding the challenge of global governance today and to try to make sense of them, so as to intelligently speculate about "what's ahead for America and the world" in the immediate post-Cold War era and beyond.

In Chapter 2, I raised the question of whether conditions in the contemporary international system were conducive to a "new multilateralism"—a new framework for global governance that might represent the next stage of global institution-building beyond the League of Nations and the United Nations that the United States helped to create in the twentieth century. I left open exactly what this might entail, taking the view that before one tries to save the planet, one should first try to develop a better understanding of what the planet looks like. That is, before one proposes prescriptions on what *ought* to be, one should have a solid grasp of reality, a diagnosis of what *is*, in terms of both the deep historical forces that have given rise to nation-states, international organizations, and multinational corporations as well as the current forces at work. Hence, I first attempted to provide a "birds-eye" overview of the contemporary system that replaced the Cold War system, pointing out the mix of constraints and opportunities that are likely to inform any effort at improved global governance and noting that, while the need for global institutions may be greater than ever, central guidance mechanisms may be harder to come by in some respects than in previous eras due to recent systemic developments. I referred to four current system properties specifically that have introduced greater complexity into world politics than existed in the post-World War II period: (1) a growing diffusion of power, with the demise of one "superpower" and the other finding it hard to flex its muscles; (2) a growing fluidity of alignments, with the East-West and North-South axes of conflict giving way to less readily definable fault lines; (3) an ever expanding agenda of issues, with traditional military-security matters increasingly having to compete for attention with economic, environmental, and other issues; and (4) a growing importance of nonstate actors (IGOs, NGOs, MNCs, etc.) increasingly competing with states in shaping outcomes in the international arena.

I suggested that perhaps the central question of our time was whether—based on the first two trends (the breakup of the postwar power and bloc structure)—we were witnessing merely the déjà vu transformation of the international system from bipolarity back to the more normal, pre-1945 historical pattern of multipolarity, *or* whether—based on the other two trends (the new agenda of issues and the new set of actors)—we were on the threshold of a much more profound, epic transformation, namely a change not only *in* the Westphalian system but *of* the Westphalian system and its centuries-old underlying operating principles. In other words, is the early twenty-first century a "Westphalian moment"? Some observers answer in the affirmative, that we are living at a special time. Friedman, describing the 2000 presidential election in the United States, comments:

> Although our current election comes at the dawn of the information and biotech revolutions, you'd never quite know it from the presidential campaign. . . . There is a general sense that not much is at stake . . . and that we have entered an era of good feelings and tiny differences. This is an illusion. My gut tells me that by 2008 we will look back at the Clinton years as a fool's paradise—the quiet interlude after the cold war and before all the forces unleashed by e-commerce . . . and global integration reached their critical mass and ushered in a period of radically new political choices and issues in U.S. and global politics. . . . We are all increasingly connected but nobody's quite in charge. And when everyone is more tightly connected, but not more tightly governed, small units can wreak huge havoc . . . which is why this new era is going to actually demand more global governance, not less.[6]

Some argue otherwise, that the more things change the more they stay the same and that what we are seeing is business as usual. Kenneth Waltz: "Challenges at home and abroad test the mettle of states. Some states fail, and other states pass the tests nicely. In modern times, enough states always make it to keep the international system going as a system of states. The challenges vary; states endure. They have proved to be hardy survivors."[7] Ditto Robert Jackson and Alan James: "Nowadays no less than previously the population of the world is divided into separate, independent States each with their own identities, territories, and symbols which mark them off from one another. The vast majority of people still owe their allegiance to [these entities]. . . . There is nothing to indicate that in the foreseeable future such entities will not continue to be the preferred and predominant form of political organization. . . . The fundamental characteristics of the international society formed by such . . . entities therefore give no indication of soon changing into something different."[8]

In Chapter 3, I conducted a closer examination of the international system in historical and contemporary perspective, showing that *both* sides are right, that we are truly straddling "two epochs." One can find theoretical potency and empirical evidence to support both the realist or neorealist, state-centric position as well as the liberal or neoliberal, pluralist position. We can debate whether the billiard ball paradigm, with its focus on some 200 actors, or the cobweb paradigm, with its focus on thousands of actors, more accurately reflects reality, but a compelling case can be made that each offers a useful lens for conceptualizing world politics. Likewise, we can volley bits of data back and forth, but it is probably a futile exercise. Yes, for all the talk of globalization, it is true that "the United States is still almost 90 percent an economy that produces goods and services for its own use"[9]; and, yes, it is also true that "foreign corporations and individuals now receive almost 50 percent of all the patents issued by the U.S. Patent and Trademark Office, nearly twice as many as in 1980."[10] We obviously still live in a state system, but one that is being chipped away at daily. It is premature to guess how this will ultimately play out, how long we will be in limbo between two epochs, or even if these tensions will ever be resolved and a post-Westphalian system will ever fully materialize. Only time will tell.

In Chapter 4, I tried to indicate how, meanwhile, we might live and cope with these paradoxes. I argued that intergovernmental organizations (IGOs) can be best understood as the key nexus points between the state-centric Westphalian culture and the more pluralistic post-Westphalian culture, and that they were likely to provide the key vehicles in the twenty-first century whereby nation-states could essentially retain their sovereignty while managing to continue to function in a global political space in which human transactions and concerns figured to increasingly transcend national borders. As Inis Claude had written after World War II, the historic role of IGOs such as the UN was not that they were clearly precursors to world government, but rather that they were an adaptation of the state system which could make world government unnecessary, if such arrangements among sovereign states could be made to work in a way that responded to human needs.[11] Hence, global governance was about "shooting pool and pooling sovereignty," improving "global policy processes" whereby international regimes could be produced as collective responses to shared problems. If the reader will pardon my mixing metaphors, international relations has long been characterized by "bowling alone" pressures; but the growth of IGOs over time demonstrates the recognition that states cannot function by simply acting alone through unilateral policies. In Chapters 5, 6, and 7, I then proceeded to discuss a series of challenges facing the nation-state today in the areas of war and peace, economic welfare, and the environment, and tried to flesh out what the dynamics of global policy agenda setting, formulation, adoption, and implementation looked like in these three domains. I noted that billiard ball and cobweb elements could be found in all three issue-areas, albeit in differing degrees as one went from high-politics to low-politics concerns; the lower the politics, the greater the congeries of actors that are likely to be involved, although, as the concept of "security" broadens, these distinctions may become less clear-cut in the future.

In the remainder of this chapter, I will peer into the new millennium and consider "solutions" to our puzzle, examining how humanity might be organized to deal with a range of local and global concerns, small problems and big problems, low-politics and high-politics issues. I will fill in what I mean by a "new multilateralism." Finally, I will indulge in some speculation on the implications of all this for America and the world, keeping in mind the Romanian proverb that it is always hard to predict anything, especially the future. And especially—to quote a Chinese proverb—when we live in such exciting times.

THINKING ABOUT THE FUTURE

In conjecturing about the world politics of the future, it is helpful to think in terms of "alternative world order models," ways in which human beings could conceivably organize themselves politically.[12] Two basic questions are posed here: (1) What alternative world order models are *possible?* (2) Which are *desirable?* The first is an empirical question, calling for a judgment about what kind of world one can realistically expect to see in the future. The second is a normative question, calling for a value judgment about what kind of world one ideally would like to see; this question relates to our query about how much government we want, and what level (supranational, national, or subnational) is optimal for satisfying our wants.

Regarding the empirical question, it is almost as difficult today for the average person to envision a world without nation-states as it was for people in an earlier time to envision a world that was round rather than flat. Yet, the historical record shows that the nation-state and state system have not always existed, and logic dictates that they will not necessarily be with us for all time. In tracing the origins of the nation-state, Chapter 2 discussed various ways political space can be organized, ranging from a highly decentralized, anarchical set of arrangements to a highly centralized, hierarchical governing structure and including a less neatly configured feudal mode of organization. Given the trends discussed in this book, what might the world look like during the course of this century?

Regarding the normative question, many arguments can ensue over the criteria to be applied in evaluating the merits of alternative world order models. The "world order values" that often come to mind are: peace, individual freedom and dignity, economic justice, and ecological balance.[13] Others, however, might add such goals as cultural diversity, national unity, or economic efficiency. A political system that is conducive to one set of values might well be detrimental to another set of values, or at least might maximize certain values more than others. For example, do we put the emphasis on peace, or justice? Although many would argue that these two goals serve each other, at least one observer has commented that "peace will serve justice better than justice will serve peace,"[14] meaning that general economic well-being cannot occur in the absence of a stable order and that the latter cannot exist where armed force is used in the name of equality. Then, too, there is the matter of whether we should adopt a Grotian "society of states" morality, which stresses obligations states have toward each other (e.g., the obligation not to intervene in each other's affairs, and the obligation to try to narrow the rich-poor gap between states), or a "cosmopolitan" morality, which takes a more holistic view of humanity and the obligations people have toward each other (e.g., the obligation to promote human rights, including supporting humanitarian intervention in civil wars where genocide is occurring and supporting closing the rich-poor gap within states).[15] What kind of world should we be striving for in this century?

In contemplating what is possible and desirable, people tend to become either overly cynical and resigned to the present reality or overly optimistic and idealistic about what could be. The former are "bad realists," obsessed with what is, and are incapable of opening up their minds to new possibilities; the latter are "bad idealists," preoccupied with what ought to be, to the exclusion of what can practically be attained.[16] The field of international relations, which has revolved around competing strands of realism and idealism, has had its share of both bad realists and bad idealists, Cassandras and Panglossians. It could be argued that observers of late have tended to err more on the side of the former than the latter. Who can claim to have foreseen in 1945, at the end of World War II, that France and Germany, centuries-old rivals, would within a dozen years be engaged in a regional integration project that would reduce the probability of war between them to almost zero, and would by the end of the century share a common currency? And who can claim to have foreseen in 1981, when a Cold Warrior entered the White House decrying the "evil empire" that was the Soviet Union, that both the Cold War and the Soviet Union would be gone within a decade and that this transformation of the bipolar international system would occur so quietly, without a shot being fired?

Although in the long run the least likely future is the present, it is, of course, quite possible—many would say probable—that the contemporary, post-Cold War international system will continue to exist in its basic characteristics for quite some time, that is, a world whose dominant feature remains the competition between the governments of sovereign nation-states, albeit a contest played increasingly with a wider circle of participants, over wider stakes, and with ever more complex rules. There are different variants of this system that can be envisoned; for example, Charles Kupchan talks of "benign unipolarity" and "stable multipolarity,"[17] similar to Samuel Huntington's "uni-multipolarity" I alluded to earlier.[18] Whether unipolar, bipolar, multipolar, or whatever, is the state system the best of all worlds? Kenneth Waltz thinks so, asserting that "the sovereign state with fixed borders has proved to be the best organization for keeping peace and fostering the conditions for economic well-being."[19] Robert North disagrees, contending that "one may entertain serious doubts whether the competitive, often violent nation-state system as it now exists is any longer safe for the human race."[20]

One can rightly ask: If not the nation-state, then *what*? How else might, or should, human affairs be organized? Let us examine for a moment a number of alternative world order models, in each case attempting to assess the likelihood of the world's resembling that model within the span of the next several decades, as well as whether the model would necessarily represent an improvement on the current system in terms of various world order values we might wish to promote.

ALTERNATIVE WORLD ORDER MODELS

Regionalism

An alternative to the nation-state system is a system of regional units. If integrative trends should progress further, then instead of some 200 nation-states, the world's people might be organized in five or six region-states—the United States of Europe, the United States of Africa, and so forth. Regionalism is a significant phenomenon in international relations, with regional organizations growing far more rapidly than global organizations.[21] It is not inconceivable that sometime in the future, because of mutual security or economic concerns, national units might merge into larger regional political communities, although enormous language and other barriers obviously would have to be overcome. Such regionalization is likely to be an uneven process, because the transfer of loyalty and authority to regional institutions is likely to occur in some geographical areas sooner than in others. Clearly, to the extent this scenario is in the process of materializing, it is the furthest along in Western Europe, where (as discussed in Chapter 3) the European Union has taken on many attributes of a supranational entity, including not only a common currency but a common decision-making apparatus. Although the EU has not yet made good on its vow to establish "a single foreign and security policy czar [who] would speak for Europe and carry out the military will of European leaders,"[22] nor is there any immediate likelihood that the EU will become a "European Federation" with a "European government,"[23] there is nonetheless movement toward a single Europe as the "nation-state is losing ground":

> It is still early, and nobody is suggesting that France has suddenly been expunged from the heart of the Frenchman. But . . . the widening appreciation of a body of European law that takes precedence over national legislation seems to be spurring a new consciousness. "There has been a qualitative jump in the sense of European identity [remarks one observer]. What you are seeing are the first signs of shared beliefs, rights and responsibilities among young Europeans." "It was an absolute discovery . . ." said Tanja Kreil, the 23-year-old German woman whose campaign to be allowed to bear arms in the German Army was upheld by the European Court of Justice . "I used to think of myself as German. Now I feel a little European, too." . . . At the European Court of Justice, whose jurisdiction is the 376 million citizens of the European Union, judges and lawyers are swamped, with the number of cases growing by more than 10 percent a year and over 1,000 cases pending.[24]

Similar, though more glacial, movement can be seen on the other side of the Atlantic, where the U.S.-Canada trade agreement of 1989 created a "free-trade zone . . . stretching from the Arctic Circle to the Rio Grande,"[25] and the 1993 NAFTA agreement extended the area to Mexico, with some obervers envisioning the eventual inclusion of the entire Western Hemisphere as a single economic if not political space.

As a world order model, regionalism would still be a decentralized system, with sovereignty residing in the individual regional units. Would this necessarily be a better world than the current one? Because it would be a somewhat more centralized political system in which agreeement would have to be reached among fewer actors, it would probably be a more manageable world in many respects. Such a system would be particularly effective in dealing with problems that are primarily regional rather than global in scope. Some have also suggested that regional units would represent "stepping stones" toward a global community and world government, or at least would be "islands of peace." There is evidence to suggest that the regional arrangements that have developed thus far, modest as they are, have helped "to control certain types of conflicts among their members and prevent them from spreading."[26]

Others, however, argue that regional units would simply be nation-states writ large, with the same propensity for conflict and with far more firepower with which to pursue their interests. Conflicts that today might be confined to a relatively localized area on the world map would in a future regionalized system pit very large areas of the globe against each other. There is already mounting concern over the prospect of possible trade wars between such regional blocs as the EU, NAFTA, and the Asian economies in APEC. Regionalism poses other problems. As difficult as it is today for many national leaders to sustain national unity and patriotism among their people, loyalty to a regional state would be even more diluted and difficult to maintain. It is not clear, either, whether regionalism would promote values of economic justice and individual freedom.

World Government

If "McWorld" trends were to be carried to their ultimate conclusion, we could get world government—a political system in which one set of institutions would preside over all human beings and political units on the planet. Several variations of this model have been considered. The most ambitious proposal calls for nation-states surrendering total sovereignty to a supreme global authority that would rule directly over all citizens of the world. Almost equally ambitious would be a federation, in which nation-states would share power and authority with a central world government; the world government would be delegated specific powers in certain areas (e.g., maintenance and deployment of armed forces) and the nation-states allowed to exercise jurisdiction over other areas (e.g., education or health care). This would resemble the model used by the founding fathers of the United States in creating a nation in 1787. Another possibility would be a confederation, in which a world government would enjoy some limited degree of power and authority, but the bulk would be clearly retained by the constituent nation-state units. Still another approach to world government might be the creation of several separate global authorities in different functional areas, along the lines of the International Seabed Authority called for in the UN Law of the Sea Treaty (the Montego Bay Convention).[27]

Various model constitutions have been drafted over the years to flesh out what the elements of a world government might look like in terms of legislative, executive, and judicial organs. For example, Grenville Clark and Louis Sohn of the Harvard Law School, in *World Peace Through World Law*, envisioned a permanent world police force with a monopoly on the legitimate use of force.[28] Richard Hudson of the Center for War/Peace Studies has proposed a "binding triad" arrangement that would empower the UN General Assembly to make binding decisions upon approval of three concurrent majorities, one based on the current one state-one vote formula, another based on a formula weighted by a state's contribution to the regular UN budget, and a third proportioned by national population.[29] Marc Nerfin, a former staff member of the UN Secretariat, has proposed a tripartite Assembly consisting of a Princes Chamber, in which national governments would be represented and security issues would predominate; a Merchants Chamber, in which major economic actors would be represented, including state entities, Bretton Woods institutions and other IGOs in the economic field, and multinational corporations and private bodies; and a Citizens Chamber, representing grassroots associations, with equal participation by men and women.[30] Jan Tinbergen, a Nobel Prize-winning economist, has called for a World Treasury, a World Central Bank, a World Ministry of Agriculture, and other global executive agencies, while another Nobel Laureate economist, James Tobin, has suggested a global tax on all foreign exchange transactions, to be utilized by the UN to combat global poverty.[31] Other global taxes that have been suggested have been a world income tax (for general revenue purposes), a global carbon tax (to fund environmental programs), a global tax on arms sales (to fund peacekeeping), a global tax on international air or sea travel (to fund air and ocean safety programs), and a global tax on distant e-mails (to fund the Internet wiring of developing countries).[32]

Fanciful as all this sounds, it is not just ivory-tower academics who are sounding like World Federalists. The globalist statements of bottom-line oriented multinational corporation executives were cited in earlier chapters; about these elites, one writing notes "the new generation of planetary visionaries, unlike globalists of earlier days, come to their prophetic calling not by way of poetic imagination, transcendental philosophy, or Oriental mysticism but by solid careers in electrical circuitry, soap, mayonnaise, and aspirin."[33] Even the "political class," with the most vested interest in sovereignty-based institutions, at times seems prepared to write off the nation-state; a U.S. Deputy Secretary of

State for Global Affairs in the 1990s was quoted as saying that "all countries are basically social arrangements. Within the next hundred years, nationhood as we know it will be obsolete. All states will recognize a single global authority. A phrase briefly fashionable in the mid-20th century, citizen of the world, will have assumed real meaning at the end of the 21st."[34]

Still, notwithstanding the growing globalization of the international economy, the spread of the World Wide Web, and other globalizing trends, speculating about the prospects for world government at this moment admittedly borders on science fiction. By the year 2500—the setting for *Star Trek*—humankind's sense of the universe may have expanded to the point where earthlings will view each other as one people with a common destiny. However, short of a Martian invasion, the vision of a single supranational community under one roof is not likely to materialize anytime soon.

Even if a world government were possible, though, would it necessarily be a panacea for all our problems? It is true that a centralized system would facilitate a more concerted global effort to deal with environmental and other problems; it would be less possible, for example, for states to offer "flags of convenience" to shippers seeking to evade maritime safety and pollution rules. Such a system also might allow for a more equitable distribution of wealth, although probably at the expense of some individuals and states that are now in a privileged position. There is serious question whether such a system would promote freedom and democracy. Who would determine the nature of the political institutions? Where would the "capital" be located? There are complaints today that even in a democracy such as the United States the average person has little access to the decision-making centers of power. One would imagine the problem would be greatly magnified with a world government. A world government would be in a better position to enforce the Universal Declaration of Human Rights and other human rights regimes than the UN is today, because national governments that practice oppression could not then invoke sovereign privileges against foreign interference in their internal affairs, yet some of these same governments might be the ones controlling the world government and defining the nature of the rights enjoyed by Americans and other peoples.

The one value that a world government would most likely maximize, according to conventional wisdom, is peace. However, just as central governments of nation-states today are often incapable of preventing the outbreak of large-scale domestic violence and civil war—and, indeed, at times find themselves presiding over failed states—there is no reason to assume that a world government could necessarily keep its house in order. In fact, some have suggested that the more "amalgamated" a political community is (in terms of having a common set of governmental institutions), the more prone it can be to instability and disintegration; instead, it might be better to work toward a "pluralistic" community with constituent units sharing common values and interests but not necessarily tied together under one government.[35]

Polis

Regionalism and world government models presume increased centralization of the global political system. If "Jihad" trends become more pronounced, another possibility is increased decentralization, with political life revolving around even smaller and more fragmented units than the current nation-states. Each of the roughly 1,500 distinct nationality or ethnic groups in the world might seek to form its own state.[36] This scenario, unlikely as it is, gained a measure of credibility in the 1990s with the growing ethnic unrest in places as diverse as Canada and Rwanda and the breakup of Yugoslavia and the Soviet Union. The "ministate" phenomenon has been much commented on. The United Nations currently has thirty-nine member countries with populations of one million or less (e.g., five European states—Andorra, Monaco, Vatican City, San Marino, and Lichtenstein—have a combined population smaller than Little Rock, Arkansas' 170,000 people). Ethnic-based secessionist movements could add substantially to the proliferation of ministates.

Smaller units might be based not on common ethnicity but on the special needs of local populations. The "states rights" movement in the United States, aimed at giving more power back to states and localities, is paralleled by recent calls for greater regional autonomy on the part of Northern Italians unhappy with the Italian government's tax and other policies that have the effect of redistributing resources from the highly industrialized, wealthy North to the less developed, poorer South. Jihad forces can be seen as well in the recent threats made by Staten Islanders to secede from New York City and by the denizens of the San Fernando Valley to loosen their ties to Los Angeles, and also in the increased number of gated communities with their own private charters springing up throughout the United States.

Robert Kaplan comments: "Nations as we know them have existed for only a few hundred years. But cities have been with us since the dawn of civilization. And while the future of the city is not in doubt, modern nations will probably continue to weaken in the 21st century. By 2100, the organizing principle of the world will be the city-state. . . . Indeed, loyalty toward the polis will gradually overwhelm the traditional state patriotism of the twentieth century."[37] Some observers have noticed a trend toward the evolution of "microregions" emerging not only within national boundaries but in some cases across national boundaries. James Rosenau remarks:

> [One can see] the emergent role of certain cities and "natural" economic zones as subtle and nascent forms of transnational rule systems that are not sponsored by states and that, instead, emerge out of the activities of other types of actors. . . . An insightful example along these lines is provided by the developments that have flowed from the success of a cooperation pact signed in 1988 by Lyon [in France], Milan [in Italy], Stuttgart [in Germany], and Barcelona [in Spain], developments that have led one analyst to observe that "a resurrection of 'city-states' and

regions is quietly transforming Europe's political and economic landscape, diminishing the influence of national governments and redrawing the continental map of power for the twenty-first century." . . . Some argue that, as a result, the emerging urban centers and economies are fostering "a new historical dynamism that will ultimately transform the political structure of Europe by creating a new kind of 'Hanseatic League' that consists of thriving city-states." One specialist forecasts that there will be nineteen cities with at least twenty million people in the greater metropolitan area by the year 2000, with the result that "cities, not nations, will become the principal identity for most people in the world."[38]

An even smaller microregion than the four-city axis Rosenau mentions is the so-called "Alpine Diamond," made up of Lyon and Geneva, Switzerland, and Turin, Italy.[39] Similarly, Seyom Brown speaks of "geographically concentrated clusters of economic activity, which may not fall within the borders of a particular country and in which the major sectors engage in a high degree of coordination to advance the prosperity of the region. . . . Examples of such flourishing regional clusters are the San Diego and Tijuana corridor . . . and the 'growth triangle' linking Singapore and some of the nearby islands of Indonesia."[40]

Although a world order system comprised of subnational local entities or transnational microregions as the dominant political units is conceivable, it seems at least as unlikely as world government. The world might be organized in smallish communes after a nuclear war, as Jonathan Schell has suggested in *The Fate of the Earth*.[41] Otherwise, it would seem a utopian idea. As a utopian model, one can again ask whether it would necessarily be an improvement on the current system or any of the other alternative world order models that have been mentioned. Leopold Kohr, in *The Breakdown of Nations*, thinks so, urging "instead of union, let us have disunion."[42] Those who believe greater decentralization would be a positive development include "New Left" thinkers who seek greater democracy in the workplace and in other areas, as well as some "limits to growth" thinkers who urge a "small is beautiful" approach to living.[43] The common thread is a concern that the world has become too big and complicated for individuals to relate meaningfully to it, and a resultant desire to return to smaller, "human-scale" communities—along the lines of the ancient Greek city-states, which stressed the concept of "polis." (Recall Aristotle's admonition that the optimal size of a polity should not exceed 100,000 persons.)

Such a model could prove dystopian, however. Although decentralization might well maximize individual freedom, democracy, and economic justice, some central guidance mechanism would still be needed to address global issues such as greenhouse warming and other ecological problems that are not likely to disappear from the planet. Traditional security concerns would also have to be addressed somehow. The specter of Peoria or Poughkeepsie, or the San Diego-Tijuana corridor, saber rattling with nuclear weapons is hardly any more reassuring than the likes of the United States and Russia doing it. As hard as it is to forge agreement on nuclear arms control among 200 sovereign actors, it would be all the more cumbersome and daunting a task if several hundred or several thousand actors had to be consulted. Given the nature of the global problematique, a "stop the world, I want to get off" approach does not seem workable. Some degree of decentralization might be both possible and desirable, but only within limits.

Other World Order Models

All of the models discussed thus far tend to assume a territorial basis for human organization. Even world government models generally assume that, in addition to a global orientation, people will retain some degree of identity with smaller territorial units, be they regional, national, or subnational. However, other futures are conceivable. As discussed in Chapter 6, many globalization thinkers already see the world organized around nonterritorial principles, with transnational economic elites and the pursuit of corporate interests overshadowing national governments and the pursuit of national interests. Although these theorists seem to underestimate the forces of nationalism, it is possible that at some time in the future, if the multinational corporation phenomenon continues to grow, the world political map might consist of units defined more by corporate logos than geographical boundaries. In this world society, human beings would be primarily employees and managers of MNCs rather than citizens of nation-states or other territorialities. The General Motors auto worker in St. Louis would feel a greater bond of community with his fellow GM worker in Brazil than with his next-door neighbor employed by Ford Motors. As Raymond Vernon, Stephen Kobrin, and others have suggested, the "strategic alliances" between MNCs across nations and regions may render mute the concept of "home country" and may, indeed, mean "the end of geography." [44]

In a variety of ways, the future world system could be based on "networks" of nongovernmental organizations. Today, various groups around the world—not only MNCs but terrorist organizations and more benign actors—already meet and communicate on a regular basis that is challenging state control, abetted increasingly by the wonders of cyberspace. Although the NGO network is still heavily dominated by the developed world—evidenced by the fact that "only 251 of the 1,550 NGOs associated with the UN Department of Public Information come from the South"[45]—the network's tentacles are likely to spread more evenly over time into the developing world. An emergent "global civil society" is contributing to growing complexity of human relationships, which some see taking humanity back to a pre-Westphalian, medieval-type system of overlapping hierarchies of authority and multiple affiliations and loyalties.[46] The simultaneous occurrence of integrative and disintegrative dynamics—"fragmegration," to use Rosenau's appropriately awkward phrase[47]—further fuels such speculation. Although the European Union is ordinarily described as a manifestation of a new regionalism, it could just as easily be viewed as the leading edge of a "new feudalism," given the convergence of both McWorld and Jihad forces that define the EU (where supranational institutions in Brussels must contend not only with competing nationalisms but also with the evolution of microregions and the commitment to the principle of "subsidiarity" that urges public policy decisions be taken as much as possible by bodies closest to the people).[48]

It is not clear what the implications of a "new feudalism" scenario would be for various world order values. In an MNC-centered world, for example, although there would seemingly be less international conflict as we know it, there might be intensified transnational class conflict. Although the drive for profit maximization would presumably contribute to economic growth and some economic efficiencies, concerns about economic justice and environmental protection would probably suffer. How would *government* function? In a world of overlapping hierarchies of authority, the lines of accountability might be so blurred that it might be difficult to hold officials responsible for decisions, and hence democracy would be difficult to sustain in the face of the "democratic deficits" that would be produced by such variegated arrangements.[49] To the extent there is a "power shift" toward nongovernmental elites, including scientific authorities in epistemic communities, where will they derive their legitimacy from?

Normatively and empirically speaking, where does this foray into alternative world order models leave us? Robert Jackson, writing at the outset of the post-Cold War era, tried to put things into proper perspective:

> Granted the States system can be exploited by abusive or corrupt elites, often encourages national parochialism and prejudice, and has periodically—some would say regularly—led to devastating wars and other kinds of human suffering. But no human institution is fail-safe or foolproof. The States system still remains a remarkably flexible political arrangement that has accommodated . . . the greatest freedom and certainly the highest living standards ever recorded in human history. The affluent and democratic countries of the West are proof of what can be achieved within the framework of independent statehood. Why should anyone expect such a system to be abandoned at the very moment of its greatest success?[50]

Whether the state system survives will depend on whether it can continue "the long peace" in the twenty-first century and can extend it beyond developed states to less developed ones, whether it can address rich-poor gaps between and within countries, whether it can avert environmental disaster, and whether it can generally be seen as meeting human needs. Whether it is "flexible" enough to be up to the challenge of global governance in our time will be sorely tested in the coming years and decades. Putting aside long-term speculation, what can be done in the immediate, near-term to strengthen global governance within the framework of the contemporary state system?

AMERICA, THE WORLD, AND A NEW MULTILATERALISM

Maurice Strong, who was given prime responsibility for organizing the 1992 Earth Summit, wrote shortly before the event:

> The need for international cooperation is inescapable, and growing almost exponentially. This in turn has focused renewed attention on the principal instruments through which such cooperation is carried out. Most notable are the United Nations and its system of agencies . . . . These organizations provide the indispensable structure and fora on which international cooperation depends. They are the newest, least understood, least appreciated, and least supported of all the levels of our hierarchy of governance—and the most removed from the people they serve. They represent not the precursors of world government but the basic framework for a world system of governance which is imperative to the effective functioning of our global society.[51]

A similar passage, written by Richard Benedick in connection with the Montreal Protocol on ozone, was cited at the end of the previous chapter, begging the question "will the need forge a way?" Benedick offered the Montreal Protocol as a possible model for future global governance, which prompted me to raise a number of questions about the design. Those questions, and more, need to be addressed in any scheme that purports to furnish a framework for improved global governance.

If IGOs are the key vehicles for pooling sovereignty, it is practically a given that the United Nations is the logical linchpin of the IGO system, best positioned to facilitate global public policy processes across the broadest possible range of actors and issues, with the aim of producing international regimes in various problem areas. Imperfect as it is, the UN, if it did not exist, would have to be invented. All we need do is reinvent it through reform. Hence, the call here for a new multilateralism—if you will, an overarching regime that can be the engine for generating issue-specific regimes. There are few more daunting undertakings one can imagine than attempting to get Iraq, its neighbors, and everybody else to agree to the "mother" of all regimes that would be a next-generation central guidance system. Although a new multilateralism hopefully will be able to accommodate the participation of nonstate actors, I am realistic enough to recognize that any "game" that gets played over UN reform in the foreseeable future will itself be of the high-politics variety, heavily driven by national interests, national power, and statecraft (as suggested in the abbreviated examination of UN Security Council reform in Chapter 3).

Still, by focusing on the UN, I realize I am opening myself up to the charge of "bad idealism." I would only remind my accusers that the UN is an empirical fact that can be understood as the resultant of large-scale, long-term technological and other forces contributing to the establishment of the "habit of international organization" in the nineteenth century and the creation of global organization in the twentieth century. Whether this historical pattern of growing formalization and universalization of international politics continues, and can be given an accelerated push, will depend upon several factors. The past dynamics of international institution-building suggests that major innovation in the development of the international political system, in terms of new macrolevel governance arrangements resulting from human design, tends to be associated with the existence of a systemwide crisis combined with the existence of a critical mass of actors disposed toward and capable of moving the system. These conditions do not seem to exist today. There is no clear systemwide crisis akin to World War I or World War II that can serve as a catalyst to jar us into action. Indeed, the very thought of the "obsolescence of war," at least among highly developed societies, may be cultivating a sense of complacency rather than any reformist imperative. Moreover, we have observed how in some respects central guidance through global organization is more problematical than previously, given the diffusion of power along with the multitude of nation-state actors now claiming a seat at the global bargaining table and the increasingly convoluted relationships evolving between their governments and a host of nonstate actors enmeshed in complex interdependence.

Although the *constraints* are formidable, at the same time, the contemporary international system may hold out certain fresh *opportunities* for enhanced institution-building at the global level that perhaps we can seize. While power has become more diffused, there still remains a considerable concentration of power sufficient to constitute a dominant coalition of actors (national governments) capable of moving the system. Notwithstanding the "loss of control" experienced by today's governments, enough states still have enough "capacity" to act. What has been lost in power concentration in the waning of the superpower era has been more than offset by the reduced rigidity and polarization of alignments and reduced thinkability of great-power war, allowing more creative possibilities for an enlightened "concert of power" approach to world order.[52] As pointed out in Chapter 2, less than a dozen states account for the bulk of the planet's military and economic resources. These states constitute a virtual proprietorship over the "policing" instruments in the world body politic (as measured by their 75 percent share of global arms expenditures), while also accounting for much of the planetary economic product (70 percent of total GNP) and—relevant to legitimacy considerations and the use of soft power—well over a majority of the world's population.[53] At the core of the world's "power centers" is the Group of Seven, the leading industrialized democracies (lately renamed the G-8, to reflect the inclusion of Russia among the elite). And at the core of this group remains the United States.

When Samuel Huntington talks of a "uni-multipolar system" and Joseph Nye talks of the United States as having to settle for the role of "sheriff of the posse" rather than that of the Lone Ranger, they are conceptualizing a world today in which the United States cannot quite claim to be a hegemonic superpower but is at the very least the first among equals.[54] David Wilkinson puts it in Rousseauian terms, that "the strongest is never strong enough to be always the master."[55] In the context of UN reform, this means the United States is in a position to lead but not necessarily dominate deliberations over global governance. It is clearly a veto-state, one which cannot by itself dictate change but which can effectively block change. Given the fact that the United States is relied upon for roughly 25 percent of the UN regular budget, any meaningful reform proposals will likely have to pass through Washington.

There remains the problem of complacency. Power alone does not confer a global leadership role. One must also have the *will*, specifically the willingness to invest one's resources in steering the system and to absorb the costs of providing collective goods despite "free-riding" by some members. Describing the absence of leadership in the period between the two world wars, and the decision of the United States to remain relatively aloof from efforts to engage the international system in institution-building despite rising American power capabilities, Charles Kindleberger noted "the United Kingdom could not [lead]; the United States . . . would not."[56] Will history be repeated? Although it would appear a compelling case presently can be made for the United States treating improved global institution-building as an important foreign policy goal worthy of increased attention and resources (see the cost-benefit analysis conducted in Chapter 2), U.S. policy toward the UN in the post-Cold War era has been marked by indifference. Not only does the U.S. government continue to be in arrears of its UN dues payments, but—other than defense spending—it has evidenced declining interest in international affairs generally, even as the world becomes more interdependent. This is reflected in the fact that the international affairs portion of the federal budget (covering UN dues and contributions to multilateral agencies, State Department embassies and operations, and foreign aid programs), which is no more than 1 percent of the overall budget to begin with, "has plunged nearly 50 percent since the 1980s."[57] There almost seems to be a retreat from multilateralism, as Washington lately has been a visible nonparty to the Comprehensive Nuclear Test Ban Treaty, the Biodiversity Treaty, the Ottawa Treaty on landmines, the treaty establishing an International Criminal Court, and other global regime efforts (although it is true Washington has ratified several other agreements, such as the Chemical Weapons Convention, the Marrakesh Treaty creating the WTO, and the Montreal Protocol). Politics is supposed to stop at the water's edge when it comes to the really big foreign policy issues facing a country, such as defining its strategic vision in the world, but bipartisanship can be difficult to achieve when there is no obvious external enemy or threat. There is currently little consensus within the American political system, even within the Bush administration itself, as to what role the United States should play today in a world it can neither dominate nor withdraw from,[58] and little sense of urgency about it, as the country "casts about for an anchor in the waters of the post-Cold War world" to replace the containment of communism as a centerpiece of U.S. policy.[59]

One such anchor could be a new multilateralism that prepares the United States to cope with the complexity of a world in transition between a Westphalian and post-Westphalian landscape. John Mearsheimer wrote in 1990 that "we may wake up one day lamenting the loss of the order that the Cold War gave to the anarchy of international relations."[60] In the twenty-first century, in the new world disorder, we may wake up one day lamenting the passing of a window of opportunity we had to produce a more mature anarchy. One hates to think what a wake-up call would look like. One scholar observes that "history does not move forward without catastrophe."[61] Another observes that "man is a strange creature who does not see the handwriting on the wall until his back is up against it."[62] The next catastrophe may be too late to spark action, since it may be the last.

What might be the shape of a bargain struck in a game the United States plays over UN reform that would be normatively appealing and would also be cognizant of current realities both at home and abroad? A new multilateralism could have the following broad elements:

- First, in the war/peace area, emphasize the UN Charter's provisions pertaining to Chapter VI (peaceful settlement) or Chapter VI 1/2 (peacekeeping) rather than Chapter VII (collective security). As compelling as collective security is as a concept, it invites charges of hypocrisy and double standards, since the permanent members of the Security Council (especially the most powerful members) are unlikely ever to be the targets of UN action. Besides, most hostilities today are intrastate in nature rather than of the interstate variety that collective security was premised upon. In either case, preconflict peace maintenance (preventive deployment), mid-conflict peacemaking and peacekeeping, and postconflict peacebuilding—as articulated in Boutros Ghali's *Agenda for Peace* proposal—figure to be less heat-generating and more doable than branding and punishing "aggressors." It is in these areas that UN capabilities should be more fully and carefully developed to avoid the mistakes of past blue-helmet missions in Sierra Leone and elsewhere. In all these situations, and in the rare instance where collective security might be appropriate, it would be better for both the United States and the international community if Washington limited its contribution to money and technical support rather than manpower, since this would defuse the hot-button issue of American troops serving under a foreign commander.
- Second, play down "humanitarian intervention" insofar as it is perceived as posing an Article 2(7) threat to the integrity of lesser states in an international system where the one value that continues to command universal acceptance among governments is national sovereignty, eroded or not. Typical is the recent comment by the foreign minister of Namibia, responding to UN Secretary-General Kofi Annan's support for humanitarian intervention in Kosovo and other places: "What I hear is not my idea of the new world order. The idea of a right to humanitarian intervention is a threat to small nations and to the sacred principles and purposes of the

Charter itself."[63] The so-called Clinton Doctrine, that "if somebody comes after innocent civilians and tries to kill them en masse because of their race, ethnic background, or religion, and it's within our power to stop it, we will stop it," sounds like a noble call to combat genocide. However, if applied selectively, as in Europe but not Africa, it can breed cynicism; if applied consistently everywhere, it can produce imperial overstretch. It seems to lack enthusiastic support both among the American public (who were unwilling to tolerate American bloodshed in Kosovo) and within the international community at large. The "shifting sands of sovereignty," reflected not only in the new norm of humanitarian intervention but also in the recent creation of an International Criminal Court with the power to try government leaders for actions taken against their own people, threaten to undermine the underlying principle upon which the Westphalian system is ordered, without replacing it with any comparable ordering device.[64] As we navigate our way toward a post-Westphalian world, we need to think through how we can promote human rights through the use of various tactics (e.g., widely publicizing violations of human rights regimes, along the lines of the "mobilization of shame" tactics that have been successfully utilized at times by Amnesty International; offering the inducement of most-favored-nation trade status) which do not constitute a frontal assault on the Westphalian order.

- Third, in regard to economic, environmental, and other non-military areas of concern, focus on a few achievable goals rather than staging a never-ending "road show" of social summits, city summits, earth summits, and other global extravaganzas which cannot be adequately staffed by most states and which too often produce inflated rhetoric and empty gestures, only adding to the cynicism surrounding the organization. For example, an enhancement of its disaster relief capabilities would seem to attract a broad consensus among the UN membership and provide a strong raison d'être for the organization. The successful practice in the environmental field of hooking states on cooperation first through framework conventions, and then following-up with more explicit protocols should be pursued in other fields as well. It might be helpful to revisit the *Successor Generation* study funded in the 1980s by the Ford Foundation, which was the victim of poor timing, with its Cold War assumptions overtaken by the events that immediately followed its publication. The study contained many useful ideas for restructuring the UN—not only the General Assembly but especially the Economic and Social Council and the Advisory Committee on Coordination that links the specialized agencies to the UN proper—to deal with functional, non-war/peace concerns.[65] Among the proposals worth further consideration is the creation of a UN Bureau of Global Watch that would regularly monitor and report on evolving "human security" concerns, in the service of a 25-member Ministerial Board composed of high-level, national cabinet ministers meeting periodically to discuss issues within their substantive domain (somewhat along the lines of the relationship between the European Commission and the Council of Ministers in the EU).

- Fourth, related to the third element, treat the UN as a regime-processing center, a fulcrum for managing international public policy processes (agenda-setting, policy formulation, adoption, and implementation) and providing a degree of central guidance compatible with the systemic environment in which it is likely to operate for much of this century. Not all concerns are global in scope and require global solutions. The UN is uniquely situated to serve as a general facilitator of decisions by the international community as to what type of regime instrument is possible and desireable in a given problem area (in terms of norms/soft law, rules/hard law, organizations, programs, or other outputs) as well as what the regime scope might be (global or subglobal). It should be possible to improve the capacity of the international system as a whole to respond to problems confronting humanity, without foreclosing or limiting local or regional efforts. Global and subglobal approaches should not be mutually exclusive or competitive but should have a synergistic relationship, with global-level agencies stimulating subglobal activities (as in the case of the Regional Seas program sponsored by UNEP) and subglobal projects providing "laboratory" settings for experiments in international collaboration which if successful might be applied elsewhere in the system (along the lines of the function often attributed to the political subdivisions in the United States and other federal systems).

- Fifth, insist on administrative reform and greater efficiencies in the UN Secretariat, to minimize waste, overlap, and duplication. In almost every issue area, there is a bewildering array of IGOs and affiliated bodies that have been established to address concerns. "Sunset" procedures should be adopted to review whether some of these agencies have outlived their usefulness or have ever been useful. Just as the world does not need bigger governments so much as better governments, it needs higher quality intergovernmentalism. Bureaucratic politics is unavoidable in any large bureaucratic setting, and the reform or elimination of international bureaucracies pose special problems. But UN officials and staff, constituting the international civil service, have a special obligation to demonstrate dedication and competence in carrying out tasks with which they are entrusted. If the United States or any other member states are to be expected to increase their support for the UN, there has to be greater confidence that money will be well spent. At the same time, member states have to take the organization seriously enough to demand that the UN house be put in order and to see to it that necessary changes are made.

- Sixth, any efforts to improve the management of global policy processes must take into account the polyarchic characteristics of the international system. This means ensuring that various interests (both state and nonstate actors) are broadly represented in governance arrangements; utilizing primarily noncommand, consensus-based decision-making procedures where possible; and generally minimizing threats to sovereignty. At the same time, if, in the wake of the proliferation of state and nonstate actors pushing myriad demands, institutional overload and paralysis is to be avoided, some streamlining of decision-making machinery is needed. Regarding nation-state actors, some can barely pay the rent and utility bills of their UN delegations much less meaningfully participate in global conferences. (Reportedly, the minister of the Mission of Guinea-Bissau recently was forced to rely on a flashlight and cell phone to work at his New York office since the landlord had cut off all electricity and utilities due to nonpayment of rent. Because of "sovereign immunity," the landlord could not prosecute or forcibly evict the tenant.)[66] Other states, such as Liechtenstein, may be wealthy but are so small in the number of people they represent that they hardly seem entitled to the same voting power as a China. Overcrowding at the global bargaining table is creating pressures against the kind of rigid state-centric egalitarianism embodied in one state-one vote formulas as in the UN General Assembly, so that associate or consultative membership status, weighted voting formulas, and other devices will probably have to be explored. As for NGOs and nonstate actors, ways must be found to involve these players more systematically and constructively in global policy processes. There needs to be a review of the procedures utilized to accredit these organizations to UN conferences, with some organizations, based on their representativeness, expertise, and other criteria, more deserving of full participation than others. Better use should be made of NGOs to help supplement state capacity, particularly in helping to implement international regimes and monitor compliance.[67] Kofi Annan, in recently offering a "millennial vision" that he confessed was "absurdly ambitious," has urged "imaginative efforts among states, nongovernmental organizations, and the private sector to fight poverty and disease."[68] The UN Development Program, in seeking to narrow rich-poor gaps, has called for "redistributing the costs and responsibilities of care—to family, state, and corporation."[69]

- Seventh, in order to move all this, we need to consider the matter of "the sheriff and the posse." The prospects for peace and peaceful change can be greatly enhanced by the collective leadership provided by a dominant coalition of states (a concert of power) able and willing to steer the system in a manner that not only serves their interests but offers incentives for others to follow. The coalition must be broad enough to possess sufficient material resources to support the demand load and, at the symbolic level, to make a reasonable claim to the aura of legitimacy, but not so broad as to be incapable of action and susceptible to breaking down. It may be possible to put off for awhile longer the single most contentious issue in UN reform, but the moment of decision cannot be avoided indefinitely on the future expansion of the Security Council. The current composition of the Council is the most glaring anachronism left over from the post-World War II era. The world, and Europe, would not seem quite ready for an IGO—the European Union—and Japan to take over the seats occupied by the UK and France. As I suggested earlier, a "prominent solution" to this part of the UN reform game might consist of adding Japan and Germany (the number 2 and number 3 financiers of the organization) as permanent members; allocation of a permanent seat each to Latin America, Asia, and Africa, with the regional caucus group in each case asked to make the selection; and the addition of two nonpermanent seats from the developing world rotating biennially. A Security Council of twenty-two members, with each permanent member having a more circumscribed veto power, would seem the maximum size compatible with operability; although paralysis might still be a concern, there is much to be said for the organization not acting without the significant backing of major players in both the developed and developing worlds. Insofar as the expanded Security Council would likely represent over a majority of the world's people, as well as planetary product, military firepower, and UN budget contributions, the plan could claim to satisfy both realist and idealist desiderata. The closer that global governance arrangements come to reflecting an intersubjective image of fairness and reasonableness, the more workable they are likely to be.

- Eighth, economic resource transfers will be especially critical. Dominant coalition members will not only have to pay their full assessments as currently calculated but must be prepared to accept a bigger burden, both to provide necessary side-payments to the bulk of the UN membership (in the form of debt relief or some other quid pro quo) to attract initial support for reforms as well as to maintain a reformed system once it is in place. Major donor states might be willing to overcome the pattern of delinquency in paying their assessed dues and might be willing to convert more voluntary funding into assessed funding, thereby putting UN budgets on much more solid footing, if they could be assured of greater control over the budget process, not necessarily as final arbiters but at least as gatekeepers able to screen spending proposals. For the United States, at a minimum, it must be prepared to pay the roughly $1 billion it owes the UN in arrearages; this is closer to chump change than it is an act of great national sacrifice, and it is a sine qua non for the United States positioning itself to have leverage over the institutional reform process. Hard cash is one price to pay for exercising soft power.

These ideas are not as radical as others that have been floated. They can be thought of as "micropractices" in the ongoing project of global institution-building, not far removed from what Richard Gardner once called "practical internationalism," that is, a blending of "bilateral, regional, 'plurilateral' and global approaches" to problem-solving.[70] In its capacity as a regime-processing center, the UN would be a place where emerging problems could be identified, monitored, and proposed for consideration on the global agenda; where bargaining could occur (and two- and three-level games played) which would indicate the degree of consensus mobilizable in support of international action; and where signals ultimately would be furnished as to whether global solutions are possible or whether regime-making should be pursued at some level lower in the system. A new multilateralism could go a long way toward promoting not only a more peaceful world order but a more just order.

SOME FINAL THOUGHTS ON COPING WITH AMBIGUITY

Lord Caradon, the former British ambassador to the UN, once remarked: "There is nothing fundamentally wrong with the United Nations—except its members."[71] There is much truth to this observation that the UN, although in some respects an autonomous actor on the world stage in the same way that Ford Motor or other nonstate actors can be conceptualized today, is ultimately the sum of its parts. Pat Buchanan and American xenophobes to the contrary, it is not a world government but an inter-state organization. The "parts" are still mainly nation-states—formally, legally, and otherwise. It is through the latter that we human beings are all "members" and hold the fate of global governance in our hands.

Whether the nation-state as we know it will remain the primary repository of our hopes and fears throughout this new century is unclear. Human beings almost everywhere are experiencing a steady, almost inexorable interconnectedness across geographical, cultural, and other divides even as we seek to maintain the distinctiveness and separateness of our individual communities.[72] This is causing a growing dislocation of identity, which in turn may be contributing to a growing "citizen disaffection" with existing governments, even where there is the most democracy and prosperity to be found, as in the United States, Western Europe, and Japan. Public disenchantment with the latter political systems is being manifested statistically by lowered electoral turnouts, weakened political party affiliation, and opinion polls showing reduced trust of political institutions throughout the First World.[73] There is good reason to assume that public disenchantment with politics elsewhere, in political systems where there is less democracy and prosperity, is much higher, although hard statistics can be harder to come by to support such a conclusion. In many cases these people are voting with their feet (or, as in the case of the Cuban and Haitian boat people, their paddles), reflected in an unprecedented flood of political and economic refugees worldwide.[74] Often becoming wards of the American welfare state or European welfare states through legal or illegal entry, they add to the muddling of identities and borders and to the discomforting perception in Washington and other capitals that, like it or not, problems over democracy deficits and rich-poor gaps in *their* societies are becoming inescapably *our* problems.

Perhaps what we are witnessing is more a case of anxiety, a sense of vulnerability and helplessness in the face of powerful currents of change, than disenchantment or disillusionment. This may just be a fleeting trend—a "feeling in the air," as mentioned at the outset of this book. But it may prove to be deep and enduring, grounded in the complex puzzle I have tried to elucidate that is likely to be with us for a long time. The more we come to understand the nature of this puzzle and come to grips with it, the less disorienting, and less disillusioning, the world will seem. That is the epochal challenge facing us.

Today's typical undergraduate, were he or she to live that long, would be roughly 96 years of age when the USA is scheduled to celebrate its tricentennial in 2076. Modern medical technology has already extended life expectancy on average to nearly 80 years in some countries, one of the many blessings the nation-state era has produced, so that it is quite thinkable for the contemporary college student to envision being around to participate in America's 300th birthday party. The question is whether the USA will be around. And, if so, will it be at all recognizable, not just in terms of lifestyle and the consumer gadgets we have at our disposal (faster remote controls and the like) but in terms of governance? Will we still have deliberative democracy based on popular sovereignty? Will we still be a "nation" with all the pageantry that has come to be associated with the Fourth of July, complete with special citizenship-conferring ceremonies and red-white-and-blue fireworks? Or, in singing the national anthem at ballgames on the Fourth of July and every other day of the year, do we find ourselves already merely going through the motions of celebration, participating in token, ritualized observances but not heartfelt actions? Patriotism is having to compete with other belief systems and, even more so, with a postmodern mood of nihilistic disbelief.

Vaclav Havel, the president of the Czech Republic, appeared in the United States to give a July Fourth speech recently, in which he issued a "declaration of interdependence," stating that we are living at a time when "everything is possible and almost nothing is certain." He went on to say that, while recognizing the counterforces at work, he envisioned eventually "a single interconnected civilization [based on] the miracle of Being, the miracle of the universe, and the miracle of our own existence."[75] In calling for unity amidst diversity, Havel was an especially suitable messenger. He had personally played a leadership role in the mindboggling—some would say miraculous—events of the late-twentieth century, and was in the middle of the crucible of change. He had helped to bridge the East-West divide by leading Czechoslovakia from communist dictatorship to liberal democracy at the end of the Cold War in 1989; had presided over a nation-state torn by competing nationalisms that resulted in the peaceful, "velvet divorce" of the Czech Republic and the Slovak Republic in 1993; had gone on to grapple with the forces of globalization and subgroupism ranging from resisting the attempt by Anheuser-Busch (Budweiser) to take over the local Budvar brewery to resisting demands for autonomy by the Gypsies and other indigenous ethnic populations; and had formally applied for Czech entry into the European Union. Like the rest of the world, his country continues to be a work in progress. His words in his speech reflected his background as a poet who came belatedly to the job of statesman. The qualities of the poet and the statesman will both be needed in the twenty-first century if we are to blend idealism and realism.

A pessimist has been called an optimist with experience. Recent experience suggests that, on balance, there are more grounds for optimism than pessimism. In the end, which one proves to be warranted will be for us to determine through our action or inaction. There is admittedly a tendency for every generation to be temporocentric, that is, to assume that it is at the crossroads of history and that its decisions will be the pivotal ones on which the entire future of humanity will hinge. We, in the age of Starbucks and Star Wars, can be forgiven our vanity, considering we are living at the beginning of a new millennium and at a time when we have the potential to take the human race to an unparalleled level of well-being or to extinguish it. The following, written on January 1, 2000, nicely captures where we stand, not just those living in the American metropolis described in the passage below, but all of us:

> We will turn soon enough to the tasks that await us. Even now, the monumentality of this moment fades in the old familiarity of morning and afternoon. The sun has barely begun to gather itself after the winter solstice, and the light over the city and the country is so fragile that it threatens to splinter and fall like flakes to the ground, as it always threatens to do in January.
>
> And yet something about the sound of 2000 draws past and future near in a way that we have never quite known before. So here we are now, . . . just next door to yesterday and yet somehow in a different world. . . . Soon we will have slept a full night in this strange-sounding year, and then another. We cannot know how the new millennium will end, but we do have the power to determine how it begins and, perhaps, what it will remember of us.[76]

Dawn has arrived. We have a long way to go. We had better get started.

APPENDIX

Discussion Questions for the Twenty-First-Century Chat Room

Imagine you have a pen pal living in Upper Volta (the former name of Burkina Faso), Down Under (Australia), Outer Mongolia (the former name of Mongolia), any inner city in America, or, for that matter, anywhere else on the planet. It is likely that at some point in the twenty-first century you will be able to communicate with that person, wherever he or she may be located, on the Internet. What follows are some questions, drawn from each chapter in this book, that would seem worth mulling over in a twenty-first-century "chat room." Some suggested selected bibliography accompanies each set of questions.

CHAPTER 1

1. A student was once asked: "What's worse, ignorance or apathy?" The student responded: "I don't know, and I don't care!" Does this define your attitude toward foreign policy issues and international affairs in the post-Cold War era, at a time when, at least in the United States, there does not seem to be the kind of highly visible external threat that preoccupied the country for much of the half-century following World War II? To the extent that the United States is facing problems or threats today, are they mainly internal or external in nature? Regarding external concerns—"the global problematique"—what problems would you list, in what order? Do people in other countries share the view of the global problematique that the average American has?

2. How can we reconcile the traditional, still ingrained way of thinking about international relations—that is, as a "game" played by nation-states, revolving around such concepts as national power, national interests, national security, sovereignty, and citizenship—with the growing contemporary reality of cyberspace, a globalized world economy of multinational corporations, and other phenomena that seem to be blurring national boundaries and national identities and rendering the traditional concepts increasingly anachronistic? Do you find all of this confusing, or does it all make perfectly good sense to you? How good is your handle on the world?

3. How much government do you want in your life? In what areas do you think government has a role to play in regulating the behavior of the members of society? To the extent you believe government has a role to play in dealing with problems in some area (e.g., crime, the environment, poverty, education, disease), which *level* of governance is best equipped to address that set of concerns (local, state, national, regional, global)? For example, if you are a U.S. citizen, are you prepared to pay increased gasoline taxes to the federal government to dampen fossil fuel use and help promote cleaner air? What about a global carbon tax, to be collected by the United Nations and used to help countries develop energy alternatives that will lessen the chances of global warming?

4. Do you believe in the slogan "think globally, act locally"? If so, what are you doing about it?

Suggested Bibliography

The Commission on Global Governance, *Our Global Neighborhood* (Oxford: Oxford University Press, 1995).

James N. Rosenau, "Governance in the Twenty-First Century," *Global Governance*, 1 (Winter 1995), pp. 13–43.

Joseph S. Nye, "In Government We Don't Trust," *Foreign Policy* (Fall 1997), pp. 99–111.

Claude Moisy, "Myths of the Global Information Village," *Foreign Policy* (Summer 1997), pp. 83–95.

CHAPTER 2

1. Charles Dickens famously wrote, in *A Tale of Two Cities*, (to paraphrase) that "it was the best of times and the worst of times." Today, can we say the same? Is it the best of times? The worst of times? Both? How so?

2. What are the key trends in world politics in the post-Cold War era, in terms of the distribution of power and other variables? For example, is the United States now "the lone superpower," or is power so elusive today that no state can claim that title?

3. With the fall of the Berlin Wall and the end of the Cold War, have we wit-

nessed merely the déjà vu transformation of the international system from bipolarity back to the more normal, pre-1945 historical pattern of multipolarity, *or* are we on the brink of a much more epic, profound transformation, namely the unraveling of the very fabric of the state system itself and the underlying principles of political organization that have dominated human governance over the past several centuries, at least as far back as the Peace of Westphalia in 1648? Are we witnessing the beginning of the end of the nation-state? In other words, is this a "Westphalian moment"?

4. Do you think current conditions in the contemporary international system are very hospitable, or not very hospitable, for improved global institution-building and for promoting at the very least what Barry Buzan has called "a more mature anarchy"?

Suggested Bibliography

John Mearsheimer, "Why We Will Soon Miss the Cold War," *The Atlantic Monthly* (August 1990), pp. 35–50.

Francis Fukuyama, "The End of History?," *The National Interest*, 16 (Summer 1989), pp. 3–16.

Max Singer and Aaron Wildavsky, *The Real World Order*, rev. ed. (Chatham, N.J.: Chatham House, 1996).

Paul Kennedy, "The Future of the Nation-State," Chapter 7 in *Preparing for the Twenty-First Century* (New York: Random House, 1993).

Samuel P. Huntington, "The Clash of Civilizations," *Foreign Affairs*, 72 (Summer 1993), pp. 22–49; and his book by that name, published by Simon and Schuster in 1996.

James N. Rosenau, *Turbulence in World Politics* (Princeton: Princeton University Press, 1990).

Joseph S. Nye, *Bound to Lead: The Changing Nature of American Power* (New York: Basic Books, 1990).

CHAPTER 3

1. How would you define what is meant by the term "nation-state"? "Nation"? "State"? Roughly how many nation-states (countries) are there in the world today? How many distinct ethnic groups do you think there are? Do you think nationalism (patriotism) is on the rise or on the decline in the United States? What about worldwide?

2. Would you characterize yourself as a "realist" or an "idealist" in terms of your general orientation toward world politics?

3. If you had to choose, which "paradigm" do you think makes more sense as an accurate representation of contemporary world politics—the billiard ball paradigm (which stresses the continued primacy of sovereign nation-states as the dominant actors, concerned mainly about their phys-

ical security and survival in an anarchic environment) or the cobweb paradigm (which assumes a more complex, richer set of actors and issues, including nonstate actors competing with national governments, and economic and other issues competing equally with security issues for attention)? Why? What is the evidence to support one or the other?

4. It has often been said that what differentiates foreign policy from domestic policy in the United States and many other countries is that domestic politics (public opinion, interest groups, and the like) play a lesser role in decision making in the former case than in the latter case, since when it comes to the formulation and conduct of foreign policy, politics supposedly "stops at the water's edge" as decisions are more likely to be based on bipartisan, "national interest" calculations. However, Robert Putman has argued that diplomats at a bargaining table always necessarily play to two audiences when advancing proposals—their diplomatic counterparts from rival states seated across the table with whom they are attempting to reach agreements, as well as various bureaucratic and other domestic interests seated within their own delegation whom they must try to please if they are to maintain support back home. Is the importance of domestic politics in the foreign policy process greater today, or smaller, compared with previous eras? Has the end of the Cold War had the effect of undermining the "glue" holding the U.S. political system and many other political systems together, thereby giving greater play to internal, domestic politics since leaders cannot as easily manipulate citizens to "rally round the flag"?

5. To the extent the nation-state as an institution is threatened today, is it mainly being threatened by transnational forces from without (e.g., multinational corporations) or by subnational forces from within (e.g., ethnic separatism)? Would you say the dominant trend in the world today is integration (what Benjamin Barber has called the forces of "McWorld") or disintegration (what Barber has called the forces of "Jihad")? In other words, are we witnessing the emergence of a global village, or global villages, or both at once?

Suggested Bibliography

John Vasquez, ed., *Classics of International Relations*, 3rd ed. (Upper Saddle River, N.J.: Prentice-Hall, 1996), Part I on "Morality and Politics" and Part II on "Debates Over Methods and Theory."

Charles W. Kegley, Jr., "The Neoliberal Challenge to Realist Theories of World Politics," in Kegley, *Controversies in International Relations Theory* (New York: St. Martins Press, 1995), pp. 1–24.

Charles Tilly, ed., *The Formation of National States in Western Europe* (Princeton: Princeton University Press, 1975).

Kenneth N. Waltz, "Globalization and Governance," *PS* (December 1999), pp. 693–700.

Janice E. Thomson and Stephen D. Krasner, "Global Transactions and the Consolidation of Sovereignty," in Ernst-Otto Czempiel and James N. Rosenau, eds.,

Global Changes and Theoretical Challenges (Lexington, Mass.: Lexington Books, 1989), pp. 195–219.

Robert H. Jackson and Alan James, eds., *States In a Changing World* (Oxford: Clarendon Press, 1993).

Robert O. Keohane and Joseph S. Nye, *Power and Interdependence*, 2nd ed. (Boston: Scott Foresman, 1989).

Mark Zacher, "The Decaying Pillars of the Westphalian Temple: Implications for International Order and Governance, in James N. Rosenau and Ernst-Otto Czempiel, eds., *Governance Without Government* (Cambridge, Eng.: Cambridge University Press, 1992).

Articles by Vincent Cable ("The Diminished Nation-State"), Susan Strange ("The Defective State"), and Vivien Schmidt ("The New World Order Incorporated") in a symposium on "What Future for the State?" in *Daedalus*, 124 (Spring 1995).

Jessica Matthews, "Power Shift," *Foreign Affairs* (January/February 1997), pp. 50–66.

Benjamin Barber, "Jihad Vs. McWorld," *The Atlantic Monthly* (March 1992), pp. 53–63; and Barber's book by that name, published by Random House in 1995.

CHAPTER 4

1. Do you have much faith in international organizations such as the United Nations? How useful are global organizations? What purposes do they serve?

2. Some observers speak of promoting a "pooling of sovereignty" among countries so that they might collaborate in solving mutual problems. What is meant by this? Is it a contradiction in terms, or is it a meaningful concept?

3. Is there such a thing as a "global policy process" whereby international regimes (agreements) are created and implemented? If so, what are the various stages of the process? How do problems (e.g., deterioration of the ozone layer) become widely perceived as global concerns and elicit global responses?

4. Can we speak of some international issues as being "high-politics" in nature, and other issues as involving "low-politics"? What is meant by these terms? What kinds of issues would be examples of each? Are concerns about economic well-being and environmental quality so critical and salient today that these deserve to be viewed as involving the highest "national security" stakes no less than traditional war/peace concerns? On what kinds of issues would one expect the "billiard ball" paradigm, as opposed to the "cobweb" paradigm, to be most relevant and useful in helping one understand the political dynamics at work?

Suggested Bibliography

Harold K. Jacobson, *Networks of Interdependence*, 2nd ed. (New York: Knopf, 1984).

Inis L. Claude, Jr., *Swords Into Plowshares*, 4th ed. (New York: Random House, 1984).

Marvin S. Soroos, *Beyond Sovereignty: The Challenge of Global Policy* (Columbia, S.C.: University of South Carolina Press, 1986).

Mark W. Zacher and Brent A. Sutton, *Governing Global Networks: International Regimes for Transportation and Communications* (Cambridge, Eng.: Cambridge University Press, 1996).

Stephen D. Krasner, ed., *International Regimes* (Ithaca, N.Y.: Cornell University Press, 1983).

Robert D. Putnam, "Diplomacy and Domestic Politics: The Logic of Two-Level Games," *International Organization*, 42 (Summer 1988), pp. 427–460.

CHAPTER 5

1. Is the world getting more war-prone, or less? What should we make of the fact that around 1990, contrary to almost all "realist" theory and historical patterns, a distinct era of international politics gave way to a new era—the Cold War international system gave way to the post-Cold War system—without any major war serving as an engine of change, and virtually without a shot being fired?

2. The period since World War II has been called "the long peace," meaning that it is the longest continuous stretch of time since the beginning of the modern state system in the seventeenth century that one cannot find a single instance of direct exchange of actual military hostilities between "great powers." Do you think the long peace will continue throughout the twenty-first century? Has major war become obsolete, at least among highly developed societies? Or, as realists contend, is there still a strong possibility we will see the existence of another great-power rivalry (say, between the United States and Russia or the United States and China) that may well eventuate in all-out war as has happened so often with such classic competitions in the past?

3. Thomas Friedman has advanced what he calls "the golden arches theory" of war, arguing that no two countries that have each had a McDonalds have ever gone to war with each other, presumably because they are too invested in a mass consumption culture (as symbolized by Big Macs) to find it worth their while to engage in the kind of violence that could destroy their way of life. Is this a silly theory, or is there something to this?

4. A "nation" has sometimes been defined as the largest unit one is willing to die for. Are you willing to die for your country? Or have we reached the point where, as Richard Lamm has put it, "in the event of a major war in the nuclear age, you will no longer be dying for your country but with your country"? Does this mean the end of what Edward Luttwak has called "heroic warfare"? Could a massive military operation along the lines of D-Day during World War II still be conducted today, or do we now have

such low tolerance for battlefield casualties in the United States and other developed democratic states that such a campaign would be unthinkable?

5. Should the United States, whether unilaterally or multilaterally through the United Nations, engage in "humanitarian intervention" in another country's internal affairs when the people of that country are suffering from a deadly civil war or are experiencing genocidal treatment by the regime that is in power? Is there enough blood and treasure in the United States and in the international community generally to rectify problems in all the world's failed states? How does one choose which ones to help—what should be the criteria for involvement?

6. It is said that one person's terrorist is another's national liberation hero. Any comment on this?

7. Are we making any progress in reducing ABC (atomic or nuclear, biological, and chemical) weapons proliferation in the world? Should the United States be more concerned about the "loose nukes" in the former Soviet Union or about the potential development of chemical and nuclear weapons by "rogue" states such as North Korea or Libya?

8. By "collective security" is meant the obligation of all countries in the world to form a grand coalition to fight against any other member or members of the international community that commit aggression in violation of the UN Charter. Is this a workable principle? Has it ever been put into practice?

9. If you had to identify some "nonstate" actors (intergovernmental organizations, nongovernmental organizations, and multinational corporations) who have had important impacts in the war/peace issue area, who would they be? How powerful have these actors been in affecting the development of international regimes (agreements) in this issue area? Have they been a positive force or a negative force—a part of the solution or a part of the problem?

Suggested Bibliography

Boutros Boutros-Ghali, *An Agenda for Peace*, UN Documents A/47/277 and S/24111, June 17, 1992.

Joseph S. Nye, "Conflicts After the Cold War," *Washington Quarterly* (Winter 1996), pp. 1–17.

Ted Gurr and Barbara Harff, *Ethnic Conflict in World Politics* (Boulder: Westview Press, 1994).

John Mueller, *Quiet Cataclysm* (New York: HarperCollins, 1995).

James Lee Ray, "The Abolition of Slavery and the End of International War," *International Organization*, 43 (Summer 1989), pp. 405–439.

Edward Luttwak, "Toward Post-Heroic Warfare," *Foreign Affairs*, 74 (May/June 1995), pp. 109–122.

CHAPTER 6

1. What is meant by "globalization"? Is it good or bad—a trend we should try to promote, or try to reverse? If we wanted to stop globalization, could we? Or does the idea of a world without borders (in terms of the free flow of trade and investment across national boundaries) already have such momentum behind it, driven by powerful technological forces, that there is no stopping it?

2. How does globalization affect the functioning of the welfare state? If nation-states feel they have to be "lean and mean"—that is, reduce taxes and regulations on businesses in order to attract new companies (and jobs) from abroad as well as keep one's own indigenous companies (and jobs) from moving overseas—then won't this make it more difficult for a national government to generate enough revenue to support a safety net for the poor and to engage in other activities associated with the modern welfare state?

3. Raymond Vernon many years ago wrote a book entitled *Sovereignty at Bay*, in which he suggested that multinational corporations (MNCs) were challenging the sovereignty of nation-states. Another observer, Charles Kindleberger, around the same time, said "the nation-state is finished as an economic unit," referring to how MNCs were spreading their tentacles across the globe and penetrating so pervasively into national economies that the latter were losing their identity. Do you feel the autonomy and power of MNCs has been exaggerated, or are these actors truly eroding the sovereignty of nation-states? How powerful are MNCs relative to national governments?

4. American MNCs are often thought by foreigners to be an arm of U.S. foreign policy and agents of U.S. "imperialism." However, when Coca-Cola or IBM or any other MNC based in the United States makes decisions about where to locate plants or factories, to what extent does the top management of the company worry about promoting American "national interests"? Is there not a "love-hate" relationship between MNCs and their "home" government? What about the relationship between MNCs and "host" governments in countries in which they have overseas subsidiaries?

5. If your boss is a very patriotic American and urges you to buy an "American" car, which would be a proper response to his directive—buying a Honda made in Maryville, Ohio or a Ford made in Ontario, Canada?

6. Is the "rich-poor gap" between countries widening or narrowing? What about the "rich-poor gap" within countries such as the United States? What obligations do governments have to narrow both these gaps?

7. What is meant by "Third Way"?

8. What side do you support in the skirmishes (e.g., the 1999 "battle of Seattle") over the issue of whether the U.S. government should continue promoting the expansion of global free trade principles as enforced by the

World Trade Organization, even if they may undermine labor and environmental standards? Is the average American worker likely to be helped or hurt by the WTO? What about workers in other developed countries? Less developed countries?

9. If you had to identify some "nonstate" actors (intergovernmental organizations, nongovernmental organizations, and multinational corporations) who have had important impacts in the economic issue area, who would they be? How powerful have these actors been in affecting the development of international regimes (agreements) in this issue area? Have they been a positive force or a negative force—a part of the solution or a part of the problem?

Suggested Bibliography

Thomas Friedman, *The Lexus and the Olive Tree: Understanding Globalization* (New York: Farrar, Straus, Giroux, 1999).

Richard J. Barnet and John Cavanaugh, *Global Dreams: Imperial Corporations and the New World Order* (New York: Simon and Schuster, 1994).

Joan E. Spero and Jeffrey A. Hart, *The Politics of International Economic Relations,* 5th ed. (New York: St. Martins Press, 1997).

Bruce E. Moon, *Dilemmas of International Trade* (Boulder: Westview Press, 1996).

John Ruggie, "International Regimes, Transactions, and Change: Embedded Liberalism in the Postwar Economic Order," in Stephen D. Krasner, ed., *International Regimes* (Ithaca, N.Y.: Cornell University Press, 1983), pp. 195–231.

Geoffrey Garrett, "Global Markets and National Politics: Collision Course or Virtuous Circle?," *International Organization,* 52 (Autumn 1998), pp. 787–824.

Paul Doremus, Louis Pauley, and Simon Reich, *The Myth of the Multinational Corporation* (Princeton: Princeton University Press, 1998).

D. Korten, *When Corporations Rule the World* (West Hartford: Kumarian Press, 1995).

Raymond Vernon, "Sovereignty At Bay: 20 Years After," *Millennium,* 20 (Summer 1991), pp. 191–195.

Dani Rodrik, "Sense and Nonsense in the Globalization Debate," *Foreign Policy* (Summer 1997).

CHAPTER 7

1. What is the nature and magnitude of the environmental problems facing Americans and others on the planet? Are we pushing up against the earth's "limits" and "carrying capacity," or have these threats been exaggerated in the media?

2. Is "sustainable development" a meaningful concept, or a way to avoid making the hard choices between economic growth and environmental quality?

3. The North tends to blame many environmental problems on overpopu-

lation in the South, while the South tends to blame these problems more on overconsumption in the North. Who deserves to be blamed for what?

4. Given the likelihood that China, India, and most other less developed countries will be seeking to emulate the United States and other developed countries in the twenty-first century—with increasing numbers of cars, refrigerators, VCRs, and other consumer goods, all requiring substantially increased energy consumption—how will the world avoid global warming and other adverse environmental effects associated with the mass consumption culture? Can the world afford for China and all other countries to look like the United States, where one-third of all households have at least two cars? Yet how can Americans tell others to reduce consumption when we have shown little willingness to do so ourselves through carpooling or other conservation measures? Are you willing to sacrifice your car and other creature comforts to the larger cause of "Spaceship Earth"?

5. When countries enter into agreements to, say, eliminate all ozone-destroying chemicals or reduce CO_2 emissions by a certain date, how is compliance monitored and enforced? Does each party trust the other to report honestly whether it has fulfilled its treaty obligation and met the targeted goal, or are there neutral third parties that can be relied on for verification, which can involve complex measurement procedures? In the case of less developed countries, even if they are well-intentioned, do they have the necessary economic and technical resources to carry out their treaty obligations? Does the United States risk being a martyr if it commits to reducing its carbon dioxide emissions by 8 percent by 2010, and takes costly steps to do so, with no assurance that its efforts will be reciprocated by others?

6. If you had to identify some "nonstate" actors (intergovernmental organizations, nongovernmental organizations, and multinational corporations) who have had important impacts in the environmental issue area, who would they be? How powerful have these actors been in affecting the development of international regimes (agreements) in this issue area? Have they been a positive or a negative force—a part of the solution or a part of the problem?

Suggested Bibliography

Brundtland Commission, *Our Common Future* (New York: Oxford University Press, 1987).

Peter M. Haas, Robert O. Keohane, and Marc A. Levy, eds., *Institutions for the Earth* (Cambridge: MIT Press, 1993).

Lawrence E. Susskind, *Environmental Diplomacy* (New York: Oxford University Press, 1994).

Gareth Porter and Janet Welsh Brown, *Global Environmental Politics*, 2nd ed. (Boulder: Westview Press, 1996).

Richard E. Benedick, "Ozone Diplomacy," *Issues in Science and Technology* (Fall 1989); and his book by that name, published by Harvard University Press in 1998.

Christopher D. Stone, *The Gnat Is Older Than Man* (Princeton: Princeton University Press, 1993).

Lester R. Brown et al., *Vital Signs: The Trends that Are Shaping Our Future,* an annual publication of the Worldwatch Institute.

CHAPTER 8

1. Allan Goodman, in *A Brief History of the Future,* predicts that "the twenty-first century will encompass the longest period of peace, democracy, and economic development in history." What do you think is the basis for such a rosy forecast? Are you optimistic or pessimistic about the future of the world? The future of the United States? *Your* future? Do you think the world will be a better place, say in the year 2050, than it is today?

2. Given the pace of change today, is there any more unrealistic, unlikely, impossible future than the present? Yet most of us assume we will continue to live much as we have for centuries, in a world of nation-states. If not the nation-state, how else might human beings be organized politically to govern their affairs? In other words, what are some "alternative world order models" that are possible? Given the emergence of regional trade blocs such as the European Union (EU) and the North American Free Trade Agreement (NAFTA), is regionalism the dominant trend, so that instead of some 200 nation-states we might see five or six region-states in the future? Or does the development of such institutions as the World Trade Organization (WTO) suggest globalism—perhaps even a single world government—will be triumphant? At the other extreme, if more and more states disintegrate as the Soviet Union and Yugoslavia did in the 1990s, and ever smaller ethnic groups increasingly call for self-determination and autonomy, might we end up with a world of city-states? Or might we be moving toward a "new feudalism," with a complex web of overlapping hierarchies of authority and multiple loyalties, or toward a nonterritorial order altogether in which the units on a world map are defined more by corporate logos than by geographical boundaries? How probable are any of these scenarios by the end of the century, and how desirable would they be? Would any be an improvement over the "Westphalian state system"?

3. What are the values you believe humanity should be trying to maximize? If you had to rank order the importance of the following—peace, economic prosperity, economic equality, individual freedom and democracy, environmental quality—what would be your ranking? How would the suggested alternative world order models promote or hinder the achievement of these values? Should we be promoting a "society of states" morality that mainly focuses on improving relations between states (e.g., honoring the obligation not to interfere in any state's internal affairs), or a "cos-

mopolitan" morality that takes a more holistic view of humanity and the obligations people have toward each other (e.g., insisting that all governments observe human rights)? If the latter, how does one go about getting a universal definition, acceptance, and enforcement of human rights?

4. Inis Claude has said that the historic role of international organizations such as the United Nations is not that they are precursors to world government, but rather that they are an adaptation of the state system which could make world government unnecessary, if such arrangements can be made to work in a way that responds to human needs. Should the United States pay its UN dues in full, rather than continue to owe roughly $1 billion to the organization? If you were to do a cost-benefit analysis of what the UN costs the United States relative to the benefits it derives, what would it look like?

5. What kinds of reforms in global institution-building in general and the UN in particular do you believe are feasible and desirable?

6. Henry Kissinger has asserted that the major challenge for U.S. foreign policy in the post-Cold War era is to carve out a role for itself in a world which "for the first time in her history . . . she cannot dominate, but from which she cannot simply withdraw." What stance should the United States take in the world today—isolationist, unilateralist, multilateralist, or what?

Suggested Bibliography

Yale H. Ferguson and Richard W. Mansbach, "Global Politics At the Turn of the Millennium: Changing Bases of 'Us' and 'Them'," *International Studies Review*, 1, no. 2 (Summer 1999), pp. 77–107.

John Newhouse, "Europe's Rising Regionalism," *Foreign Affairs*, 76 (January/February 1997), pp. 67–84.

Ronnie D. Lipschutz, "Reconstructing World Politics: The Emergence of Global Civil Society," *Millennium*, 21, no. 3 (1992), pp. 389–420.

Michael Edwards, *Future Positive: International Cooperation in the Twenty-First Century* (London: Earthscan, 2000).

Barry B. Hughes, *International Futures: Choices in the Creation of a New World Order* (Boulder: Westview Press, 1993).

Robert Kaplan, "The Coming Anarchy," *The Atlantic Monthly* (February 1994), pp.44–76.

Robert L. Heilbroner, *An Inquiry Into the Human Prospect*, 2nd ed. (New York: W.W. Norton, 1991).

James Traub, "W's World," *New York Times Magazine* (January 14, 2001), pp. 28–34.

Endnotes

Chapter 1: Introduction: A New World Order, or Disorder?

1. Winston Churchill, radio broadcast, London, October 1, 1939.
2. Frederic S. Pearson and J. Martin Rochester, *International Relations in the Twenty-First Century*, 4th ed. (New York: McGraw-Hill, 1998), p. 80.
3. Cited in Henry A. Kissinger, "We Live In An Age of Transition," *Daedalus*, 124 (Summer 1995), p. 99.
4. Most international relations scholars consider 1648 as marking the beginning of the modern state system, although many note that the roots of the Westphalian system could be traced back much further to earlier in the feudal era. For example, Bruce Bueno de Mesquita has argued that it was the Concordat of Worms in 1122 that led to a system of sovereign states since it was then that the Pope surrendered to monarchs the right to appoint bishops in their respective realms. See Bruce Bueno de Mesquita, "The Concordat of Worms and Westphalia," paper delivered at annual meeting of the International Studies Association, Washington, D.C., February 18, 1999. For a discussion of the feudal era and the emergence of nation-states, see Charles Tilly, *Coercion, Capital and European States A.D. 900–1990* (Cambridge, Eng.: Basil Blackwell, 1990); Tilly, "Reflections on the History of European State-Making," in Tilly, ed., *The Formation of National States in Western Europe* (Princeton: Princeton University Press, 1975), pp. 3–83; and Henrik Spruyt, *The Sovereign State and Its Competitors* (Princeton: Princeton University Press, 1994).
5. The extension of the Westphalian state system into Asia, Africa, and other parts of the globe is discussed in Hedley Bull and Adam Watson, eds., *The Expansion of International Society* (Oxford: Oxford University Press, 1985).
6. See James A. Nathan, "The New Feudalism," *Foreign Policy*, no. 42 (Spring 1981), pp. 156–166; and Susan Strange, "The Defective State," *Daedalus*, 124 (Spring 1995), pp. 55–74.
7. The "states as billiard balls" metaphor owes to Arnold Wolfer's discussion in *Discord and Collaboration* (Baltimore: Johns Hopkins University Press, 1962). I discuss the "billiard ball" paradigm in Chapter 3.
8. See Kenneth Waltz, *Theory of International Politics* (Reading, Mass.: Addison-Wesley, 1979), pp. 138–160.
9. See James A. Field, "Transnationalism and the New Tribe," *International Organization*, 25 (Summer 1971), pp. 355–356.

10. Janice E. Thomson and Stephen D. Krasner, "Global Transactions and the Consolidation of Sovereignty," in Ernst-Otto Czempiel and James N. Rosenau, eds., *Global Changes and Theoretical Challenges* (Lexington, Mass.: Lexington Books, 1989), p. 198.

11. See Seyom Brown, *New Forces, Old Forces and the Future of World Politics*, post-Cold War ed. (New York: Harper and Row, 1995), pp. 257–269.

12. The concept of regimes is discussed in Stephen D. Krasner, ed., *International Regimes* (Ithaca, N.Y.: Cornell University Press, 1983).

13. Ronnie D. Lipschutz, "Reconstructing World Politics: The Emergence of Global Civil Society," *Millennium*, 21, no. 3 (1992), pp. 389–420.

14. Paul Streeten, monograph on International Governance, IDS, University of Sussex, Silver Jubilee Papers (1992), p. 2, cited in Erskine Childers, *Renewing the United Nations System*, Dag Hammarskjold Foundation, Uppsala, Sweden, 1994, p. 17. A similar remark was made by Daniel Bell in "The World of 2013," *New Society* (December 8, 1987), p. 35.

15. This is captured in the report of The Commission on Global Governance, entitled *Our Global Neighborhood* (Oxford: Oxford University Press, 1995).

16. *An Agenda for Peace*, Report of the Secretary-General on the Work of the Organization, UN Doc. A/47/277 and S/24111, June 17, 1992, p. 5.

Chapter 2: An Overview of the Contemporary International System

1. On the failure of international relations theory to anticipate and account for the end of the Cold War, see John Lewis Gaddis, "International Relations Theory and the End of the Cold War," *International Security*, 17 (Winter 1992–1993), pp. 5–58; and Charles W. Kegley, Jr., "How Did the Cold War Die: Principles for an Autopsy," *Mershon International Studies Review*, 38 (April 1994), pp. 11–41.

2. Zbigniew Brzezinski, *Game Plan: A Geostrategic Framework for the Conduct of the US-Soviet Contest* (Boston: Atlantic Monthly Press, 1986), p. xiii.

3. The term "post-international politics," referring to the transformation of the Westphalian state system into a completely new set of relationships not predicated upon the nation-state as the preeminent actor, was coined by James Rosenau in *Turbulence in World Politics* (Princeton: Princeton University Press, 1990), p. 6.

4. Charles Maynes, "The New Pessimism," *Foreign Policy* (Fall 1995), pp. 33–49.

5. Julian Simon, *The Ultimate Resource* (Princeton: Princeton University Press, 1982).

6. Max Singer and Aaron Wildavsky, *The Real World Order*, revised ed. (Chatham, N.J.: Chatham House, 1996).

7. Allan E. Goodman, *A Brief History of the Future* (Boulder: Westview Press, 1993).

8. John Mueller, *Retreat from Doomsday: The Obsolescence of Major War* (New York: Basic Books, 1989).

9. James Lee Ray, "The Abolition of Slavery and the End of International War," *International Organization*, 43 (Summer 1989), pp. 406–439.

10. Francis Fukuyama, "The End of History?," *The National Interest*, 16 (Summer 1989), pp. 3–16.

11. John J. Mearsheimer, "Why We Will Soon Miss the Cold War," *The Atlantic Monthly* (August 1990), pp. 35–50; and "Back to the Future: Instability in Europe After the Cold War," *International Security*, 15 (Summer 1990), pp. 5–56.

12. Samuel P. Huntington, "The Clash of Civilizations," *Foreign Affairs*, 72 (Summer 1993), pp. 22–49; and *The Clash of Civilizations and the Remaking of World Order* (New York: Simon and Schuster, 1996).

13. Robert Kaplan, "The Coming Anarchy," *The Atlantic Monthly* (February 1994), pp. 44–52; and *The Ends of the Earth* (New York: Random House, 1996).

14. Paul Kennedy, *Preparing for the Twenty-First Century* (New York: Random House, 1993).

15. Robert Heilbroner, *An Inquiry Into the Human Prospect*, 2nd ed. (New York: W.W. Norton, 1991). Heilbroner's first edition, written in 1975, had painted a grim portrait of the future. The second edition, which took as its subtitle "Looked At Again for the 1990s," was no more hopeful than the earlier work.

16. Cited on the eve of the 1992 Earth Summit by Maurice Strong, Secretary-General of the conference. Statement to Second Session of the Preparatory Committee for the UN Conference on Environment and Development, April 2, 1991, p. 13.

17. John G. Ruggie, "International Structure and International Transformation: Space, Time, and

Method," in Ernst-Otto Czempiel and James N. Rosenau, eds., *Global Changes and Theoretical Challenges* (Lexington, Mass.: Lexington Books, 1989), p. 32.

18. Roger Hilsman, *The Politics of Policy Making in Defense and Foreign Affairs* (New York: Columbia University Press, 1971), p. 5. Secretary of State Henry Kissinger, *U.S. Department of State Bulletin*, 69 (December 10, 1973), p. 708.

19. "I still believe he [President Lyndon Johnson] found it viscerally inconceivable that what Walt Rostow [one of Johnson's chief national security advisors] kept telling him was 'the greatest power in the world' could not dispose of a collection of night-riders in black pajamas." Quoted from Arthur Schlesinger, Jr., "The Quagmire Papers," *New York Review of Books*, December 16, 1971, p. 41.

20. On the United States as the lone superpower in the post-Cold War era, see Charles Krauthammer, "The Unipolar Moment," *Foreign Affairs*, 70, No. 1 (1991), pp. 23–33; remarks of U.S. Secretary of Defense Richard Cheney, "The United States as A Superpower," *Defense Issues*, 5 (May 7, 1990), pp. 5–8; and Robert W. Tucker and David C. Hendrickson, *The Imperial Temptation: The New World Order and America's Purpose* (New York: Council on Foreign Relations, 1993). Susan Strange, writing in 1995, noted that "five years of post-Cold War 'order' have only confirmed what I have always believed: there is only one superpower, the U.S." "ISA as a Microcosm," *International Studies Quarterly*, 39 (September 1995), p. 293. Earl Ravenal, in a lecture at the University of Missouri-St. Louis on November 17, 1995, stated that "the U.S. is the only country on earth whose foreign policy choices are still determinative of the shape of the international system."

21. A fundamental assumption of Robert Keohane's *After Hegemony* (Princeton: Princeton University Press, 1984) is that it is highly unlikely any single state will emerge in the foreseeable future as a hegemon. The term "post-superpower age" is from Jonathan Clarke and James Clad, *After the Crusade: American Foreign Policy for the Post-Superpower Age* (New York: Madison Books, 1995); also see Christopher Layne, "The Unipolar Illusion: Why New Great Powers Will Rise," *International Security*, 17 (Spring 1993), pp. 5–51; the "subpower" term is from William Safire, "Clinton Flinched from Bosnia Duty," *St. Louis Post-Dispatch*, July 16, 1995, p. C3.

22. Joseph S. Nye, "Conflicts After the Cold War," *Washington Quarterly* (Winter 1996), p. 2. Nye acknowledges that the United States in many respects remains a superpower in a privileged position, but feels Washington will need to act through building coalitions rather than alone if it is to exercise power successfully. The "sheriff of the posse" analogy is also used by Richard Haass in *The Reluctant Sheriff: The United States After the Cold War* (New York: Council on Foreign Relations, 1997).

23. Henry Kissinger, *American Foreign Policy*, 3rd ed. (New York: W.W. Norton, 1977), p. 416, alluded to the emergence of multiple power centers well before the "decline of U.S. hegemony" literature started appearing in the 1980s; Kissinger most recently has added India as a sixth power center, suggesting "we are now living in a world composed of six or seven major global players." Kissinger, "We Live in an Era of Transition," *op. cit.*, p.102. In Chapter 8 of *The Rise and Fall of the Great Powers* (New York: Random House, 1987), which was the most prominent "declinist" work of the 1980s, Paul Kennedy speculated about the ability of the United States, the former Soviet Union, the European Union, China, and Japan to exercise world leadership in the twenty-first century.

24. See the previous note.

25. In 1998, U.S. Secretary of State Madeleine Albright justified the possible need for Washington to take military action against Iraq, despite lukewarm support from the international community, as arising out of the fact the United States was "the indispensable nation." Remarks at Ohio State University, February 18, 1998.

26. See Richard A. Higgott and Andrew F. Cooper, "Middle Power Leadership and Coalition Building," *International Organization*, 44 (Autumn 1990), pp. 589–632.

27. The "unit veto" system, in which each state had nuclear weapons, was one of the models delineated by Morton Kaplan in *System and Process in International Politics* (New York: John Wiley, 1957).

28. Statement by then UN Ambassador Madeleine Albright, reported in the *St. Louis Post-Dispatch*, August 4, 1995, p. 8.

29. Kenneth N. Waltz, "The Emerging Structure of International Politics," *International Security*, 18 (Fall 1993), p. 54.

30. Kissinger, "We Live in An Age of Transition," *op. cit.*, p. 102. Theodore Moran, in "An Economic Agenda for Neorealists," *International Security*, 18 (Fall 1993), p. 211, states that economic power is "probably the most important source of power, and in a world in which military conflict between major states is unlikely, economic power will be increasingly important in determining the primacy or subordination of states." Also see Richard N. Rosecrance, *The Rise of the Trading State: Commerce and Conquest in the Modern World* (New York: Basic Books, 1986).

31. "Soft power" is discussed in Joseph S. Nye, *Bound to Lead: The Changing Nature of American Power* (New York: Basic Books, 1990); the quote is from G. John Ikenberry and Charles A. Kupchan, "Socialization and Hegemonic Power," *International Organization*, 44 (Summer, 1990), p. 284.

32. Robert Dahl, *Who Governs: Democracy and Power in An American City* (New Haven: Yale University Press, 1961). Seyom Brown borrows the term and applies it to the international system, referring to the diffusion of power among both state and nonstate actors in *New Forces, Old Forces, and the Future of World Politics*, post-Cold War ed. (New York: HarperCollins, 1995). On the continued search for Number 1 status, see the articles by Robert Jervis, "International Primacy: Is the Game Worth the Candle?" and Samuel P. Huntington, "Why International Primacy Matters," in *International Security*, 17 (Spring 1993).

33. These data are discussed in J. Martin Rochester, *Waiting for the Millennium: The United Nations and the Future of World Order* (Columbia, S.C: University of South Carolina Press, 1993), pp. 57–68. The Group of Seven has been informally expanded recently to permit a degree of participation by Russia, so that it is sometimes referred to as the Group of Eight.

34. This would be modeled after the Concert of Europe, which helped restore order following the end of the Napoleonic Wars in the early nineteenth century and was a precursor to the League of Nations and the United Nations. On the "concert" concept and its applicability to today's world, see Charles A. Kupchan and Clifford A. Kupchan, "Concerts, Collective Security, and the Future of Europe," *International Security*, 16 (Summer 1991), pp. 114–161.

35. Mearsheimer, "Why We Will Soon Miss the Cold War," *op. cit.*, p. 35.

36. Abba Eban, "The UN Idea Revisited," *Foreign Affairs*, 74 (September/October 1995), p. 50.

37. The term "bimultipolarity" was coined by Richard N. Rosecrance, "Bipolarity, Multipolarity, and the Future," *Journal of Conflict Resolution*, 10 (September 1966), pp. 314–327.

38. Nicholas Kristof, "China Sees 'Market-Leninism' As Way to Future," *New York Times*, September 6, 1993.

39. Craig N. Murphy, "The United Nations' Capacity to Promote Sustainable Development: The Lesson of A Year That Eludes All Facile Judgment," in Albert Legault et al., *The State of the United Nations: 1992* (Providence, R.I.: Academic Council on the UN System, 1993), p. 63. Also, see Gerald Dirks et al., *The State of the United Nations: 1993* (Providence, R.I.: Academic Council on the UN System, 1993); Mark T. Berger, "The End of the 'Third World'?," *Third World Quarterly*, 15 (June 1994), pp. 257–275; and the special issue of *Third World Quarterly* entitled "The South in the New World (Dis) Order," 15 (March 1994).

40. See note 12. For Huntington's latest thinking on his "clash of civilizations" thesis, see his "The Lonely Superpower," *Foreign Affairs*, 78 (March/April 1999), pp.40–49.

41. On the "end of history," see note 10. On the "end of geography," see Richard O'Brien, *Global Financial Integration: The End of Geography* (London: Pinter, 1992).

42. Earl C. Ravenal, "The Regionalization of Power: General Unalignment in the Future International System," paper presented at the annual meeting of the International Studies Association, Washington, D.C., April 14, 1990.

43. See Michael T. Klare and Daniel C. Thomas, *World Security: Challenges for A New Century*, 2nd ed. (New York: St. Martin's Press, 1994).

44. Stanley Hoffmann, "Choices," *Foreign Policy* (Fall 1973), p. 5.

45. Robert Keohane and Joseph S. Nye, *Power and Interdependence* (Boston: Little, Brown, 1977), Chapter 2.

46. The quote is from Daniel Bell in the Fall 1990 issue of *Dissent*, cited in Huntington, "Why International Primacy Matters," *op. cit.*, p. 81.

47. On the "long peace," see John Lewis Gaddis, "Great Illusions, The Long Peace, and the Future of the International System," in Charles W. Kegley, Jr., ed., *The Long Postwar Peace* (New York: HarperCollins, 1991), pp. 25–55. Also see Mark W. Zacher, "The Decaying Pillars of the Westphalian Temple: Implications for Global Order and Governance," in James N. Rosenau and Ernst-Otto Czempiel, eds., *Governance Without Government* (Cambridge: Cam-

bridge University Press, 1992). According to one analysis, toward the end of the 1990s "the world had fewer active conflicts than at any time since World War II." *The Defense Monitor*, XXVII, No. 1 (1998), p. 1.

48. Leslie Gelb, "Teacup Wars," *Foreign Affairs* (November 1995). Also see Peter Rodman, "Points of Order," *National Review*, May 1, 1995, p. 37.

49. See Sean M. Lynn-Jones and Steven E. Miller, eds., *Global Dangers: Changing Dimensions of International Security* (Cambridge: MIT Press, 1995).

50. On subnational actors, see for example John Barkdull, "Globalization and Texas," paper delivered at annual meeting of the International Studies Association, Minneapolis, March 20, 1998.

51. Depending on the criteria used, the number of IGOs may exceed 1,000, and the number of NGOs may exceed 28,000. See Harold K. Jacobson et al., "National Entanglements in International Governmental Organizations," *American Political Science Review*, 80 (March 1986), pp. 141–159; and the Commission on Global Governance, *Our Global Neighborhood* (Oxford: Oxford University Press, 1995), p. 32. See Chapter 3 for further discussion.

52. On the special importance of NGOs at Rio, see Jessica Matthews, "Power Shift," *Foreign Affairs* (January/February, 1997), pp. 50–66.

53. Robert Putnam has noted "the politics of many international negotiations can usefully be conceived as a two-level game [one pitched at the international level and the other at the domestic level, aimed at constituencies back home]." Robert D. Putnam, "Diplomacy and Domestic Politics: The Logic of Two-Level Games," *International Organization*, 42 (Summer 1988), p. 434. Maria Cowles has shown that in some cases, such as European Union negotiations, there is a complicated three-level game operating, involving not only subnational and state actors but also transnational actors at the supranational level. Maria Cowles, *The Politics of Big Business in the European Community*, Ph.D. dissertation, The American University, 1994.

54. For example, when the Group of Seven leaders arrive at their annual economic summits these days, they no longer enjoy quite the aura of statesmanship which surrounded them during the Cold War era. The growing public distrust of and alienation from national governments, found not only in the United States but throughout Western Europe, and already evident by the 1980s, has only become more pronounced in the 1990s and 2000s. On this phenomenon, and its relationship to the end of the Cold War, see Joseph S. Nye, "In Government We Don't Trust," *Foreign Policy* (Fall 1997), pp. 99–111. It is unlikely that an article such as Aaron Wildavsky's "The Two Presidencies," *Transaction*, 4 (December 1966), pp. 7–14, predicated on the special power the U.S. president enjoys in the foreign policy realm relative to the domestic policy arena, would be written in today's climate. Also see Michael C. Desch, "War and Strong States, Peace and Weak States," *International Organization*, 50 (Spring 1996), pp. 236–268.

55. On these contradictory integrative and disintegrative trends, see Boutros Boutros-Ghali, *An Agenda for Peace*, UN Doc. A/47/277 and S/24111, June 17, 1992, p. 3; and Benjamin Barber, *Jihad vs. McWorld* (New York: Times Books, 1995).

56. Susan Strange, "The Defective State," *Daedalus*, 124 (Spring 1994), pp. 56–57.

57. In Chapter 1, the author quoted Stephen D. Krasner and Janice Thomson as noting that there has never been any "golden age of state control." Krasner and Thomson have tried to make the case that in some respects national sovereignty has increased of late. See "Global Transactions and the Consolidation of Sovereignty," in Czempiel and Rosenau, *Global Changes, op. cit.*, pp. 195–219.

58. Rosenau, *Turbulence in World Politics, op. cit.*

59. James N. Rosenau, "Governance in the Twenty-First Century," *Global Governance*, 1 (Winter 1995), p. 13.

60. Gorbachev's proposal for a comprehensive system of international security that would include not only war/peace concerns but environmental and other concerns was floated in the September 17, 1987 issues of *Pravda* and *Izvestia*, the official Communist Party and government newspapers, as well as before the 43rd UN General Assembly on December 7, 1988. Gorbachev entitled the article "Realities and Guarantees for A Secure World." The Shevardnadze statement was reported in *Pravda*, September 28, 1988.

61. Barry Buzan, *People, States and Fear* (Chapel Hill, N.C.: University of North Carolina Press, 1983), p. 97.

62. Inis Claude, "The Record of International Organizations in the Twentieth Century," Tamkang Chair Lecture Series, No. 64, Tamkang University, Taiwan (mimeo), pp. 4–5.

63. Lynn H. Miller, *Global Order*, 2nd ed. (Boulder: Westview Press, 1990), p. 29.
64. The concept of "veto state" is discussed in Gareth Porter and Janet Welsh Brown, *Global Environmental Politics*, 2nd ed. (Boulder: Westview Press, 1996). The authors note, on p. 14, that in many issue-areas "there is one state or a group of states whose cooperation is so essential to a successful agreement for coping with the problem that it has the potential to block strong international action."
65. Robert W. Gregg, *About Face? The United States and the United Nations* (Boulder: Lynne Rienner, 1993), p. 50.
66. Inis Claude, "The Record of International Organizations in the Twentieth Century," *op. cit.*, p. 53; also see Claude, "Collective Legitimization as a Political Function of the United Nations," *International Organization*, 20 (Summer 1966), pp. 367–379.
67. Stephen D. Krasner, *Structural Conflict: The Third World Against Global Liberalism* (Berkeley, Calif.: University of California Press, 1985).
68. Although the vast majority of the some 8,000 international agreements the United States is a party to are bilateral, there are approximately 1,000 which are multilateral, including many major regimes.
69. The international regimes governing transportation and communications generally have been favorable to the United States. See Mark W. Zacher and Brent A. Sutton, *Governing Global Networks* (Cambridge: Cambridge University Press, 1996).
70. Jonathan Wilkenfeld and Michael Brecher, "International Crises 1945–1975: The UN Dimension," *International Studies Quarterly*, 28 (March 1984), pp. 45–67; also see Ernst B. Haas, *Why We Still Need the United Nations: The Collective Management of International Conflict, 1945–1984*, Policy Papers in International Affairs, No. 26 (Berkeley, Calif.: Institute of International Studies, 1986).
71. U.S. Secretary of State Henry Kissinger, *U.S. Department of State Bulletin*, 69 (December 10, 1973), p. 708.
72. David Kennedy, "The Move to Institutions," *Cardozo Law Review*, 8 (April 1987), pp. 841–988, describes the growth of IGOs in the twentieth century. On the special American role, see John Ruggie, "Multilateralism: The Anatomy of An Institution," *International Organization*, 46 (Summer 1992), p. 584.
73. Henry A. Kissinger, "Clinton in the World," *Newsweek*, February 1, 1993, p. 45.
74. For a good statement of current American interests, see Thomas L. Friedman, "A Manifesto for the Fast World," *New York Times Magazine*, March 28, 1999, pp. 41ff; and Friedman, "The Powell Perplex," *New York Times*, December 19, 2000.
75. Eban, "The UN Idea Revisited," *op. cit.*, p. 55.

Chapter 3: Billiard Balls and Cobwebs

1. On the concept of "nation-state," see Alan James, *Sovereign Statehood* (London: Allen and Unwin, 1986); Mostafa Rejal and Cynthia Enloe, "Nation-States and State-Nations," *International Studies Quarterly*, 13 (June 1969), pp. 140–158; and Gideon Gottlieb, *Nation Against State* (New York: Council on Foreign Relations Press, 1993), and Gottlieb, "Nations Without States," *Foreign Affairs*, 73 (May/June 1994), pp. 100–112.
2. Reported in the *New York Times*, May 31, 1999, p. A9.
3. Daniel Boorstin, in *The Americans* (New York: Vintage Books, 1974), discusses the transcontinental railroad on p. ix and the moon landing on pp. 593–596. For a discussion of the U.S. pursuit of "manifest destiny" in the nineteenth century, see Albert K. Weinberg, *Manifest Destiny* (Baltimore: Johns Hopkins University Press, 1935); the term was first coined in 1845 by John O'Sullivan in *The Democratic Review*, a Jacksonian paper. The reference to "meeting their destiny" is attributed to U.S. Senator Robert Kerr, who in 1961 predicted that President Kennedy's just-announced space program would "enable Americans to meet their destiny." Cited in Boorstin, *op. cit.*, p. 596.
4. Cited in Boorstin, *op. cit.*, p. 596.
5. So-called "resident aliens"—foreigners permitted entry into a country to live there for an extended stay—can in fact be drafted into that country's armed forces, depending on the latter's laws.
6. http://www.ins.usdoj.gov/natz/natznews.pdf. Accessed on 5/9/99.
7. *St. Louis Post-Dispatch*, July 4, 1999, p. B2.

8. Robert B. Reich, *The Work of Nations: Preparing Ourselves for 21st Century Capitalism* (New York: Knopf, 1991), p. 8.
9. Charles R. Morris, "The Coming Global Boom," *The Atlantic Monthly*, 264 (October 1989), p. 51.
10. Joseph Grunwald and Kenneth Flamm, *The Global Factory* (Washington, D.C.: The Brookings Institution, 1985).
11. There are a few unusual exceptions that can occur. For example, in recent years Taiwan, which due to opposition from the People's Republic of China (Communist China) is recognized by very few governments, has been permitted to participate under the banner of "Tapei City." Some non-sovereign territories such as Puerto Rico have been allowed to participate. Some recognized states have been at times denied participation, such as South Africa, when its apartheid policies made it a pariah state internationally during much of the Cold War era.
12. Thomas S. Kuhn, *The Structure of Scientific Revolutions*, 2nd ed. (Chicago: University of Chicago Press, 1970). On the subject of paradigms and "research programs," see Imre Lakatos and Alan Musgrave, eds., *Criticism and the Growth of Knowledge* (Cambridge, Eng.: Cambridge University Press, 1970), especially Lakatos, "Falsification and the Methodology of Scientific Research Programmes." One author notes the term "paradigm" is somewhat imprecise, as Kuhn used it twenty-one different ways. Margaret Masterman, "The Nature of a Paradigm," in Lakatos and Musgrave, *op. cit.*, pp. 61–65; cited in Steve Smith, "The Self-Images of a Discipline," in Ken Booth and Steve Smith, eds., *International Relations Theory Today* (University Park, Pa.: Pennsylvania State University Press, 1995), p. 15.
13. Kuhn, *op. cit.*, p. 4.
14. James N. Rosenau and Mary Durfee, *Thinking Theory Thoroughly* (Boulder: Westview Press, 1995), p. 6.
15. *Ibid.*, pp. 2 and 7.
16. Thomas J. Biersteker, "Eroding Boundaries, Contested Terrain," *International Studies Review*, 1 (Spring 1999), pp. 3–4.
17. An overview of these debates and the development of international relations as a discipline is provided in William Olson's "Growing Pains of a Discipline: Its Phases, Ideals, and Debates," in Olson et al., eds., *The Theory and Practice of International Relations*, 6th ed. (Englewood Cliffs, N.J.: Prentice-Hall, 1983), pp. 391–401; and K.J. Holsti, *The Dividing Discipline: Hegemony and Diversity in International Theory* (London: Unwin and Allen, 1985).
18. For an excellent discussion of all these schools, including extensive bibliography, see Michael Brecher, "International Studies in the Twentieth Century and Beyond: Flawed Dichotomies, Synthesis, Cumulation," *International Studies Quarterly*, 43 (June 1999), pp. 213–264.
19. See Ray Maghroori and Bennett Ramberg, *Globalism Versus Realism: International Relations' Third Debate* (Boulder: Westview Press, 1982); also see Charles A. McClelland, "On the Fourth Wave: Past and Future in the Study of International Systems," in James N. Rosenau et al., eds., *The Analysis of International Politics* (New York: Free Press, 1972), pp. 15–40.
20. Harold K. Jacobson, *Networks of Interdependence*, 2nd ed. (New York: Knopf, 1984), p. 14.
21. Yale H. Ferguson and Richard W. Mansbach, *Polities: Authority, Identities, and Change* (Columbia, S.C.: University of South Carolina Press, 1996); also see their paper "Beyond Inside/Outside" presented at the annual meeting of the International Studies Association, Chicago, February 1995.
22. Richard J. Barnet and Ronald E. Muller, *Global Reach* (New York: Simon and Schuster, 1974), p. 13.
23. Geoffrey Barraclough, *An Introduction to Contemporary History* (Baltimore: Penguin, 1967), p. 110.
24. Lynn Miller, *Global Order*, 3rd ed. (Boulder: Westview Press, 1994), pp. 21–23.
25. K.J. Holsti, *International Politics: A Framework for Analysis*, 3rd ed. (Englewood Cliffs, N.J.: Prentice-Hall, 1977), p. 54.
26. John Agnew, "The Territorial Trap: The Geographical Assumptions of International Relations Theory," *Review of International Political Economy*, 1 (Spring 1994), p. 60.
27. The Congress of Westphalia actually met from 1642 to 1648 before producing the peace treaties that would conclude the war. For a detailed description of the conference and the peace treaties, see Stephen D. Krasner, "Westphalia and All That," in Judith Goldstein and Robert O. Keohane, eds., *Ideas and Foreign Policy* (Ithaca, N.Y.: Cornell University Press, 1993), pp. 240–246.

28. See *ibid.*, pp. 246–247.
29. Charles Tilly, *Coercion, Capital, and European States: A.D. 900–1990* (Cambridge, Eng.: Basil Blackwell, 1990); and Tilly, "Reflections on the History of European State-Making," in Tilly, ed., *The Formation of National States in Western Europe* (Princeton: Princeton University Press, 1975), pp.3–83. Also see Gianfranco Poggi, *Development of the Modern State* (Stanford: Stanford University Press, 1978).
30. Bruce Bueno de Mesquita, "The Concordat of Worms and Westphalia," paper presented at the annual meeting of the International Studies Association, Washington, D.C., February 18, 1999.
31. John H.Herz, *International Politics in the Atomic Age* (New York: Columbia University Press, 1959).
32. Krasner, "Westphalia and All That," *op. cit.*, pp. 246–247.
33. *Ibid.*, p. 253.
34. See Henrik Spruyt, *The Sovereign State and Its Competitors* (Princeton: Princeton University Press, 1994).
35. K.J. Holsti, *Peace and War: Armed Conflicts and International Order, 1648–1989* (Cambridge, Eng.: Cambridge University Press, 1991), p. 25.
36. Leo Gross, "The Peace of Westphalia, 1648–1948," *American Journal of International Law,* 42 (January 1948), p. 28.
37. Miller, *op.cit.*, p. 203.
38. As Inis Claude suggests, the Hague Conferences of 1899 and 1907, convened to discuss ways of settling disputes peacefully, symbolized the shifting nature of the international system at the turn of the century: "Whereas the first conference was attended by only twenty-six states and was preponderantly European in composition, the second involved representatives of forty-four states, including the bulk of the Latin American republics [as well as Asian states]." Inis L. Claude, *Swords Into Plowshares*, 4th ed. (New York: Random House, 1971), p. 29.
39. "States' finances were driven by the preparation for and conduct of war. During the major wars of the eighteenth century, military expenditures accounted for between 61 and 74 percent of public spending in Britain. During the Great Northern War, Peter the Great spent 90 percent of Russia's revenues on the military." Stephen D. Krasner, "Economic Interdependence and Independent Statehood," in Robert Jackson and Alan James, eds., *States In A Changing World* (Oxford: Clarendon Press, 1993), p. 305.
40. Ephraim Lipton, "The Age of Mercantilism," in Lipton, *The Economic History of England*, vol. III (London: Macmillan, 1956); cited in Vincent Cable, "The Diminished Nation-State: A Study in the Loss of Economic Power," *Daedalus*, 124 (Spring 1995), p. 25.
41. Adam Markham, *A Brief History of Pollution* (New York: St. Martin's Press, 1994), p. 10.
42. On mercantilism and the relationship between power and wealth, see Jacob Viner, "Power vs. Plenty as Objectives of Foreign Policy in the Seventeenth and Eighteenth Centuries," *World Politics*, 1 (1948), pp. 1–29.
43. Tilly, "Reflections on the History of European State-Making," *op. cit.*
44. Peter J. Katzenstein, "Domestic Structures and Strategies of Foreign Economic Policy," *International Organization*, 31 (Autumn 1977), p. 892; Stephen D. Krasner, *Defending the National Interest* (Princeton: Princeton University Press, 1978), p. 57; and Joel S. Migdal, *Strong Societies and Weak States* (Princeton: Princeton University Press, 1988).
45. Migdal, *op. cit.*, pp. 4–5.
46. Seymour Martin Lipset, *The First New Nation* (New York: W.W. Norton, 1979).
47. In *The End of Liberalism* (New York: W.W. Norton, 1979), Theodore Lowi argues that the period from the end of the Civil War through the New Deal in the 1930s resulted in the founding of the "Second Republic"—a quiet revolution that shifted power from the state capitals to Washington, D.C., and permitted a more expansive federal state. Prior to that, Lowi argues, the phrase "the American state" was almost an oxymoron.
48. Francis Fukuyama, "The End of History?," *The National Interest*, 16 (Summer 1989), p. 3.
49. Inis L. Claude, "The Record of International Organizations in the Twentieth Century," Tamkang Chair Lecture Series, Number 64, Tamkang University, Taiwan, January 1986 (mimeo), p. 2.
50. Inis L. Claude, *Swords Into Plowshares*, 4th ed. (New York: Random House, 1984), p. 448.
51. John G. Ruggie, "Multilateralism: The Anatomy of An Institution," *International Organization*, 46 (Summer 1992), p. 584.

52. "The Character of Independent Statehood," in Robert Jackson and Alan James, eds., *States In A Changing World* (Oxford: Clarendon Press, 1993), p. 4.

53. John Maynard Keynes, *The General Theory of Employment, Interest, and Money* (London: Macmillan, 1957), p. 383.

54. Hans J. Morgenthau, *Politics Among Nations* (New York: Knopf, 1948).

55. John Vasquez et al., "Color It Morgenthau: A Data-Based Assessment of Quantitative International Relations Research," paper presented at the annual meeting of the International Studies Association, St. Louis, March 1973; and Vasquez, "Coloring It Morgenthau: New Evidence for An Old Thesis on Quantitative International Politics," *British Journal of International Studies* (1979), pp. 210–228. Similarly, in "The Dialectics of World Order: Notes for A Future Archeologist of International Savoir Faire," *International Studies Quarterly*, 28 (June 1984), pp. 121–142, Hayward Alker and Thomas Biersteker noted that the vast majority of works appearing on the reading lists of international relations courses offered at American universities were based on Morgenthau's ideas.

56. Noting the parallels between the dynamics of the Greek city-state system and the dynamics of the Westphalian nation-state system, one writer confesses that "in honesty, one must question whether or not twentieth-century students of international relations know anything that Thucydides and his fifth-century compatriots did not know about the behavior of states." Robert Gilpin, *War and Change in World Politics* (Cambridge, Eng.: Cambridge University Press, 1981), p. 227.

57. It was not Morgenthau but Arnold Wolfers who suggested the billiard ball imagery in *Discord and Collaboration* (Baltimore: Johns Hopkins University Press, 1962).

58. Oran R. Young, "The Actors in World Politics," in James N. Rosenau et al., eds., *The Analysis of International Politics* (New York: Free Press, 1972), p. 125.

59. Hedley Bull, *The Anarchical Society* (New York: Columbia University Press, 1977), p. 8.

60. The definition is attributed to David Lilienthal; cited in Yair Aharoni, "On the Definition of A Multinational Corporation," in Ashok Kapur and Phillip D. Grub, eds., *The Multinational Enterprise in Transition* (Princeton, N.J.: Darwin Press, 1972).

61. Graham T. Allison, *Essence of Decision* (Boston: Little, Brown, 1971), pp. 4–5.

62. Rosenau and Durfee, *op. cit.*, p. 12.

63. Graham T. Allison, "Conceptual Models and the Cuban Missile Crisis," *American Political Science Review*, 63 (September 1969), p. 689.

64. Rosenau and Durfee, *op. cit.*, p. 13.

65. This is consistent with Aaron Wildavsky's "The Two Presidencies" article, which argued that in the American political system the U.S. president enjoys far more decision latitude and power to make decisions in the area of foreign policy than in the area of domestic policy. Aaron Wildavsky, "The Two Presidencies," *Transaction*, 4 (December 1966), pp. 7–14. Written during the Cold War, the question remains how pertinent the argument is today in the post-Cold War era. See note 54 in Chapter 2.

66. In *The Political System* (New York: John Wiley, 1953), David Easton defined politics as "the authoritative allocation of values," taking national political systems as his reference point. Sociologist Max Weber once defined the state as that entity which enjoys "a monopoly on the legitimate use of armed force" within its borders.

67. Hans J. Morgenthau, *Politics Among Nations*, 5th ed. (New York: Knopf, 1973), p. 27.

68. Thucydides, *The Peloponnesian War*, trans. Rex Warner (New York: Penguin, 1978), p. 402; Niccolo Machiavelli, *The Prince*, trans. Luigi Ricci and revised E.R.P. Vincent (Fairlawn, N.J.: Oxford University Press, 1935), Chapter 12.

69. For example, Albert Zimmerman, *The League of Nations and the Role of Law 1918–1935* (London: Macmillan, 1936). Woodrow Wilson became closely associated with the idealist school. See R.S. Baker, *Woodrow Wilson and World Settlement* (Gloucester, Mass.: P. Smith, 1922).

70. Michael Banks, "The Inter-Paradigm Debate," in M. Light and A.J.R. Groom, eds., *International Relations* (London: Pinter, 1985), pp. 14–15. See Ian Clark, *The Hierarchy of States* (Cambridge, Eng.: Cambridge University Press, 1988), especially Chapter 3 on "Kant and the Tradition of Optimism."

71. E.H. Carr, *The Twenty Years' Crisis, 1919–1939* (London: Macmillan, 1939).

72. Realist theory has at times been criticized for claiming to be an *empirical* theory that describes and explains the workings of the state system, yet, in many realist writings, often has the look of a *normative* or *prescriptive* theory, i.e., it urges policymakers to pursue, say, balance

of power policies even though they might be driven by liberal internationalist impulses to try less threatening multilateral diplomacy. In other words, realists acknowledge that real-world policymakers frequently act contrary to what realist theory would predict. On the many uses of "the balance of power" concept, see Ernst B. Haas, "The Balance of Power: Prescription, Concept, or Propaganda," *World Politics*, 5 (July 1953), pp. 442–477.

73. Among well-known realist disciples of Morgenthau were George Kennan and Henry Kissinger. Kennan, in *American Diplomacy, 1900–1950* (Chicago: University of Chicago Press, 1951), noted the "moralistic-legalistic" tendencies of U.S. foreign policy historically, and urged that policymakers resist such idealistic impulses. Kissinger, in *American Foreign Policy: Three Essays* (New York: W.W. Norton, 1969), also urged that American policymakers resist such idealistic impulses.

74. Prominent examples of neorealism are Kenneth Waltz, *Theory of International Politics* (Reading, Mass.: Addison-Wesley, 1979); Gilpin, *op.cit.*; and John J. Mearsheimer, "Back to the Future: Instability in Europe After the Cold War," *International Security*, 15 (1990), pp. 5–56.

75. The theory of hegemonic stability posits that a hegemonic state is able to maintain stability through a combination of coercion (i.e., threatening to use armed force against any state violating norms or rules established by the hegemon) and positive inducements (i.e., conferring economic and other benefits on states that cooperate in preserving order). See Gilpin, *op. cit.*; G. John Ikenberry and Charles A. Kupchan, "Socialization and Hegemonic Stability," *International Organization*, 44 (Summer 1990), pp. 283–316; and Charles P. Kindleberger, *The World in Depression, 1929–1938* (Berkeley, Calif.: University of California Press, 1973). The problems hegemons face in sustaining their power are discussed in Paul Kennedy, *The Rise and Fall of the Great Powers* (New York: Random House, 1987).

76. John J. Mearsheimer, "Why We Will Soon Miss the Cold War," *The Atlantic Monthly* (August 1990), pp. 35–50.

77. A useful discussion of the "prisoners' dilemma" game and other games is Glenn H. Snyder and Paul Diesing, *Conflict Among Nations* (Princeton: Princeton University Press, 1977).

78. Waltz, *op.cit.*, p. 105. Also, see Joseph Grieco, "Anarchy and the Limits of Cooperation: A Realist Critique of the Newest Liberal Institutionalism," *International Organization*, 42 (Summer 1988), pp. 486–507.

79. John J. Mearsheimer, "The False Promise of International Institutions," *International Security*, 19 (1994–95), pp. 5–49.

80. Examples of neoliberalism are Robert O. Keohane, *After Hegemony: Cooperation and Discord in the World Political Economy* (Princeton: Princeton University Press, 1984); and Robert Axelrod, *The Evolution of Cooperation* (New York: Basic Books, 1984). Keohane particularly examines how cooperation under anarchy is feasible in the absence of a hegemon. On the debate between neorealists and neoliberals generally, see Charles W. Kegley, Jr., ed., *Controversies in International Relations Theory: Realism and the Neoliberal Challenge* (New York: St. Martin's Press, 1995).

81. Bull, *op. cit.*

82. *Ibid.*, p. 16.

83. The term "complex interdependence" is taken from Robert O. Keohane and Joseph S. Nye, *Power and Interdependence* (Boston: Little, Brown, 1977). See especially Chapter 2. Keohane and Nye themselves drifted in the 1980s and 1990s between "billiard ball" and "cobweb" paradigms, finding it hard to break completely from the traditional Westphalian paradigm. See Nye, "Neorealism and Neoliberalism," *World Politics*, 40 (January 1988), pp. 235–251.

84. Samuel P. Huntington, "The Lonely Superpower," *Foreign Affairs* (March/April 1999), pp. 47–48.

85. On trends in the number of states, see the data in J. David Singer et al., *Explaining War* (Beverly Hills, Calif.: Sage, 1979), p. 65; and Arthur S. Banks, *Political Handbook of the World 1992* (Binghamton, N.Y.: CSA Publications, 1992). On the "low annihilation rate of states since World War II," see Janice E. Thomson and Stephen D. Krasner, "Global Transactions and the Consolidation of Sovereignty," in James N. Rosenau and Ernst-Otto Czempiel, eds., *Global Changes and Theoretical Challenges* (Lexington, Mass.: Lexington Books, 1989), pp. 206–207. The United States was able to mobilize the UN against Iraq in the 1991 Gulf War partly because, in seeking to incorporate all of Kuwait within Iraq's boundaries, Saddam Hussein violated what was seen as a sacred norm of the international system.

86. The first was a Gallup poll taken on June 25, 1999; the second was a Public Agenda poll taken on September 3, 1998, compiled by the Roper Center. Even in Western Europe, where

the development of the European Union has aimed to create a sense of European solidarity beyond the nation-state, nationalism remains a powerful force. For example, in the 1970s, "survey data [showed] that in all [states in the European Community] . . . more than half of the respondents gave their nation as either their first or second identification," far ahead of "Europe" or "the world," although some respondents did list their locality ahead of their national affiliation. Reported in Jacobson, *op. cit.*, pp. 384–385. More recent Euro-Barometer polls have reported similar findings. On the continued vitality of nationalism, see William Pfaff, *The Wrath of Nations* (New York: Simon and Schuster, 1993).

87. Peter Dicken, *Global Shift: The Internationalization of Economic Activity* (London: Paul Chapman, 1992), p. 198; cited in Norman Lewis, "Globalization and the End of the Nation-State," paper presented at the annual meeting of the International Studies Association, San Diego, April 1996, p. 24.

88. Lewis, *op. cit.*, pp. 24–25.

89. One writer notes that "the state in most Western countries is generally taking a large share of the GDP [gross domestic product] (after fifteen years of the Thatcherite 'revolution' in Britain and the privatization of almost all nationalized industries and utilities, the government share of the GDP—40 percent—is actually larger than when it took over from a Socialist administration!)." Cable, *op. cit.*, p. 41.

90. Thomson and Krasner, *op.cit.*, pp. 208–214.

91. Depending on how one defines an IGO, one might even count over 1,000. On trends in the growth of IGOs, see Michael Wallace and J. David Singer, "Intergovernmental Organizations in the Global System 1815–1964," *International Organization*, 24 (Spring 1970), p. 277; and the Union of International Associations, *Yearbook of International Organizations, 1999* (Brussels: UIA, 1999).

92. Based on the University of Washington Treaty Research Center Studies, reported in Richard Bilder, *Managing the Risks of International Agreement* (Madison: University of Wisconsin Press, 1981), p. 232. The growth of treaties in modern times is reflected in the fact that in 1892 the official compendium of treaties entered into by the United Kingdom numbered only 190 pages, whereas by 1960 it exceeded 2,500 pages. Michael Akehurst, *A Modern Introduction to International Law*, 6th ed. (London: Allen and Unwin, 1987), p. 25. For the international system as a whole, "treaties concluded between 1648 and 1919 fill 226 thick books, between 1920 and 1946 some 205 more volumes, and between 1946 and 1978, 1,115 more tomes." Mark W. Janis, *An Introduction to International Law* (Boston: Little, Brown, 1988), p. 11. Technically, the UN and other nonstate actors in a few cases may be parties to treaties, but this is the exception to the rule.

93. "Until 1914 a sensible, law-abiding Englishman could pass through life and hardly notice the existence of the state, beyond the post office and the policeman. He could live where he liked and as he liked. He had no official number or identity card. He could travel abroad or leave his country forever without a passport or any sort of official permission." A.J.P. Taylor, *English History: 1914–1945* (Oxford: Clarendon Press, 1965), p. 1. The reference to ground beef regulation is from *U.S. News and World Report*, February 11, 1980, p. 64; also, see Thomas R. Dye, *Politics in America*, 3rd ed. (Upper Saddle River, N.J.: Prentice-Hall, 1999), pp. 453–460.

94. Thomson and Krasner, *op. cit.*, pp. 198–206; Nicholas D. Kristof, "At This Rate, We'll Be Global in Another Hundred Years," *New York Times*, May 23, 1999; and Keith Bradsher, "Back to the Thrilling Trades of Yesteryear," *New York Times*, March 12, 1995.

95. Krasner, "Westphalia and All That," *op. cit.*, p. 318.

96. Lucian Pye, "Political Science and the Crisis of Authoritarianism," *American Political Science Review*, 84 (March 1990), p. 6.

97. Reported in Claude Moisy, "Myths of the Global Information Village," *Foreign Policy* (Summer 1997), p. 83. Typically, every year, five of the least selling newsstand issues of *Time, Newsweek*, and *U.S. News and World Report* have foreign policy or world affairs cover stories; reported by James Fallows, former editor of *U.S. News*.

98. Samuel P. Huntington, "The Clash of Civilizations," *Foreign Affairs*, 72 (Summer 1993), pp. 22–49.

99. Moisy, *op. cit.*, p. 79.

100. Paul Lewis, "UN Panel Proposes Expanding Security Council to 24 Members," *New York Times*, March 21, 1997.

101. The "cobweb" metaphor can be credited to John Burton et al., *The Study of World Society*,

Occasional Paper No. 1, International Studies Association, 1974. Also, see Richard W. Mansbach et al., *The Web of World Politics: Nonstate Actors in the Global System* (Englewood Cliffs, N.J.: Prentice-Hall, 1976).

102. James N. Rosenau, "Global Changes and Theoretical Challenges: Toward A Postinternational Politics for the 1990s," in Rosenau and Ernst-Otto Czempiel, eds., *Global Changes and Theoretical Challenges* (Lexington, Mass.: Lexington Books, 1989), p. 5.
103. John Lukacs, "The Short Century—It's Over," *New York Times,* February 17, 1991, p. IV–13.
104. Herz, *op. cit.* In a later article, "The Territorial State Revisited: Reflections on the Future of the Nation-State," *Polity,* 1 (1968), pp. 12–34, Herz retracted his thesis, confessing that he was premature in writing off the nation-state as a viable institution. However, many observers felt he was prescient in anticipating how technology might affect interdependence, long before the term "interdependence" became fashionable.
105. For example, see Raymond Vernon, ed., *The Oil Crisis* (New York: W.W. Norton, 1976).
106. Keohane and Nye, *Power and Interdependence, op. cit.,* introduced the terms "sensitivity" and "vulnerability" to characterize the extent to which states are not only increasingly touched by external forces but are at times severely impacted. See note 83. Keohane and Nye focused on nonstate actors in their edited volume *Transnational Relations and World Politics* (Cambridge, Mass.: Harvard University Press, 1972).
107. Charles P. Kindleberger, *American Business Abroad* (New Haven: Yale University Press, 1969), p. 207.
108. Raymond Vernon, *Sovereignty At Bay* (New York: Basic Books, 1971).
109. George W. Ball, "The Promise of the Multinational Corporation, *Fortune,* June 1, 1967, p. 80.
110. Hans J. Morgenthau, "The New Diplomacy of Movement," *Encounter,* 43 (August 1974), p. 57.
111. Walter Wriston, *The Twilight of Sovereignty* (New York: Scribner's, 1992); Reich, *op. cit.*
112. Richard O'Brien, *Global Financial Integration: The End of Geography* (London: Pinter, 1992); Jessica Matthews, "Power Shift," *Foreign Affairs* (January/February 1997), pp. 50–66.
113. Some of these statistics are taken from Richard Barnet and John Cavanaugh, *Global Dreams* (New York: Simon and Schuster, 1994), pp. 169 and 184–185.
114. *U.S. News and World Report,* January 2, 1995, p. 76.
115. "Electronic herd" is taken from Thomas Friedman, *The Lexus and the Olive Tree* (New York: Farrar, Straus, Giroux, 1999), Chapter 6. "Gypsy capitalism" is David Hale's term, cited in *ibid.,* p. 109. "Casino capitalism" is taken from Susan Strange, *Casino Capitalism* (Oxford: Basil Blackwell, 1986).
116. John Markoff, "Illness Becomes Apt Metaphor for Computers," *New York Times,* June 14, 1999, p. A1.
117. Maryann K. Cusimano, *Beyond Sovereignty: Issues For A Global Agenda* (New York: St. Martin's Press, 2000), p. 21.
118. Friedman, *op. cit.,* pp. 55–56.
119. Rosenau and Durfee, *op. cit.,* p. 47.
120. Kjell Skjelsbaek, "The Growth of International Nongovernmental Organization in the Twentieth Century," *International Organization,* 25 (Summer 1971), pp. 435–436.
121. Cusimano, *op. cit.,* p. 217. Also, see Harold K. Jacobson et al., "National Entanglements in International Governmental Organizations," *American Political Science Review,* 80 (March 1986), pp. 141–159. See note 91 in this chapter.
122. Claude, "The Record of International Organizations," *op. cit.,* p. 25.
123. Craig N. Murphy, *International Organization and Industrial Change: Global Governance Since 1850* (New York: Oxford University Press, 1994).
124. Jacobson, *Networks of Interdependence, op. cit.,* p. 49.
125. The classic formulation of functionalist theory is David Mitrany, *A Working Peace System: An Argument for the Functional Development of International Organization* (London: Royal Institute of International Affairs, 1943). Also, see Ernst B. Haas, "International Integration: The European and the Universal Process," in *International Political Communities* (New York: Doubleday Anchor, 1966), pp. 93–130.
126. Robert O. Keohane, "International Institutions: Can Interdependence Work?," *Foreign Policy,* 110 (1998), p. 82.
127. James A. Field, Jr., "Transnationalism and the New Tribe," *International Organization,* 25 (Summer 1971), pp. 355–356.
128. Jacobson, *Networks of Interdependence, op. cit.,* p. 10.

129. The 28,000 figure is from The Commission on Global Governance, *Our Global Neighborhood* (Oxford: Oxford University Press, 1995), p. 32.

130. Lester M. Salomon, "The Rise of the Nonprofit Sector," *Foreign Affairs* (July/August 1994), pp. 109–122.

131. Remarks of a UN official, cited in Donald Puchala and Roger Coate, *The Challenge of Relevance: The UN in a Changing World Environment* (Hanover, N.H.: Academic Council on the UN, 1989), p. 95.

132. See P.J. Simmons, "Learning to Live with NGOs," *Foreign Policy* (Fall 1998), p. 84. Also see Matthews, *op. cit.*; and Margaret E. Keck and Kathryn Sikkink, *Activists Beyond Borders: Advocacy Networks in International Politics* (Ithaca: Cornell University Press, 1998).

133. Cited in Simmons, *op.cit.*, p. 91.

134. Duane Kujawa, "International Business Education and International Studies," paper presented at annual meeting of the International Studies Association, Cincinnati, March 25, 1982.

135. *The Economist*, July 30, 1994; cited in Cusimano, *op. cit.*, p. 268.

136. Data are from Stephen Gill, "Globalization, Market Civilization, and Disciplinary Neoliberalism," *Millennium*, 24, no. 3 (1995), p. 405; *Fortune*, 132 (August 7, 1995), pp. 23ff.; D. Korten, *When Corporations Rule the World* (West Hartford: Kumarian Press, 1995), p. 124; "A Survey of Multinationals," *The Economist*, March 27, 1993; and Joan E. Spiro and Jeffrey Hart, *The Politics of International Economic Relations* (New York: St. Martin's Press, 1997), pp. 97–98.

137. Friedman, *op.cit.*, p. 185.

138. *New York Times*, January 13, 1999, p. C18; found in Jonathan F. Galloway, "Is It the Global Economy, Stupid?," paper presented at annual meeting of the International Studies Association, Washington, D.C., February 16, 1999, p. 8.

139. Cited in Barnet and Muller, *op. cit.*, p. 16.

140. Barnet and Cavanaugh, *op. cit.*, p. 14.

141. Cited in Barnet and Muller, *op. cit.*, p. 16.

142. Robert Gilpin, *The Political Economy of International Relations* (Princeton: Princeton University Press, 1987), p. 379.

143. Benjamin Barber, *Jihad vs. McWorld* (New York: Times Books, 1995). Similarly, Friedman, *op. cit.*, p. 27, speaks of the competing forces of globalization (symbolized by the "Lexus" automobile) and traditional culture (symbolized by the "olive tree").

144. Among those who have drawn attention to "nonrational" factors are Allison, *Essence of Decision*, *op. cit.*; Richard C. Snyder et al., *Foreign Policy Decision-Making* (New York: Free Press, 1962); Robert Jervis, *Perception and Misperception in International Politics* (Princeton: Princeton University Press, 1976); and Irving L. Janis, *Groupthink*, 2nd ed. (Boston: Houghton Mifflin, 1982). Bruce Bueno de Mesquita, in *Principles of International Politics* (Washington, D.C.: CQ Press, 2000), argues that, if one wants to understand world politics, one must focus on individual national leaders and treat them as rational decision-makers mainly concerned about maximizing *their* interests, not the national interests—particularly staying in power; hence, in contrast to realists, he sees the domestic political environment more so than the external, systemic environment as driving foreign policy.

145. See Deborah Shapley, "Technological Creep and the Arms Race: ICBM Problem A Sleeper," *Science*, 201 (September 22, 1978), p. 105; and "U.S. Accuses Soviets of Developing Four New Long-Range Missiles," *St. Louis Post-Dispatch*, October 18, 1990. On bureaucratic politics, see Morton Halperin and Arnold Kanter, eds., *Readings in American Foreign Policy: A Bureaucratic Perspective* (Boston: Little, Brown, 1973).

146. The term "intermestic" is taken from Ryan J. Barilleaux, "The President, 'Intermestic' Issues, and the Risks of Political Leadership," *Presidential Studies Quarterly*, 15 (Fall 1985), pp. 754–767.

147. President Bill Clinton, "Remarks by the President in Freedom House Speech," White House Documents Office of the Press Secretary, October 6, 1995; cited in Cusimano, *op. cit.*, p. 6.

148. Robert D. Putnam, "Diplomacy and Domestic Politics: The Logic of Two-Level Games," *International Organization*, 42 (Summer 1988), p. 434.

149. Cited in *ibid.*, p. 433.

150. Cited in *ibid.*

151. Joseph S. Nye, "In Government We Don't Trust," *Foreign Policy* (Fall 1997), pp. 99–111.

152. Cable, *op. cit.*, p. 43.

153. Rosenau and Durfee, *op. cit.*, p. 36.

154. See Earl Fry et al., *America the Vincible* (Englewood Cliffs, N.J.: Prentice-Hall, 1994), p. 312; Fry, *The Expanding Role of State and Local Governments in U.S. Foreign Affairs* (New York: Council on Foreign Relations Press, 1998); and Heidi Hobbs, *City Hall Goes Abroad: The Foreign Policy of Local Governments* (Beverly Hills, Calif.: Sage, 1994).
155. Remarks by Sylvia Porter, cited in *World Development Newsletter*, 4 (March 4, 1981), p. 1.
156. Bruce Russett and Harvey Starr, *World Politics: The Menu for Choice*, 3rd ed. (San Francisco: W.W. Freeman, 1989), p. 54. Also see Gunnan P. Nielson, "States and 'Nation-Groups': A Global Taxonomy," in Edward A. Tiryakian and Ronald Rogowski, eds., *New Nationalisms of the Developed West* (Boston: Unwin and Allen, 1985), pp. 27–56.
157. *Wall Street Journal*, September 20, 1993.
158. On the "failed state" phenomenon, see Gerald B. Hellman and Steve R. Ratner, "Saving Failed States," *Foreign Policy* (Winter 1992–93), pp. 3–20; and I. William Zartman, ed. *Collapsed States* (Boulder: Lynne Rienner, 1995).
159. Jack Levy, *War in the Modern Great Power System, 1495–1975* (Lexington, Ky.: University of Kentucky Press, 1983), p. 130.
160. See notes 8 and 9 in Chapter 2.
161. The reference is to Mark Zacher, "The Decaying Pillars of the Westphalian Temple: Implications for International Order and Governance," in James N. Rosenau and Ernst-Otto Czempiel, eds., *Governance Without Government* (Cambridge, Eng.: Cambridge University Press, 1992).
162. The first quote is from Joseph S. Nye, "Conflicts After the Cold War," *The Washington Quarterly* (Winter 1996), p. 5. The second is from Donald Kagan, cited in George Will, "Defense Cuts Reflect Liberals' Blind Optimism in Lasting Peace," *St. Louis Post-Dispatch*, July 17, 1995, p. 6B.
163. On the "democratic peace," see Bruce Russett, *Grasping the Democratic Peace* (Princeton: Princeton University Press, 1993).
164. Friedman, *op. cit.*, Chapter 10. Friedman also acknowledged that the 1999 Kosovo War, which pitted the United States and its NATO allies against Yugoslavia, involved combatants that each had McDonalds restaurants, although Friedman questions whether this was a war in the usual sense.
165. Cable, *op. cit.*, p. 37.
166. For the debate between "society of states" morality and "cosmopolitan" morality, see Charles Brown, *International Relations Theory: New Normative Approaches* (Hemel Hempstead: Harvester Wheatsheaf, 1992); and Charles Beitz, *Political Theory and International Relations* (Princeton: Princeton University Press, 1979).
167. Robert Mcnamara, when he was President of the World Bank, argued that the UN should be concerned about addressing the needs of not only the poorest 40 *states* but also the poorest 40 percent of the population *within* those states, since otherwise aid might not necessarily trickle down to the bottom, neediest segment of the population. See his *One Hundred Countries, Two Billion People* (New York: Praeger, 1973). In recent years, the annual *Human Development Report* published by the UN Development Program has drawn attention to both rich-poor gaps.
168. These statistics are cited in "Kofi Annan's Astonishing Facts," *New York Times*, September 27, 1998.
169. Jessica T. Matthews, "Are Networks Better than Nations?," *New Perspectives Quarterly* (Spring 1997).
170. Africa now accounts for 16 percent of all NGO memberships, and Asia 17 percent. *Our Global Neighborhood*, op. cit., p. 33.
171. Figures are from Michael Webb and Stephen D. Krasner, "Hegemonic Stability Theory: An Empirical Assessment," *Review of International Studies*, 15 (1989), Table 6.
172. The figures are from Friedman, *op. cit.*, p. xv. The quotation is from Michael Stewart, *The Age of Interdependence* (Cambridge, Mass.: MIT Press, 1984), p. 26.
173. Zacher, *op. cit.*, p. 89.
174. Friedman, *op. cit.*, p. xvi.
175. Ithiel de Sola Pool, *Technologies Without Borders: On Telecommunications in a Global Age* (Cambridge, Mass.: Harvard University Press, 1990), p. 71; cited in Zacher, *op. cit.*, p. 65.
176. Joseph S. Nye, "Independence and Interdependence," *Foreign Policy*, 22 (1976), p. 138. Also, see Raymond F. Hopkins, "The International Role of 'Domestic' Bureaucracy," *International Organization*, 30 (1976), pp. 405–432.

177. The quote is attributed to former Colorado Governor Richard Lamm.

178. Zartman, *op. cit.*, p.3; and Cusimano, *op. cit.*, p. 12.

179. Dye, *op. cit.*, pp. 672–673.

180. Cusimano, *op. cit.*, p. 237.

181. Freedom House, *Freedom in the World* (New York: Freedom House, 1995), p. 1. Also, see Samuel P. Huntington, *The Third Wave* (Norman: University of Oklahoma Press, 1991).

182. The remark was made by Jeffry Frieden of Harvard University, at a seminar given at the University of Missouri-St. Louis on March 26, 1998.

183. See "European Union Vows to Become Military Power," *New York Times,* June 4, 1999, which discusses the "move toward a unified defense."

184. Thomas Kamm, "You Won't Find Fans of A Borderless Europe in This Soccer Arena," *Wall Street Journal,* February 12, 1999.

185. See John Newhouse, "Europe's Rising Regionalism," *Foreign Affairs,* 76 (January/February 1997), pp. 67–84.

186. John G. Ruggie, "Territoriality and Beyond: Problematizing Modernity in International Relations," *International Organization,* 47 (Winter 1993), p. 140.

Chapter 4: Living with Paradoxes: Shooting Pool and Pooling Sovereignty

1. Marvin S. Soroos, *Beyond Sovereignty: The Challenge of Global Policy* (Columbia, S.C.: University of South Carolina Press, 1986), page 20.

2. For example, see Charles O. Jones, *An Introduction to the Study of Public Policy* (Monterey, Calif.: Brooks Cole, 1984) and James E. Anderson, *Public Policymaking: An Introduction* (Boston: Houghton Mifflin, 1990); also see Soroos, *op. cit.*, Chapter 3.

3. Eugene J. Meehan, "Policy: Constructing A Definition," *Policy Science,* 18, no.4 (1985), p. 295.

4. James N. Rosenau and Ernst-Otto Czempiel, eds., *Governance Without Government* (Cambridge, Eng.: Cambridge University Press, 1992).

5. See Clyde Sanger, *Ordering the Oceans* (Toronto: University of Toronto Press, 1987).

6. On international law compliance, see Louis Henkin, *How Nations Behave,* 2nd ed. (New York: Columbia University Press, 1979), pp. 46–47; and Abram Chayes and Antonia Chayes, "On Compliance," *International Organization,* 47 (Spring 1993), pp. 175–205.

7. Mark W. Zacher and Brent A. Sutton, *Governing Global Networks: International Regimes for Transportation and Communications* (Cambridge, Eng.: Cambridge University Press, 1996).

8. Soroos, *op. cit.*, p. 82.

9. Harold K. Jacobson, William M. Reisinger, and Todd Mathers, "National Entanglements in International Governmental Organizations," *American Political Science Review,* 80 (March 1986), pp. 157–158.

10. Graham T. Allison, *Essence of Decision* (Boston: Little, Brown, 1971), p. 176.

11. Chayes and Chayes, *op. cit.*, p. 180.

12. See Douglass Cater, *Power in Washington* (New York: Random House, 1964); and Hugh Heclo, "Issue Networks and the Executive Establishment," in Anthony King, ed., *The New American Political System* (Washington, D.C.: American Enterprise Institute, 1978).

13. David L. Larson, *Major Issues of the Law of the Sea* (Durham, N.H.: University of New Hampshire, 1976), p. 10.

14. Sanger, *op. cit.*, p. 25.

15. *Ibid.*, p. 28.

16. *Ibid.*, p. 33.

17. Maria Cowles, *The Politics of Big Business in the European Community: Setting the Agenda for a New Europe,* Ph.D. dissertation, The American University, 1994, p. 86. Also see Vivien Schmidt, "The New World Order, Incorporated," *Daedalus,* 124 (Spring 1995), pp. 75–106.

18. Theodore Lowi, "Distribution, Regulation, Redistribution: The Functions of Government," in Randall P. Ripley, ed., *Public Policies and Their Politics* (New York: W.W. Norton, 1966).

19. James Q. Wilson, *American Government,* 7th ed. (Boston: Houghton Mifflin, 1998), pp. 479–483.

20. David V. Edwards, *The American Political Experience,* 4th ed. (Englewood Cliffs, N.J.: Prentice-Hall, 1988), p. 482.

21. James N. Rosenau and Mary Durfee, *Thinking Theory Thoroughly* (Boulder: Westview Press, 1995), p. 59.

22. 1999 ISA Presidential Address by Michael Brecher, in *International Studies Quarterly,* 43 (June 1999), p. 252.

Chapter 5: Challenges to the National Security State: High Politics in the Post-Cold War Era

1. James Chace and Caleb Carr, *America Invulnerable: The Quest for Absolute Security from 1812 to Star Wars* (New York: Summit Books, 1988), p. 12.

2. Robert H. Jackson. "Continuity and Change in the State System," in Robert H. Jackson and Alan James, eds., *States in A Changing World* (Oxford: Clarendon Press, 1993), pp. 354–355 and 358.

3. Charles W. Kegley and Eugene R. Wittkopf, *World Politics: Trend and Transformation,* 7th ed. (New York: St. Martin's Press, 1999), p. 367.

4. *The Defense Monitor,* XXVII, no.1 (1998), p. 1.

5. For a discussion of problems in measurement, along with reporting of competing data, see Lester Brown, Michael Renner, and Brian Halweil, *Vital Signs 1999* (New York: W.W. Norton, 1999), p. 112.

6. Barry M. Blechman and Stephen S. Kaplan, *Force Without War: U.S. Armed Forces as a Political Instrument* (Washington, D.C.: Brookings Institution, 1979); and Kaplan, *Diplomacy of Power: Soviet Armed Forces as a Political Instrument* (Washington, D.C.: Brookings Institution, 1981).

7. The concept of "coercive diplomacy" is discussed in Alexander George et al., *The Limits of Coercive Diplomacy* (Boston: Little, Brown, 1971). The concept of "diplomacy of violence" is discussed in Thomas Schelling, *Arms and Influence* (New Haven: Yale University Press, 1966), Chapter 1. See also *Forceful Persuasion: Coercive Diplomacy as an Alternative to War* (Washington, D.C.: U.S. Institute of Peace, 1991).

8. Richard Pipes, "Why the Soviet Union Thinks It Could Fight and Win A Nuclear War," *Commentary,* 64 (July 1977).

9. Evan Luard, *War in International Society* (London: I.B. Taurus, 1986), p. 396.

10. James Lee Ray, "The Abolition of Slavery and the End of International War," *International Organization,* 43 (Summer 1989), pp. 405–439.

11. Charles Krauthammer, "B-2 Is Weapon for Our Times," *St. Louis Post-Dispatch,* November 1, 1995.

12. Edward Luttwak, "Toward Post-Heroic Warfare," *Foreign Affairs,* 74 (May/June 1995), pp. 109–122.

13. James N. Rosenau, *Turbulence in World Politics* (Princeton: Princeton University Press, 1990).

14. Thomas Friedman, "Was Kosovo World War III?," *New York Times,* July 2, 1999.

15. For example, see Josef Joffe, "Three Unwritten Rules of the Serbian War," *New York Times,* July 25, 1999; and Donald G. McNeil, "Bombing Won in Kosovo. Africa Is a Tougher Case," *New York Times,* July 25, 1999.

16. *St. Louis Post-Dispatch,* February 10, 1996.

17. Craig Whitney, in "As the Battlegrounds Shift, the Draft Fades in Europe," *New York Times,* October 31, 1999, reported that the French along with the Spanish and the Italians were in the process of joining the United States and Britain in replacing the draft with an all-volunteer army, leaving Germany as the only major state requiring national service.

18. Robert Kaplan, *The Ends of the Earth* (New York: Random House, 1996).

19. K.J. Holsti, "War, Peace, and the State of the State," *International Political Science Review,* 16 (October 1995), p. 320.

20. Brown et al., *op. cit.,* p. 112. The authors were reporting on the Conflict Data Project at the University of Uppsala in Sweden.

21. *The Defense Monitor, op. cit.,* p. 2.

22. "The World's Wars," *The Economist,* March 12, 1988, pp. 19–20.

23. Project Ploughshares, *Armed Conflicts Report 1995* (Waterloo, Canada: Institute of Peace and Conflict Studies, Spring 1995), p. 3.

24. On failed states, see I. William Zartman, ed., *Collapsed States* (Boulder: Lynne Rienner, 1995); and Tonya Langford, "Things Fall Apart: State Failure and the Politics of Intervention," *International Studies Review,* 1 (Spring 1999), pp. 59–79. On ethnopolitical conflict, see Ted Robert Gurr and Barbara Harff, *Ethnic Conflict in World Politics* (Boulder: Westview Press, 1994).

25. Melvin Small and J. David Singer, "Conflict in the International System, 1816–1977: His-

torical Trends and Policy Futures," in Charles W. Kegley and Patrick J. McGowan, eds., *Challenges to America: United States Foreign Policy in the 1980s* (Beverly Hills, Calif.: Sage, 1979), p. 100. Also see Istvan Kende, "Twenty-Five Years of Local Wars," *Journal of Peace Research*, 8, no. 1 (1971), pp. 5–22.

26. This is the finding of Alex Schmid, cited in Anthony Clark Arend and Robert J. Beck, *International Law and the Use of Force* (London: Routledge, 1993), p. 140.

27. Cited in *ibid.*

28. *Patterns of Global Terrorism 1998* (Washington, D.C.: U.S. Department of State, April 1999), p. vi. Similar definitions can be found in Arend and Beck, *op. cit.* and Andrew J. Pierre, "The Politics of International Terrorism," *Orbis*, 19 (Winter 1976), pp. 1251–1270.

29. See Claire Sterling, *The Terror Network* (New York: Holt, Rinehart and Winston, 1981).

30. *Patterns of Global Terrorism 1988* (Washington, D.C.: U.S. Department of State, March 1989), pp. 1–2.

31. *Patterns of Global Terrorism 1998, op. cit.,* p. 1.

32. Anthony Clark Arend, *Legal Rules and International Society* (New York: Oxford University Press, 1995), p. 174.

33. *Ibid,* pp. 181–182.

34. Maryann K. Cusimano, ed. *Beyond Sovereignty: Issues for a Global Agenda* (New York: St. Martin's Press, 2000), p. 31. On the international drug trade, see Rensselaer W. Lee III, "Global Reach: The Threat of International Drug Trafficking," *Current History* (May 1995), pp. 207–211; and Stephen E. Flynn, "The Global Drug Trade Versus the Nation-State: Why the Thugs Are Winning," in Cusimano, *op. cit.,* pp. 44–66.

35. Remarks by John Deutsch, cited in Cusimano, *op. cit.,* p. 67.

36. *Ibid.*, pp. 67–68.

37. Thomas C. Schelling, "Thinking About Nuclear Terrorism," *International Security*, 6 (Spring 1982), p. 76.

38. According to the U.S. Arms Control and Disarmament Agency, total world military spending reached a high (in current dollars) of $1.1 trillion in 1990. "World Arms Spending," *U.S. Arms Control and Disarmament Agency* [article online]; available from <http://www.cdi.org/ArmsTradeDatabase/Arms_Trade_Patterns_and_Trends>, accessed November 24, 1999.

39. For a discussion of the "opportunity costs" of armaments and what they could buy in social expenditures, see the annual editions of Ruth Leger Sivard, *World Military and Social Expenditures* published by World Priorities, Washington, D.C.

40. International Institute for Strategic Studies, *Military Balance, 1985–1986* (London: 1985).

41. [online article] <http://www.acda.gov/factshee/conwpn/small.htm>; accessed November 24, 1999.

42. Jean Pascal Zanders et al., "Chemical and Biological Weapon Developments and Arms Control," *SIPRI Yearbook 1997: Armaments, Disarmament and International Security* (Stockholm: SIPRI, 1997), pp. 445 and 450.

43. Andrew Cordesman, "One Half Cheer for the CWC," in Brad Roberts, ed., *Ratifying the Chemical Weapons Convention* (Washington, D.C.: Center for Strategic and International Studies, 1994).

44. William Broad and Judith Miller, "Soviet Defector Says China Had Accident at a Germ Plant," *New York Times,* March 20, 1999.

45. On nuclear proliferation, see Gary T. Gardner, *Nuclear Nonproliferation* (Boulder: Lynne Rienner, 1994), especially Chapter 9; Peter A. Clausen, "Nuclear Proliferation in the 1980s and 1990s," in Michael T. Klare and Daniel C. Thomas, eds., *World Security: Trends and Challenges at Century's End* (New York: St. Martin's Press, 1991), pp. 144–169; and Michele A. Flournoy, ed., *Nuclear Weapons After the Cold War* (New York: HarperCollins, 1993).

46. *The Defense Monitor,* XXII,, no. 1 (1993), p. 1.

47. U.S. Arms Control and Disarmament Agency data show that, as of late 1999, the United States had a total of 7,815 nuclear warheads deployed on 1,466 ICBMs (intercontinental ballistic missiles), SLBMs (submarine-launched ballistic missiles), and strategic bombers, while Russia had a total of 6,546 warheads deployed on 1,397 strategic delivery vehicles. "Weapons of Mass Destruction Factsheet," *U.S. State Department, Bureau of Arms Control* [article online]; available from <http://www.acda.gov/factshee/wmd/nuclear/start1/startagg.htm>; accessed November 25, 1999.

48. See Michael Walzer, *Just and Unjust Wars* (New York: Basic Books, 1977); and Louis Henkin et al., *Right vs. Might,* 2nd ed. (New York: Council on Foreign Relations, 1991).

49. In the case of the League of Nations Covenant, the only obligation of states to refrain from war was that they at least exhaust all peaceful settlement procedures first.

50. Louis Henkin, *How Nations Behave,* 2nd ed. (New York: Columbia University Press, 1979), p. 146.

51. Cusimano, *op. cit.,* p. 2.

52. See Arend and Beck, *op. cit.;* and Lori Fisler Damrosch, ed., *Enforcing Restraint: Collective Intervention in Internal Conflicts* (New York: Council on Foreign Relations, 1993).

53. On the Article 2 section 7 controversy, see Abiodun Williams et al., *Article 2 (7) Revisited* (Providence: Academic Council on the United Nations System, 1994); Damrosch, *op. cit.;* and Arend and Beck, *op. cit.,* Chapter 8.

54. Judith Miller, "Sovereignty Isn't So Sacred Anymore," *New York Times,* April 18, 1999.

55. *An Agenda for Peace,* UN Doc. A/47/277 and S/24111, 1992. The rapid deployment force is discussed in Joseph S. Nye, "What New World Order?," *Foreign Affairs* (Spring 1992), pp. 83–96.

56. Virginia Nesmith, "Landmines Are a Lingering Killer," *St. Louis Post-Dispatch,* December 31, 1995.

57. Landmines Fact Sheet (July 1995), published by the U.S. Campaign to Ban Landmines; also reported in *The Defense Monitor,* XXV, no. 5 (July 1996).

58. Steven Myers, "Land-Mine Ban Has Trouble Getting Off the Ground," *New York Times,* September 5, 1999.

59. Reported in *The Interdependent,* 22 (Summer 1996), p. 4. Others have tried to argue that nuclear weapons are covered under the body of customary and treaty law prohibiting the use of weapons that inflict indiscriminate damage on civilians. See Burns H. Weston, "Nuclear Weapons and the World Court: Ambiguity's Consensus," *Transnational Law and Contemporary Problems,* 7, no. 2 (1996); and Ved P. Nanda and David Krieger, *Nuclear Weapons and the World Court* (Ardsley, N.Y.: Transnational Publishers, 1998).

60. This is the characterization of the U.S. Arms Control and Disarmament Agency. "The Comprehensive Test Ban Treaty," *U.S. Arms Control and Disarmament Agency* [article online]; available from <http://www.acda.gov/ctbtpage/quotes .htm>; accessed November 24, 1999.

61. Cited in Cusimano, *op. cit.,* pp. 265–266. Similar remarks were made by Robert Lawson, Canada's chief negotiator at the Ottawa talks, at the annual meeting of the International Studies Association in Washington, D.C., on February 18, 1999.

62. For a discussion of the role of domestic politics in the war-peace area, see Jo L. Husbands, "Domestic Factors and De-Escalation Initiatives," in Louis Kriesberg and Stuart Thorson, eds., *Timing the Deescalation* (Syracuse: Syracuse University Press, 1992), pp. 97–116.

63. Abram Chayes and Antonia Chayes, "On Compliance," *International Organization,* 47 (Spring 1993), p. 180.

64. Robert J. Mathews and Timothy L.H. McCormack, "Entry Into Force of the Chemical Weapons Convention," *Security Dialogue,* 26, no. 1 (1995), p. 93. The Organization for the Prohibition of Chemical Weapons homepage calls the treaty "the first disarmament agreement negotiated within a multilateral framework that provides for the elimination of an entire category of weapons of mass destruction under universally applied international control." "The Chemical Weapons Convention," *Organization for the Prohibition of Chemical Weapons* [article online]; available from <http://www.opcw.nl/guide.htm#history1>; accessed November 25, 1999.

65. J.P. Perry Robinson, "Origins of the Chemical Weapons Convention," in Benoit Morel and Kyle Olson, eds., *Shadows and Substance: The Chemical Weapons Convention* (Boulder: Westview Press, 1993), p, 40.

66. Much of this early historical discussion draws on Robinson, *op. cit.,* and the *Organization for the Prohibition of Chemical Weapons* website at <http://www.opcw.nl/guide .htm#history1>.

67. Statement by Will Irwin, uttered in 1926, cited by Amy Smithson in her testimony before the U.S. Congress in 1994. *Hearings Before the Committee on Foreign Relations, U.S. Senate,* June 9, 1994, p. 130.

68. There is some evidence that chemical weapons might have been used in a limited fashion by Italy against Ethiopia in the 1930s and by Japan against China during World War II, but the historical record generally supports the view that the Geneva Protocol was largely abided by in the decades following World War I. For a weighing of rumor and fact, see Robinson, *op. cit.,* pp. 40–44.

69. *Ibid.,* p. 37.

70. *Ibid.*, p. 47.
71. *Ibid.*, p. 51.
72. Office of Technology Assessment, *The Chemical Weapons Convention: Effects on the U.S. Chemical Industry* (Washington, D.C.: U.S. Government Printing Office, August 1999), p. 8.
73. Much of this discussion on the role of the CMA and nonstate actors in the CWC negotiations is based on a personal interview I conducted on November 1, 1999, with Will Carpenter, a Monsanto Company executive who headed CMA during the 1980s and 1990s. Also, see Will Carpenter and Michael Moodie, "Industry and Arms Control," in Ray Zilinska, ed., *Biological Warfare: Modern Offense and Defense* (Boulder: Lynne Rienner, 2000).
74. The quotation is attributed to Will Carpenter, referred to in note 73. Carpenter indicated that U.S. Defense Department officials were becoming increasingly nervous about on-site inspection in the late 1980s, and in testimony before Congress attributed their nervousness to concerns raised by the chemical industry, when in fact the chemical industry was being "scapegoated," insofar as it had already accepted the need for intrusive inspections. In "Playing Politics with the Chemical Weapons Convention," *Current History*, 96 (April 1997), p. 163, Amy Smithson discusses attempts by right-wing opponents of the CWC to scapegoat the U.S. chemical industry. Also, see Office of Technology Assessment, *op. cit.*, pp. 10–11; and Will Carpenter, "The Perspective of the Western Chemical Industry," in Morel and Kyle, *op. cit.*, pp. 115–120.
75. On domestic politics, see Smithson, "Playing Politics," *op. cit.*; "Clinton Pressures GOP to Act on Chemical Arms Ban," *Congressional Quarterly Weekly Report*, 55 (March 1, 1997), pp. 545–550; and David Morrison, "Political Chemistry," *National Journal*, 26 (May 14, 1994), pp. 1131–1134.
76. Morrison, *op. cit.*, p. 1133.
77. Marie Isabelle Chevrier and Amy Smithson, "Preventing the Spread of Arms: Chemical and Biological Weapons," in Jeffrey A. Larsen and Gregory T. Rattray, eds., *Arms Control Toward the 21st Century* (Boulder: Lynne Rienner, 1996), p. 203.
78. "Evaluating the CWC in the Post-Cold War Security Context," in Brad Roberts, ed., *Ratifying the Chemical Weapons Convention* (Washington, D.C.: Center for Strategic and International Studies, 1994), p. 195.
79. U.S. national interests are discussed in Donald A. Mahley, "The CWC and the U.S. National Interest," in Roberts, *op. cit.* On Germany and its chemical industry, as well as the Australian perspective, see Detlef Mannig, "At the Conclusion of the Chemical Weapons Convention: Some Recent Issues Concerning the Chemical Industry," in Morel and Kyle, *op. cit.*, pp. 127–135; and Mathews and McCormack, *op. cit.*, pp. 93–107. On the Russian and developing country perspectives, see Nikita Smidovich, "The Russian and Other Perspectives," in Morel and Kyle, *op. cit.*, pp. 55–63.
80. See Smithson, "Playing Politics," *op. cit.* Smithson blames President Clinton for waiting until late in his first term before sending the treaty to the Senate for ratification, which gave the treaty opponents time to mobilize.
81. On implementation problems, see Walter L. Busbee, "Now for the Heavy Lifting: Destroying CW Stockpiles in the United States and Russia," in Roberts, *op. cit.*, pp. 105–110. Also see Amy Smithson, "Rudderless: The Chemical Weapons Convention at 11/2," *Stimson Center* [article online]; available from <http://www.stimson.org/pubs/cwc/execsum.htm>; accessed October 31, 1999.
82. David E. Sanger, "High-Tech Exports Hit Antiquated Speed Bump," *New York Times*, June 13, 1999.

Chapter 6: Challenges to the National Welfare State: Middle Politics in the Post-Cold War Era

1. Paul Lewis, "UN Lists 4 Lands At Risk over Income Gaps," *New York Times*, June 2, 1994, p. A7.
2. *New York Times*, June 3, 1999, citing World Bank data.
3. The figure for Mexico is from Norman Lewis, "Globalization and the End of the Nation-State," paper delivered at annual meeting of the International Studies Association, San Diego, April 16, 1996. The U.S. figure is cited in Thomas L. Friedman, *The Lexus and the Olive Tree* (New York: Farrar, Straus, Giroux, 1999), p. 250.

4. Robert Gilpin, *The Political Economy of International Relations* (Princeton: Princeton University Press, 1987), p. 31.
5. Jacob Viner, "Power Versus Plenty as Objectives of Foreign Policy in the Seventeenth and Eighteenth Centuries," *World Politics*, 1 (October 1948), p. 10.
6. Cited in Gilpin, *op. cit.*, p. 180.
7. *Ibid.*, pp. 181–182.
8. Asa Biggs, "The World Economy: Interdependence and Planning," in C. L Mowat, ed., *The New Cambridge Modern History*, vol. 12 (Cambridge, Eng.: Cambridge University Press, 1968); cited in Kenneth N. Waltz, *Theory of International Politics* (Reading: Mass.: Addison-Wesley, 1979), p. 140.
9. Erich Marcks, *Manner and Zeiten* (Leipzig, 1911); cited in Geoffrey Barraclough, *An Introduction to Contemporary History* (Baltimore: Penguin Books, 1967), p. 53.
10. Cited in Craig N. Murphy, *International Organization and Industrial Change* (New York: Oxford University Press, 1994), p. 66.
11. See Gilpin, *op. cit.*, Chapter 2, for an excellent summary of these three IPE "ideologies."
12. This thesis was most forcefully presented in Charles P. Kindleberger, *The World in Depression, 1929–1938* (Berkeley, Calif.: University of California Press, 1973).
13. For West-West and East-West trade patterns, see Joan E. Spero, *The Politics of International Economic Relations*, 4th ed. (New York: St. Martin's Press, 1990), Chapters 3, 7, and 10; David H. Blake and Robert S. Walters, *The Politics of Global Economic Relations*, 4th ed. (Englewood Cliffs, N.J.: Prentice-Hall, 1992), Chapter 2; and *Handbook of Economic Statistics 1989* (Washington, D.C.: U.S. Central Intelligence Agency, 1989), tables, section 12.
13. On the reliance of most developing countries on primary products for the bulk of their export revenues, see Blake and Walters, *op. cit.*, Chapter 2; and *Handbook of International Economic Statistics 1992* (Washington, D.C.: U.S. Central Intelligence Agency, 1992), p. 170. For West-South trade flows, see International Monetary Fund, *Direction of Trade Statistics Yearbook 1995* (Washington, D.C.: IMF, 1995), p. 16 and p. 170.
15. Spero, *op. cit.*, p. 176; World Resources Institute, *World Resources 1994–95* (New York: Oxford University Press, 1994), p. 255; and *Handbook of Economic Statistics 1989, op. cit.*, pp. 180–181.
16. Lewis, *op. cit.*, p. 24.
17. Sources and targets of direct foreign investment are discussed in Spero, *op. cit.*, pp. 106 and 250–251; and Blake and Walters, *op. cit.*, p. 93.
18. John Gerard Ruggie, "International Regimes, Transactions, and Change: Embedded Liberalism in the Postwar Economic Order," in Stephen D. Krasner, ed., *International Regimes* (Ithaca: Cornell University Press, 1983), pp. 195–231.
19. Daniel Bell, *The End of Ideology* (New York: Free Press, 1965).
20. *New York Times*, November 21, 1999.
21. *New York Times*, August 10, 1998.
22. *New York Times*, July 25, 1999.
23. *New York Times*, January 18, 2000.
24. *New York Times*, September 16, 1999.
25. See Nicholas Kristof, "China Sees 'Market-Leninism' As Way to Future," *New York Times*, September 6, 1993.
26. F.A. MacKensie, *The American Invaders* (London: Oxford University, 1902); J.J. Servan-Schreiber, trans. Ronald Steel, *The American Challenge* (New York: Atheneum, 1968).
27. In the 1970s, Richard Barnet, with Ronald Muller, wrote *Global Reach: The Power of the Multinational Corporation* (New York: Simon and Schuster, 1974). In the 1990s, Barnet, with John Cavanaugh, offered a sequel, *Global Dreams: Imperial Corporations and the New World Order* (New York: Simon and Schuster, 1994).
28. UN Development Program, *UN Development Report 1994* (New York: Oxford University Press, 1994), p. 61.
29. World Bank, *World Development Report 1994* (New York: Oxford University Press, 1994), p. 92.
30. *Fortune*, July 30, 1990, p. 268.
31. Friedman, *op. cit.*, p. 8.
32. See note 142 in Chapter 3.
33. D. Held and A. McGrew, "Globalization and the Liberal Democratic State," in Y. Sakamoto, ed., *Global Transformation: Challenges to the State System* (New York: United Nations Press, 1994), p. 66.
34. Friedman, *op. cit.*, pp. 86–88.

35. *New York Times*, December 10, 1996.
36. *New York Times*, January 20, 2000.
37. Geoffrey Garrett, "Global Markets and National Politics: Collision Course or Virtuous Circle?," *International Organization*, 52 (Autumn 1998), pp. 787–824.
38. Friedman, *op. cit.*, p. 134.
39. Stephen D. Krasner, "Economic Interdependence and Independent Statehood," in Robert H. Jackson and Alan James, eds., *States In A Changing World* (Oxford: Clarendon Press, 1993), p. 303.
40. Kenneth P. Thomas, *Capital Beyond Borders* (New York: Macmillan, 1997).
41. Earl H. Fry et al., *America The Vincible* (Englewood Cliffs, N.J.: Prentice-Hall, 1994).
42. Spero, *op. cit.*, p. 237.
43. There is disagreement in the scholarly literature as to whether MNCs or national governments have the upper hand. See Thomas, *op. cit.*, for the view that MNCs, due to capital mobility, tend to dominate the relationship. For the opposite view, see Theodore H. Moran, *Multinational Corporations and the Politics of Dependence: Copper in Chile* (Princeton: Princeton University Press, 1974); and Moran, ed., *Governments and Transnational Corporations* (London: Routledge, 1993).
44. "Europe's Deal Frenzy Tends to Stop at National Borders," *New York Times*, March 25, 1999.
45. *New York Times*, December 3, 1998.
46. In *The Political Economy of National Security* (New York: McGraw-Hill, 1992), p. 21, Ethan Kapstein notes how Louis XIV's chief advisor, Colbert, "built state-owned arsenals and shipyards," although in the end "France remained dependent on imports of both raw materials and finished ships."
47. K.J. Holsti, "Change in the International System: Interdependence, Integration, and Fragmentation," in Ole R. Holsti et al., eds., *Change in the International System* (Boulder: Westview Press, 1980), p. 37; and Peter Kresl, "Canada-United States Investment Linkages," paper presented at annual meeting of the International Studies Association, Cincinnati, March 26, 1982, p. 6.
48. Rick Salutin, "Keep Canadian Culture Off the Table—Who's Kidding Who," in Laurier LaPierre, ed., *If You Love This Country* (Toronto: McClelland and Stewart, 1987), pp. 205–206; cited in Bruce E. Moon, *Dilemmas of International Trade* (Boulder: Westview Press, 1990), p. 141.
49. "The Buying of America," featuring a hypothetical "For Sale" sign on the Statue of Liberty, was the cover story of the November 27, 1978, issue of *Newsweek*. See Fry, *op. cit.*
50. UN Center on Transnational Corporations, *Foreign Direct Investment, the Service Sector and International Banking* (New York: United Nations, 1987), pp. 5–6; also, see *Economic Report of the President 1990* (Washington, D.C.: 1990), pp. 125ff; and Spero, *op. cit.*, p. 113. An excellent review essay examining writings on the theme of increased foreign penetration of the U.S. economy is Robert Kudrle, "Good for the Gander? Foreign Direct Investment in the United States," paper presented at the annual meeting of the International Studies Association, Washington, D.C., April 13, 1990.
51. Excerpted material taken from Earl Fry, "Foreign Direct Investment in the United States: Public Policy Options," paper presented at the annual meeting of the International Studies Association, Washington, D.C., April 13, 1990, pp. 1–2.
52. Lewis, *op. cit.*, p. 24, reports extensive data on this point, based on W. Ruigrok and R. Van Tuldr, *The Logic of International Restructuring* (London: Routledge, 1995).
53. Lewis, *op. cit.*, pp. 25–26.
54. Paul Doremus, Louis Pauley, and Simon Reich, *The Myth of the Multinational Corporation* (Princeton: Princeton University Press, 1998).
55. Reported in *Newsweek*, March 31, 1997, p. 38.
56. Raymond Vernon, "The Multinationals: No Strings Attached," *Foreign Policy*, 33 (Winter 1978–79), p. 121.
57. Kathryn J. Ready, "NAFTA: Labor, Industry and Government Perspectives," in Mario Bognanno and Kathryn J. Ready, *The North American Free Trade Agreement* (Westport, Ct.: Praeger, 1993), p. 12.
58. *New York Times*, December 31, 1995, p. 10.
59. See Barnet and Muller, *op. cit.*, pp. 77 and 87–89, for a discussion of several such incidents.
60. Stephen Kinzer, "Caspian Lands Back A Pipeline Pushed by West," *New York Times*, November 19, 1999.

61. Raymond Vernon, "The Role of U.S. Enterprise Abroad," *Daedalus*, 98 (Winter 1969), p. 129. Vernon later revisited his "sovereignty at bay" thesis in "Sovereignty At Bay: 20 Years After," *Millennium*, 20 (Summer 1991), pp. 191–195.

62. On the growing complexity of "strategic alliances," see Stephen J. Kobrin, "Strategic Alliances and State Control of Economic Actors," paper presented at the annual meeting of the International Studies Association, Chicago, February 24, 1995.

63. Vincent Cable, "The Diminished Nation-State: A Study in the Loss of Economic Power," *Daedalus*, 124 (Spring 1995), p. 31.

64. D. Korten, *When Corporations Rule the World* (West Hartford: Kumarian Press, 1995), p. 125.

65. Cited in James N. Rosenau, *Turbulence in World Politics* (Princeton: Princeton University Press, 1990), p. 255.

66. Charles Lipson, "International Cooperation in Economic and Security Affairs," *World Politics*, 37 (October 1984), p. 12. A similar observation is made by Robert Jervis in "Security Regimes," *International Organization*, 36 (Spring 1982), pp. 357–378.

67. Vernon, "Sovereignty At Bay: 20 Years After," *op. cit.*, p. 195.

68. Sir Roy Denman, head of the European Community mission to the United States; cited in *Washington Post National Weekly Edition*, September 22, 1986, p. 19, upon the opening of GATT's Uruguay Round negotiations.

69. Paul Krugman, "DOA at IMF," *New York Times*, March 1, 2000, p. A31.

70. A billiard ball, national interest interpretation of the NIEO debate is offered in Stephen Krasner, *Structural Conflict: The Third World Against Global Liberalism* (Berkeley, Calif.: University of California Press, 1985).

71. Brandt Commission, *North-South* (Cambridge, Mass.: MIT Press, 1980), p. 32.

72. UN Development Program, *UN Development Report 1999* (New York: Oxford University Press, 1999), p. 3.

73. *St. Louis Post Dispatch*, February 14, 2000.

74. Maryann Cusimano, *Beyond Sovereignty* (New York: St. Martin's Press, 2000), p. 262. Also see Julie Fisher, *Nongovernments: NGOs and the Political Development of the Third World* (West Hartford: Kumarian Press, 1998).

75. Paul Wapner, *Environmental Activism and World Civic Politics* (Albany: State University of New York Press, 1996), pp. 109–110.

76. Claudia Deutsch, "Unlikely Allies with the United Nations," *New York Times*, December 10, 1999.

77. Thomas L. Friedman, "Don't Mess with Moody's," *New York Times*, Febraury 22, 1995, p. A19.

78. Barbara Crossette, "Why the UN Became the World's Fair," *New York Times*, March 12, 1995.

79. Ernest H. Preeg, *Traders in A Brave New World* (Chicago: University of Chicago Press, 1995), p. 185.

80. *Ibid.*, p. 53.

81. *Ibid.*, p. 58.

82. *Ibid.*, p. 2.

83. *Ibid*, p. 10.

84. *Ibid*, p. 6.

85. Barnet and Cavanaugh, *op. cit.*, p. 326.

86. Christopher C. Meyerson, "Domestic Politics and International Relations in Trade Policymaking: The United States and Japan and the GATT Uruguay Round Agriculture Negotiations," paper presented at the annual meeting of the International Studies Association, Washington, D.C., February 1999, p. 23.

87. *Ibid.*, p. 3.

88. Richard Grant, *From Blair House to the Farm House: Negotiating Agricultural Trade in the European Union* (Washington, D.C.: Institutute for the Study of Diplomacy, 1995), p. 5.

89. *Ibid.*, p. 4.

90. Preeg, *op. cit.*, p. 65.

91. *Ibid.*, p. 161.

92. Cited in *ibid.*, p. 175.

93. *Ibid.*, p. 176.

94. Quoted in Robert Dodge, "Grappling with GATT," *Dallas Morning News*, August 8, 1994; cited in Bruce E. Moon, *Dilemmas of International Trade* (Boulder: Westview Press, 1996), p. 91. On the strange coalitions generally, see Friedman, *op. cit.*, Chapter 18.

95. A remark made on "Both Sides," a TV show hosted by Jesse Jackson on April 4, 1999.

96. The tension between free trade and environmental concerns is treated in C. Ford Runge, *Freer Trade, Protected Environment* (New York: Council on Foreign Relations, 1994); Daniel C. Esty, *Greening the GATT* (Washington, D.C.: Institute for International Economics, 1994); David Vogel, *Trading Up* (Cambridge: Harvard University Press, 1995); and Preeg, *op. cit.*, pp. 147–152.

97. Molly Ivins, "Time to Begin Building Labor, Human, and Environmental Rights on A Global Scale," *St. Louis Post-Dispatch*, November 30, 1999.

98. See "Seattle Talks on Trade End with Stinging Blow to U.S.," *New York Times*, December 5, 1999.

99. Quoted in "Clinton Gives a Pass to 'Globaphobia,'" *Wall Street Journal,* January 31, 2000.

100. "Rich Brazilians Rise Above Rush-Hour Jams," *New York Times*, February 15, 2000. Also see "Cashing In On Security Worries," *New York Times,* July 24, 1999.

101. Preeg, *op. cit.*, p. 209.

102. *St. Louis Post-Dispatch,* January 30, 2000, p. 1.

103. Robert Kaplan, "The Coming Anarchy," *Atlantic Monthly*, February 1994, p. 58.

Chapter 7: Challenges to the National Ecological State: Low Politics in the Post-Cold War Era

1. These and other historical examples of early environmental consciousness are found in Adam Markham, *A Brief History of Pollution* (New York: St. Martin's Press, 1994).

2. Report of the Club of Rome, *The Limits to Growth* (New York: Universe Books, 1972).

3. The World Commission on Environment and Development (Brundtland Commission), *Our Common Future* (New York: Oxford University Press, 1987).

4. Lester R. Brown et al., *State of the World 2000* (New York: W.W. Norton, 2000), p. 4.

5. Brundtland Commission, *op. cit.*, p. 27.

6. See Everett Carl Ladd and Kathryn H. Bowman, *Attitudes Toward the Environment* (Washington, D.C.: American Enterprise Institute, 1995); and Russell Dalton, *The Green Rainbow* (New Haven: Yale University Press, 1995).

7. Comments made by Lee Thomas in testimony before the U.S. Senate, Committee on Foreign Relations Hearings, February 19, 1988; and George Mitchell, statement in U.S. Senate, 1988; cited in Richard E. Benedick, *Ozone Diplomacy*, enlarged ed. (Cambridge: Harvard University Press, 1998), p. 1.

8. Brown, *op. cit.*, p. 5. An overview is provided in Chapter 1, "Challenges of the New Century."

9. W. Jackson Davis, *The Seventh Year* (New York: W.W. Norton, 1979), p. 109.

10. Hilary F. French, "Clearing the Air," in Lester R. Brown et al., *State of the World 1990* (New York: W.W. Norton, 1990), p. 98.

11. G. Tyler Miller, *Living in the Environment*, 10th ed. (New York: Wadsworth Publishing, 1998), p. 314.

12. Brown, *op. cit.*, pp. 5–6. For discussion of trends in global warming and other atmospheric problems, and for surveys of environmental problems generally, see the biennial editions of *Environmental Data Report* published by the UN Environmental Program and *World Resources* published by the World Resources Institute.

13. See Brown, *op. cit.*, pp. 6–7 and the general reference sources cited in Note 12, as well as Sandra Postel, *Last Oasis* (New York: W.W. Norton, 1992); and "Next, Wars Over Water," *World Press Review* (November 1995), pp. 8–10.

14. Andre van Dam, "The Future of Waste," *International Studies Notes*, 4 (Winter 1977), p. 17.

15. "Next, Wars Over Water," *op. cit.*, p. 8. Another author counts only 26 "water scarce" countries; see Sandra Postel, "Facing A Future of Water Scarcity," in John Allen, ed., *Environment 1995/96* (Guilford, Conn.: Dushkin, 1996), pp. 170–180. On China and India, see Brown, *op. cit.*, p. 7.

16. Michael G. Renner, "Shared Problems, Common Security," in Charles W. Kegley and Eugene Wittkopf, eds., *Global Agenda* (New York: St. Martin's Press, 1992), p. 337.

17. *Newsweek,* July 5, 1999, p. 52.

18. Cited in Jeremy Rifkin, *Biosphere Politics* (San Francisco: HarperCollins, 1991), p. 56.

19. See Ann Platt McGinn, "Charting A New Course for Oceans," in Lester R. Brown, *State of the World 1999* (New York: W.W. Norton,, 1999), pp. 78–88. See also "U.S. Fishing Fleet Trawling Coastal Water Without Fish," *New York Times*, March 7, 1994, p. 1.

20. Miller, *op. cit.*, pp. 555–556.

21. Christopher D. Stone, *The Gnat is Older Than Man* (Princeton: Princeton University Press, 1993), p. 19.
22. Janet N. Abramowitz, "Sustaining the World's Forests," in Lester R. Brown et al., *State of the World 1998* (New York: W.W. Norton, 1998), p. 22.
23. Miller, *op. cit.*, p. 342.
24. Abramowitz, *op. cit.*, p. 22.
25. See Norman Myers, *The Primary Source: Tropical Forests and Our Future* (New York: W.W. Norton, 1992).
26. Peter Raven, "A Time of Catastrophic Extinction," *The Futurist* (September/October 1995), p. 38. On measuring extinction rates, see Miller, *op. cit.* pp, 668–669.
27. Miller, *op. cit.*, p. 665.
28. *Ibid.*, p. 668.
29. Bill McKibben, "A Special Moment in History," *The Atlantic Monthly* (May 1998), p. 72.
30. See Ruth Sivard, *World Military and Social Expenditures 1985* (Washington, D.C.: World Priorities, 1985), p. 27. On estimates of malnourishment, see Joseph Collins, "World Hunger: A Scarcity of Food or a Scarcity of Democracy?," in Michael T. Klare and Daniel C. Thomas, eds., *World Security: Risks and Challenges at Century's End* (New York: St. Martin's Press, 1991), p. 345; and Brundtland Commission, *op. cit.*, p. 118.
31. For food production trends, see Lester R. Brown, "Feeding Nine Billion," in Brown et al., *State of the World 1999* (New York: W.W. Norton, 1999), pp. 115–132. For a competing view that questions whether there is an impending food crisis, see Dennis T. Avery, *Saving the Planet with Pesticides and Plastics: The Environmental Triumph of High-Yield Farming* (New York: Hudson Institute, 1995).
32. Brundtland Commission, *op. cit.*, p. 99.
33. Reported in *St. Louis Post-Dispatch*, February 22, 1994.
34. Joel E. Cohen, "How Many People Can the Earth Support?," *The Sciences* (November/December 1995), pp. 18–23.
35. For population projections, see Brundtland Commission, *op. cit.*, Chapter 4. Among the more alarmist writings on population is Paul Ehrlich and Anne Ehrlich, *The Population Explosion* (New York: Simon and Schuster, 1990).
36. Seth Mydans, "Bangkok Opens Skytrain, But Will It Ease Car Traffic?," *New York Times*, December 6, 1999. Also see Thomas Friedman, "Bangkok Bogs Down," *New York Times*, March 20, 1996. On "the urban challenge" generally, see Brundtland Commission, *op. cit.*, Chapter 9.
37. Hilary F. French, "Coping With Ecological Globalization," in Lester R. Brown et al., *State of the World 2000* (New York: W.W. Norton, 2000), p. 185.
38. Cited in Marvin Soroos, *Beyond Sovereignty* (Columbia, S.C.: University of South Carolina Press, 1986), p. 305.
39. One author notes "if we include bilateral and multilateral instruments . . . there are more than 870 international legal instruments that have one or more provisions addressing environment." Edith Weiss Brown, "Global Environmental Change and International Law: The Introductory Framework," in Weiss, ed., *Environmental Change and International Law* (Tokyo: UN University Press, 1992), p. 9. See Weiss for a good discussion on the development of international law in this area over time. Using a narrower definition of environmental regimes, the UNEP Register in the 1990s listed more than 120 international agreements in the environmental field. Lawrence E. Susskind, *Environmental Diplomacy* (New York: Oxford University Press, 1994), p. 16.
40. See Michael Grubb et al., *The Earth Summit Agreements: A Guide and Assessment* (London: Earthscan Publications, 1993). Also see James Speth, "A Post-Rio Compact," *Foreign Policy*, 88 (Fall 1992), pp. 145–161. On the politics of the Global Environmental Facility, see Susskind, *op. cit.*, pp. 37–41.
41. See *Environmental Data Report 1993–1994* (Oxford, UK: Blackwell, 1993), pp. 24–25.
42. A good case study of European acid rain is Marc A. Levy, "European Acid Rain: The Power of Tote-Board Diplomacy," in Peter M. Haas, Robert O. Keohane, and Marc A. Levy, eds., *Institutions for the Earth* (Cambridge: MIT Press, 1993), pp. 75–132. Levy argues that, although the United Kingdom did not formally sign the Helsinki Protocol, it was shamed by adverse European-wide publicity into reducing its SO_2 emissions.
43. On the politics of global warming, see Ian H. Rowlands, *The Politics of Global Atmospheric Change* (New York: Manchester University Press, 1995), Chapters 3, 6, 9, and 12.
44. On international fisheries management and oil pollution at sea, see the articles by M.J.

Peterson and Ronald Mitchell in Haas, Keohane, and Levy, *op. cit.* Also see "Gaps in Sea Laws Shield Pollution by Cruise Lines," *New York Times,* January 3, 1999.

45. See Peter M. Haas, *Saving the Mediterranean* (New York: Columbia University Press, 1990).
46. Kal Raustiala and David Victor, "The Future of the Convention on Biological Diversity," *Environment* (May 1996), pp. 17–20 and 37–45.
47. *New York Times,* March 13, 1998.
48. See Betsy Hartmann, *Reproductive Rights and Wrongs: The Global Politics of Population Control,* rev. ed. (Boston: South End Press, 1995); and the article by Barbara B. Crane in Haas, Keohane, and Levy, *op. cit.*
49. See Detlef Sprinz and Tapani Vaahtoranta, "The Interest-Based Explanation of International Environmental Policy," *International Organization,* 48 (Winter 1994), pp. 77–105.
50. Susskind, *op. cit..* p. 8.
51. *Ibid.,* p. 18.
52. *Ibid.,* p. 107.
53. Examples of noncompliance with environmental regimes are discussed in Peter H. Sand, ed., *The Effectiveness of International Environmental Agreements* (Cambridge: Grotius Publications, 1992); Abram Chayes and Antonia Chayes, "On Compliance," *International Organization,* 47 (Spring 1993), pp. 175–205; and Susskind, *op. cit.,* Chapter 6.
54. See Allison B. Morrill, "National Capacity for International Environmental Agreements with Countries in Transition: Lessons from Montreal for Kyoto?," paper presented at the annual meeting of the International Studies Association, Washington, D.C., February 20, 1999. Also, on state capacity, see Haas, Keohane, and Levy, *op. cit.*
55. For an excellent treatment of the emergent role of nonstate actors in the politics of food, population, energy, and the environment, see the two "Global Arena" series edited by James Harf and Thomas Trout in the 1980s, one published by Holt, Rinehart and Winston and the other by Duke University Press. Also see Gareth Porter and Janet Welsh Brown, *Global Environmental Politics,* 2nd ed. (Boulder: Westview Press, 1996).
56. Statistics on the number of NGOs participating in 1972 and 1992 are from Jacqueline V. Switzer, *Environmental Politics: Domestic and Global Dimensions* (New York: St. Martin's Press, 1994), p. xv.
57. Peter Haas, "The Future of International Environmental Governance," paper delivered at the annual meeting of the International Studies Association, San Diego, April 17, 1996, p. 16.
58. Following Rio, the Business Council for Sustainable Development expanded to become the World Business Council for Sustainable Development, which included many of the largest MNCs in the world. Some observers question how committed these MNCs are to "green" policies. See Matthias Finger and J. Kilcoyne, "Why Transnational Corporations Are Organizing to Save the Global Environment," *The Ecologist,* 27 (1997), pp. 138–142.
59. Speth, *op. cit.,* p. 146.
60. Grubb et al., *op. cit.,* p. 44.
61. Porter and Brown, *op. cit.,* p. 58.
62. On the role of nonstate actors at Rio, see Speth, *op. cit.;* Grubb et al., *op. cit.,* Chapters 4 and 5; and Susskind, *op. cit.,* pp. 47–52.
63. Susskind, *op. cit.,* p. 48. Susskind notes that NGOs played an important role at Rio, but not quite as far-reaching as some had hoped. On NGO activity in the environmental issue area, see Thomas Princen and Matthias Finger, eds., *Environmental NGOs in World Politics* (London: Routledge, 1994); Ken Conca, "Greening the UN: Environmental Organizations in the UN System," in Thomas E. Weiss and Leon Gordenker, eds., *NGOs, The UN, and Global Governance* (Boulder: Lynne Rienner, 1996), pp. 103–119; Paul Wapner, *Environmental Activism and World Civic Politics* (Albany: State University of New York Press, 1996); and Kal Raustiala, "States, NGOs, and International Environmental Institutions," *International Studies Quarterly,* 4 (December 1997), pp. 719–740.
64. Susskind, *op. cit.,* p. 24.
65. A case study of Greenpeace can be found in Wapner, *op. cit.,* Chapter 3.
66. See Morrill, *op. cit.;* and Raustiala, *op. cit.*
67. Raustiala, *op. cit.,* p. 728.
68. Jessica Matthews, "Power Shift," *Foreign Affairs,* 76 (January/February 1997), p. 55.
69. Susskind, *op. cit.,* p. 62. See his Chapter 4 on "The Need for a Better Balance Between Science and Politics."
70. On "green gold," see Curtis Moore and Alan Miller, *Green Gold: Japan, Germany, the United*

States, and the Race for Environmental Technology (Boston: Beacon Press, 1995); and Haas, "The Future of Environmental Governance," *op. cit.*, pp. 34–37.

71. McKibben, *op. cit.*, p. 72.
72. See Peter Newell, "Environmental NGOs, TNCs, and the Question of Governance," paper presented at the annual meeting of the International Studies Association, Washington, D.C., February 17, 1999. On complex linkages in the global warming issue area, see Ian H. Rowlands, "Energy Companies and Climate Change Politics," paper given at the annual meeting of the International Studies Association, Washington, D.C., February 17, 1999.
73. Jennifer Clapp, "The Global Recycling Industry and Hazardous Waste Trade Politics," paper given at the annual meeting of the International Studies Association, Washington, D.C., February 16, 1999. Also see Charles E. Davis, *The Politics of Hazardous Waste* (Englewood Cliffs, N.J.: Prentice-Hall, 1993).
74. Haas, *Saving the Mediterranean, op. cit.*
75. See Rachel M. McCleary, *Development Strategies in Conflict: Brazil and the Future of the Amazon* (Washington, D.C.: Carnegie Council on Ethics and International Affairs, 1990).
76. Dan Morgan, *Merchants of Grain* (New York: Viking Press, 1979).
77. Richard E. Benedick, "Ozone Diplomacy," *Issues in Science and Technology* (Fall 1989), p. 43.
78. *Ibid.*
79. Benedick, *Ozone Diplomacy, op. cit.*, p. 9. Much of my case study draws on the work of Benedick.
80. Benedick, "Ozone Diplomacy," *op. cit.*, p. 43.
81. Benedick, *Ozone Diplomacy, op. cit.*, p. 315.
82. *Ibid.*, p. 42.
83. *Ibid.*, pp. 59–60. Benedick reports that U.S. Under Secretary of State for Economic Affairs Allen Wallis tried to persuade Secretary of State Shultz to withdraw his support for the United States signing the Vienna Convention.
84. *Ibid.*, pp. 51–52. Also see Karen Litfin, *Ozone Discourses: Science and Politics in Global Environmental Cooperation* (New York: Columbia University Press, 1994).
85. *Ibid.*, pp. 57–58.
86. Edward A. Parson, "Protecting the Ozone Layer," in Haas, Keohane, and Levy, *op. cit.*, p. 40.
87. *Ibid.*, p. 43.
88. *Ibid.*
89. Benedick, *Ozone Diplomacy, op. cit.*, pp. 101–102.
90. *Ibid.*, pp. 100–101.
91. *Ibid.*, p. 390. For the ratification process, especially as regards the developing countries, see Chapters 12 and 16.
92. The quote is from Peter M. Haas, "Policy Responses to Stratospheric Ozone Depletion," *Global Environmental Change* (June 1991), p. 228; cited in Michele M. Betsill, "Explaining Environmental Cooperation: The Contribution of International Relations Theory," paper delivered at the annual meeting of the International Studies Association, San Diego, April 16, 1996, p. 11. Betsill does a good job of dismantling the pure realist explanation.
93. Benedick, *Ozone Diplomacy, op. cit.*, p. 314.
94. *Ibid.*, p. 114. For an elaborate discussion of the role of epistemic communities and science, see Chapter 9.
95. Wapner, *op. cit.*, p. 53.
96. Benedick, *Ozone Diplomacy, op. cit.*, p. 169.
97. *Ibid.*, pp. 194–195.
98. *Ibid.*, p. 247.
99. "Severe Loss To Arctic Zone," reported on April 7, 2000, via Internet from the www .oceanspace@spearhead.co.uk website.
100. Morrill, *op. cit.*, p. 18. Also, see Benedick, *Ozone Diplomacy, op. cit.*, Chapter 17 on compliance problems.
101. Problems with the effectiveness of the ozone regime are discussed in Mark Dowie, "A Sky Full of Holes," *The Nation*, July 8, 1996, pp. 11–12 and 14–16.
102. Benedick, *Ozone Diplomacy, op. cit.*, pp. 220–223.
103. Susskind, *op. cit.*, p. 71, says that "in two decades of debate over ozone depletion, the focus was on scientific rather than political issues. . . . All of this was unusual."
104. Benedick, "Ozone Diplomacy," *op. cit.*, p. 50.
105. Stanley Hoffmann, *Primacy or World Order* (New York: McGraw Hill, 1978), p.193.

106. The quote is attributed to Fred Hoyle.
107. *New York Times*, May 23, 2000, pp. C1 and C4.
108. Cited in Molly O'Meara, "Exploring A New Vision for Cities," in Lester R. Brown et al, *State of the World 1999* (New York: W.W. Norton, 1999), p. 147.
109. *Ibid.*, p. 148.
110. *Ibid.*, 149.
111. "Justices Weigh Issue of States' Making Foreign Policy," *New York Times*, March 23, 2000.

Chapter 8: Summing Up and Moving On: World Politics and Global Governance in the New Millennium

1. *Newsweek*, May 15, 2000, p. 73k.
2. Robert D. Putnam, *Bowling Alone* (New York: Simon and Schuster, 2000). The book is an expansion of his earlier article in *The Journal of Democracy*, 6 (January 1995), pp. 65–78.
3. On the problems associated, for example, with e-commerce and "governance in a digital world," see Stephen J. Kobrin, "Electronic Cash and the End of National Markets," *Foreign Policy* (Summer 1997), pp. 65–77.
4. Thomas L. Friedman, *The Lexus and the Olive Tree: Understanding Globalization* (New York: Farrar, Straus, Giroux, 1999), p. 25.
5. The Commission on Global Governance, *Our Global Neighborhood* (New York: Oxford University Press, 1995), p. 2.
6. Thomas L. Friedman, "The Parallel Universe," *New York Times*, May 12, 2000.
7. Kenneth N. Waltz, "Globalization and Governance," *PS* (December 1999), p. 697. Also see Waltz, "Globalization and American Power," *The National Interest* (Spring 2000).
8. Robert H. Jackson and Alan James, "The Character of Independent Statehood," in Jackson and James, eds., *States in a Changing World* (Oxford: Clarendon Press, 1993), pp. 6–7. Also, for a somewhat different take on the same theme, see Stephen Krasner, *Sovereignty: Organized Hypocrisy* (Princeton: Princeton University Press, 1999).
9. Paul Krugman, "Competitiveness: A Dangerous Obsession," *The Shape of World Politics* (New York: W.W. Norton, 1997), p. 166.
10. Earl H. Fry et al., *America the Vincible* (Englewood Cliffs, N.J.: Prentice-Hall, 1994), p. 5.
11. See Chapter 2, Note 62.
12. "Alternative world order models" were first discussed by scholars involved in the World Order Models Project (WOMP) during the 1970s. See Richard A. Falk, *This Endangered Planet* (New York: Random House, 1972); Rajni Kothari, *Footsteps Into the Future: Diagnosis of the Present World and A Design for An Alternative* (New York: Free Press, 1974); and Saul H. Mendlovitz, *On the Creation of a Just World Order: Preferred Worlds for the 1990s* (New York: Free Press, 1975).
13. See *ibid.*
14. Judge C. de Visscher, cited by Louis Henkin, in *How Nations Behave*, 2nd ed. (New York: Columbia University Press, 1979), p. 164. Henkin adds that "but justice, perhaps, must come not too long after, if peace is to endure."
15. See my discussion in Chapter 3. For differing perspectives on this, see Charles Beitz, *Political Theory and International Relations* (Princeton: Princeton University Press, 1979); Terry Nardin, *Law, Morality, and the Relations of States* (Princeton: Princeton University Press, 1983); and Robert Tucker, *The Inequality of Nations* (New York: Basic Books, 1977).
16. The terms "bad realists" and "bad idealists" are from Giovanni Sartori, *Democratic Theory* (New York: Praeger, 1965).
17. Charles A. Kupchan, "After Pax Americana: Benign Power, Regional Integration, and the Sources of A Stable Multipolarity," *International Security*, 23 (Fall 1998), pp. 40–79. Also see Ronald Tammen et al., *Power Transitions: Strategies for the 21st Century* (London: Chatham House, 2000).
18. See Note 84 in Chapter 3.
19. Waltz, "Globalization and Governance, *op. cit.*, p. 697.
20. Robert C. North, *The World That Could Be* (New York: W.W. Norton, 1976), p. 136. Also see his *War, Peace, Survival* (Boulder: Westview Press, 1990).
21. See Note 124 in Chapter 3.
22. *New York Times*, June 4, 1999.

23. German Foreign Minister Joschka Fischer, on May 14, 2000, called for a centralized European government ruling over the 15-member EU. *New York Times,* May 15, 2000.

24. Roger Cohen, "A European Identity: Nation-State Losing Ground," *New York Times,* January 14, 2000.

25. *Christian Science Monitor,* January 4, 1989, p. 1.

26. Joseph S. Nye, *Peace in Parts* (Boston: Little, Brown, 1971), p.199.

27. For a discussion of approaches to world government, see Louis Rene Beres and Harry R. Targ, *Reordering the Planet: Constructing Alternative Futures* (Boston: Allyn and Bacon, 1974), Chapter 6.

28. Grenville Clark and Louis Sohn, *World Peace Through World Law: Two Alternative Plans,* 3rd ed. (Cambridge: Harvard University Press, 1966).

29. Richard Hudson, "Give UN the Power to Make Peace," *St. Louis Post-Dispatch,* July 20, 1990. Also see the World Federalists' *Fourteen-Point Program of the Campaign for UN Reform* (Wayne, N.J.: Campaign for UN Reform, 1978).

30. Marc Nerfin, "The Future of the UN System—Some Questions on the Occasion of An Anniversary," *Development Dialogue,* 1 (1985), p. 21.

31. See UN Development Program, *Human Development Report 1994* (New York: Oxford University Press, 1994), p. 88.

32. A number of these proposals are discussed in Christopher Stone, *The Gnat Is Older than Man* (Princeton: Princeton University Press, 1993), pp. 206–211.

33. Richard J. Barnet and Ronald E. Muller, *Global Reach* (New York: Simon and Schuster, 1974), pp. 19–20.

34. Comments by Strobe Talbott, cited by Pat Buchanan in a speech before the Boston World Affairs Council on January 6, 2000.

35. See Karl W. Deutsch et al., *Political Community and the North Atlantic Area* (Princeton: Princeton University Press, 1957).

36. Citing Ted Gurr's definition of a "communal group," one writer notes that "if a nation is defined as a population with a 'distinctive and enduring collective identity based on cultural traits and lifeways that matter to them and to others with whom they interact,' then by some counts the world contains anywhere from 3000 to 5000 nations." Seyom Brown, *New Forces, Old Forces, and the Future of World Politics,* post-Cold War ed. (New York: HarperCollins, 1995), p. 162.

37. Robert D. Kaplan, *New York Times,* December 27, 1999.

38. James N. Rosenau, "Governance in the Twenty-First Century," *Global Governance,* 1 (Winter 1995), pp. 25–26. Also see Saskia Sassen, *The Global City* (Princeton: Princeton University Press, 1991); and Earl H. Fry et al., *The New International Cities Era: The Global Activities of North American Municipal Governments* (Provo, Utah: Brigham Young University Press, 1989).

39. See William Drozdiak, "Regions on the Rise," *Washington Post,* October 22, 1995; and John Newhouse, "Europe's Rising Regionalism," *Foreign Affairs,* 76 (January/February 1997), pp. 67–84.

40. Brown, *op. cit.,* pp. 154–155. Also see Kenichi Ohmae, "The Rise of the Region-State," *Foreign Affairs,* 72 (Spring 1993), pp. 78–87.

41. Jonathan Schell, *The Fate of the Earth* (New York: Knopf, 1982).

42. Leopold Kohr, *The Breakdown of Nations* (London: Routledge and Kegan Paul, 1957), p. 57.

43. On the virtues of "decentralization to protect the environment," see Paul Wapner, *Environmental Activism and World Civic Politics* (Albany: State University of New York Press, 1996), pp. 34–38.

44. On "strategic alliances," see Note 62 in Chapter 6. On "the end of geography," see Note 41 in Chapter 2. Also see Jan Aart Scholte, "Global Capitalism and The State," *International Affairs,* 73 (1997), pp. 427–452.

45. Michael Edwards, "Globalization, States, and Civil Society: False Dawn or Future Positive?," paper prepared for Conference on Development and the Nation-State, Washington University, St. Louis, February 2000, p. 16.

46. On "the emergence of global civil society," see Ronnie D. Lipschutz, "Reconstructing World Politics: The Emergence of Global Civil Society," *Millennium,* 21, no. 3 (1992), pp. 389–420. On the "new feudalism," see the works cited in Note 6 in Chapter 1; and Hedley Bull, *The Anarchical Society* (New York: Columbia University Press, 1977), p. 254.

47. James N. Rosenau, *Turbulence in World Politics* (Princeton: Princeton University Press, 1990).

Others speak of "fission/fusion." See Yale H. Ferguson and Richard W. Mansbach, "The Past As Prelude to the Future: Identities and Loyalties in Global Politics," in Yosef Lapid and Friedrich Kratochwil, eds., *The Return of Culture and Identity in IR Theory* (Boulder: Lynne Rienner, 1996), pp. 39–40.

48. Although Robert Kaplan, *op. cit.*, speaks of a future of "city-states," he ends his article by predicting something more complex, that the twenty-first century "will be the age of high-tech feudalism."

49. "Nonterritorial actors" and their relationship to world order values is discussed in Richard A. Falk, "A New Paradigm for International Legal Studies: Prospects and Proposals," in Falk et al., eds., *International Law: A Contemporary Perspective* (Boulder: Westview Press, 1985), pp. 651–702. The problem of "democratic deficits" is discussed in Alan Gilbert, *Must Global Politics Constrain Democracy?* (Princeton: Princeton University Press, 2000).

50. Robert H. Jackson, "Continuity and Change in the States System," in Jackson and Alan James, eds., *States in a Changing World* (Oxford: Clarendon Press, 1993), p. 367.

51. "What Place Will the Environment Have in the Next Century?—And At What Price?," *International Environmental Affairs* (Summer 1990), p. 1.

52. See Note 34 in Chapter 2.

43. See Note 33 in Chapter 2. Paul Hirst notes, for example, that the international economy "remains sufficiently concentrated in the key national states for . . . governance to be possible." See his "The Global Economy—Myths and Realities," *International Affairs*, 73 (1997), pp. 409–425.

54. On Huntington, see Note 84 in Chapter 3. On Nye, see Note 22 in Chapter 3; and *Bound to Lead: The Changing Nature of American Power* (New York: Basic Books, 1990).

55. David Wilkinson, "Unipolarity Without Hegemony," *International Studies Review*, 1, no. 2 (Summer 1999), p. 143.

56. Charles P. Kindleberger, "Hierarchical Versus Inertial Cooperation," *International Organization*, 40 (Autumn 1986), p. 841.

57. Kevin Baron, "Coalition Works to Support American Engagement," *The Interdependent* (Spring 1999), p. 11. On the continued underpayment of UN dues, see *New York Times*, June 23, 1999. Also, on public disengagement, see Note 97 in Chapter 3.

58. See Note 73 in Chapter 2.

59. *Wall Street Journal*, March 27, 2000, p.1. Also see James Traub, "W's World," *New York Times Magazine*, January 14, 2001, pp. 28–34.

60. John J. Mearsheimer, "Why We Will Soon Miss the Cold War," *The Atlantic Monthly* (August 1990), p. 35.

61. S. Pollard, *The Idea of Progress* (Hammondsworth, Eng.: Penguin, 1971).

62. Remark by Kenneth Boulding at the annual meeting of the International Studies Association, St. Louis, March 16, 1977.

63. Reported in *New York Times*, December 31, 1999.

64. The "shifting sands of sovereignty" phrase is from the International Institute for Strategic Studies, *Strategic Survey 1999/2000* (New York: Oxford University Press, 2000). Also see Gene Lyons and Michael Mastanduno, eds., *Beyond Westphalia? State Sovereignty and International Intervention* (Baltimore: Johns Hopkins University Press, 2000).

65. *A Successor Vision: The United Nations of Tomorrow* (New York: United Nations Association-USA), 1987).

66. "Landlords Around the UN Find Diplomacy Doesn't Pay," *New York Times*, December 25, 1999.

67. An interesting look at global civil society and global governance is provided by Michael Edwards in *Future Positive: International Cooperation in the 21st Century* (London: Earthscan, 2000).

68. *New York Times*, editorial, April 9, 2000.

69. UN Development Program, *Human Development Report 1999* (New York: Oxford University Press, 1999), p. 80.

70. Richard Gardner, "Practical Internationalism," *Foreign Affairs*, 66 (Spring 1988), p. 830.

71. Cited in Richard Gardner, "To Make the World Safe for Interdependence," *UN 30* (New York: United Nations Association-USA, 1975), p. 16.

72. On multiple identities, see Yale H. Ferguson and Richard W. Mansbach, "Global Politics at the Turn of the Millennium: Changing Bases of 'Us' and 'Them,'" *International Studies Review*,

1, no. 2 (Summer 1999), pp. 77–107; and Thomas M. Franck, "Tribe, Nation, World: Self-Identification in the Evolving International System," *Ethics and International Affairs,* 11 (1997), pp. 151–169.

73. Data to support the observation that there is growing "citizen disaffection" in the United States, Europe, and Japan are provided in Susan J. Pharr and Robert D. Putnam, *Disaffected Democracies: What's Troubling the Trilateral Countries?* (Princeton: Princeton University Press, 2000). Also see Joseph S. Nye, "In Government We Don't Trust," mentioned in Note 54 in Chapter 2.

74. The Office of the UN High Commissioner for Refugees counted 27 million refugees who were receiving UN aid annually in the late 1990s, although some of these were persons displaced from their homes within their own country. *A Global Agenda: Issues Before the 51st General Assembly of the United Nations* (Lanham, Md.: Rowman and Littlefield, 1996), p. 7.

75. Speech in Philadelphia on July 4, 1994; reported in *Newsweek,* July 18, 1994, p. 66. The reference to "declaration of interdependence" is *Newsweek's* characterization of the speech.

76. *New York Times,* editorial, January 1, 2000.

Index